The Subject of Revolution

Envisioning Cuba

Louis A. Pérez Jr., *editor*

Envisioning Cuba publishes outstanding, innovative works in Cuban studies, drawn from diverse subjects and disciplines in the humanities and social sciences, from the colonial period through the post–Cold War era. Featuring innovative scholarship engaged with theoretical approaches and interpretive frameworks informed by social, cultural, and intellectual perspectives, the series highlights the exploration of historical and cultural circumstances and conditions related to the development of Cuban self-definition and national identity.

A complete list of books published in Envisioning Cuba is available at https://uncpress.org/series/envisioning-cuba.

The Subject of Revolution

Between Political and Popular Culture in Cuba

. . . .

JENNIFER L. LAMBE

The University of North Carolina Press Chapel Hill

© 2024 The University of North Carolina Press
All rights reserved
Set in Charis by Westchester Publishing Services
Manufactured in the United States of America

Complete Cataloging-in-Publication Data for this title is available from
the Library of Congress.

ISBN 978-1-4696-8114-6 (cloth: alk. paper)
ISBN 978-1-4696-8115-3 (pbk.: alk. paper)
ISBN 978-1-4696-8116-0 (epub)
ISBN 978-1-4696-8117-7 (pdf)

Cover art: Barbara Walters interviewing Fidel Castro, c. 1977 (Everett
Collection Inc. / Alamy Stock Photo)

Contents

Illustrations

Acknowledgments

This book, like the subject it features, sits atop a world-altering event—several, in fact. It would not have been written were it not for the generosity, forbearance, and wisdom of the four grandparents who taught my husband and me how to navigate new parenthood in the thick of a global pandemic. We depended in all ways on their willingness to change diapers, carry babies (then toddlers), and provide assurances that things would eventually get better. I am equally grateful to my two boys, Max and Tommy, who served as the first and, inevitably, least judgmental audience for many of the ideas that appear here, and to my husband Alex, whose enthusiasm, insight, and companionship sustained me along the way.

Though much of this book was written in the quiet hours of the early morning, its genesis depended on the encouragement and guidance of many, starting with the undergraduate and graduate students at Brown University who helped me work through these ideas in embryonic form. In this respect, I must acknowledge the special contributions of Lily Hartmann, who witnessed the evolution of this project from beginning to end and provided outstanding research assistance along the way, and Laura Muñoz and Eileen Artigas, who served as expert interviewers. The feedback and camaraderie of Javier Fernández Galeano, Thamyris Almeida, René Cordero, Juan Betancourt, Fernando Norat, and Marina Dias Lucena Adams buoyed me at many stages of the research process; René and Fernando also made important contributions as research assistants. In fall 2019, I benefited from conversations with participants in the Revolutions in History panel series, generously funded by the Brown Department of History, Cogut Institute for the Humanities, Herbert H. Goldberger Lectureship Fund, and Program in Science and Technology Studies; my thanks to Jeanne Ernest for her astute engagement and enthusiastic collaboration.

This book would not have been possible without the expertise and assistance of librarians and archivists in Cuba, the United States, and Canada, who responded to emails, hunted down references, and otherwise made the research for this book not only possible but pleasurable. In Cuba, I would like to thank colleagues at the Biblioteca Nacional and the Archivo

General del Ministerio de Cultura, who kindly facilitated my research, and representatives and members of the Workers Social Clubs, who took time to speak with me. The Fundación Antonio Núñez Jiménez served as a warm and energizing base for my research in Cuba. All arguments presented in this book are exclusively my own, and I am solely responsible for any errors or misinterpretations contained therein.

In Miami, I benefited from the hospitality and camaraderie of friends at the Cuban Heritage Collection, which continues to serve as a vibrant epicenter for Cuban studies. The professionalism and courtesy of staff at the John F. Kennedy Library, Hoover Institution Library and Archives, and Holt-Atherton Special Collections and Archives (University of the Pacific) made those research trips fun and fruitful. My thanks also go to librarians and archivists at the Wisconsin Historical Society, Rockefeller Archive Center, Columbia University Archives, Lyndon B. Johnson Library, John Hay Library, David M. Rubenstein Rare Book and Manuscript Library (Duke University), Kenneth Spencer Research Library (University of Kansas), Bentley Historical Library (University of Michigan), Library and Archives Canada, and the University of Texas Archives for fielding requests and questions. Christopher Cook provided instrumental research assistance at Library and Archives Canada, as did Richard Denis at the Cuban Heritage Collection.

Research and writing were made possible thanks to generous support from the Dean of the Faculty, the Department of History, and the Cogut Institute for the Humanities at Brown University, which provided a warm intellectual home during the early stages of the writing process. I am especially grateful to Amanda Anderson for facilitating a stimulating conversation about an early version of chapter 1, and to all of the Cogut Fellows who offered motivating feedback. This book would never have moved forward had it not been for the dedicated and assiduous work of many at Brown's Rockefeller Library, who fielded ILLiad requests, hunted down books, and, in the doldrums of COVID, made weekly trips to pick up those books a pleasure.

In the course of writing (and rewriting) this book, I accumulated significant intellectual debts. First and foremost, I must recognize—in alphabetical order, because it would be impossible to rank their contributions—Michael Bustamante, James N. Green, and Lillian Guerra, who participated in a transformative manuscript workshop on this book. Their perceptive comments and general enthusiasm delivered a jolt of energy at a crucial moment in this project's development; their support, guidance, and friendship over the long term has been equally critical to my development as a scholar. My sincere thanks to Ethan Pollock for his encouragement and counsel, and to Cherrie Guerzon and Julissa Bautista, who handled all the details that made the workshop possible. I am also grateful to the anonymous reviewers for the University of North Carolina Press who provided constructive feedback and helpful references, and to Elaine Maisner, Andreina Fernandez, Debbie Gershenowitz, and JessieAnne D'Amico for thoughtfully shepherding this book to review and completion. Finally, I would like to thank Lindsay Starr, Michelle Witkowski, Varsha Venkatasubramanian, and Jessica Ryan, who directed the design, copyediting, indexing, and proofreading processes, respectively.

I owe the deepest appreciation to everyone, here and there, who agreed to be interviewed for this book. In Cuba, I also benefited from conversations with friends from whom I have learned so much over the years. Many scholars of Cuba offered feedback and fellowship along the way. I am grateful to work alongside them in a field that has prized judicious engagement and intellectual generosity in spite of the sometimes significant odds.

My thanks to colleagues at Brown University who make the other activities that consume our working days a welcome diversion, and to faculty and students at the University of Miami, Yale University, Kenyon College, and Swarthmore College—notably Lillian Manzor and Kate Ramsey, Gil Joseph and Stuart Schwartz, Thamy Almeida, and Diego Armus, respectively—who posed thought-provoking questions. Elizabeth Schwall deserves special mention for her generative comments on various iterations of this project. Debbie Weinstein and Debby Levine were a crucial audience for some of the sidebars that became the seed of this book. Alejandro de la Fuente and Lou Pérez graciously lent their support to early funding applications. Elizabeth Mirabal offered perceptive reflections and toddler-friendly explanations of windmills. Reinaldo Funes continues to model collaborative historical inquiry. Jorge Macle memorably explained, among so many other things, the special relevance of Foucault to Cuban history.

Portions of the introduction and chapter 3 appeared in "The Revolution's Fourth Face on the Fourth Network: Feuding over Cuba on U.S. Educational Television, 1959–1970," *Journal of American History* 107, no. 3 (December 1, 2020): 636–57; and "Drug Wars: Revolution, Embargo, and the Politics of Scarcity in Cuba, 1959–1964," *Journal of Latin American Studies* 49, no. 3 (2017): 489–516. An earlier version of chapter 2 was published as "The Medium Is the Message: The Screen Life of the Cuban Revolution, 1959–1962,"

Past and Present 246, no. 1 (February 2020): 227–67. I am grateful to the reviewers and colleagues who provided feedback on those submissions.

Some debts are built on lessons learned, others on the instigation to learn more. A book about knowledge production cannot help but reflect on both process and outcome. Above all, I am grateful to the many Cubans who, over the years, have issued the humbling and galvanizing referendum (*tú no sabes na'*) that not only inspired me to keep looking but also, in different ways, became the very subject (and "Subject") of this book.

The Subject of Revolution

Introduction

"The director is getting impatient. The camera is ready, awaiting the famous call: 'Lights, sound, camera, ACTION.' But something is missing. . . . Why is this chair vacant? Is there no plot? Of course, there is . . . or should I say . . . there will be."[1]

In May 1961, Cuban cultural officials launched a competition—one among many in the years that would follow—to identify a script of "national interest." With a prize of 1,000 pesos at stake and a jury staffed by prominent writers (Alejo Carpentier, José Soler Puig, José Valdés Rodríguez) and directors (José Massip, Julio García Espinosa), the call went out across the island, recruiting ordinary Cubans as prospective authors of the revolutionary epic. Fresh off victory over the Bay of Pigs invasion, the implications of this invitation exceeded the cinematographic. As filmmakers mobilized to document the Revolution's achievements and promote popular identification, the directive to pen a script with national interest was effectively superfluous.

The competition thus promoted both imaginative and ideological work. Aspiring screenwriters responded in kind, threading together personal and political dramas in such submissions as "Por fin somos iguales" (At last we are equal), "Todos tenemos cabida en la Revolución" (We all belong in the revolution), and, most straightforwardly, "Patria" (Fatherland) and "Libertad" (Freedom).[2] It is also notable, however, that none of these scripts seems to have been published, and a few were *censurados*. Indeed, the real prize—the promise that the winning entry would be made into a film—appears never to have been awarded.

How does a revolution become a Revolution, at once political theory and popular experience? From television to travel bans, academic exchange, and popular music, *The Subject of Revolution* explores how knowledge about the 1959 Cuban Revolution was generated and how the Revolution in turn shaped ways of knowing and being. Throughout, I argue that revolutions in general, and the Cuban Revolution in particular, have transformed not only political and social structures but also epistemological orders. In France, Haiti, Mexico, and Russia, world-making revolutions overturned governments *and* recast the prevailing "*imago mundi*," as María del Pilar Díaz Castañón writes.[3] It thus fell to those who led and lived them to fabricate meaning anew, from the efforts of political leaders to produce usable knowledge about the populace—and render them governable subjects—to the associated vehicles through which ordinary people construed their realities. The "Subject of Revolution," I propose, can be understood as the evolving, not always consonant, amalgam of the imaginaries constructed by its many subjects, from state officials to professionals from a variety of disciplines and ordinary people within and beyond the island's borders.

To trace knowledge production from above and below, this book centers the interactive channels through which the Revolution acquired meaning for its constituents. The first three chapters of the book take up mediums (the written press, television, and radio) that served as a crucible for revolutionary process and were in turn transformed by it, as the new government nationalized and politicized the cultural landscape it had inherited. In their interaction with these technologies and other mediums of revolutionary engagement (travel and research, school and work, music and dance), people across the hemisphere, and most especially Cubans themselves, became mediums in turn—transfigurative vessels for relating and reframing revolutionary change—and thus subjects of Revolution.[4]

Overall, I contend that the outsized global mark made by the Cuban Revolution was not exclusively a function of its ideological content but also the ways in which it channeled the era's most pressing debates (over socialism, civil rights, mobility and immobility, intellectual freedom, and popular culture) through its most pervasive mediums. From transnational press wars to solidarity radio outreach, the Revolution spoke to a broad set of international actors, among whom its exile community figured centrally, and constituted new "imagined communities": publics and counterpublics organized around the "reflexive circulation of discourse."[5] As Lillian Guerra has proposed, despite the symbolic significance attached to combat, the Revolution was thus, in the words of her Cuban interlocutors, "mostly made by talking."[6]

The transnational reach of the Cuban Revolution also drew on a shared sense of its singularity. In part, and not for the first time, foreigners looked to Cuba to perform difference—from US imperialism or Jim Crow–style racism, Soviet orthodoxy, and Marxist-Leninist formalism. The fact that US officials worked so insistently to overturn the Revolution only reinforced this commitment to its importance. US hostility in turn compelled Cuban officials to court international audiences: both geostrategic allies against diplomatic and economic isolation, and passionate fellow travelers—many located in the United States—to burnish the Revolution's political potency.[7]

Yet Cuba's international outreach did not prompt universal acclaim; many across the hemisphere (and beyond) came to define their politics in critical relation to the Revolution. At the same time, island leaders bemoaned the contaminating effect of the foreign and sought to delimit its domestic reverberations. In short, the virtual and embodied interactions between the Revolution's international and Cuban subjects were ripe with interpretive possibility and rampant misinterpretation. Meanwhile, as foreigners considered the proper way to "love" (or hate) the Revolution, the fact of being *subject to* revolutionary authority inevitably shaped how Cubans uniquely came to know the subject of Revolution.[8]

This book thus attends to the Revolution's global projections in relation to the specific experiences of its island subjects. For Cubans, revolutionary world building was informed not only by au courant transnational debates but also by the ubiquitous and authoritarian character of revolutionary politics. In their totalizing aims, however, revolutionary officials did not act on a blank canvas. The early abandonment of partisan institutions, electoral practices, and the traditional pillars of civil society made culture, broadly conceived, an especially vital seat for political extension *and* popular epistemologies. At times, culture also served as an avenue for the expression of dissent alongside other modes of popular understanding and participation.

An orientation to knowledge production thus allows us to glimpse what often remains otherwise imperceptible: the channels, frameworks, and vocabularies through which Cubans processed revolutionary change. Interpretation is not equivalent to revision or resistance, but it is a definitionally active and analytically significant form of engagement.[9] Not everyone took a stab at writing the revolutionary story, and even fewer were able to sit in the director's chair, but the Cuban Revolution interpellated many subjects, both within and beyond its borders, as prospective readers of the realities it had created.[10] Cubans in turn developed their own scripts, public and hidden, for inhabiting the Subject of Revolution and thus became subjects—actors and, however boundedly, agents—on the revolutionary stage.

Knowing and Being

"My first reading of the script gave me the impression that I had seen this text before. . . . As I went over it more carefully, recollections dawned on me. No, I had not seen this particular movie, but I had come across many like it. . . . The intent was always the same—to whitewash totalitarian excesses and to support a regime of terror, while concealing this in a false context of impartiality and objectivity."[11] So concluded self-taught propaganda expert Edward Hunter following his examination of the 1965 documentary *Three Faces of Cuba*, directed by Robert Carl Cohen. Hunter had risen to prominence in Cold War US politics thanks to his purported discovery of Chinese "brainwashing." On this basis, the Truth about Cuba Committee, an anticommunist Cuban exile group, had contracted him to weigh in on *Three Faces of Cuba*, a film he ultimately classified as "black"—that is, covert enemy—propaganda.

Three Faces of Cuba, which first aired on educational television stations across the country in 1965, had been commissioned by a Chicago affiliate of National Educational Television (NET), a recently debuted initiative to raise the standards of US television through civic-minded programming. The film offered a unique window onto early revolutionary Cuba following the rupture of diplomatic relations with the United States. Amid documentary footage, the movie featured the perspectives of the titular three Cubans, including one from the exile community. Yet this effort to bring together a variety of voices did not sit well with many viewers. The televised broadcast of *Three Faces of Cuba* provoked a firestorm of controversy, particularly among Cuban exiles. Their campaign against the film would spur not only public outcry but also government hearings and an FBI investigation.

To give their grievances credibility, the Truth about Cuba Committee enlisted Hunter to assess the film's claims to objectivity. In the thick of the Cold War, this was no mere academic matter: objectivity was a category with serious ideological baggage. In the new arena of television news, for example, the Departments of State and Defense molded media representations behind the scenes, even as the US government worked to present capitalism as the natural seat of objectivity. At the same time, in the spirit of fighting communism, the American public was encouraged to accept the dependence of press freedom on corporate underwriting, as Nancy Bernhard has argued.[12] This served to define objectivity as apolitical *and* anticommunist—a framing that many intellectuals independently adopted—all while obscuring the politicking on which it depended.[13] The seeming obviousness of this construction belied the myriad connotations attached to objectivity: impartiality and balance, anticommunism—but also the renunciation of ideology.

Yet the conflation of anticommunism with truth in representation was not only imposed by US cold warriors like Hunter. In the early 1960s, the flight of Cubans from the island led to the formation of a uniquely power-ful exile community, centered in South Florida and stretching well beyond it. Though members of other exile groups, notably the Hungarian refu-gees of the late 1950s, had also mobilized to intervene in US political debates, the sheer size of the Cuban out-migration—with 273,868 island Cubans heading north between 1959 and 1964, and many more thereafter—quickly dwarfed its predecessors.[14] But the political authority afforded to Cuban exiles was also a function of the significant representation of profes-sionals, college graduates, and urban dwellers within their ranks. In the context of the high-profile standoff between Cuba and the United States, exiles thus acquired an unprecedented visibility in US politics. They also assumed a leading role in shaping international depictions of the Revolu-tion itself, as the island government extended its outreach over the air-waves, and Cubans in the United States mobilized to counter its influence.

In their efforts (at times lukewarm) to defend *Three Faces of Cuba* from the media storm it had unleashed, NET representatives adhered to the dis-puted ideal of balance. The film, they insisted, had modeled balance in its focus on the three Cubans, with the exile's narration occupying exactly half of the film's duration, and the other half devoted to supporters of the revo-lution. Only by hearing from the proverbial "other side," they maintained, could the public apprehend the era's complex global issues. This imagined "view from nowhere"—what Lorraine Daston has called "aperspectival objectivity"—thus comprised incommensurate views from "somewhere."[15] The public, they presumed, would achieve analytical synthesis by landing somewhere in the middle.

Critics of *Three Faces of Cuba*, among whom Cuban exiles occupied a prominent place, raised questions about both the structuring device of bal-ance as well as the narrators chosen to enact it. They did not, however, re-linquish the principle of objectivity. In distancing themselves from the three faces depicted in the film (including the exile, whom they branded insuffi-ciently critical), Cuban exiles often requested the opportunity to introduce a "fourth face" representing their own views. In doing so, they cited their personal knowledge of communism as the necessary precondition for repre-sentational objectivity. At the same time, revolutionary officials presented political *commitment* as the foundation for revolutionary truth. Notably, *Three Faces of Cuba*, one of the few US films made in the early 1960s with official permission, never appeared on island screens.[16]

In order to explain the contradictions of knowing Cuba—how it is that reasonable people can be convinced of irreconcilable facts—observers have long relied on some version of a truism: that multiple things can simultaneously be true; that the Revolution, particularly in its early years, was liberating for some and oppressive for others. This claim has, in turn, been critiqued as an interpretive evasion, even an attempt to whitewash revolutionary repression, US imperialism, or the forcible efforts of leaders to mold popular mentalities. It is striking, however, that supporters of the Revolution, like exile critics of *Three Faces of Cuba*, have long grounded their claims in the evidence of experience.[17] Much work has been devoted to disentangling this Gordian knot, in the hopes that we might illuminate a path to a less "partial" view.[18]

But what if we were to zoom in on, rather than back away from, the fact of subjectivity? Globally, the 1960s witnessed the cross-fertilization of "knowing" and "being" in the classic formulation of philosopher of science Michael Polanyi. Engaging a long tradition of philosophical inquiry, Polanyi proposed that our understanding of what is known and knowable is subjectively contingent and processual. In this respect, all knowledge, he suggested, is better understood as "personal knowing." It is, after all, no coincidence that the Cuban Revolution bore a strong attraction for the existentialist philosophers of its day, most notably Jean-Paul Sartre and Simone de Beauvoir, and countercultural gurus of all stripes. Even as revolutionary officials, exile leaders, and the many publics caught in between them battled over the nature and future of the Revolution, I propose that these debates—and their grounding in personal experiences and allegiances—served to fortify, rather than undermine, the sense that it was a *singular* entity, in both senses of the word. Different ways of knowing and being thus endowed the idea of revolution with an "intimation of coherence," to use Polanyi's words.[19]

The connection between objectivity and subjectivity (thinking and feeling, knowing and being) was forged in the era's most urgent polemics and popular mediums. It was a historical effect of mediation, and the translation from the personal to the political that occurred in its course. Even the most arcane debates about the Revolution were thus rooted in the intensity of personal commitments. This necessarily imperils any "aperspectival" perch observers past or present might claim to occupy—and renders suspect any single narrative of its reception.

Charting the history of revolutionary world building demands that we engage the fact of multiplicity without neglecting the operation and circulation of power. I do not aim to offer a comprehensive survey of the Revolution's potentially infinite "faces" (an impossible and intellectually dubious task), but I do seek to understand how popular imaginaries were informed by differences of race, class, gender, and ideology. In this, revolutionary projection was highly consequential, as revolutionary officials both cited and effaced the specific experiences of Afro-Cubans, mobilized to root out gender and sexual nonconformity, and cultivated new revolutionary subjects, including students, peasants, and workers, not to mention international allies. Exile leaders also drew on inclusive and exclusionary framings in forging revolutionary counterpublics, rendering some identities more visible (and politically valuable) than others.[20]

As I argue across these chapters, the Subject of Revolution came to intersect with a variety of affiliated causes, from the battle against racial discrimination to global anti-imperialism, and interpellated a vast and sometimes incongruous group of subjects. At the same time, political officials often silenced the assertion of meaningful particularity, whether the right to think differently or to acknowledge the ongoing inequalities and differential experiences that shaped individual worldviews. Overall, this book centers both the *breadth* of the Revolution's epistemological reach and the *narrowness* of the master narratives that island leaders (as well as their counterparts in Miami and Washington) crafted in response.[21] But it also aims to capture the dialectic between knowing and being from below: how the subjects of Revolution, broadly conceived, framed their own, inevitably disparate, engagement with revolutionary experience—and truth.

Vikings, Worms, and Other Revolutionary Icons

In the 1960s, *Aventuras*, directed by small-screen veteran Erick Kaupp, was one of the most popular programs on Cuban television, having brought the beloved and politically opportune stories of Robin Hood and Zorro to island audiences. In 1967, the series featured the epic saga of the Vikings, transmitted live from a small television studio. "Los Vikingos" presented a unique spin on the epic tale, departing liberally from the historical record. The action begins with the sudden death of King Ragur, which plunges the Vikings into a succession crisis. Erik is the next in line to the throne but must face off against Harald, who is plotting Erik's death. When Erik is away, Harold installs a repressive dictatorship, and it falls to Erik and his allies to confront him.[22]

For its Cuban audience, the relevance of this story was clear. In vanquishing the treacherous Harold, Erik enacted the Revolution's victory over its own North American foe.[23] The lyrics to the show's theme made these

SON LAS SIETE Y MEDIA
Y LOS TELEVISORES SE ABREN
AL MUNDO DE INSOLITAS
AVENTURAS DE LOS

¡VIKINGOS!

A 1967 ad for the "Los Vikingos," a popular installment of the
Cuban television show *Aventuras*. *Cuba*, no. 9 (September 1967): 2.

resonances overt, declaring that "without liberty, a people cannot be
at peace."[24] As children across the island donned capes and swords, the
Comité de Defensa de la Revolución (CDR, Committee for the Defense of
the Revolution)—a neighborhood vigilance organization—set out to draw
even more direct parallels between the tenth-century hero and his Cuban
admirers. The committee ordered the production of a pin in his likeness,
bearing a shield that pledged loyalty to the Vikings—and the CDR. But
something about the analogy drew scrutiny, as one pin owner recalls, and
the effort to cultivate political identification through the Viking precedent
was abruptly shelved.[25] Meanwhile, "Los mambises," the next installment

This 1967 Viking pin encouraged CDR members to identify with Erik's example, especially his enthusiastic defense of his people's freedom.

of *Aventuras* (1969), drew its heroes from the safer territory of Cuba's nineteenth-century struggle for independence.

This pin bears fruitful comparison to another in my personal collection, which features, as a somewhat improbable hero, a worm. By the time of its issue in the early 1960s, the term *gusano* had, following a long Cuban political tradition, been adopted as an epithet for Cubans who opposed the revolutionary government. In response, some who identified as part of that group began to reclaim the moniker as a term of ironic self-definition. The CIA hoped to capitalize on this inversion and, in planning Operation Mongoose (1962), turned to a variety of mediums, from radio to comic books and trinkets, to disseminate the symbol of the "gusano libre." They thus encouraged disaffected Cubans to take up the worm as a political icon and a spur to anti-Castro mobilization.[26] Exile commentators thereafter

Gusano pin.

incorporated the figure into political cartoons and appeals as well, and one journalist found worm-sporting key rings, reportedly "in great demand among self-styled and defiant gusanos," being "sold openly on Havana streets."[27] But it remains hard to know how many island Cubans embraced these pins (along with the associated armbands, pencils, and other trinkets) as markers of not only alienation from but active resistance to the revolutionary government.[28]

By their very nature, revolutions challenge received wisdom, unsettling public and private frameworks for understanding the world. But for revolutions to become a "way of life," they need to penetrate the realm of culture, infusing artistic practice and popular habits.[29] Unsurprisingly, the revolutionary governments with the greatest longevity have made significant investments in the culture industries, spawning innovations and debates in literature, the visual arts, and film.[30] Yet state patronage of the arts was rarely envisioned as an end in itself. Rather, leaders turned to culture as the most direct means to reshape worldviews. The audience for such representations likewise stretched beyond national borders. The virtual potentialities of the era's mass mediums allowed revolutionary officials (along with their political antagonists) to reach allied audiences near and far, with less sympathetic observers often listening in, too.

Like their Mexican and Bolshevik counterparts before them, Cuban leaders sought to harness culture to the project of revolutionary integration, an inescapable term that condensed formal participation and ideological training. This mission inspired novel investments in—and political scrutiny of—new cultural institutions, such as the Cuban Institute of Cinematographic Art and Industry (Instituto Cubano de Arte e Industria Cinematográfico, ICAIC). Indeed, the big screen played host to some of Cuba's most celebrated artistic achievements and heated polemics, with directors and cultural bureaucrats regularly sparring over the parameters of revolutionary filmmaking.[31] The intensity of these debates reflected the political potential revolutionary leaders had ascribed to film, famously described by Vladimir Lenin as the "most important of all the arts," as well as the ambitions of the adventurous directors who sometimes clashed with them. The aesthetic avant-garde was similarly bent toward political and popular ends in other state-sponsored mediums, such as poster art and photography. Tasked with recording and promoting revolutionary "uplift," the image thus channeled, in José Quiroga's words, a "certain kind of *knowledge* that would be used to produce more *knowledge* in turn."[32]

The field of Cuban studies now boasts extensive coverage of the artistic output and political battles attached to revolutionary culture.[33] We can count on equally comprehensive analysis of the US government's cultural footprint across the hemisphere.[34] Indeed, the very vitality of these fields has made culture one of the most debated subjects in the broader corpus of Revolution studies. Yet despite the massifying aims of revolutionary leaders and their counterparts in Washington, the audience for such representations has more rarely figured into scholarly accounts. At the same time, popular culture has been a mostly spectral presence in discussions of the Revolution's political and economic trajectory.[35]

If revolutionary leaders and their antagonists turned to culture as a vehicle of ideological incorporation, the question of how the populace received such efforts is especially pressing. I propose that the Revolution—and popular interpretations thereof—were decisively shaped by the state-sponsored spillover between political and popular culture. Though the meanings associated with these concepts have long been subject to debate, here I deploy both terms as inclusively as possible, with a focus on political concepts and behavior on one hand and cultural systems and practices on the other, especially in their variously "mass," "subaltern," and "folk" forms.[36] In charting this interface, I heed Gilbert M. Joseph and Daniel Nugent's framing of state formation and popular culture as "each connected to, as well as expressed in, the other," with hierarchical relations of power infusing their meeting.[37]

The urgency attached to revolutionary (and counterrevolutionary) programs prompted officials to embed what they viewed as transparent ideological messages in cultural platforms. Yet even in these politicized circumstances, listeners, readers, and viewers did not always decode the resulting artifacts—Vikings, worms, and otherwise—in predictable ways.[38] This book thus treats popular culture as an inherently unwieldy template for political projection, which catalyzed ideological integration, disintegration, and translation on both sides of the Florida Straits.

This orientation opens up space for new historical actors. In a diasporic political universe inhabited almost exclusively by men, the cultural work of revolutionary extension was often performed by women, from teachers to phone operators, librarians, letter writers, and more.[39] Meanwhile, the geographical reach of these debates and mediums allowed a diverse (and often distant) cast of actors—workers, peasants, and students, as well as activists, correspondents, scholars, and ordinary people across the hemisphere—to tune in to the Subject of Revolution. Though the crossfire between Havana and Washington/Miami looms large here, I also draw inspiration from a vibrant field of inquiry into the Revolution's Latin American, European, and Global South constituencies.[40] This book thus relies on new and previously unutilized archives in Cuba, the United States, and Canada, as well as recently declassified sources, including a Freedom of Information Act request I submitted about the activists discussed in chapter 4.

In the spirit of my orientation to the *how* of revolutionary knowledge production and the relations of power bound up in it, I also seek to denaturalize the terms of our archival engagement. Sometimes this has led me to reframe classic secondary sources as objects of primary analysis, most notably in my discussion of experts in chapter 5. Elsewhere, I trace the genesis of classic archives of the Revolution, including those attached to radio and print media. Following some of the historical actors who appear in chapter 1, I propose that understanding the means of archival production is a necessary precondition to harnessing such sources to our analytical ends.

The island side of this story relies especially on sources about the revolutionary cultural bureaucracy. Recent scholarship has drawn on these records to illuminate the conflictive and politically consequential interactions among artists, intellectuals, and cultural bureaucrats.[41] Here I frame them as a window onto revolutionary efforts to bridge political and popular culture. If cultural officials played a leading role in generating knowledge about ordinary Cubans while attempting to rally them behind the revolutionary cause, this archive offers evidence, however sporadic, of the diverse responses such efforts encountered among the public.

These sources bear fruitful comparison with a collection of interviews I assembled in collaboration with two undergraduate students. With no pretense at rigorous sampling, we asked a group of several dozen Cubans, both on the island and in the diaspora, to share their most important cultural memories and experiences. These discussions turned up more than a few surprises, capturing moments of cultural and political inflection largely invisible in other accounts. They have thus provided valuable context, as well as a salutary reminder not to rely exclusively on official sources.[42]

Reading across these diverse sources, I explore how political officials and the Revolution's many subjects mobilized culture as a vehicle of ideological struggle and epistemological consolidation. In this, they built on an established tradition of revolutionary politics that featured cultural forms—literature and poetry in the late nineteenth century, photography and essays in the 1920s and '30s, and radio in the 1940s and '50s—and novel constructs, from "racelessness" to revolutionary nationalism, to recruit followers at home and abroad.[43] They also contributed to, and often spearheaded, the kind of "culture wars" that would come to define the 1960s and '70s across the hemisphere.[44] Personalizing the political—and politicizing the personal—thus ran straight through the fertile terrain of popular culture.

Mediums of Revolution

To understand the interplay between political and popular culture, this book centers on *mediums* and *paradigms*, as well as their dynamic interaction. Over the course of seven chapters, I trace how the individuals who engaged them collectively produced the Subject of Revolution and thus became, in different ways, its subjects. This book aims to capture their epistemological and affective contributions to that construct while also disaggregating the very notion of a revolutionary (or counterrevolutionary) public. Several themes—the weaponization of the media (chaps. 1–3 and 7), solidarity and its limits (chaps. 3–5), socialist transition and translation (chaps. 5–7), and the definition of the popular (chaps. 2 and 7)—underpin multiple chapters and serve as important analytical bridges. So, too, do key terms that acquired or renewed their salience in revolutionary times, including *truth* (chaps. 1 and 5), *betrayal* (chaps. 1–3 and 5), *integration* (chaps. 6–7), and *the people* (chaps. 1–3 and 7). Throughout, these categories connect, narratively and analytically, the Revolution's experimental and institutionalizing phases, as well as its domestic and transnational publics: partisans, opponents, and those who fell in between.

The book's early chapters follow the evolution from an early ideological openness to the political and economic radicalization associated with the escalation of hostilities with the United States (1959–61). This process culminated in the April 1961 Bay of Pigs invasion and the declaration of the Revolution's socialist and then Marxist-Leninist (December 1961) character. These years also saw the debut of signal revolutionary initiatives, such as the reduction of urban rents and related housing measures, agrarian reform, public health extension, educational overhaul, and the battle against racial discrimination, launched in March 1959 and concluded two years later.

As Fidel Castro consolidated his hold over political power, his government moved to nationalize the cultural industries as it battled with journalists, radio hosts, and TV producers over the future of civil society. The first three chapters thus engage mediums in the most literal sense, from the written press (chap. 1) to television (chap. 2) and radio (chap. 3). Yet each chapter also introduces debates that played out in the space of these mediums—over freedom of the press, the politics of "the people," and solidarity—as well as the ways in which they channeled revolutionary participation and knowledge production.

Chapter 1, for example, highlights how media depictions of the revolutionary project functioned as a political agent, dating to the original stirrings of the revolutionary movement against Fulgencio Batista. After 1959, the written press played host to enduring transnational battles over the "truth about Cuba," as leaders drew on press contestation to make their case for political radicalization and a tightly controlled public sphere. Chapter 2 follows these debates onto the small screen, the unlikely but powerful seat for Fidel Castro's political outreach. From 1959 to 1961 and beyond, Castro took to television to shape popular understandings and to face off against his foes. In the process, he redefined the boundaries for media engagement in the Revolution and enduringly linked political participation to spectatorship.

By 1962, the media (radio, television, the written press) was in the hands of the government, and new cultural institutions—especially the Consejo

Nacional de Cultura, led by long-standing members of the Partido Socialista Popular (Popular Socialist Party, or PSP)—had launched initiatives to expand access to the arts while deploying culture as an ideological tool. Chapter 3 picks up in the aftermath of the media wars, as domestic and foreign observers confronted a constrained sphere for public engagement. In this context, both US and Cuban governments moved to weaponize knowledge about their antagonists through covert radio outreach. These efforts contributed to the constitution of transnational networks of furtive listeners, who wrote letters, celebrating or critiquing what they had heard on the air. Such correspondence consolidated new forms of communication with—and emotional connections to—revolutionary and oppositional causes alike.

The middle chapters of the book are rooted in the mid-1960s, which, amid waxing and waning relations with the Soviet Union, saw expanding revolutionary entanglements abroad and battles at home between advocates for Soviet-style economic planning and those favoring the more radical proposal—associated with Che Guevara—to build socialism and communism simultaneously. The rapidly shifting landscape of the mid- to late 1960s witnessed the high-profile campaign to forge a "new man" and related efforts to briefly expand—and then, more decisively, constrain—political and cultural expression. This was most notoriously realized in the camps of the Unidades Militares de Ayuda a la Producción (Military Units to Aid Production), run in the central province of Camagüey from 1965 to 1968, where religious believers, political dissidents, and gender and sexual nonconforming individuals were sent to remake themselves through compulsory productive labor.

These processes shaped how both international and domestic observers came to interact with the Subject of Revolution, catalyzing battles over freedom of movement and expression, the status of intellectuals, and the diverse form(s) of Cuban socialism. These debates, as they transpired in the written press, on television, and on radio, also flowed through other mediums of revolutionary engagement, including travel, expertise, and work. Chapter 4, for example, extends the discussion of solidarity politics to clashes over immobility, specifically as experienced by activists against the US travel ban (notably the Student Committee for Travel to Cuba [SCTC]) and island Cubans. By the mid-1960s, as two highly publicized SCTC trips to the island ended in legal prosecution in the United States, the 1965 Camarioca boatlift drew renewed attention to curbs on Cubans' movement. In the process, travel bans became an important prism through which people assessed the Revolution itself, prompting new forms of allegiance, identification, disaffection, and dissent.

Among the most important travelers to the island throughout the 1960s were Western intellectuals who sought to actualize their solidarity with Cuba. With a focus on the mid- to late 1960s, chapter 5 traces how the interaction between experts and the Revolution came to influence and, in some respects, define the shape of Cuban socialism. Yet as these scholars quickly discovered, their professional contributions were welcome up to the point where they did not conflict with political imperatives. By the late 1960s, the encounter between the Revolution and its experts had inexorably soured, turning intellectual freedom into an enduring political battleground.

These cultural and political shifts closely followed economic policy of the mid- to late 1960s, which had witnessed a dramatic turn in the Guevarist direction amid the buildup to a programmed ten-million-ton sugar harvest in 1970. The failure of that effort inspired more than a decade of economic and political integration with the Soviet bloc. Domestically, the 1970s brought not only new openings and opportunities—from an era of modest socialist plenty to initiatives to formalize popular participation in politics—but also campaigns to homogenize popular understandings.[45] Culture sat at the center of many of these efforts, underpinning campaigns to integrate the public into revolutionary politics on the one hand (as in the aficionado, or amateur arts, movement) and to enforce ideological orthodoxy on the other. The infamous *quinquenio gris* ("five-year gray period," dated 1971–76, but often extended earlier to 1968) thus saw the rise of *parametración*, or the purging of ideologically and sexually nonconforming artists and intellectuals.[46]

Covering this period from the late 1960s through the 1970s, chapters 6 and 7 chart the fraught interplay between political consolidation and popular culture. Chapter 6, for example, explores the development of Cuban socialism as experienced by ordinary Cubans, foregrounding two concepts adapted from Soviet precedents: *superación*, or self-improvement, and *emulación*, or socialist competition. These categories channeled official efforts to make culture a universal site of individual cultivation and work, especially of the productive variety, an essential value in revolutionary culture. A new culture of work (and the work of culture) bore political implications, promoting new forms of socialist discipline, actualized in embodied practice, and enacting revolutionary consolidation through culture.

Chapter 7 also approaches culture as an arena of political integration, as the island government moved to bring popular culture under its sponsorship and authority. In a country whose international reputation had long been tied to its cultural output, specifically the music and dance innovated by Cubans of African descent, this effort had direct political consequences. In the 1960s and '70s, officials integrated leisure spaces along lines of race while also restricting the circulation of content they viewed as antithetical to their goals. Such efforts in turn shaped subaltern perspectives, inspiring both identification and disidentification with the Revolution's course. Underpinning the resulting debates was a question first raised in the earliest years of the Revolution: when it came to culture—or politics, for that matter—what, exactly, was "popular"?

On Commitments

It has become common in books like this to begin with a discussion of vocabulary, in part to explain to readers (and editors) why scholars of Cuba refer to "Fidel" or "Castro," cite the "embargo" versus the "blockade," or adhere to the grammatically incorrect practice of capitalizing the word "Revolution." Since I and others have discussed these issues elsewhere, here I will add only that I conceive of this book as a partial response to the final question.[47] But the need to contextualize terms speaks to a broader problem: that of the subjectivity attached to our academic production. In writing about the Revolution, we, like many who have come before us, enter a metatextual universe in which our choice of words, topics, and subjects is held to signal political, and therefore personal, attachments.

Accounts of the Revolution's past and present inevitably seem to turn on judgments of culpability: most notably, whether one should hold the US or Cuban government accountable for the circumstances faced by ordinary Cubans today. These debates have assumed a timeless character, yet they are rooted in assumptions that, from a popular perspective, feel out of touch.[48] The zero-sum discourse about responsibility and blame is, moreover, a fundamentally historical construction. It is therefore ripe for the contextual analysis and archival scrutiny that historians prize.

Yet the terms of these battles feel particularly unsatisfying at this historical moment. Following several summers of popular unrest and a historic out-migration from the island, the need for economic and political change in Cuba (*and* in US policy toward Cuba) has never been so apparent.

Cubans have themselves taken to the streets in unprecedented numbers to protest shortages, blackouts, and the denial of political freedoms. Cuba has long borne the weight of external ideological commitments; since 1959, many people around the world have come to hold a stake in the Revolution. But we cannot propose to write about the Subject of Revolution without featuring those subjects who lived its consequences on the front lines. The principal "subjects of Revolution" are, and have always been, Cubans themselves. In the end, they are thus the subject of this story, too.

1 The Truth about Cuba

. . . .

"If words could destroy," mused Joseph Hansen, "a single day's production of 'hate Cuba' language in the American capitalist press would suffice to make Havana look like Hiroshima on the evening of August 6, 1945. Even the staid newspapers," the US Trotskyist wrote in the *Militant* in 1960, "those that believe a public image of dignity pays off best, are at the firing line, bucket in one hand, filth in the other." In its intent and effect, US press coverage of the Revolution amounted to a full-fledged "Operation Brainwash," Hansen argued, fueled by the interests of those who stood to lose economically with the Revolution's success. Following his 1960 trip to the island, he pledged to offer his own insights so that readers might finally discover "the truth about Cuba," as he titled his piece.[1]

Roughly a year later, a very different organization emerged to make claims on that truth. The Truth about Cuba Committee (TACC), founded in 1961 by Cuban exile Luis Manrara, also proposed to "divulge the truth about Cuba." Yet where Hansen located truth in solidarity with the Cuban Revolution, the committee advanced a "total war against Cuba's Communist regime," waged in and through the media.[2] The committee, as an English-language bulletin from 1961 explained, aimed to "disseminate factual information to the American people, so that they [would] better understand and, therefore, be able to more intelligently evaluate, what has happened and is happening in Cuba under a communist regime."[3] To that end, the TACC launched several major offensives to monitor and shape coverage of Cuba in the US media.

Before Hansen and Manrara, however, there was Fidel Castro, who in January 1959 inaugurated Operation Truth, the first of many such campaigns that propelled the Revolution's first year. As the new government set out to prosecute and, in some cases, execute *batistianos* accused of serious crimes, island officials were dismayed by the resulting outcry in the US press. To court a more sympathetic international reception, Castro invited nearly 400 correspondents from across the hemisphere to come and see the trials for themselves. The hope was that they would thus "witness, with their own eyes, the truth," as Castro proclaimed at a massive public rally on

January 21. "If it's necessary," he added, "we'll give them a permanent invitation . . . because here we don't have anything to hide from the world."[4]

In retrospect, the accumulation of these divergent claims to the truth about Cuba—not to mention Castro's "permanent invitation" to international journalists—can have a disorienting effect, familiar to anyone living in polarized times. For the last six decades, Cuba has offered a paradigmatic case study of how information can be mobilized to serve partisan, and often contradictory, ends. Yet media fracture around the Revolution has been so persistent that it is easy to forget that it, too, has a history. Here I trace how reporting on Cuba became politicized to begin with, as island and international (especially US) journalists waged a battle to report the—or *their*—truth about Cuba. From 1959 to 1961, I argue, the written press served as a key forum for defining and polemicizing the essence of the Revolution, both inside and outside Cuba.[5]

In explaining that politicization, many involved in these battles cited bias or, in the parlance of the time, "interests." The work of journalists, they proposed, was guided not by professional objectivity but rather by corporate or political allegiances. For outside observers, those loyalties might have been to the US businesses threatened by the economic program of the Revolution or to the anticommunist line that governed US policy. On the island, revolutionary officials issued similar charges against independent papers, accusing writers and editors who critiqued the course of the Revolution of selling out to imperialist interests.

The historical context in which the early years of the Revolution were reported indeed guaranteed that strong interests would come to bear on the press. Most directly, journalists on both sides of the Florida Straits forged relationships with their country's intelligence services, putting their work at the service of Cold War security objectives. Though we do not know how common these partnerships were, we can assume that such motivations, or at least the presumption of their existence, decisively shaped the work of reporters. But this is less a story of intrigue and conspiracy than of escalating political warfare. From growing hostility between the US and Cuban governments to the radicalization of the Revolution itself, ideological breaches widened over time, both in Cuba, where dissent was equated with counterrevolutionary commitments, and in the United States, where the opposite logic applied. Over the course of the Revolution's first two years, these positions continued to harden in an increasingly tense dialectic. The resulting debates undermined the very prospect of neutrality.

There is no question that some members of the US and international press misreported the Revolution in these early years. It may not have added up to an organized "campaign of calumnies," as revolutionary officials alleged, but such coverage indelibly shaped the perspectives of many across the hemisphere. Evidence of journalistic malpractice in turn left many on the island defensive about external reporting, abetting the conflation of critical and counterrevolutionary perspectives. Island leaders specifically cited the convergence of foreign and Cuban critiques of communism to justify attacks on the domestic press, both in the pages of newspapers affiliated with the government and in Fidel Castro's public addresses. Shrinking tolerance for dissent, alongside the assertion of dishonesty in foreign reporting, thus rendered untenable any publicly uncommitted stance.

Paradoxically, the battle for the truth about Cuba would end with the literal burial of the island's independent papers. Before they were interred, however, they were deluged with the so-called *coletillas* of early 1960, in which newspaper workers appended "notes" to stories they regarded as contrary to the interests of the Revolution. The coletillas were framed as an assertion of workers' freedom of expression, but owners quickly found them to infringe on their own ability to publish. The clash over coletillas brought to a head the conflict over press freedom in Cuba, triangulated through international and especially US critics. But it also drew attention to the seemingly incompatible truths of some newspaper workers, who condemned criticism of the Revolution as inaccurate and politically divisive, and owners, who insisted on its essential importance.

As scholars of the Revolution have long argued, the impact of newsroom confrontations reached far beyond journalism as such.[6] The writers and political officials pulled into these struggles knew that they were arguing not only about the place of reporting in a revolutionary society but also about the right and responsibility to define its very nature. In turn, freedom and truth in expression became leitmotifs of more encompassing political conversations, essential to evaluating the Revolution itself.

But where others have examined the press wars in terms of their implications for politics and civil society, here I draw attention to their epistemological effects. Waged in the name of a populace with limited opportunities to intervene, these transnational battles framed the truth about Cuba as dependent on the content and *context* of its production, evaluable based on a source's politics and provenance. As any cursory scan of the news would suggest, the terms of this discourse have proved enduring. Indeed, the

historical Cuban press wars have provided the language and, to a significant degree, the archive through which contemporary scholars and observers of Cuba continue to pursue our own facts—and, perhaps, truths.

The Thirteen

When the revolutionary movement against Fulgencio Batista erupted in the
1950s, the context of journalistic production—namely, imperialist intervention and influence—had long granted Cuba a prominent place in US newspapers. For decades, the American press had played a central role in both
publicizing and catalyzing events on the island. During the final Cuban war
of independence (1895–98), US papers had spearheaded the print jingoism
that would come to be known as "yellow journalism." Their coverage of
Cuban victimization at Spanish hands helped to consolidate support for
North American intervention. But US press involvement was not only imposed but actively solicited by Cuban leaders such as Máximo Gómez, who
hoped to use foreign attention to their advantage. They did not, however,
always exercise influence over the messaging itself. Though many in the
US reading public experienced solidarity with Cuban independence fight-
ers, such depictions were infused with paternalistic sentiments that did
not soon fade.[7] Even as the journalistic profession began to professional-
ize, imperialist blinders often shaped US coverage of Cuba, including when
directed toward more politically radical ends.[8]

The struggle against Fulgencio Batista, who had returned to power in a
1952 coup, once again drew foreign correspondents onto the stage. In the
face of government censorship, rebel leaders courted a foreign and, especially, US audience to raise awareness of their struggle and drum up support.
As Van Gosse has documented, US observers responded by casting Fidel Castro and other revolutionaries in a variety of molds, including the archetypal
"rebel with a cause."[9] These representations helped to render the anti-Batista
movement palatable and intelligible to an international audience.

The classic story in this regard is that of *New York Times* reporter
Herbert L. Matthews, whose interview with Castro's troops in the Sierra
Maestra helped convince both the US and Cuban public that the revolutionary leader was alive, despite government rumors to the contrary, and
spearheading a viable movement to topple Batista. Matthews—a veteran of
previous frontline engagements, such as the Spanish Civil War—quickly became identified with the revolutionary struggle. This provoked regular

conflict in his relationship with *Times* administrators, with whom he sparred in the late 1950s over their decision to relegate him to the editorial pages. The self-declared objective "style" maintained by the *Times* was, of course, "time-honored, successful and right," Matthews conceded. "But if I will be forgiven for saying so, the reputation of *The Times* has also been brought to its present level by the men who have broken through the rigid concepts of what is 'editorial' or 'impartial' or 'objective.'"[10]

Matthews was only the first in a succession of foreign (and Cuban) journalists, many inspired by him, who journeyed behind rebel lines. This came to include thirteen US correspondents at a variety of heritage papers and popular magazines, as well as several Latin American reporters, one of whom—Ecuadorian journalist Carlos Bastidas—was allegedly killed by Batista's secret police.[11] Throughout the struggle, Fidel Castro and other leaders courted journalists to draw positive attention to their cause. By multiple accounts, Castro also saw them as impressionable. As Leonard Teel notes, US correspondents offered no apologies for partial reporting on the rebels. Some explicitly abandoned any pretense to objectivity; most made no effort to cover "all sides."[12] According to Jay Mallin—an American correspondent for *Time* who had grown up in Cuba—"Virtually all the American journalists that visited Oriente leaned toward the rebels," including, he says, himself.[13]

In traveling to the sierra, foreign correspondents became protagonists of the revolutionary struggle and, in some cases, heroes by their own account.[14] This did not always contribute to rigorous reporting, but it certainly served the rebel cause. In the early flush of success, Fidel Castro drew regular attention to the role played by US journalists. The first revolutionary edition of *Bohemia* magazine celebrated four of them—Matthews, Mallin, Jules Dubois (*Chicago Tribune*), and Andrew St. George (*Life*)—as "[friends] of Cuba."[15] During Fidel Castro's April 1959 trip to the United States, the thirteen US correspondents were even honored with gold medals at the Cuban embassy in Washington, D.C.[16]

Yet in the months to come, many of these journalistic friends would become publicly bitter enemies. In doing so, they helped to consolidate an emerging revolutionary narrative about the treachery of former press allies. Among them, only Herbert Matthews maintained a complex but lifelong support for the Revolution, a position that garnered him notoriety, hate mail, and death threats. Meanwhile, Jules Dubois, the foreign correspondent who, besides Matthews, had perhaps most endeared himself to the revolutionary leadership, was turned into a symbol of foreign meddling. For his part, Andrew St. George became deeply disillusioned with the direction the Revolution had taken.[17] Only two years after *Bohemia* featured Matthews, Mallin, Dubois, and St. George as allies of Cuba, another article in the magazine accused Mallin and several others of being "CIA agents."[18]

Among the thirteen US correspondents, Dickey Chapelle (the only woman in the group) traveled to the sierra for *Reader's Digest*. Her sympathetic reporting on the rebel struggle was shaped by previous war zone engagements in the Pacific, Hungary (where she was in solitary confinement for over a month), and Algeria.[19] Though she did not speak Spanish, Chapelle felt a strong sense of identification with the Cubans she encountered in the mountains, and especially the female rebels among them, noting that she had "never [been] more proud to be a woman than when [she] marched with Fidel Castro's Cuban guerrillas."[20] But by late 1959, Chapelle had literally crossed enemy lines, living among exiled Cubans in South Florida, planning commando raids to Cuba, and even reportedly manufacturing bombs.[21]

In the thick of that evolution, Chapelle sought to account for why reporting on the Revolution had become so difficult. Admittedly, she pointed out, there was still an "almost total lack of knowledge in the US about the real causes of the Cuban Revolution," leading to what she viewed as hasty judgments of the January 1959 executions. But that ignorance, Chapelle insisted, was largely the result of deliberate obfuscation by Cuban leaders. Revolutionary officials offered "no hard-fact news sources," leaving foreign correspondents with only "rumors" to go by. Increasingly, Castro and other leaders refused meetings, and, Chapelle bemoaned, the "press found its needs pointedly ignored." But the most direct evidence of changing tides came from Carlos Franqui, a close Castro ally and editor of the official daily, *Revolución*. Franqui had been Chapelle's liaison to the rebel forces, and she was thus chagrined to hear his assessment that the government no longer intended to accommodate foreign reporters. Such outreach, he insisted, was "just a propaganda device" and one that had run its course.[22]

After 1959, many foreign correspondents in Cuba came to echo Chapelle's criticisms, characterizing revolutionary leaders as reluctant and even hostile interlocutors. Meanwhile, over the course of 1959, unfavorable foreign coverage became a regular target of revolutionary leaders and reporters alike. By summer 1959, Cuban journalistic associations had begun to decry an international "campaign of defamation" against the Revolution.[23] That resolution capped a process by which foreign reporting became inherently suspicious, in both its content and the political interests to which it was said to answer.

Many of these critiques came to center on the person of Jules Dubois. A longtime Latin America observer for the *Chicago Tribune*, Dubois had earned his stripes by denouncing Batista-era censorship in the Inter-American Press Association (IAPA, known in Latin America as SIP, the Sociedad Interamericana de la Prensa). In his reporting for the *Tribune*, he had also helped to craft a portrait of Fidel Castro as a legitimate leader with a broad following.[24] By the time Batista fled the country, Dubois was, by Leonard Teel's estimation, the "most informed journalist covering the revolution" and one of the few with a direct line to Batista.[25] These credentials helped to earn him the first interview with Fidel Castro following Batista's departure, a slight that Herbert Matthews never forgot. Dubois's unique access to Fidel also allowed him to write one of the first sanctioned biographies of the revolutionary leader.

Yet that book, published in 1959 with the subtitle "Rebel, Liberator, or Dictator?," helped to consolidate a turn in Dubois's portrayal of Castro. This shift, combined with his anticommunist politics, soon turned him into an official antagonist of the Revolution. As early as January 1959, the Communist daily *Noticias de Hoy* had been the first to publicly critique Dubois, citing his history of "interventionism" and self-aggrandizement.[26] At the heart of the paper's antagonism was a long-running feud between Dubois and Carlos Rafael Rodríguez, an editor at the paper and a longtime member of the Cuban Communist Party (renamed in 1944 as the Popular Socialist Party [PSP, Partido Socialista Popular]). Their enmity reflected not only political differences but also personal slights, including Dubois's efforts to exclude Rodríguez from the 1950 IAPA meeting in New York. But Rodríguez also seeded the accusation that would be perpetually attached to the journalist's name in Cuba: namely, that he was a covert intelligence agent.

That claim was hardly new. Though it remains difficult to confirm whether Dubois worked directly for the CIA, some US and Western reporters certainly did so, with diverse intentions and outcomes.[27] But Dubois *was* a colonel in the US Army and an instructor of the Latin American class at the General Staff School (Fort Leavenworth, Kansas), where he taught Carlos Castillo Armas. Castillo Armas, whom Dubois regarded as one of his "best students," went on to lead a military coup against the government of Jacobo Árbenz in Guatemala.[28] Yet nothing about the journalist's military or political background was hidden from view. In fact, Dubois had long relished the efforts of critics across Latin America to paint him as a Nazi, an "imperialist spy," or, in Rafael Trujillo's Dominican Republic, a Communist and "continental agitator."[29] Throughout the 1940s, he had made enemies of political leaders in Mexico, Guatemala, Venezuela, Panama, and especially Argentina, where Juan Perón's government published the condemnatory *Libro azul y blanco* (1945/51), with some ninety-seven pages devoted to him. Dubois responded by suing Perón for libel.[30]

Throughout spring 1959, these battles found renewed life in revolutionary Cuba.[31] By June, Dubois was openly sparring with Che Guevara in the pages of *Bohemia* over his alleged CIA affiliation.[32] In August, the revolutionary press turned up the heat on Dubois in response to his public criticism of Manuel Urrutia's resignation from the presidency, which he characterized as a "televised coup."[33] That allegation earned him the designation of "persona non grata" by the National Guild of Journalists (Círculo Nacional de Periodistas).[34] Finally, at the twenty-fourth national meeting of the Confederation of Cuban Workers (Confederación de Trabajadores de Cuba, CTC), workers approved a measure repudiating Dubois's presence on the island, and members of the gastronomic union vowed not to serve him in restaurants.[35] Dubois told officials in the US embassy that the resulting boycott had "had considerable effect."[36] As Fidel Castro and other revolutionary leaders continued to portray Dubois as a "hypocrite" and a "traitor,"[37] a public demonstration was staged against him, "[stopping] traffic" and culminating in a group of protesters singing the national anthem. At that point, the *Tribune* finally replaced him as their Cuba correspondent.[38]

The Cuban campaign against Jules Dubois formed part of a new media offensive mounted by revolutionary journalists and officials alike, who, by late 1959, contended that onetime friends like Dubois had become complicit in spreading falsehoods and brandishing the specter of Communism to undermine the Revolution on the international stage. They did so, critics argued, at the behest of allies in the US government and business sector, sacrificing journalistic integrity to "special interests."[39] If the thirteen correspondents played an outsized role in these early battles with the US press, the media war in turn quickly expanded beyond them, pushing revolutionary officials and reporters on the one hand and many Western correspondents on the other into their ideological barricades.

The Paper Curtain

In January 1959, revolutionary leaders had opened the doors to foreign reporters with Operation Truth. Those correspondents had responded, they maintained, by perpetrating "Operation Lie."[40] An April 1960 article in *Revolución* alleged that periodicals like *Time* and *Newsweek* employed a "technique of defamation," routing the "dispatches of their Latin America correspondents" to a "special department" for revision according to "what [was] convenient to the interests that represent both magazines."[41] Cuban journalists and officials also denounced the international wire services, especially the Associated Press (AP) and United Press International (UPI), and characterized their stories on the Cuban economy as "'[fabricated]' . . . 'on command,' based on ridiculously false information"[42]—and misleading or partial statements from political figures.[43] The government-allied *Diario Nacional* ran a regular feature titled "What the Wire Services Don't Say," while stationery circulated with the words "If you see A.P. or U.P.I., you are looking at a lie."[44]

In response, revolutionary leaders moved to establish their own wire service, soon to be born as Prensa Latina. Roughly a decade earlier, Juan Perón of Argentina had made a related but abortive attempt to assert Latin American control over the international distribution of news. One veteran of that enterprise, Jorge Masetti, joined the Revolution first in the sierra and then as a founding member of Prensa Latina. His response to the politicization of Revolution coverage was to assert an "objective, but not impartial," stance. The CIA conceded as much in its assessment of Prensa Latina, concluding that the reporting was factual, if prone to "neutral" reporting on Communism and unfavorable coverage of the United States.[45] On these grounds, as well as the financial support provided by the revolutionary government, Jules Dubois raised doubts about the agency, earning him another round of press criticism in Cuba. But the success of Prensa Latina can perhaps be measured by the fact that media all over the world, including the *Times* and the Associated Press itself, eventually relied on it to cover events in Cuba.[46]

But was "Operation Lie" real? In 1963, Maurice Zeitlin and Robert Scheer set out to answer that question by analyzing US press coverage of the Revolution through October 1960. Surveying *Life*, *Time*, and *Newsweek*, as well as three newspapers of different political orientations (*San Francisco Examiner*, *San Francisco Chronicle*, and *Washington Post*), they concluded that the materials "offered an excellent subject for the study, not of the Cuban Revolution, but rather of propaganda about the Revolution."[47] Having uncovered no articles "about the claimed positive social and economic achievements of the revolution," they instead noted a preponderance of propagandistic visuals, "name-calling," "fictionalized news," "half-truths,"

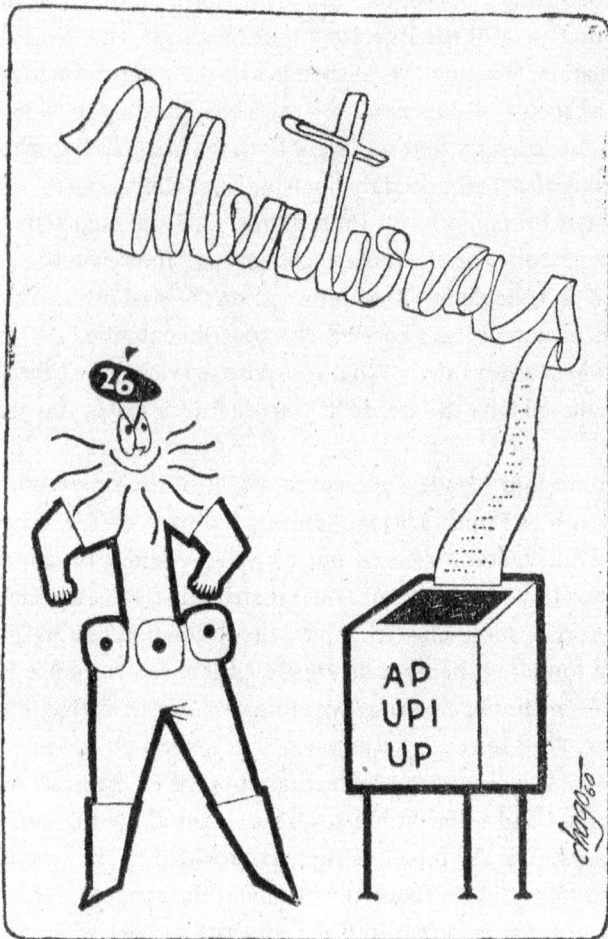

Featuring the character Julito 26, this political cartoon by
Chago Armas presents the Western wire services as generators
of "lies" rather than news. Chago, "Mentiras," *Revolución*,
May 25, 1960, 3.

and "fantasy (lies)."[48] Zeitlin and Scheer acknowledged that the "paper
curtain," as they called it, was not necessarily the result of willful obfuscation. Foreign correspondents preferred to be stationed in Havana, which
meant that the Revolution's footprint in the countryside was invisible to
them. Most also displayed a bias toward "scoops" and relied on the AP and
UPI to get them.[49] Yet the result was, in their view, the same. "Had our
press been government-controlled, carefully censored, and its writers

regimented," Zeitlin and Scheer posed, "would it have reported the Cuban Revolution very differently from the way it has?"[50]

This assessment, like those offered by other critics of the US press, presumed a largely homogeneous journalistic corps. But one of the most notable demarcations in early coverage of the Revolution was the one separating the so-called mainstream press from Black American papers. Many associated outlets, such as the *Afro-American* (Baltimore), the *Chicago Defender*, and the *New York Amsterdam News*, sent their own correspondents to Cuba, who drew positive attention to the revolutionary campaign against racial discrimination launched in March 1959. Black journalists also critiqued US coverage of the Revolution based on their own experiences with media misrepresentation. In the words of Thomas J. Davis, editor of the *Cleveland Call and Post*, "Negroes in America are quite used to the battle cry of the big press of calling any movement that demands fairness for all people regardless of race, creed, color or financial position, Communists."[51] These positive assessments were in turn amplified in the island press, even as Afro-Cuban journalists continued to draw attention to persistent racial disparities.[52]

Some constituencies thus had strong, and historically rooted, reasons to offer more positive coverage of the early Revolution. As Davis's words suggest, that disposition could leave journalists open to criticism. Indeed, where more sympathetic observers saw a "paper curtain" or, in Herbert Matthews's judgment, a "Cuban wall," other readers discerned revolutionary manipulation.[53] On these grounds, the *New York Times*—and Herbert Matthews in particular—became regular targets of exile protests, charged with bringing Castro to power and keeping him there.[54] Yet Rafael Rojas has pointed out that even the *Times*, which offered the "most extensive coverage of the island's political process," was divided in its portrayal of the Revolution, with Matthews pulling the editorial page in a more positive direction and correspondents such as Ruby Hart Phillips adopting a more critical stance.[55]

Ultimately, as Michael Francis proposed in his 1967 study of US coverage of the Revolution, "what the papers saw in the events of Cuba" was perhaps a function of "their own political ideologies."[56] Surveying seventeen major US newspapers between January 1959 and April 1961, Francis found relevant diversity in their depictions of agrarian reform, the rupture of diplomatic relations, the embargo, and even Fidel Castro himself. Even so, most of the papers "remained basically friendly to Castro for months after the revolution," he concluded.[57] Friendliness, however, did not translate into depth of coverage. Francis noted that most US newspapers dedicated little attention to internal Cuban dynamics, or even the major policy issues attached to US-Cuban tensions.[58] This left them poorly equipped to inform policy debates about the Revolution.

The 1961 Bay of Pigs invasion presents a key case in point. Though most US newspapers had spent months ridiculing Castro's allegations that covert preparations were afoot, Francis concluded that the US-sponsored intervention, in which a force composed largely of Cuban exiles unsuccessfully attempted to topple the island government, represented the "worst-kept secret in the history of modern 'black hand' diplomacy."[59] Even as relations between the United States and Cuba deteriorated, few papers had publicly supported a military intervention in Cuba. But editors and reporters collaborated with the Kennedy administration to prevent the news of the impending engagement from breaking. Only the *Nation* punctured that firewall, thanks to a report from Ronald Hilton, a Stanford professor of Romance languages who had witnessed CIA preparations for the invasion during a trip to Guatemala.[60]

The results were notoriously catastrophic. During the campaign, the US government refused to speak to the press, even on background.[61] Recently declassified documents suggest that the CIA may have even seeded false wire stories about the invasion.[62] And while a few prominent voices critiqued the pact of media silence that had allowed the botched plan to go forward, the US press largely stood by Kennedy in its aftermath.[63] Following a series of foreign policy failures, including the Cuban Missile Crisis and intervention in Vietnam, this kind of "news management" would soon galvanize press reformers who sought to adopt a more "adversarial" relationship with the state.[64]

Paradoxically, however, the tidal wave that the Bay of Pigs helped to unleash barely grazed coverage of the Revolution. The same events that insinuated doubts about press loyalty in the United States also precipitated the arrest and expulsion of many Western journalists from Cuba.[65] This included the eight US correspondents still in residence on the island at that point: Harold "Heine" Milks and Robert Berrellez of the AP, Henry Raymond and Martin Houseman of UPI, Ruby Hart Phillips, Dick Valeriani of NBC, Robert Perez (a stringer for the Mutual Broadcasting System), and Jay Mallin.[66]

With important exceptions—notably Juan de Onís of the *New York Times*—for years to come, correspondents who covered the island did so largely from a distance, "sometimes dishonestly bearing Havana datelines."[67] Many awaited invitations from Castro himself, propelling them to jump through the legal hurdles associated with acquiring a US visa.[68] Once in Cuba, they had to navigate not only the strings attached to their invitation—including the understanding that the government would foot the bill for their stay—but also predictable political dynamics.[69] Critics of these visits alleged that participants were suspiciously friendly to the Revolution in their reporting and might be receiving bribes.[70] Meanwhile, following a 1966 conversation with Ministry of the Interior chief Ramiro Valdés, Herbert Matthews noted that Valdés remained "firmly convinced that it is impossible for an American newspaperman to be objective even if he wanted to be."[71]

A Revolution in Journalism

Battles between Cuban officials and US correspondents consumed significant airtime in these early years, but they did not crowd out even more important changes in the world of Cuban newspapers. Between 1959 and 1961, the island's media landscape was indelibly altered by the Revolution. What began as a honeymoon between the press and the state soon morphed into an all-out war, as Cuba's independent papers found themselves on the wrong side of emergent political orthodoxies. But the transformation of Cuban journalism occurred not only at the hands of the new government but also in the clashes—some old, some new—*between* newspapers. These debates established a highly politicized standard for practicing journalism in the Revolution.

Dating back to the struggle against Spanish colonialism and slavery in the nineteenth century and the interaction with US imperialism in the early decades of the twentieth, Cuba's press had long hosted fiery political battles.[72] But it was the grassroots activism leading up to the Revolution of 1933, as well as the press censorship enacted by dictator Gerardo Machado (1926–33), that established the island's papers as a medium and catalyst for popular mobilization writ large. The first half of the twentieth century thus saw the consolidation of a lively and sometimes contentious press, periodically muzzled by authoritarian governments.[73]

The antagonism between press and state came to a head during Fulgencio Batista's final presidential tenure, as he unleashed unprecedented if inconsistent media repression. Censorship was first imposed during a state of emergency, proclaimed in the immediate aftermath of Batista's March 1952 coup, and lifted that fall. But the Law of Public Order No. 997, which allowed the government to punish such crimes as "disrespect," "false rumors," "defamation," and "calumny," remained in force as a latent threat.[74] A more formal order of censorship, instituted in response to the 1953 storming of the Moncada barracks by Fidel Castro and his allies, soon extended its reach,

This circular, issued by the Directorio Nacional of the Movimiento Resistencia Cívica, encouraged Cubans "not to buy censored newspapers," characterizing "freedom of expression" as a "precious democratic achievement." It directed Cubans to seek out the "only uncensored press, the revolutionary one, and help it to circulate." "Cubano, no compres periódicos censurados," Jay Mallin Papers, box 1, folder 20, Cuban Heritage Collection.

which waxed and waned over the course of the decade. Yet state censorship proved largely counterproductive.[75] Rebel leaders relied on the foreign media to disseminate the news that could not be published at home and also established media outlets of their own, including the underground newspaper *Revolución* and Radio Rebelde, thereby turning the media into a privileged venue for oppositional militancy.[76]

The symbiotic relationship between the Revolution and the media only intensified in the early months of 1959. Lillian Guerra proposes that periodicals such as *Bohemia* "played a pivotal role in securing public trust" for the new government.[77] They did so by graphically exposing the horrors of Batista's dictatorship, as *Bohemia* editor Miguel Ángel Quevedo opened his safe and published once-forbidden exposés on political violence and torture.[78] But editors at *Bohemia* and *Revolución* were committed to documenting *and* interpreting the recent past. In framing the struggle against Batista, they focused on Castro and the sierra front to the exclusion of the urban resistance and also, "[promoted] undivided loyalty to Fidel months before Fidel himself did."[79]

The press thus assumed a key role in validating the new state while also drawing attention to urgent and still unresolved issues, including racial discrimination.[80] It also called on ordinary citizens to mobilize on behalf of signal revolutionary initiatives. One early example was the "Colecta de la Libertad," launched by *Bohemia* magazine in March 1959 to enlist popular sponsorship of agrarian reform. As María del Pilar Díaz Castañón has argued, the Colecta not only helped to build support for the Revolution's land redistribution program; it also rescripted the relationship between the state and the populace. Though the many small monetary contributions of ordinary people did not prove consequential in the long run, Díaz Castañón observes that the "myth of popular decision-making power" nonetheless endured, fueling ordinary Cubans' conviction "that their participation was decisive."[81]

The influence of the press on the Revolution was mutually felt. After 1959, the revolution that had been waged through journalism sparked a revolution *in* journalism. It began with a formal end to press censorship and the arrest of the most notorious executors of that policy.[82] Newspapers that had been driven underground began to reemerge, notably the Communist paper *Hoy* and the onetime Orthodox Party outlet *La Calle*, which had been closely affiliated with Fidel Castro following his 1955 release from prison.[83] In March 1959, they were joined by *Combate*—an organ of the 26th of July Movement—and several new provincial papers. The early weeks of 1959 also saw the intervention of newspapers linked to the Batista government, including *Ataja, Alerta, Pueblo,* and *Mañana. Tiempo de Cuba,* owned by the notorious Batista ally Rolando Masferrer, was "destroyed by the indignant populace."[84] As *Revolución* set up shop in the former workroom of *Alerta*, radio stations owned by *batistianos* and in one case Batista himself were also taken over, soon replaced by new revolutionary frequencies, such as Radio Rebelde and Radio Mambí.[85]

Early on, Castro targeted the state subsidies that had sustained many Havana papers and magazines in the preceding decades. Of the city's sixteen outlets, only three (*Bohemia, Prensa Libre,* and *Times of Havana*) had declined funding from the Batista government, as the Cuban public discovered in late January in the pages of *Revolución*. Official support for the press, moreover, was not limited to formal subsidies but also included so-called *botellas*, or phantom government positions, for many Cuban journalists. Newspaper subsidies dated back to the 1930s and had once channeled a "progressive" mission to "sustain a healthy democracy and encourage debate about political issues," as Michael Salwen observes.[86] Yet political leaders ultimately relied on the subsidies to inhibit rather than promote press independence, fueling support for their elimination after 1959.

Official interventions continued apace in the early months of 1959, first targeting accused Batista ally Gaspar Pumarejo, whose media empire included TV station Channel 12.[87] In January, national and Havana-based journalistic associations also decreed the expulsion of known *batistianos* from their ranks, though some complained that purges had not proceeded quickly enough.[88] In June 1960, a Revolutionary Code of Sanctions was approved by the National and Provincial (Havana) Guilds of Reporters. That code inspired the punishment and removal of over 200 journalists for such crimes as collaboration with Batista, participation in his security forces, and public "counterrevolutionary attitudes."[89]

The revolution in journalism thus began to reach beyond those directly aligned with the dictatorship, as new political fault lines emerged. Already in late January 1959, some papers, notably *Prensa Latina*, were urging revolutionary leaders to proceed cautiously in enacting measures such as agrarian reform. The first agrarian reform of May 1959 was indeed relatively moderate in its aims, but it was consequential enough to provoke more open criticism in the pages of the conservative *Diario de la Marina*.[90] Even before then, however, *Diario* had relinquished its hopes that the bourgeois and industrial classes it represented would benefit from revolutionary reform. The early months of 1959 thus saw the paper's evolution, as Katya Rodríguez Gómez relates, from "initial support for the Revolution, defending private property . . . to [opposition] to the revolutionary regime . . . [giving] space to anyone in disagreement with the process."[91]

As newspapers like *Prensa Libre* and *Diario de la Marina* found themselves in open conflict with the revolutionary government, they were also drawn into battles with its defenders in the press, notably *Revolución* and *Hoy*. These debates raged throughout 1959 and 1960, forcing many journalists to brandish their revolutionary credentials in print. As Michael Bustamante has argued, asserting political bona fides was as much about the past as it was the present, given that most of Havana's newspapers had entered the revolutionary period with historical baggage.[92] In this respect, *Diario* was a notoriously easy target, given its support for Spanish colonialism in the nineteenth century and a variety of conservative causes in the twentieth. Even before *Diario* began to voice open criticism of revolutionary measures, it thus found itself on the defensive, with *Hoy* taking a particularly aggressive stance.[93] Writers at *Hoy* and *Revolución* pulled stories directly from the *Diario* archive to show how often the paper had found itself on the wrong side of history, a strategy they also deployed in their clashes with other papers.

This reaching to the past took on a palimpsest quality, as old political divisions were given new life—and renewed urgency—in a revolutionary context. *Prensa Latina* may have had sterling anti-Batista credentials (though even these would be disputed in the months to come), but the anti-Communism of its editors Sergio Carbó and Humberto Medrano garnered it special opprobrium in the pages of *Hoy* and other outlets aligned with the revolutionary government, who referred to the paper as "Panza Libre" (Fat Gut).[94] In turn, *Prensa Latina* and other voices in the liberal press fired back at *Hoy* for the Communist Party's onetime alliance with Batista, as well as its initially dismissive attitude toward the revolutionary movement against him. Meanwhile, *Revolución* launched attacks at just about everyone, including, in early 1959, the editors of *Hoy*.[95]

Sparring over the past was an inevitable result of the "retrospective" politics of the early Revolution.[96] But it also functioned as a diversion of sorts, buying time for those who found themselves unsettled by the new government's direction. It was safer to attack *Hoy* for its past allegiance to Batista, for example, than to challenge Communist influence on the new government. In March 1959, observers at the US embassy noted that a "voluntary censorship" had set in among the island's papers. "Voluntary" may not have been the right word to describe what appears to have been a more systematic effort to prevent criticism from appearing in print, specifically at the hands of Ernestina Otero, Fidel Castro's "unofficial press secretary," and *Revolución* director Carlos Franqui. Otero's and Franqui's phone calls to newspaper editors seem to have averted the publication of more oppositional perspectives. Undoubtedly, many editors were also cowed by the knowledge that the government could accuse them of having collaborated with or "profiteered under" Batista.[97] By summer 1959, even oblique criticism had become taboo, though some, including Sergio Carbó, continued to defend their right to dissent.[98]

The increasingly tense relationship between the press and the revolutionary government soon gave way to open confrontation. The resulting conflict, which Juan Marrero has described as a "battle of ideas," took up not only the substance of revolutionary process—agrarian reform, anti-imperialism, persecution of government critics—but also the very question of press freedom. In the process, the revolution in journalism helped to define the Revolution through journalism. As political figures, editors, and writers sparred over the meaning of freedom of expression, enshrined as an individual right in the 1948 Universal Declaration of Human Rights (to which Cuba was a signatory), they also made the success of the Revolution dependent on its willingness to defend that liberty.

How Free Is Your Press?

The symbolic importance of press freedom to the revolutionary movement can be measured by the fact that it was one of the most consistent refrains in Fidel Castro's early speeches, beginning with his January 1959 victory march across the island. On January 1, in the Parque Central de Santiago, he promised to immediately reestablish that liberty along with all others that had been breached by the Batista government.[99] Speaking to journalists in Camagüey several days later, Castro promised to defend their right to report as a foundational principle of the Revolution: "We have freedom of the press now, because the whole world knows that as long as a revolutionary is still standing there will be freedom of press in Cuba. When we say freedom of press, we say freedom of assembly; when we say freedom of assembly, we say the right to freely choose one's own government."[100]

But Castro's commitment to press freedom was quickly drawn into question in the face of growing criticism of his government, both foreign and domestic. Though international journalists were the first to earn his ire, early skirmishes with the Cuban press raised concerns about the relationship between state officials and the media. In late January, for example, the satirical magazine *Zig Zag* published a cartoon mocking those who transferred their allegiances to any government in power. Castro was not amused; in a speech at Petrolera Shell, he lambasted "cowardly writers" and vowed that the Revolution would "not apply censorship" but greet them with "moral anathema." For his part, the publisher of *Zig Zag* was disturbed by this statement, noting that the cartoon was intended not to "hinder the work of the government, but to help it get rid of" such individuals.[101]

The *Zig Zag* controversy was the first in a series of battles to surface in the coming months, as castigating critical journalists and editors became a regular feature of Castro's speeches. By June, tensions between the Revolution's leader and the press were high enough that several prominent editors did not attend the annual celebration of World Press Freedom Day, at which Fidel was scheduled to speak, even as Jorge Quintana, head of Havana's journalist guild, proposed that it was the first time Cuba could truly celebrate the occasion.[102] At the end of that month, a public demonstration against *Diario de la Marina* (led by the woodworkers' union) culminated in a procession to the paper's offices and shouts of "Death to Volcano"—the pen name of the paper's editor, José I. Rivero.[103] Writers at *Hoy* responded to Rivero's denunciation of the incident by ridiculing his "hysterical attack of fear" and countering that the *Diario* editor had not, as he claimed, censured a similar past attack on *Hoy*.[104]

In these confrontations, participants on all sides expressed their commitment to freedom of expression. Yet the events of early 1959 revealed a growing schism in how different constituencies would actualize that liberty. As early as January 1959, writers at *Revolución* had initiated a debate over the parameters of press freedom. One "Dr. Pastor," for example, framed "objective journalism"—"neuter [*asexuado*] or invertebrate"—as the "antithesis to true press freedom." "Freedom of the press," he maintained, was meaningful only when "each social or political group had its own organs of opinion."[105] Angel Cuiña Fernández, head of organization and publicity for the journalist division of the 26th of July Movement, made the argument even more pointedly: "Freedom of the press . . . only exists for those who monopolize the national press and never for the large majority of those affected and dispossessed."[106]

By June, these debates had become more intense, with writers at *Hoy* taking the lead in advancing a materialist critique of press freedom as traditionally defined. Economic concerns had long thwarted the ability of Cuban journalists to live honorably, they argued, but capitalism itself represented a corrupting influence on the press. In a similar spirit, a writer at *Combate* proposed that it was not the revolutionary government but rather the commercial foundation of the press that had imposed "self-censorship" in Cuba.[107] To that end, Carlos Rafael Rodríguez charged international organizations such as the IAPA with weaponizing freedom of expression to undermine the Revolution. "The degree of press freedom in Cuba won't be measured by the Yankee-fied SIP," he declared, "but by the Cuban people and their journalists."[108]

Contrary to Rodríguez's determination, however, in the months to come, debates over press freedom would indeed be triangulated through external observers, especially the IAPA. For veteran media watchers in the hemisphere, this was hardly surprising, nor were the terms of the resulting controversy. Many of the players in the Cuban war with the IAPA, including Rodríguez himself, were veterans of previous battles in Latin America, especially Juan Perón's Argentina. This extended to IAPA head Alberto Gainza Paz, whose paper *La Prensa* had been taken over by Perón in 1947 following a worker strike and occupation, and Jules Dubois in his new capacity as head of the IAPA Freedom of the Press Committee. The issues at hand were familiar, too, given that Perón, citing the interests of Argentina's workers, had also targeted the country's commercial press.[109]

But there was also personal bad blood here. Following years of Latin American and, in fact, Cuban leadership, the IAPA had been restructured during a 1950 meeting in New York. Rodríguez and other *Hoy* writers often charged that this amounted to a full-fledged "coup," which had delivered the IAPA into the hands of the US State Department thanks to the personal machinations of Jules Dubois.[110] Dubois unsurprisingly painted his aims in different terms, suggesting that it was only thanks to him and other US collaborators that the IAPA had finally become independent of any government. The outcome, however, was the same in both accounts. Dubois lobbied to exclude known Communists from the 1950 meeting, arguing that "Communist newspapers were direct agents of the Soviets and not free and independent publications."[111] When Rodríguez, then IAPA treasurer, arrived in New York, he was detained and sent to Ellis Island before being forced to return to Cuba.[112] That personal insult was compounded by the meeting's political effects, which tipped the balance of power toward the organization's anti-Communist bloc.

Battles over press freedom in Cuba were thus inherently intertextual and became more so over time, connecting transnational enmities (between Dubois and Rodríguez, for example) to national ones (as in the skirmishes among Cuban newspapers) as all parties sought to clarify their relationship to the revolutionary state. A new opportunity to do so arose in July 1959 in response to concerns raised by UPI president Frank Bartholomew, who characterized the press under Batista as "robust" and decried the dependence of Cuban papers on the revolutionary government.[113] His concerns provoked an immediate condemnation from Eudaldo Gutiérrez Paula, dean of the Colegio Nacional de Periodistas, and a counter from *Bohemia* editor Miguel Ángel Quevedo, even as another satirist, Carlos Robreño of *El Mundo*, was publicly lambasted by Fidel Castro.[114]

When Bartholomew declined an invitation to come and observe the island's papers for himself, Quevedo responded by commissioning a lengthy treatment of the issue, which invited directors at Havana's major media outlets to weigh in on the state of press freedom in Cuba.[115] The majority rejected Bartholomew's accusations. Even so, there were a few notable exceptions. Jules Dubois joined José I. Rivero, Milton Guss (*Times of Havana*), Jorge Zayas (*Avance*), and Ángel Fernández Varela (*Información*) in highlighting the chilling effects of the attacks launched by Castro and his press proxies. Dubois offered perhaps the most direct criticism of this practice, proposing that the "verbal potency of doctor Fidel Castro and the force of his words on public opinion, create the impression that he's making recourse to the weapon of intimidation."[116]

Newspapers aligned with the revolutionary government presented a different diagnosis. Guillermo Jiménez of *Combate* countered that press freedoms in Cuba were stronger than ever, having been "extended to the forgotten classes of our population." Jiménez also praised the new imperative for "social utility" in Cuban journalism and insisted that it was only under such conditions that true press freedom existed. *La Calle* director Raúl Quintana went further, proposing that there was still work to be done in dismantling that "terrible and engulfing guillotine": the capitalist structure of Cuban papers. Eduardo Hector Alonso of the *Diario Nacional* in turn affirmed Fidel's "right to response" as another essential liberty.[117]

These debates between international observers and their Cuban interlocutors exploded at the October 1959 meeting of the IAPA. Island journalists were particularly incensed by Alberto Gainza Paz's classification of Cuba as a place in which press freedoms were threatened and the effort (ultimately unsuccessful) to pass a resolution to this effect.[118] José I. Rivero, who had chosen not to attend the meeting, became the focal point of many of these discussions, given the escalating conflict between the *Diario de la Marina* and the government. He responded in the pages of his paper: "There is freedom of the press today in Cuba," he averred. "Anyone who says the contrary, is covering the sun with a finger."[119] But this was a "very special" freedom, he continued. "There are no censors in the papers, and the Government doesn't send us censors, nor do we censor the information the Government provides." Nonetheless, Rivero expressed concern about hypocrisy among some political officials, who "say one thing in their house and in private[,] and in the street or the tribune express themselves differently," and the overzealousness of others in squashing critique.[120] That apprehension was seconded by Guillermo Martínez Márquez, editor of *El País* and *Excelsior*, in a report cataloguing Castro's responses to media criticism, the unlawful use of the workshops of decommissioned papers, public demonstrations and union agreements, and the preferential treatment afforded to certain papers. Yet Martínez Márquez insisted that the appropriate path forward was constructive dialogue between IAPA representatives and the Cuban government. Other conference attendees, including Jorge Zayas of *Avance*, agreed.[121]

Dissident notes were sounded by the few government-aligned journalists in attendance at the conference, along with those who insisted that the obstacles to press freedom were more pressing elsewhere in the hemisphere. From afar, Carlos Rafael Rodríguez and other *Hoy* writers continued to present biting commentary. They condemned the use of press freedom as a weapon with which to attack Cuba and criticized those who defended the right of expression for some while denying it to others, including, in their estimation, Castro himself.[122] Rodríguez was particularly incensed by the awarding of the IAPA Mergenthaler prize to the editors of *Prensa Libre* for their "unceasing fight against dictatorial tendencies in Cuba and elsewhere in the Western hemisphere."[123] Though the resolution censuring the state of the press in Cuba failed, IAPA attendees succeeded in blocking *Revolución* from joining the organization and vowed to combat Communist influence on journalism throughout the Americas.

Back in Cuba, meanwhile the independent press was more vulnerable by the day. In the wake of the meeting, government-allied papers stepped up their attacks on the IAPA, Jules Dubois, and their perceived allies among island editors and journalists.[124] The text and subtext of these battles was the increasingly politicized category of press freedom itself. In the pages of *Revolución*, its vice director Euclides Vázquez Candela, soon to be made head of the National Journalism School (Escuela Nacional de Periodismo), issued a direct repudiation of the definition held up by international and domestic critics: "Can counterrevolutionary expression be tolerated when the revolutionary state is required to combat counterrevolutionary conduct?" The answer, he concluded, was no: "In our case the notion of press freedom has to be erected not on a theoretical or idealist plane, but rather in response to a reality . . . of profound social change."[125]

For a time, editors at *Diario de la Marina* and *Avance* seemed to step back from the line of fire. They began to air their concerns, as US embassy officials observed, by "quoting the criticism of others," a practice that *Revolución* immediately attacked.[126] But as 1959 drew to a close, the campaign against the independent press culminated in a vote of censure targeting *Diario de la Marina*, *Avance*, and *Prensa Libre* at the annual congress of the CTC.[127] Though editors at all three papers objected, none of them published editorials on the December 1959 trial of Huber Matos, a widely respected revolutionary leader who had resigned from the army and been imprisoned in October for his criticism of Communist influence on the government.[128]

Meanwhile, in November, critics of independent newspapers began to literally entomb them.[129] On December 23, for example, *Hoy* reported on the recent "burial of the libelous" in San Antonio de los Baños, organized by representatives of the city's seventeen *sindicatos* as well as leadership from the 26th of July Movement and the PSP. Among the papers committed to their final rest were *Diario de la Marina, Avance, Prensa Libre, Life,* and *Time.* With some 5,000 people in attendance, the group staged a "funerary conga" as they paraded a sarcophagus through the streets, shouting "Down with Pepinillo! Down with Dubois!"[130] Newspaper burnings followed throughout the island.[131] By the turn of 1960, the government had endorsed these actions, further emboldening the PSP militants and others who organized them.[132] As Fidel remarked in February 1960, "If the people want to burn a newspaper . . . since when do I have to get involved in what people want to do with their newspapers?"[133]

Gregorio Ortega, a journalist who led the September 1960 intervention of CMQ and Radio Reloj (discussed in chapter 2), has argued that "freedom of information . . . could only be definitively achieved when the papers, the magazines, the television and radio stations were the property of all the people."[134] That framing is the logical encapsulation of the position advanced by *Hoy, Revolución,* and other government-affiliated papers over the course of 1959. Control over the means of production, they posed, was the necessary precondition for control over the production of meaning. But a parallel and equally significant thread runs through this statement and the arguments advanced by press allies of the revolutionary state. Both material and ideological hegemony, they insisted, depended on workers demanding their own freedom of expression in the name of the revolutionary state. Therein lay the truth about Cuba.

Over the first few months of 1960, the coletilla, a kind of Tweet *avant la lettre,* became the means through which typographers asserted their claim to that truth. It remains unclear who first proposed it—Alfredo Viñas, head of the Colegio Provincial de Periodistas de La Habana, credited Carlos Franqui himself—but all observers agreed that it was a sui generis phenomenon.[135] The coletilla took over the pages of the island's independent papers in the months to come and came to assume a somewhat standardized form: a "note" published at the end of an article claiming that the right to press freedom covered both its publication *and* the coletilla's critique of its contents. At the same time, newly formed Freedom of the Press Committees began to root the battle for press freedom in newspaper labor struggles. The right to express oneself was thus both the instrument and the endpoint of that militancy. Privileging workers' voices also abetted the nationalization of the press, as editor after editor gave up his paper and abandoned the country in response.

The coletilla battles began with two cables, one from the AP and the other from UPI, published in *Información* in mid-January. Both featured spokespeople for the US government discussing the threat of Communist influence in Cuba. Workers at the paper objected to this content and prepared a note to be run alongside it, but the paper's director refused to publish their response and proposed to leave the section blank. The authors of the coletilla framed this as an act of coercion, arguing that to omit any content would be to "give room to the Revolutionary Government's enemies to say that there is press censorship in Cuba." Both the cables and the coletilla were thus published under the authority of the workers, as the directorship issued its own indictment of "coercion" and asked the police to thwart this "obvious attack on freedom of the press." But workers insisted that they had drafted the coletilla precisely to exercise their right to respond to the cables, "which [were] not in accordance with the truth or the most elemental journalistic ethics."[136]

Editors at other papers who decried these events soon confronted coletillas in response, while others attempted to preempt aftershocks by removing AP and UPI cables from their pages. None, however, was able to avoid what would soon become a familiar course of events. *Avance* was the first to fall when its director, Jorge Zayas, sequestered the paper to avoid a coletilla on several letters authored by opponents of the revolutionary government, including high-profile defector Manuel Artime. Yet he was unable to block publication and went into hiding soon thereafter. His subsequent exile and denunciations of censorship inspired a far-reaching media campaign, in which revolutionary officials painted Zayas as a *batistiano* and antagonist to press freedom.[137]

By February, Freedom of the Press Committees had been established at all independent newspapers, while editors at *Diario de la Marina* and *Información* initiated (ultimately unsuccessful) legal challenges to their constitutionality. In the interim, other editors, including Guillermo Martínez Márquez, defected, and additional papers, such as *El Mundo*, were taken over by the state.[138] Led by Jules Dubois, the IAPA denounced these events, while writers at pro-government papers celebrated the coletilla as the apotheosis of revolutionary press freedom. As one representative of the Freedom of the Press Committee at *Información* told reporters from *Hoy*, the right to express oneself was now truly "quite vast. . . . Before that liberty was only enjoyed by the capitalist, the *latifundista*, etc. [but] now we can all voice our opinions without fear."[139] Doing so, a writer at *Combate* proposed, was nothing short of a "civic" act, a "[refusal] to play into the hands of our foreign enemies."[140]

Over time, the call-and-response of editorials and coletillas trended in a metatextual direction, with the coletilla itself a preferred subject.[141] In *Diario de la Marina*, José I. Rivero drafted coletillas for his own editorials and kept a running tally of those written by others. It was a source of some pride to him that his paper usually received the most such notes.[142] Journalists at *Prensa Libre*, including former Castro ally Mario Llerena, engaged in a particularly theoretical tête-à-tête with their coletilla respondents. At the forefront of these debates was satirist Carlos Robreño, recently decamped from *El Mundo*, who in mid-March boasted that he had achieved a "record"—nearly a "*coletillazo*" per day—and proposed that his "*coletilladores*" should be allotted a portion of his salary to compensate them for their efforts.[143]

Robreño acknowledged that the foreign cables published by Cuban papers were often "mendacious, deforming or exaggerating the facts." Even so, he maintained that the coletilla was not the best instrument with which to defend "revolutionary ideals." "The truth," Robreño concluded, "is always strong enough to clear its own path forward."[144] As proof, he cited the dark days of the Batista dictatorship, when newspapers slandered the rebels as "thieves" and "bandits." But "at the end," Robreño proposed, "the truth emerged resplendent, capping one of the most selfless and glorious deeds of all the American revolutions, perhaps in the history of the world."[145] He soon received an official summons to the offices of the Colegio de Periodistas, where he was notified of charges filed against him for noncompliance with the organization's Code of Professional Conduct.[146] In May 1960, when the Havana Newspaper Guild voted to terminate the coletilla, they also booted Robreño from their ranks, citing his "humorously satirical comments against 'coletilla writers.'"[147]

Two weeks earlier, the last holdouts in the combatively independent press had met their end when both *Prensa Libre* and *Diario de la Marina* were taken over by their workers. Their demise inspired a mass funerary party comprising some 100,000 participants.[148] José Rivero watched the proceedings on TV from the US embassy; he and the editors of *Prensa Libre* soon left for exile in the United States. An editorial at the *New York Times* characterized these events in familiar terms: "One of the problems is that

Premier Castro really believes there has been—and even that there is—freedom of the press in Cuba. The concept of a free press, and of how that press works in a country like the United States, is difficult for Latin Americans to grasp, yet nearly all the Latin-American countries do have what can fairly be called freedom of the press today. Cuba does not have it, and the seizure of the *Diario de la Marina* underlines the fact."[149]

Condescension aside, the *Times* report does capture one thing accurately. While we cannot know what was in Fidel Castro's mind as these battles played out, many who aligned themselves with him *did* believe that Cuba had achieved a more encompassing press freedom. To cry cynicism in some ways neglects the potency of this debate, just as the same charge, directed at the IAPA and its Cuban allies, rang foul when levied in the revolutionary press. Material and political forces may have influenced those who defended a commercial press on the one hand or sought to demolish it on the other, but at its heart this was an ideological struggle. And the stakes, as editors, writers, and readers soon found out, could not have been higher.

Ultimately, however, the stakes were not equivalent for the different actors drawn into these battles. The coletilla had provided newspaper workers with an instrument to assert their authority, drawing on a history of labor activism as well as more proximate disagreements over the radicalizing direction of the government. At the same time, the publication of coletillas presented a direct response to "Operation Lie" and the press crossfire between Cuba and the United States. By the turn of 1960, however, that back-and-forth had become entangled with a related, now official, mandate: to combat critiques of Communist influence on the government by circumscribing the bounds of public discourse, and vice versa. Grassroots efforts to enact press freedom via workers' rights thus became a paradoxical instrument to constrain Cuba's public sphere—an endpoint that many who had enthusiastically adopted the coletilla may not have anticipated.

"Your Newspapers Lie; Our Newspapers Lie"

In their feuds with representatives of the US press, revolutionary officials, and each other, Cuban journalists had elaborated a series of consequential equivalencies. What had begun as Operation Truth rapidly became the campaign to arrest "Operation Lie," as former allies in the international press corps were recast as public enemies of the Revolution. Allegations of Communist influence inspired many such ruptures, which in turn opened a rift between the island's once sympathetic press and the revolutionary government. The battle for the truth about Cuba drew fuel from such geopolitical, ideological, and personal differences, but it was also driven by a tautology of sorts. Only when the press was truly free—be it in the terms set by the IAPA on the one hand or pro-government revolutionaries on the other—could the truth about Cuba be known. Yet this made the struggle for truth contingent on a profoundly embattled category. If no one could agree on what a free press looked like, how would the truth ever come to light?

That was the concern expressed by Manolo, owner of Havana's famed restaurant La Bodeguita del Medio, in his conversation with Warren Miller, a US journalist who traveled to the island in 1960. "Truth now in this country, in the whole world, has become such a slippery thing," Manolo bemoaned, "and what was true one day seems to be untrue the next day." Manolo gently ribbed Miller for believing the spurious reports of the "Ah-Pay and the Oo-Pay" regarding food shortages and popular fear of the government. But he expressed no more confidence in the ability of the island press to convey insight into the reality of the Revolution. "*Your* newspapers lie," he despaired, "*our* newspapers lie."[150]

Evidence suggests that Manolo was not alone in his sentiments about foreign coverage on the one hand or state control of the press on the other. A February 1961 government survey, for example, revealed that newspapers were not read in 40 percent of Cuban households. Island observers attributed that result to the "pernicious influence of the imperialist press," while exile critics presented the statistic as evidence of political alienation.[151] At a 1961 IAPA meeting, one former newspaper salesman noted that he and others had taken to hawking the "official papers" not by shouting their names but by shouting the "war cry 'Papers, Papers, Papers . . . ,' the only way they could achieve any sales at all."[152]

Meanwhile, other consequential silences went largely unacknowledged. Perhaps most notably, little public attention, within or outside Cuba, was afforded to the demise of an independent Black press, along with the space previously, if inconsistently, allocated to discussions of race in the national papers.[153] When Castro declared the antidiscrimination campaign launched in 1959 to be over two years later, opportunities to transact public debates about racism dwindled alongside the public forums in which they might occur. As Devyn Spence Benson has argued, this served to render certain subjects invisible, both on the island and in exile, even as Afro-Cuban intellectuals and artists continued to push for opportunities for representation—and self-representation—in other mediums.[154]

As the content of newspapers became more uniform and politically orthodox, Cubans of all political persuasions learned to turn to alternative sources. This had been the concern of a writer in *Prensa Libre*, who bemoaned the progressive undermining of the independent press as a counterbalance to the state. "What do they want," he wondered, "that people turn their back on the official press, relying on 'Radio Bemba' [or "lip radio," the island's word-of-mouth news channel] to access truly 'deceptive' information?"[155] As chapter 3 explores in more detail, his concern was prescient; after 1961, rumors became a key source of information for many Cubans.

A state monopoly over the news irrevocably inhibited Cuban journalism, especially after most of the remaining national newspapers were merged in 1965 to form *Granma*. Wilfredo Cancio has characterized the result as a "linear transmission scheme . . . with a conception of the media as mere ideological instruments."[156] Individual writers continued to pursue consequential if not heterodox reporting, especially in the more open platform provided by magazines, some of which were established (*INRA/Cuba*) or reimagined (*Mujeres*) as vehicles for documenting and advancing revolutionary change. By the late 1960s, however, ideological regimentation in journalistic organizations had curtailed many of those opportunities as well.[157]

These processes gave rise to lasting disparities in news access, leaving much of the public in the dark. During his 1969 visit to the island, sociologist Joseph Kahl was surprised to find major US and European papers on display at Havana's Biblioteca Nacional (National Library). But a Communist Party militant whom he engaged in conversation openly recognized that the Cuban papers were "garbage." Kahl's interlocutor explained that the country was in a "state of siege" and that ideological battles, combined with economic scarcity, inevitably influenced what could be published. But above all, he suggested that the "masses were 'not yet ready' for a more balanced view of things," of the kind that was provided to party members, for example.[158]

Foreign coverage, as we have seen, fared little better. Cuban officials had raised doubts about the ability of US journalists to report the Revolution fairly, and those who traveled to the island sometimes did little to contradict them. Representatives of the US media were in turn quick to criticize former leaders of the island's independent papers for bias in their reporting from exile. Indeed, those who had once decried state interference in the Cuban press quickly found themselves navigating new political entanglements, including at times CIA funding and oversight for their media ventures. Meanwhile, a 1962 assessment by *Miami Herald* journalist Hendrik J. Berns lamented that Radio Bemba was an equally vital source for Cubans in the diaspora. "Much of what the exiles pass along as factual information is, instead, wishful thinking," Burns alleged. "It is not realism. It is emotionalism."[159] That claim, however, was entered into the record during Senate hearings to expose *pro*-Castro bias in the US media. And so the wheel turned once more.

It is not surprising, then, that the right to reply, first enacted in 1950 and affirmed by Cuba's Court of Constitutional Guarantees in its ruling on the coletilla, became such an essential entry in the press war vocabulary.[160] For many participants, asserting their truth depended on disproving someone else's; in the words of court president Juan B. More Benítez and lawyer Fernando Álvarez Tabio, this made the coletilla "simply a form of the reply[,] or reply in the face of any foreign information, that threatens our independence or offends our national dignity." They concluded that the right to reply left it to the "impartial judgment of the public to determine who defended the truth and who clung to lies or errors."[161] The resulting challenges—which pitted Operation Truth against Operation Lie, reporters against government officials and each other—helped to constitute a particularly contentious and ultimately brittle public sphere. If different parties could make divergent claims on the truth about Cuba, it stood to reason that claims to objectivity were inescapably subjective, that facts were always shaded with opinion. That, of course, was precisely Manolo's concern.

Yet his commentary also raises the question of public involvement in these debates. As late as May 1960, *Combate* dedicated an edition of its series "La juventud opina" (Young people weigh in) to the coletilla itself. Though two out of three respondents expressed support, one young woman, a teaching student, described it as "an attack on freedom of the press in a supposedly democratic country." Her response in turn earned a coletilla, which framed its publication as evidence of the "existing freedom of the press in Cuba." The coletilla writer insisted that they were drawing on the same freedom in "indicating that its contents do not conform to the truth" and represented an "[attack on] the true democracy: the Cuban Revolution."[162]

The public ultimately had little access to coletillas, which disappeared soon thereafter, but they did continue to make use of the presumed right to reply. Whenever an opportunity opened, and until it almost inevitably closed, ordinary Cubans wrote letters to their papers in the time-honored tradition, raising questions, bringing up concerns, and, above all, issuing complaints. In the pages of *Revolución*, *Bohemia*, and later *Granma* and

Juventud Rebelde, they reported medication shortages, transportation is-sues, housing problems, and other challenges that shaped their lives. Those letters that were published were rarely issued in full and tended to earn terse if not dismissive responses. But they continued to be sent and, to some degree, acknowledged.[163]

Chronicling the resurgence of "citizen letters" in the reformist 2000s, Martin Dimitrov proposes that such platforms were permitted and even augmented in this period because they served to uphold rather than under-mine the state. Writing into the papers gave Cubans the opportunity to "collectively [let] off steam" and allowed governing officials to selectively heed, and even sometimes act on, their contents. These exchanges, Dimi-trov continues, fortified the "social contract" between the populace and the government, performing a kind of "proxy accountability." They also pro-vided otherwise inaccessible information about popular opinion. Yet, he notes, published letters ultimately restricted the purview of that contract by "excluding grievances about civil and political rights from the range of the permissible complaints."[164]

The work of addressing reader letters was thus governed by expectations of restraint. A journalist tasked with drafting such responses in the late 2000s notes that her editor exercised final jurisdiction over what would be published. Few of the received complaints thus made it into print, and fewer produced tangible results.[165] From the vantage point of the 2000s, then, the potential responsiveness of Cuban officials to complaints was plausible but limited; this is perhaps even more true of earlier periods.[166] But the same journalist, who was often frustrated by her editor's intracta-bility, nonetheless believes that even the restricted scope of state response, within and beyond the column, did not necessarily undermine popular expectations. "The public," she posits, "in a kind of unconscious way, con-tinued to believe (at least some of them . . .) in the myth of the press as a fourth power."[167]

Where did this belief come from—or, better put, how did it survive the transition to a state-controlled media? The nationalization of the Cuban press and dismantling of electoral governance eliminated channels for reg-istering dissent, but such outlets for complaint fostered an expectation that the public also enjoyed a right to reply. This was a bounded right, but it was sufficient to convince ordinary citizens that someone, maybe even Castro himself, was listening. Citizen complaints thus represent a counter-weight to an increasingly closed media system as well as a form of popular "testimony": an archive, however sparse, of how ordinary Cubans viewed the press and, by extension, the Revolution itself.[168]

This counterpoint between political consolidation and popular response was also channeled through other mediums. Within Cuba, television quickly became one of the most consequential vehicles for revolutionary projection. As chapter 2 explores, Fidel Castro drew on the island's highly developed TV landscape to both challenge and circumvent traditional outlets, including the newspapers surveyed here. Small-screen connectivity facilitated not only the dismantling of Cuba's traditional press but also the translation of political practice into a distinctly virtual register. Between 1959 and 1961, TV Fidel, as I refer to it, disseminated a new and increasingly inescapable message: that spectatorship represented not only an important conduit for ideological persuasion but also, in a sense, political participation itself.

2 The Medium Is the Message
TV Fidel

· ·

"I have seen the Bouglione Circus, Cinemara atrocities by Cecil B. DeMille, Arab festivals and Broadway parades, but never," declared Swiss journalist Jean Ziegler, "have I witnessed a show to hold a candle to Fidel Castro's television marathon." Her 1960 account follows the buildup to a typical performance, from the "truckloads of bearded rebels" making their way to Havana's famed CMQ studio to the extended delays before Fidel finally appeared on-screen. He sometimes proceeded through a desultory "warm up," but eventually, she relates, "the storm [would break]": "All at once the studio is electrified and for the next six hours I sit glued to my seat, fascinated, rooted to the spot like a mouse in front of a snake. And in all Cuba . . . the same thing is happening to over four million people."[1]

For decades, the iconic image of the Cuban Revolution—Fidel Castro on a podium, a rapt audience hanging on his words—has been set in Havana's Plaza de la Revolución. This portrait undergirds a primary assumption about the Revolution: that Cubans came to embrace it by basking in Castro's unmediated presence. But the media was a central protagonist in the process of incorporation, including the written press (as we saw in chapter 1) and, equally consequentially, television. As I argue here, many came to connect to the revolutionary project not only by showing up to Revolution Square but also by tuning in to TV Fidel. The small screen in turn facilitated a process of political saturation that left Cubans, whatever their ideological inclinations, unable to tune *out*.

Chronologically speaking, this was no coincidence. The 1950s and '60s saw the global cross-fertilization of television and politics, with aspiring leaders taking to the small screen to test out new modes of public outreach. In the United States, television is often credited with promoting the rise of John F. Kennedy, who defeated the more seasoned Richard Nixon in the 1960 elections, thanks in part to his showing in the nation's first televised debates.[2] Yet Fidel Castro, a frequent antagonist and foil to Kennedy, was an even more innovative pioneer of TV politics. Flooding the airwaves, he drew on the island's highly developed media landscape, with twenty-three commercial channels and high rates of television ownership. That context was essential to Castro's immediate mobilization of the small screen, which allowed him to reach Cubans across the island in real time. But television was not just a public relations tool for Castro. It quickly became a stage for revolutionary governance, where decisions were made and public ratification courted. From 1959 to 1962, television served as both an arm of official outreach and a (virtual) vehicle for popular participation.

This chapter offers a close reading of Fidel's TV appearances, as well as their echoes in the Cuban and international media. While my primary focus is on the words and performance of Castro himself, I also situate his television career in the intertextual spirit in which it was conducted. Castro often took to TV to critique his opponents, including journalists and newspaper editors. That so many press commentators focused on his novel use of television is not surprising—they were a principal audience for, and characters in, his small-screen dramas.[3]

TV Fidel both channeled and shaped the early trajectory of the Revolution, from political radicalization and media nationalizations to the narrowing bounds of ideological engagement. Yet in explaining these outcomes, many observers have instead cited Castro's "charisma." In this view, Fidel's personal magnetism, likened to an irresistible force that held Cubans in its thrall, illuminates the process through which a broad-based revolutionary movement was precipitously remade into an authoritarian, single-party state. This version of events, which persuasively foregrounds the power of Castro's political style, nonetheless neglects the historical context that led so many contemporaries to focus on charisma, along with its inherently mediated quality. Notably, it also affords little space to his television *audience.*

In contrast, I argue that Fidel's televised outreach, as well as its reverberations on the radio and in print media, enduringly shaped both the Subject and subjects of Revolution. Much as the revolutionary forces had relied on print media and radio to cultivate support in the battle against Batista, Castro turned to television to persuade and win over ordinary Cubans. These efforts established public opinion as a powerful ideological weapon. But the small screen was not a mere filter for the work of revolutionary integration. Rather, I propose that TV Fidel consequentially redefined "the people" in virtual terms. Hailed in this capacity, Cubans took on new political identities shaped by spectatorship, but not passivity, as they sought out opportunities for interpretation, response, and even, at times, contestation.

Televised Democracy and Virtual Revolution

Since its debut, television has sparked debate and suspicion, charged with luring viewers into consumerism or the embrace of antisocial values. In undermining the viewer's critical faculties, observers proposed that television contributed to a disturbing phenomenon: the erosion of reality itself.[4] In a world of "pseudo-events," per historian Daniel Boorstin's influential account, are we performing as "actors" or "audience"?[5] These concerns had obvious political implications. Boorstin proposed that television had not only "democratized" but also "segregated" experience, supplanting participation with spectatorship. As a result, politicians could "talk [the viewer's] ear off on TV and if he wanted to respond, all he could do was write them a letter."[6]

In the context of the Cold War, these concerns came to have broad international purchase, implicating television in debates about the viability of democracy.[7] This was true in Cuba as well. Yeidy Rivero has chronicled the ambivalent 1950 debut of television on the island, where the small screen bolstered claims to "democracy, economic abundance, high culture, education, morality, and decency."[8] At the same time, the medium underwrote efforts to police the vision of nation that would be broadcast to the world: implicitly white, European, Catholic, and sexually modest. As Rivero observes, those concerns escalated in response to deteriorating political conditions following Fulgencio Batista's 1952 coup. Over the course of the 1950s, television, along with other media, was subject to government intervention, with censorship institutionalized in 1955. Censors directed their attention to "moral" matters—including, per Rivero, Afro-Cuban dance and men dressed in drag—in addition to politics.[9]

Throughout this period, the island witnessed the intense and often dialectical interaction of media and political struggles, thanks in part to Cuba's precocious broadcasting landscape. According to Louis A. Pérez, by 1955, "Cuba ranked second only to the US in per capita television ownership. By the late 1950s, Cuba ranked ninth in the world in total TV sets and fourth (after the US, England, and Canada) in the number of TV channels."[10] Though television ownership was skewed toward urban (especially *habanero*) and middle- and upper-class Cubans, many more were able to access TV content in other ways, including over the radio.[11] Pérez further indicates that the number of television *watchers* was higher than even these statistics would suggest, with a 1951 survey finding "7.9 viewers per television set."[12] One woman, born a few years after that survey, recalls that during her youth in Camagüey, televisions were scarce, but most of the children of the town managed to catch a peep through someone's window, often to their parents' chagrin.[13]

The reach of Cuban broadcasting fed a venerable tradition of media politics. Most famous were the fiery radio transmissions of Orthodox Party founder Eduardo Chibás, in which he attacked the corruption of Cuba's mainstream political parties.[14] Chibás represented an important political and theatrical influence on a young Fidel Castro until a fateful 1951 show during which, having revealed that one of his accusations could not be sustained, he shot himself three times in the chest (and died).[15] The orientation to virtual politics carried over to the struggle against Batista as well. In a 1957 attempt to overthrow the government, which claimed the lives of some of the most promising leaders of the resistance, the Directorio Revolucionario Estudiantil (Revolutionary Student Directory, DRE) stormed the presidential palace and prematurely took to the radio to declare Batista dead. In the unfolding of this tragedy, both the DRE and its opponents drew on a shared repertoire of radio-centered political practices, as Alejandra Bronfman has argued.[16]

Fidel Castro and his comrades from the 26th of July Movement took these tactics to new heights, beginning with their fateful meeting with Herbert Matthews in the Sierra Maestra. From the start, the art of waging revolution was thus mediated, and dialogic at that, promoting public support as a bona fide weapon. Even after the victory of the anti-Batista forces in January 1959, leaders continued to rely on these techniques to craft representations of the Revolution's past, present, and future. Pedro Porbén suggests that these efforts might be understood as a "campaign for affective literacy," designed to cultivate emotional practices connecting Cubans to the state.[17] Here the press played a particularly important role, churning out aphorisms and icons with which to process the recent past.[18]

In this way, the Cuban Revolution was enacted as a "dramatic, hyperreal spectacle in which citizens could participate and observe," as Lillian Guerra has proposed.[19] Traditionally, observers have rendered this dynamic in cinematic terms, not least because of the importance of film in Cuba's post-1959 cultural landscape.[20] In this early period, however, television played an even more essential role in transacting politics at the popular level. At every major crossroads of the early revolutionary period (and beyond), Castro turned to TV not only to represent what was happening but also to *make things happen*. The Revolution may have been the stuff of epic filmic gestures, but the drama of the everyday was blockbuster reality television—and Fidel Castro was its consummate star.

I do not invoke this anachronism casually. Critical observers have long bemoaned the ways in which television might confuse our sense of reality. In response, a later generation of scholars sought to recuperate the agency of the audience. Insisting that viewers were not the passive recipients of media messaging, Stuart Hall emphasized the gap between "encoding"—the injection of "dominant meanings" into media content—and "decoding," or the different ways in which spectators might digest those scripts.[21] Yet reality television seems to confound such efforts to disentangle scripted intention from audience interpretation. The genre blurs, or diffuses, the performative function of television, at once narrowing and dramatizing the connection between the small screen and the world around it. That its scholars have revived the concerns of Boorstin's generation seems, in this regard, unsurprising. Reality television is perhaps the most perfect encapsulation of the medium's founding problematic.

In what follows, I argue that Fidel Castro was a pioneer of "performing the real" on television.[22] His innovative mobilization of the small screen drew out its ideological potential, spectacularizing citizenship and politicizing spectatorship. This left many of his critics to chase the truth of public opinion, an objective sense of the gestalt beyond the purportedly distorting sheen of Castro's charisma. That quest, however, overlooked the extent to which the Revolution had already recast the public. Though observers continued to pursue an empiricist accounting of popular views, both supporters and opponents of the new revolutionary state increasingly appealed to "the people," defined in both ideological and emotional terms.

Charisma and the Shibboleth of "Public Opinion"

The long-standing orientation to Castro's charisma serves to contextualize what for some remained otherwise inexplicable: the rapid consolidation of his political power. But if charisma quickly became a truism in accounts of the Revolution, its invocation had a broader interpretive context. Dating back to the 1930s, scholars had turned to Max Weber's notion of charismatic leadership to understand the mass appeal of Hitler, Mussolini, and Roosevelt.[23] In the 1950s and '60s, politics watchers were confronted by a new populist wave, this time among Global South and postcolonial leaders— Mao, Nasser, Suharto, and Castro. Weber's theory of charisma was once again mobilized in academic debates and (sometimes overlapping) political circles. The US government and intelligence forces, among others, regarded the appeal of charismatic figures—both at home and abroad—as a pressing security matter.[24]

In reviving Weber, observers devoted particular attention to the relationship between leaders and followers. Most hoped to avoid the top-down perspectives of earlier scholars, who, departing from the spirit of Weber's work, tended to attribute limited reflective capacity to ordinary citizens. Charismatic leadership was born as much of its acolytes as of its avatar, they argued, and thus could be understood only in context. Often this took the form of a destabilizing crisis, which enabled charismatic leaders (sometimes invested with supernatural qualities) to jettison institutional forms of governance and rally supporters behind a messianic vision.[25]

Though Cuba observers sought to make charisma legible—and even, at times, legitimate—by engaging these debates, few regarded it as rational or politically substantial. In the words of Nelson Valdés, who has revisited the question multiple times over the past five decades, "Charisma becomes a cliché that substitutes style for substance."[26] Almost reflexively, more nuanced accounts have sought to avoid the issue altogether. Political scientist Richard Fagen, a regular participant in the Castro charisma debate, later repudiated the personalistic emphasis of his early scholarship. Subsequent accounts have largely followed suit, instead citing structural and contextual factors—from the political vicissitudes of the anti-Batista struggle to mass mobilization and the high-stakes standoff with the United States—to explain the course of the early Revolution.[27] Some have sought to redirect attention from Castro's leadership altogether and thus bring attention to new historical subjects and constituencies.[28]

Thanks to their efforts, the Cuban people are no longer imagined as a passive audience for Fidel's charisma, cast in just-so stories of revolutionary integration. Yet much as scholars have worked to disaggregate the archetype of the Cuban public, we might also historicize and deconstruct it. In what follows, I trace how the demise of political and commercial polling over the course of the first two years of the Revolution led to the eclipse of a measurable body politic. The impossibility of scientifically *assessing* popular sentiment in turn underwrote both the official invocation of a revolutionary collective (the people) and the external recourse to charisma to explain its emergence. In short, as popular opinion became detached from the techniques once used to evaluate it, many, especially outside Cuba, assumed that it had become increasingly irrational—that is, logically inexplicable—in form.

From the first days of 1959, public opinion was frequently advanced to make claims on behalf of the Revolution. It was not, however, an unanchored signifier. Those who mobilized it relied on polling techniques first developed in advertising, public relations, and, in close association, television.[29] Among them were Aníbal Rodríguez, a trained psychologist and early practitioner of survey taking in Cuba who experienced his incorporation into the revolutionary project as a process of professional liberation. Polling, he points out, had long been beholden to corporate purposes, and suddenly the Revolution had presented an opportunity to apply it to the public good. Indeed, surveys were omnipresent in the early months of 1959, as polling techniques developed in advertising firms were applied to measuring and validating popular support for the new government, along with its signature policies.[30]

Yet the image of scientifically validated support would be difficult to uphold over time. The radicalization of government policy—from the first agrarian reform in May 1959 to escalating hostility with the US government—produced a gradual decline in its popularity.[31] Meanwhile, the commercial underpinnings of polling were also undermined by radicalizing forces. By early 1961, according to Eugenio Pedraza Ginori, a onetime survey taker, the world of publicity had "collapsed."[32] The silence around public opinion in turn bolstered oppositional claims that the government was no longer popular.

Yet a surreptitious survey, conducted by Cuban pollsters in May 1960 on behalf of Princeton political scientist Lloyd Free, found just the opposite. The team's sample of 1,000 urban and semi-urban interviewees registered widespread support for the government.[33] Enthusiasm for revolutionary programs lay at the heart of this popularity and could be detected even among those who felt unfavorably toward the new state.[34] As Free maintained, however, it would be misleading to root the Revolution's popularity exclusively in its policies. At the time of his survey, he concluded that roughly 43 percent of the population could be said to be not only supportive of the government but *passionately* so. "Many members of this group[,] and particularly the women, bordered on the fanatic in their expressions of fervor for the Revolution and Fidel Castro," Free argued.[35]

Was support for the Revolution grounded in thinking or feeling? As Castro himself once claimed, the question contained dialectical potential masquerading as a false dichotomy. The base of mass support, he suggested in a July 1964 speech, "could be found in the accomplishments of the Revolution." Even so, popular adherence was not a matter of sterile calculation.

Cuba, Castro continued, was "not a country of fanatics, but of men and women who think and feel; a people that have made thinking and feeling one and the same thing."[36]

In *The Spellbinders* (1984)—a definitive study of charismatic leadership—Ann Ruth Willner contends that the "rhetoric dimension of political charisma . . . deals less with the message and more with the medium through which the message is conveyed."[37] Her privileging of medium over message consciously echoes Marshall McLuhan's classic 1964 essay "The Medium Is the Message," in which he made a cognate argument about television.[38] McLuhan described television as a fundamentally "cool" medium: absorbing and engaging. It thus contained, he insisted, the "power . . . to involve an entire population in a ritual process."[39] He in turn cited Castro's Cuba as a prime example of this effect.

Without neglecting the significance of what Fidel said, we might direct further attention to *how* and *where* he said it. I propose that television served as an early seat for revolutionary governance and for the construction of Revolution as a lived (but also virtual) reality. At the center of Castro's media strategy were his late-night TV appearances, in which he worked to shape popular understandings of events at hand. He thereby tapped into a unique form of political and affective communication with his audience, whom he called out as the Revolution's natural constituency. As the Cuban public ceased to be a measurable analytic, "the people" thus became an ideological touchstone and a central character in the Revolution's screen life.

The Revolution's Screen Life

In the 1950s, Cubans had prided themselves on their precociously developed—and highly entertaining—television lineup. This vision followed many islanders into exile, where it both fueled and channeled nostalgia. After 1959, however, observers on the island were more likely to argue just the opposite: that Cuban TV needed a dose of revolution. Across the political spectrum, critics decried its reliance on "canned" (*enlatado*) programming, especially US shows and films dubbed into Spanish.[40] Equally shameful were the Cuban programs themselves, from imitative, overwrought dramas to ad-heavy variety shows and mirthless comedies.[41] "Cuba," wrote television scholar Carmelina Rey in 1959, was "rich in televisions" but poor in content.[42] Yet she also held out hope that the small screen might yet be harnessed to bring education and cultural uplift to the masses.

The Revolution would become the self-appointed steward of this transformation. Ironically, as Yeidy Rivero has shown, it did so for almost two years in symbiotic collaboration with privately owned television channels.[43] In the days and weeks following Fulgencio Batista's flight from the island, television was at the center of the revolutionary accession to power. When Fidel Castro ordered newspapers across the country to pause production for three days as his troops made their way to Havana, radio and television continued to broadcast.[44] Popular reception of this coverage was nothing short of euphoric, including a first interview with Fidel himself, live transmission of the rebels' entrance into Havana (with television cameras stationed along their route), and, perhaps most poignantly, an "avalanche of messages to friends and relatives in the interior from people in Havana."[45] These intraisland communications highlight the lateral potentialities of television, which linked Cubans not only to the Revolution's leaders but also, literally and figuratively, to one another.[46]

Meanwhile, TV programs both old and new were put to the service of revolutionary integration. Shows that had been censored under Batista resumed production, and tele- and radionovelas centered on political themes began to appear on air.[47] More novel programming was also born out of this conjunction, from *El pueblo pregunta*, a show grounded in dialogue between government officials and the populace, to seemingly interminable "telemaratones (telethons)," including one raising funds for Operation Arms and Planes for Cuba, which broke records with its 132 consecutive hours of broadcast.[48]

Indeed, the Revolution supplied a new context and content for Cuban TV, tracking leaders in action and documenting important political events. An early milestone was registered with the trials of notorious *batistianos* in late January and early February 1959. Part of Operation Truth, the government, as discussed in chapter 1, invited hundreds of international journalists to document the trials. Many visitors came away alarmed at the spectacle of the summary executions. Yet the trials—and their small-screen broadcasts— were must-see viewing among Cubans, who judged them favorably against past instances of revolutionary vigilantism.[49] They also established a precedent, to be repeated on multiple occasions in the years to come, for transacting high-profile legal proceedings on the air.

Inarguably, the most consequential star of these and other features of revolutionary television was Fidel Castro himself. There were times in these early years when it was nearly impossible to avoid his face on-screen; as Carlos Franqui put it, "like God he was everywhere."[50] In a 1962 account, Tad

Szulc also depicted Fidel as "something of an electronic household deity to millions of Cubans—and an electronic nightmare to a rapidly swelling element." "The average Cuban viewer," Szulc observed, "seems to be watching him on television almost every day, or even several times a day, in every conceivable form. . . . The result is reminiscent of an Orwellian 'Big Brother' situation in reverse: it is not Dr. Castro who watches the nation . . . it is the nation that watches him."[51]

To achieve this ubiquity, the new government depended on the sophisticated media landscape that it had inherited, which it also studiously enhanced. Leaders even "[sponsored] the distribution of television sets in small country towns and common buildings on estates confiscated from *batistianos* for collective viewings of Fidel's almost nightly performances."[52] One reporter noted that the government had also "installed [television sets] in nearly all police stations and army posts, and on innumerable public squares and in government buildings."[53] By August 1959, in the estimation of Ruby Hart Phillips, Castro was "reaching 95 per cent of the people in his lengthy broadcasts."[54] "It was possible," she later remarked, "to walk down any street in Havana and not miss a word of a speech by Castro since the television set in every house or commercial establishment was turned on at full volume."[55]

Fidel's April 1959 international travels, first to the US and then to Argentina, provoked particularly rhapsodic coverage, beginning with the pioneering simulcast of the leader's appearance on *Meet the Press*.[56] Shortly thereafter, a new first was registered when, en route from the United States to South America, Castro addressed the nation from a plane 20,000 feet above Havana.[57] Of the live coverage of Fidel's return to Havana in early May, *Diario de la Marina* TV critic Alberto Giro reported: "Through the cameras, from the intimacy of home . . . it was a total and absolute identification between the viewer and the prime minister, by means of television." For Giro, the majesty of the moment was amplified, not diminished, by virtue of its virtual quality: "Only the televised image, an exact replica of reality, could allow us to understand that we were facing the most magnificent demonstration that a people can offer its leader."[58] Via televised mediation, the Revolution had become more visceral, more immediate, than reality itself.

Indeed, it was on television that Fidel Castro carried out what he viewed as his most important task: persuasion.[59] His supporters more often called this "education"; his critics, "manipulation" or "propaganda."[60] But Castro regarded it as essential to the survival of the Revolution, particularly in

ENTRE TELEVIDENTES   Por Roseñada

—Chico, no me digas nada, tú también, como yo, oíste a Fidel estos dos noches.

Roseñada, "Entre televidentes," *Diario de la Marina*, June 10,
1959, 4-A.

Havana, with its reputation for "being somewhat inconsistent." As he later
claimed in a May 1968 speech, this changeability had in the early years "required our appearing on television with a certain frequency in order to
explain every kind of problem, major or insignificant."[61] Lee Lockwood, a
longtime observer, traced this orientation to Castro's training as a lawyer,
which allowed him to conceive of himself as a "creator of opinions."[62]

With this mission in mind, Fidel took to the small screen multiple times
a week, and often for several hours at a stretch. These appearances trans-
fixed (or paralyzed) Cubans in front of their televisions until the early hours
of the morning, producing a few jokes about the resulting hit to worker productivity.[63] This was the object of a *Diario de la Marina* cartoon, titled "Between TV Viewers": "Man," a bleary-eyed man addresses his companion,
"don't say a word, you and I both listened to Fidel these last two nights."

As for the political work thereby accomplished, it is perhaps useful to
turn to an anecdote recounted by journalist Victor Franco during his 1961
visit to the island. Sitting in a bar, his companion Anita and a waiter urged

LLEGO EL PREMIER.   por Arroyito.

—Arturito, más vale que vuelvas a desayunar en el café de la esquina
que ya llegó Fidel.

A May 1959 *Bohemia* cartoon skewers the gendered coordinates of
Castro-watching: a housewife sitting in front of a screen informs
her husband that he should "go back to eating breakfast at the
corner café since Fidel has returned" from his international
travels. Arroyito, "Llegó el premier," *Bohemia*, May 10, 1959, 98.

him to watch Fidel's upcoming TV appearance. Franco replied that he
planned to "read about his speech in the newspapers" the next day. That,
both the waiter and Anita declared, would be insufficient; one must *"listen
to Fidel,"* they insisted. Anita, Franco reluctantly submitted, was "in love
with Fidel Castro," a conclusion he reached after watching her view the
prime minister on television.[64]

The sexist overtones of this judgment should not obscure its explanatory
power. One female viewer, a self-professed opponent of the revolutionary
government, conceded that though she "[hated] Fidel," she found his
televised appearances to be irresistible: "If I turn on the TV while he's talking, I have to watch to the end."[65] She was far from alone in responding
to the erotic charge of Castro's screen presence. Victor Franco seemed to

acknowledge as much when, upon meeting Fidel for the first time, he blurted out: "You're exactly as you appear on television." To this, Fidel responded with laughter, adding, "I'm a revolutionary, not an actor."[66] Yet it is clear that in important ways, he was both.

Drawing on ratings surveys, Yeidy Rivero has posited that this programming was particularly appealing to female and working-class viewers.[67] The prevalence of women among television spectators—common to many other sites—would persist beyond this period as well.[68] But the seductive power of watching Fidel reached beyond female viewers. On many other fronts, Cuba's new revolutionary subject was defined as masculine and heteronormative. From the battleground to the cane fields, the "new man," even before Che Guevara explicitly identified him as such, distinguished himself though *activity* in the service of Revolution.[69] Yet TV Fidel interpellated Cubans, male and female, in a different—and implicitly feminine—register: as spectators and even fans. And the related pleasures (and displeasures) were as likely to be experienced in intimate and domestic spaces as in the public and collective ones otherwise associated with the Revolution.

The experience of watching Castro on TV was decidedly physical, even libidinal, in nature. Across social and political divides, one finds unanimity in the importance attached to Fidel's bodily presence, as well as its unlikely congruence with his chosen medium. In part, the success of this pairing stemmed from Castro's disdain for televisual artifice. Fidel, Szulc declared, "[lived] before the cameras as if he were completely unaware of their presence."[70] According to one US journalist, this preternatural comfort with the small screen allowed him to "[break] every rule. He never appears on time and always talks far too long. He cares not a whit for make-up, seldom has good lighting, sometimes turns his back on the camera and usually pitches his message somewhere below the soap opera level." But no one, he continued, could "doubt his effectiveness."[71] A member of the US diplomatic corps assessed one appearance thus: "He left the impression that this was the true, intimate Castro, with all concealments discarded and his innermost thoughts revealed."[72] Breaking with generic expectations, Fidel thus drew on his physicality to convey authenticity. That performance of naturalism also drove an innovative mode of revolutionary governance, set on television.

Government on/by Television

Longtime Cuba observer Herbert Matthews claimed to have coined the phrase "government by television."[73] In a televised debate with Matthews,

Jules Dubois in turn denounced the practice as "one of the most complete and methodical campaigns of cerebral softening . . . ever attempted in the contemporary history of Latin America."[74] Indeed, televised Revolution was the subject of many reports on Cuba during these years. As Szulc hypothesized, government by television was at the heart of the emergent formulation of "direct democracy," in which elections were jettisoned in favor of a mediated dialogue between Fidel and the Cuban people. His skillful deployment of television, Szulc maintained, had enabled him to "persuade millions of Cubans that, when he [advanced] an idea or a policy in a televised speech, he [was] actually asking for advice"—and, thus, that more formal structures of representation were thus superfluous.[75]

But Castro's TV appearances were not mere speeches. They were immersive, real-time stages of governance, where actual policy decisions were made and enacted. The theatricality inherent to the Revolution's screen life thus worked to bridge not only leadership and populace but also thinking and feeling. Staging revolutionary politics on the small screen allowed leaders to cultivate popular support for its substance by drawing on the medium's emotional effects. Novel political formations were thus built through television, as popular involvement was channeled through the emotional experience of watching.[76]

One of the most infamous such episodes involved the July 1959 forced resignation of Manuel Urrutia, a lawyer who had been selected as the first president of revolutionary Cuba. Increasingly vocal about his anti-Communist sentiments, including in a July 13 television program, where he "praised Fidel and condemned the reds," Urrutia had drawn the ire of the Communist Party and, ultimately, Fidel, who drafted a plan to execute his replacement.[77] In the lead-up to the July 26 anniversary of the 1953 storming of the Moncada barracks, Fidel unexpectedly stepped down as prime minister on July 17. That news provoked a day of incessant speculation, mobilization, and, of course, television viewing across Cuba.[78]

As protests mounted outside the presidential palace, the Council of Ministers gathered there and sat down in front of a television.[79] They watched Castro, ringed by a panel of journalists, attack Urrutia as a "traitor" for having "stirred up the phantom of Communism without any justification, inviting foreign aggression on our soil."[80] After a lengthy opening disquisition by Fidel, several of the panelists pushed him to clarify what would need to happen for him to consider returning to office; did the future of Cuba, one posed none too subtly, not "depend on the decision of a certain person?"[81]

With telegrams of support arriving at the CMQ studio and indignant crowds raging outside the presidential palace, Urrutia, who had wavered all day about how to proceed, finally prepared his resignation letter, which was delivered to Fidel by an emotional moderator. The news was greeted by the enthusiastic approval of the studio audience, which "spontaneously . . . rose to sing the National Anthem," followed by the hymn of the 26th of July Movement (Fidel led the chorus).[82] Observing an overjoyed crowd of thousands, someone related the decision to Fidel, remarking, "This is another survey, like *Bohemia*'s." "A survey? These were general elections, and the Revolution just won," Fidel replied.[83]

In the aftermath of Urrutia's fall, Osvaldo Dorticós was appointed Cuba's new president. Soon thereafter, Fidel returned to the position of prime minister, and the overall effect, Lillian Guerra contends, was to consolidate his leadership and further identify anti-Communism with counterrevolutionary convictions.[84] The broadcast, however, also established television as a tool in Castro's hands, a way to obviate traditional political structures and stage government directly for the people. This drama would subsequently be repeated on multiple occasions. As the foregoing might indicate, however, it was not a one-way street. In the televised theater of denunciation, the Cuban people would also make their voices heard.[85]

Another signal broadcast from January 1960 led to the on-air dismissal of Spanish ambassador Juan Pablo de Lojendo. That night, Castro appeared on television to, among other things, present accusations that the US and Spanish embassies had colluded with counterrevolutionary forces in Cuba. Lojendo refused to suffer the attack in silence. He demanded to be driven to the television studio and burst into the room where Fidel was broadcasting live.[86] Viewers heard a voice announcing his arrival, and the ambassador requested permission to respond, which Castro "[refused] categorically."[87] Lojendo continued to insist he had been slandered, and the studio audience rose up against him, decrying his lack of "respect." Across the country, screens suddenly went blank, as shouts of "*Fuera!*" (Out with him!) continued to sound.[88] When the transmission resumed, Lojendo had already "left the studio [accompanied] by Rebel Army officers and the commander-in-chief of the army himself." To the applause and anti-Spanish jeers of the crowd—which, that night, included foreign dignitaries and visitors such as US boxer Joe Louis—Fidel denounced the ambassador's behavior. "I want to make it understood," he continued, "that this ambassador will leave the country within twenty-four hours." President Dorticós at once ratified the decision on live television.[89]

And so, almost immediately, did viewers from all over Cuba. The response kicked off with a note signed by luminaries of the anti-Batista struggle and continued throughout the rest of the broadcast. Members of the studio audience, including the American visitors, raised their hands to register support. Telegrams poured in from all over Cuba, so many that Castro expressed irritation at the constant interruption of his discussion with the moderators. And the press, even those papers increasingly at odds with the government, signaled their approval the following day, as Lojendo returned to Spain and the Cuban ambassador, José Miró Cardona, made his way back to the island.[90]

Judging by audience reactions to the broadcast, this episode, like Urrutia's resignation before it, was the stuff of compelling viewing. But what was it about Fidel's screen presence that made him must-see TV? In a foundational text of television studies, Raymond Williams argues that what distinguishes television as a medium is its grounding in "flow," a "*sequence or set of alternative sequences.*" For this reason, we can say that we are "watching television"; the total experience has become bigger than the sum of its parts.[91]

Following Williams, Yeidy Rivero posits that the "disturbances" Castro presented to commercial television "[initiated] the dismantling of Cuba's commercial television flow" and the rise of a "new television routine."[92] "Liveness" played an important role in consolidating these new small-screen rhythms. According to Jane Feuer, the experience of live broadcast linked studio audience and home audience, performer and spectator, and the microcosm of the program to the nation as a whole.[93] Through immersion in television real time, viewers might forget they were "watching" at all.[94] Undeniably, Castro was compelling on television for all the reasons foreign observers pointed to—his intense eyes, large stature, and captivatingly awkward gestures—but also for others that could not so easily be pinned down. The ineffable residue usually described as "charisma" might, I propose, be better conceptualized as the effect of flow. After 1959, Cuban television migrated away from the component pieces of its capitalist past, but its cadence was not diminished but rather enhanced by the programming that took its place.

On the surface, Fidel's late-night TV appearances may seem the very antithesis of planned broadcasting sequences. Despite their improvised qualities, however, they nonetheless pivoted around a recognizable discursive center, from denunciations of political antagonists and US imperialism to dissertations on sugar policy and agricultural plans. These rhetorical units were the building blocks of a new experience of flow: one could now "watch Fidel" as one had "watched television" in the past. Here, Castro's rhetorical excesses, which critics mocked, converged powerfully with the demands of the medium. His very rhetorical style, wherein he would repeatedly return to a framing syntactical structure, theme, or metaphor to drive home his point, enhanced this effect. So, too, did his tendency to greet panelists' questions with long, digressive responses.[95]

Yet the rhetorical linchpin of Fidel's television performances was undoubtedly the Cuban people, whom he treated as both interpolated object and interpellated subject. To "the people," Castro often claimed to speak in a spirit of complete disclosure.[96] Bristling on one occasion at a *Bohemia* article that invoked the specter of Hitler in analyzing mass politics, he argued that the Cuban public should be trusted, not feared: "Why fear the crowd?" he mused. "How can we be democratic while fearing democracy?"[97]

In both addressing and aligning himself with the public, Fidel encouraged identification on the part of his audience. This was also the term most frequently employed by those seeking to describe his televisual effect. An October 1959 cartoon titled "Identification" depicted televisual rapport in a family so engrossed by Fidel on-screen that they had each sprouted his iconic beard. In 1965, Che Guevara cast this "dialectical unity" in notably mechanical terms: as the "dialogue of two tuning forks whose vibrations interact, producing new sounds."[98]

Identification was certainly one locus of audience experience, but we might also approach it, per one influential account, in terms of "transportation," or the "process of becoming fully engaged in a story." Sometimes it is the escapist potential of transportation, of leaving behind one's circumstances, that produces pleasure. Equally, however, transportation provides the opportunity for "transformation," for "exploring and experimenting with alternate selves."[99] Castro's dramatization of political process undoubtedly channeled both escapism and engagement. But it also abetted transformation: the categorical shift that recast spectators as political agents, and political agents as spectators.

If Castro's TV appearances were calculated to mold popular views, they also frequently enacted them, constructing public opinion as a virtual object. In this respect, the dialectic of persuasion was itself a transformative agent. Over and again, Fidel and his interlocutors acted out televised dramas of persuasion, through which he sought to shape the perspectives of viewers and enlist them as vicarious agents of revolutionary influence. Through identifying with Castro in this capacity, Cubans in turn came to

IDENTIFICACION   Por FORNES

Fornes, "Identificación," *Revolución*, October 22, 1959, 8.

A photograph of the audience at a taping of a Castro TV appearance reveals a range of reactions and, perhaps, interpersonal dynamics that might have shaped the "live" interaction with TV Fidel. Andrew St. George Collection, George A. Smathers Library, University of Florida.

understand persuasion as a political exercise to be mobilized against the Revolution's opponents—and a performance to which they should bear witness.

The Last Stand of the Virtual Opposition

The classic literature on persuasion positions the media as its most natural purveyor. The "public sphere," once constituted, becomes the locus of sparring "influencers," from advertisers to politicians and beyond. Though in many sites this dynamic dates to the nineteenth century, scholars have identified a period of intensification during the early to mid-twentieth century with the emergence of world war.[100] Indeed, the modern (political) definition of "propaganda" dates to this period.[101] In both capitalist and socialist societies, the cross-fertilization of advertising techniques, psychological theories, and Cold War politics thereafter made the battle for individual minds ever more urgent. The media—from newspapers to radio and television—often served as a host for their encounter.

We tend to distinguish democratic from authoritarian regimes by invoking the opposition between propaganda and persuasion. Unsurprisingly, Cold War antagonists freely lobbed these terms at each other. Democratic governments, the argument went, rightfully conducted persuasive exercises in the service of publicly beneficial goals. Conversely, authoritarian governments relied on propaganda to indoctrinate their subjects. The political character of this debate tended to obscure the underlying fuzziness of the distinction. What, definitionally, separated persuasion from propaganda besides the ascription of ethical legitimacy to the former and illegitimacy to the latter?[102]

In this final section, I explore the synchronicity of persuasion and propaganda in the Revolution's early screen life. More concretely, I consider how Fidel Castro introduced some of the defining features of propaganda—most notably, government control over the media—by repeatedly staging dramas of persuasion on Cuban television.[103] The most frequent target of and foil to these performances were holdout Cuban newspapers and journalists, who in turn ramped up their coverage of the erosion of press freedoms. Yet the televised drama of persuasion also came to bear on high politics, as in the 1961 trial of Bay of Pigs captives. Such programming suggested that even the Revolution's sworn enemies could be won over to its cause.

Though Fidel's television career is usually depicted as a succession of speeches, in these early years it was often waged interpersonally, through live engagement with journalists and panel moderators. Castro drew preferentially on the celebrated panel show *Ante la prensa* (a spin-off of the pioneering NBC program *Meet the Press*), which had become a leading defender of democratic freedoms under Batista.[104] Returning to the air after 1959, *Ante la prensa* offered a powerful if paradoxical vehicle for Castro's attacks on rival media, dramatized through the presence of his TV interlocutors.

The most famous was Jorge Mañach, a prominent intellectual and long-time host of *Ante la prensa*, whose early support for the Revolution did not stop him from occasionally defending the papers Castro critiqued. Others, albeit the minority, pursued an aggressive stance of televised confrontation.[105] But even panelists who did not object to Castro's denunciations were nonetheless engaged as debate partners, whom Fidel pushed, prodded, and cajoled. He frequently arrived for TV appearances armed with evidentiary material—secret cables, letters, newspaper articles—to mount a lawyerly case. But Castro's ability to influence also depended on its theatrical quality: the staging of persuasion as a televised drama.

A typical night of Fidel on television quickly escalated from pleasantries and softball questions to overheated answers. By setting up his interlocutors as rhetorical antagonists, Castro engaged in a hypnotic dance of rhetorical jousting, with the erosion of resistance functioning as both its text and its subtext. Take the following exchange between Castro and Jorge Mañach from a May 1959 episode of *Ante la prensa*. A discussion of Castro's recent trip to the United States and his refusal to ask for money there inspired a short rebuttal of charges that the cost of living in Cuba had gone up in 1959. Another panelist, Nicolás Bravo, proposed that any such accusations would be considered "counterrevolutionary," to which Castro replied that the "increase in the costs of living in all of Latin America was so great that his words got stuck in his mouth."[106] Nonetheless, he continued, the Revolution had in fact "lowered" the cost of living in Cuba. That correction was followed by a lull.

Mañach moved to clarify: "Doctor Castro, might I interpret any pause to mean that you have finished answering the question and that we might pass to the next[?]" Fidel responded that "he wouldn't go on" if Mañach "didn't want him to." Mañach prodded again: "Sometimes it's difficult to know when you've finished. There's some timidity." Castro replied forcefully: "Don't say there's timidity because then they'll claim there's no freedom of the press." Bravo interjected once more: "I would like to say that there has never been any timidity[;] the panelists sitting on this panel have never felt timidity, merely respect and nothing more." Castro in turn insisted that he would "shut up" and "adhere to time limits" when it was desired. He concluded, however, with a final jab at Mañach, whom he implicitly lumped with the skeptical "minority" for whom such broadcasts were staged: "They can't say that I haven't been courteous with that minority, whose faith [in the Revolution] grows day by day."[107]

Accounts of Castro's TV appearances have tended to focus on their presumed text: namely, his long responses to interviewers' questions. Lost in translation was the live experience of these interstitial moments, in which Fidel drove home his points by circumlocution, disputation, and even play. The subtextual drama of confrontational TV was particularly vivid on *Ante la prensa*, where Fidel went to deliver critiques of newspapers like *Diario de la Marina*, *El Mundo*, and *Avance*. This was somewhat ironic, given that the program's moderator, Jorge Mañach, was himself a columnist for *Diario de la Marina*. This often put him in a thorny position, as in June 1959, when the director of *El País* demanded to appear on *Ante la prensa* to respond to Castro's allegations. In that instance, Mañach had demurred, citing his obligation to maintain journalistic impartiality.[108]

This stance, however, would be difficult to uphold when his own paper became a target of condemnation. As we have seen, though *Diario* had long served as a bastion of conservative opinion, in early 1959 it pursued a mostly peaceful coexistence with the revolutionary leadership. Leading up to the first agrarian reform of May 1959, however, tensions between *Diario* and the government began to grow. Often Fidel took to television to extend such battles. In an October 1959 episode of *Ante la prensa*, Castro condemned the complicity of *Diario de la Marina* and other papers with counterrevolutionary forces and, he alleged, its efforts to censor its writers. The program that night was interrupted by news that workers at several papers, including *Diario*, had sent a telegram to express their support for the Revolution, and Mañach also echoed Castro's critique of financial interest in newspaper publishing. But an open media was limited by other factors as well, Fidel claimed; freedom of the press "was very relative when three hundred people worked at the papers and only the owner could express himself." On this point, Mañach felt the need to respond, indicating that he, along with other journalists, had "defended the Revolution from the pages of *Diario*" and that he would continue to do so if his freedom was "respected." Raúl Castro rose from the audience to counter this view, citing evidence that *Diario* employed reporters whom it did not allow to "write freely." Mañach objected that he had never been censored or refused publication but rather encouraged to write "freely" about Cuba's contemporary reality.[109]

In these appearances, Castro and the journalistic corps frequently battled over the meaning of speaking "freely." This debate would in turn provoke the most consequential televised feud of the early revolutionary period between Castro and Luis Conte Agüero, a celebrated radio broadcaster known as the "Voice of Oriente." Conte Agüero thus became one of the first, and perhaps the last, to challenge Castro's dominance in Cuban television politics. Their confrontation triggered not only Conte Agüero's exile from Cuba but also the nationalization of one of the island's last independent TV networks.

It was a surprising end to what had once been a celebrated partnership. Fidel's relationship with Conte Agüero extended back to his imprisonment following the 1953 Moncada barracks attack. In letters sent from prison, Castro sought to expand awareness and coverage of his battle against Batista. In the press and on his popular radio show, Conte Agüero joined others in praising Fidel, contributing to his lionization in the public eye.[110] After 1959, Conte Agüero's boosterism only rose in volume, especially on his recently launched television show on CMQ-TV, which soon became a favored forum for Castro.

Yet there were early signs of strain in their relationship, stemming from both personal and ideological differences. Fidel expressed misgivings about Conte Agüero's reissuing of his prison letters, which he ordered to be "recalled and destroyed" after a first publication run of 50,000 books. At issue was Conte Agüero's celebration of revolutionary "humanism," which he juxtaposed with the threat of Communist influence.[111] Implicitly, his broadcasts in turn drew attention to the inconsistencies of Fidel's evolution on this front, from his early proclamations of an "olive green" Revolution to the increasingly pervasive conflation of anti-Communism with counterrevolutionary sentiment.

By early 1960, these tensions had escalated into all-out media warfare, pitting Conte Agüero against radio commentators and writers at *Revolución* and the Communist daily *Hoy*. With the encouragement of his CMQ patrons, Conte Agüero decided to address the issue openly. In a March 1960 broadcast, he revealed that he would read a letter to Fidel in his upcoming TV appearance. On the radio the next day, he appealed directly to Castro to free himself of Communist influence and "save the revolution."[112] He then resigned and began to prepare for his final TV appearance. But he never made it to CMQ. A group of students and workers surrounded the studio to protest his appearance, where they were met by a counterprotest of University of Havana students.[113] While Conte Agüero turned to the media to advance his claim that Communists planned to turn Cuba into the next Hungary, Castro issued a television denunciation of his own, alleging that Conte Agüero had crossed over into enemy lines.[114]

CMQ also faced the fallout from this battle. As Conte Agüero took refuge in the Argentine embassy, ultimately to make his way to exile in the United States, the bank accounts of Goar and Abel Mestre, CMQ's owners, were suddenly frozen.[115] On March 31, Abel Mestre appeared on *Ante la prensa* to read a declaration in defense of freedom of speech, where he also decried Communist infiltration in the government.[116] The Mestres then hastily departed Cuba, leaving CMQ behind. Soon thereafter, it would become the last television station to be nationalized by the revolutionary government.[117]

In making his last stand, Conte Agüero had attempted his own version of televisual political persuasion, even insinuating that it was Fidel who was powerless before a Communist propaganda campaign. In responding to his media foes, Castro presented the same argument in reverse. Mañach and Conte Agüero, he contended, were the purveyors of bad faith and false consciousness. But the outcome of these battles pointed to an increasingly inescapable conclusion: that the persuasive dialectic that Fidel had long staged on Cuban TV was being supplanted by a one-man show.

El Pueblo Pregunta

The apotheosis of the Revolution's screen life, however, was still to come. For five thrilling days in late April 1961, Fidel Castro enacted the ultimate drama of persuasion: the live, televised interrogation of forty prisoners taken captive during the Bay of Pigs invasion. The broadcasts drew on all the conventions of TV Fidel, from the immersive spectacle of the trial, complete with a panel of journalist-questioners, to audience participation.[118] Interrogations were frequently interrupted by telegrammed allegations from viewers, who had identified among the captives a torturer or henchmen from the Batista government. One of them was even confronted by an audience member, who accused him of having murdered her partner. Live on air, she was escorted out of the room in the throes of a "nervous breakdown."[119]

Yet the objective of the interrogations was less to reveal the culpability of the prisoners than to prove the "duplicity" of the United States.[120] Participants provided detailed evidence that US officials, contrary to their public statements, had sponsored and organized the invasion. More broadly, however, interrogators presented many prisoners as victims of US propaganda. Though there were real villains among those brought before the panel, most portrayed themselves as having been "tricked" and "misled."[121] The narrative arc of the trial was thus not the indictment of individual captives so much as persuasion itself.

The final day of the broadcast brought the prisoners face-to-face with Fidel and made them unlikely panelists on the most epic *Ante la prensa* episode ever aired. At their urging, Castro launched into lengthy explanations of revolutionary policy and broadcast evidence that the United States had sponsored the invasion. But even in the face of sustained pressure, some of the prisoners held fast to their views. Several went so far as to question him about the postponement of elections and communist influence on his (now openly socialist) government.[122] Strikingly, in April 1961, popular support for the Revolution was robust enough for leaders to broadcast and, later, publish the words of their antagonists, encouraging Cubans to confront such perspectives head-on.[123]

In this respect, the broadcasts projected revolutionary adhesion— "most of the populace," Castro encouraged the prisoners to acknowledge, "was with the Revolution"—even as they archived potential counternarratives.[124] But in Castro's person, they also staged persuasion as revolutionary praxis. In a suggestive climax, many captives, who only days earlier had attempted to overthrow the revolutionary government, enacted their own performance of solidarity and conversion. Concluding the trial, one prisoner declared that they would "stand with the people of Cuba to fight against any foreign enemy who comes to tread on our soil," language that notably transitions from an exclusive ("stand *with* the people of Cuba") to an inclusive ("*our* soil") framing of their relationship to the revolutionary body politic.[125] The Bay of Pigs trial thus consolidated, dramatized, and ratified popular support for the Revolution, even among those who were once its sworn enemies.

After 1961, though other officials (especially Che Guevara) continued to make regular and even candid small-screen appearances, Castro began to appear less often on television. His absence, which he attributed to a busy schedule, produced speculation among foreign observers. The obvious explanation, however, was that such appearances had become unnecessary. Over the course of the Revolution's first two years, Castro had turned to television to construct a political reality straddling affect and ideology. In providing a forum for the medium of Fidel, television had helped to incorporate the populace into revolutionary process, interpellating Cubans as audience and virtual protagonists. Meanwhile, by staging persuasion, Castro had consolidated state control over the media, making the drama previously attached to it superfluous.

Even as its function changed, however, television remained a critical weapon in the hands of the government. The mobilization of television to ideological ends intensified during periods of crisis. During the 1962 Cuban Missile Crisis, for example, both Castro and Kennedy took to the small screen in a high-stakes diplomatic chess game. Much has been made of Kennedy's novel use of on-screen diplomacy over the course of the conflict, as well as Castro's televised demand for a preemptive Soviet strike. Yet their small-screen showdown also highlighted the limits to Castro's media power; in the end, his bold—or, as he would later concede, reckless—performance was no match for the nuclear might of the two superpowers, whose secret agreement to draw back won out, to Castro's dismay.[126]

The screen life of the early Revolution had proven to be must-see television. Very quickly, its effect changed. But before it became a script—another entry in the sacralized corpus of Fidel Castro's rhetoric—the Revolution's screen life was transacted through compelling and often unpredictable improvisation. Early on, this functioned to identify some Cubans with the leader who skillfully enacted it, while binding all Cubans to the medium where it took place. Whatever one's political affiliations, television came to constitute an inescapable fulcrum of political and social life.[127] As Simone Lueck highlights in his haunting images of contemporary island screens, "In Cuba, television is a national pastime. . . . Whether used for information or as a background for socializing and drinking rum, during broadcast hours, all TVs in Cuba are ON."[128]

I have argued here that the small screen played a signal role in helping to dismantle Cuba's traditional media while delimiting the bounds of revolutionary belonging. By constantly appealing to "the people" on television, Fidel Castro helped to bring that category into existence. In part, the revolutionary public was defined through opposition to domestic and foreign foes, from critical journalists to US policymakers and even a Cuban president. Yet it also came into being through the kind of identification Castro encouraged in his live, seemingly unscripted presence. In this respect, televised dramas of conversion were an obvious synecdoche for the broader process of revolutionary consolidation. Their intertextual connection to media controversies helped to naturalize the virtual reach of revolutionary politics and the narrowing bounds of press engagement.

Yet it would be a mistake to reason from the evidence of Fidel's intentionality to an analysis of effect. The ephemeral archive attached to the early screen life of the Cuban Revolution might instead offer an object lesson to historians of post-1959 Cuba. From the vantage point of high politics, the function of televised governance might be transparent and a natural match for the presumptions long embedded in accounts of revolutionary charisma or, on the other hand, indoctrination. But what did the Revolution look like, feel like, from the perspective of its most eager—and even its most reluctant—television viewers? That we cannot answer the question in any obvious way may itself be the moral of the story.

· · · · · ·

The tranquility of a Friday night. With your family, seated on your favorite armchair, you're watching TV. For some time now the singers and hosts have been battling it out with your drowsiness. Suddenly the shiny box sparks your interest. . . . On the screen a minister has appeared. He's answering questions about his activities. Any question that the public formulates from their homes. The telephones don't stop ringing and the man doesn't stop answering. "Now this is great," you think.[129]

In 1967, amid a political and cultural opening, producers at Cuba's Channel 6 launched a program that quickly became a smash hit. *El pueblo pregunta*, which aired every other Friday night, featured the island's governing officials in what TV producer and journalist Eugenio Pedraza Ginori dubbed the "world's biggest press conference."[130] With a dedicated team of female telephone operators fielding calls from all over the island, alongside a live audience of some 500 viewers, the show promised to revive and even augment televised Revolution as it was first pioneered in the early 1960s. On the small screen, government figures took up matters ranging from women's shoes to public health, hydraulic problems, and Cuba's participation in the V Pan American Games.

Audience response was, unsurprisingly, robust. In its first broadcast in June 1967, viewer questions reached the impressive tally of 600 in a mere eight hours. The volume of viewer queries quickly became so high that producers launched a separate written forum in *Granma*, where questions that went unaddressed on the show could be answered. "No one will be left without a response," they promised. Notably, calls to the program also featured complaints. Yet one of the show's producers suggested that most were the product of an "absence of correct information[,] or 'disinformation.' . . . We must combat that," she concluded. "That's what the program is for."[131]

Observers praised *El pueblo pregunta* for the "true dialogue" it staged between the "masses and their leaders." Among them, Pedraza Ginori framed the show as a key node in a field of political connectivity: "The people, directly informed, contribute. The healthy revolutionary climate protects the exchange between the people and their government."[132] Yet as he has recently written, there were limits on the transparency of this connection. On one December 1967 episode, Lisandro Otero, vice president of the Consejo Nacional de Cultura, was confronted on air by a caller, who, having promised to ask a different question, accused Otero of having been a "sinecurist" (*botellero*) under the Batista government. Though other panelists attempted to ignore and deflect from the question—heard live all over Cuba—the damage was done.[133] Producers of the show, "fearing that the situation could repeat itself," responded by censoring incoming questions, and "nothing," Pedraza Ginori writes, "was ever the same. With its corseted script, with everything tied up before the program even aired, the program lost the freshness of its beginnings . . . and it entered a freefall."[134]

Like its antecedents, *El pueblo pregunta* suggested that it was the audience who wrote the script. Yet in transacting politics on television, revolutionary officials continued to promote *response* as a mode of popular engagement. Posing questions, as hundreds of Cubans did live and then through intermediaries, may not have moved the needle when it came to the most pressing issues of the day, especially when those questions were not heard. But what happened when audience responses were broadcast instead of buried?

Chapter 3 explores radio propaganda crafted by the Castro government and its exile antagonists to address this very question. In their efforts to cultivate support across the hemisphere, radio programs on both sides of the Florida Straits came to feature the voices of listener-correspondents, who wrote in to register support and, at times, opposition. Programs dedicated to audience letters were quickly developed to amplify emergent solidarities. Yet the very fact of broadcast also created opportunities for alternative views to appear on air and, at times, divergent understandings of solidarity to implicate their hosts. The very importance attached to radio outreach thus created openings for the expression of popular opinion on all sides, whose dissemination had political effects—even when no one heeded it.

3　Radio Revolution

Political Reception and Solidarity Channels

. . . .

In the world of Cuban media, opportunities for reinvention were rarely hard to find. Soon after his departure from the island, Goar Mestre of CMQ began to build a Latin American TV empire, stretching from Puerto Rico to Argentina.[1] Luis Conte Agüero, fresh off his battle with Castro, was not far behind. Weeks after arriving in the United States, Conte Agüero submitted to a polygraph test administered by the CIA, which hoped that he might be a useful intelligence asset.[2] Conte Agüero's initial forays into exile politics, including a stint as propaganda chief for the Cuban Revolutionary Council (the community's principal, highly fractious outlet) soon turned him off organization work, and his relationship with the US intelligence services was similarly fraught. Nonetheless, he quickly realized that collaboration was the best hope for amplifying his message.

In the United States, Conte Agüero established a newly prominent perch—a nightly radio show broadcast on WRUL (New York)—and the CIA was eager to capitalize on his island audience. He in turn drew on agency resources for his political outreach, spanning publications, speaking tours, and, most importantly, radio. Similar overtures would catapult other former press luminaries, notably *Prensa Libre* editors Sergio Carbó and Humberto Medrano and the exiled staff of *Bohemia* magazine, to new radio careers in the United States, often with covert CIA backing.[3] The hope was that they, like their predecessors in the world of Soviet emigre politics, could bring their compatriots into the ranks of the opposition.

Both within and beyond Cuba, the political deployment of radio had a long and controversial history. With the onset of the Cold War, that politicization turned toward overt weaponization. Radio became not only a vehicle for a variety of local, national, and even global struggles but a tactical agent in those struggles as well, mobilized in campaigns to either discredit or disseminate Soviet messaging. As transistors, including shortwave units, became cheaper and more accessible, the audience for radio grew accordingly. Radio did not demand print literacy, and it expanded horizons, putting distant contexts within earshot. Moreover, the medium was ideally suited not only to building community—listening to broadcasts from abroad could be a shared and even social activity—but also to surreptitious consumption for those whose media preferences put them on the wrong side of political lines.

Architects of radio propaganda may have imagined it as a largely one-way street: a way to reach and, ideally, change the minds of listeners. Yet from the mid-century explosion of amateur (ham) radio to cross-platform exchanges between bitter foes, the medium was more interactive than this framing would suggest. The dialogic potential of radio was amplified by its interaction with a much older technology: mail. Those who did not take to the air to convey their thoughts were nonetheless able to do so by writing in to share praise, complaints, and feedback of all kinds.

Here I explore the mixed media attached to Cold War radio transmissions, especially the transnational circulation of letters written in response to propaganda broadcasts. In the Cuban context and beyond, politicized transmissions were in fact designed not only to *speak to* listeners but also to *hear from* them. Audience response was thus encouraged and integrated into the broadcasts themselves. In Cuba and the United States, radio programs featured listener letters as evidence of the righteousness of their respective causes and the efficacy of their messaging.

On both the CIA-sponsored radio network organized to counter the Revolution from afar and Radio Habana Cuba—the international station launched by the revolutionary government in 1961—programs dedicated to audience correspondence connected authorial intention to audience reception. Letters from listeners proved that broadcasts by Cuban revolutionaries or exiles in the United States had succeeded in defying the technological and political obstacles to deliver their message. They also suggested that their ideas arrived untarnished by ideological interference. But the aims of radio broadcasters did not always match the experiences of their audience.

Though both sides begrudgingly admitted to receiving hate mail, equally prevalent were those responses that echoed their scripts but transposed to a more personal key. These included, for example, letters to Radio Habana Cuba expressing solidarity in terms of individual rather than political identification. As Renata Keller has written about Mexican fan mail to Fidel Castro, such letters, though "ostensibly about the Cuban Revolution," tell us "more about political culture and society in 1960s Mexico."[4] This, I propose, was the very nature of solidarity; feeling *for* the Revolution required that listeners feel *like* the Revolution. In a similar spirit, island letters to anti-Castro programs in the United States often echoed their warnings about the imminent fall of the Revolution or the foibles of revolutionary leaders. Yet they also demanded that broadcasters engage in a kindred exercise of translation: that they imagine and even experience life on the island on the terms set by their listeners.

Examining the correspondence attached to Cuban broadcasting thus provides rare, if mediated, access to political reception—not only what was heard but how it was received by ordinary listeners. Unlike the more public participants in left-wing, Black radical, or exile political circles who often feature in histories of Cold War solidarity, radio's different constituencies— oppositional or disaffected island Cubans, North American Revolution sympathizers, and the many Latin Americans who fell somewhere in between—may have exercised little influence over the hemispheric power struggles that shaped their lives.[5] But the very act of listening and writing back broadcasted, if it did not always actualize, their political agency. By someone, somewhere, to some limited degree, the people were heard.

Radio War: Origins

By the time the United States began aiming transmitters at Cuba (and vice versa), radio had for decades been pulled into global power struggles. During World War II, all the major powers turned to the medium to convert and recruit, building on the radio outreach of leaders like Franklin Roosevelt in the preceding decade.[6] Allied concerns about the reach of Nazi propaganda led to the 1942 establishment of the Voice of America (VOA), a short-wave outlet of the US government with a strictly international mission. Together with the BBC, VOA broadcasting proposed to offer an informational—and "inspirational"—portrait of the ongoing conflict.[7] Latin America was no stranger to those efforts. The Nazis had targeted the region with some twelve hours of daily programming, and so the United States mobilized its own response.[8] Inspired by the framework of the Good Neighbor Policy, radio broadcasting formed part of a broader US media campaign to foment hemispheric goodwill.[9]

By the early 1950s, the emergent Cold War conflict between the United States and the Soviet Union inspired policymakers to revive the operational role of radio. Compared to other media, radio propaganda could travel far and reach a large audience, particularly when conveyed over shortwave frequencies. To this end, the VOA (under the auspices of the newly founded United States Information Agency, or USIA) and the BBC geared up to battle the Soviet Union over the airwaves, be it through hard-hitting reporting, political commentary, or jazz music. Their efforts were often greeted by intentional interference, also known as "jamming," on the part of the intended receiving country.[10]

Appealingly, radio could conceal its point of origin; it was the ideal vehicle for messaging that sounded unofficial. Leaders in the United States and the Soviet Union could thus camouflage their sponsorship of scripted political content. This was the case, for example, at the two US radio outlets most closely associated with the early Cold War: Radio Free Europe, which started broadcasting to Czechoslovakia in 1951 (followed by Poland, Hungary, Romania, and Bulgaria), and Radio Liberty, which launched its programming directed at the Soviet Union in 1953. Both of these stations employed Soviet exiles to "[broadcast] freedom" to their former countrymen and women.[11] Under the oversight of the CIA, the stations were tasked with countering Soviet propaganda with "fact based, balanced, and credible" reporting, guidelines they often flouted in practice.[12] In fact, one of the most controversial chapters in the history of Radio Free Europe was its broadcasting during the Hungarian Revolution of 1956, during which it transmitted false information encouraging Hungarians to revolt.[13]

This potential for radio battles to spill over into actual combat followed the medium to Latin America. After a decade of "good neighbor" engagement, in the late 1940s US policy toward the region reflected a more bellicose anti-Communism. Purportedly in the interest of combating Soviet influence, the US government adopted increasingly interventionist methods to thwart nationalist and socially progressive reform in the region. Over the next several decades, this would turn the Latin American Cold War into one of the most violent fronts of the international superpower contest.[14]

The US-sponsored deposal of President Jacobo Árbenz in Guatemala (1951–54) served as ground zero for such tactics. Though Árbenz had been democratically elected, US policymakers and business interests, especially the United Fruit Company, objected to his program for agrarian reform. Soon thereafter, the CIA began plotting to overthrow Árbenz's government. Operation PBSuccess included plans for a military invasion headed by Carlos Castillo Armas, who was subsequently installed as Guatemala's president, but its cornerstone was an unprecedented campaign of psychological warfare. As the United States blanketed Latin America with anti-Árbenz propaganda, the CIA outlet Radio Liberación began to broadcast recorded messages from neighboring Honduras, claiming to provide live coverage from inside Guatemala. Radio Liberación narrated and, in doing so, helped to instigate an invasion after its broadcasts had demobilized the Guatemalan military and populace.[15]

Many of the strategies and players first deployed in Guatemala would be resurrected to undermine Cuba's revolutionary government. In November 1959, CIA director Allen Dulles presented a "Cuba propaganda project" centered on, among other things, subversive radio programming.[16] By March of the following year, President Eisenhower had signed on to the CIA's Program of Covert Action against the Castro Regime, with psywar—and an invasion of the island—at its heart. Under the leadership of David Atlee Phillips and E. Howard Hunt—two veterans of the anti-Árbenz effort—the plan was Guatemala redux.[17] Even the directors of VOA programming were convinced to forgo their "objective, honest, and nonbelligerent" stance to bolster anti-Castro efforts.[18]

As bilateral relations between the United States and Cuba continued to unravel, radio psyops escalated accordingly. By February 1961, the US government had at its disposal more than twelve shortwave USIA transmitters, several commercial stations based in the United States, and a covert medium-wave radio station located on Swan Island, a territory jointly claimed by Honduras and the United States.[19] As VOA director Henry Loomis explained in a 1961 memo, the VOA shortwave broadcasts, pitched with an "objective and unexcited" orientation, were intended for a broad Latin American audience, while Radio Swan existed "for Cubans to talk to Cubans . . . to excite its listeners and to ridicule and undermine the regime."[20] Meanwhile, Cuba broadcasting on the commercial frequencies also targeted island audiences but was "designed to be more objective, more certain of its accuracy, and quieter in tone."[21] Cuban exiles interviewed upon arrival to the United States indicated that VOA had a particularly broad audience, due both to successful jamming of Radio Swan and the fact that Swan often trafficked in untruths. Nonetheless, Loomis reported that both the VOA and Radio Swan had "wide audiences. Many listen to both; to VOA for confirmation; to Swan for titilation [sic]."[22] Those titillations included such outright falsehoods as the October 1960 announcement that the Cuban government intended to sequester and "indoctrinate" children.[23] This inspired the exodus of some 14,000 Cuban children, which would come to be known as Operation Pedro Pan.

In this respect, Radio Swan, which debuted in May 1960, represented the closest cognate to Radio Liberación. Because the US Navy had helped to install the station on Swan Island, it could not be run clandestinely, so a commercial cover, the Gibraltar Steamship Corporation, was established, headed by former United Fruit president Thomas Dudley Cabot.[24] No one, however, was fooled. In addition to initiating successful jamming, Fidel Castro issued a formal protest at the September 1960 meeting of the United Nations, where he charged that the US presence on Swan Island and the radio station itself represented a "violation of international law"—that is, the 1960 North American Regional Broadcasting Agreement (signed by Cuba and the United States), which prohibited medium-wave broadcasting to Cuba from the United States.[25]

But Castro's most consequential response to Radio Swan's provocations was to initiate his own strategic broadcasting. With an eye toward cultivating a hemispheric audience, La Voz del INRA (The voice of INRA), headed by Antonio Núñez Jiménez, director of the National Institute for Agrarian Reform (Instituto Nacional de Reforma Agraria), "adopted a popular commercial format with Cuban music, news, radio plays, and even advertising," alongside ample political content.[26] The island's international roster of stations soon expanded to include CMBL, which countered the radio messaging of Dominican dictator Rafael Trujillo, and CMGS (Radio Varadero), aimed at the eastern United States. But the government's capacity for long-range outreach expanded dramatically when Swiss-made transmitters were put at the service of La Onda Experimental Cubana—soon to be renamed Radio Habana Cuba—which launched in February 1961.[27]

Radio Habana debuted just in time to serve at the front lines against US invasion. As in Guatemala, the planned April 1961 landing of Brigade 2506 at the Bay of Pigs was to proceed with both air cover (which never arrived) and radio coordination, with Radio Swan providing an ongoing, often fictionalized play-by-play. To listeners, however, Radio Swan's programming sounded more like gibberish than operational code. Its most infamous segment featured the "red fish," chosen by CIA planners as an appropriately "Christian" symbol for Brigade B2506.[28] When the invasion began, Radio Swan advised listeners to "Look well at the rainbow. The fish will rise very soon."[29] E. Howard Hunt, apparently inspired by BBC wartime broadcasts, intended for the message to "deceive Castro into thinking the underground was about to rise."[30] But the Cuban government knew the invasion was coming, and since the anticipated rebellion never occurred, island forces achieved a swift victory over Brigade 2506. Little dissuaded by defeat, Radio Swan "continued to broadcast mysterious orders to nonexistent battalions," much to the annoyance of those who had participated in the landing.[31] Cuba's new international station immediately took to the air to condemn the attack and announce its defeat, punctuated by the pronouncements of Fidel Castro and other revolutionary leaders.[32]

Radio Swan took some heat for its failure to deliver another Guatemala, but it quickly underwent what David Wise and Thomas B. Rose have described as a "process akin to alchemy."[33] Though its administrative cover—along with a massive CIA operational force—relocated to Miami, what would thereafter be known as Radio Americas remained on Swan Island for the duration of its life span. For years to come, it continued to face off against Radio Habana Cuba, battling for hearts and minds across the hemisphere and even the world. The Bay of Pigs was only the beginning of what would become a protracted radio war.

Radio Habana Cuba: The Sound of Solidarity

"I was so happy to hear you during the invasion," wrote a listener from British Columbia. "Like all the progressive workers of the world, I wish the workers and people of Cuba all kinds of success in repelling the invaders." A Colombian fan echoed that excitement, noting that he had "[listened] to all of the interrogations, of the mercenaries," without "[missing] a single one."[34] Their letters, along with those of other Radio Habana Cuba listeners across the hemisphere, helped to forge a network of solidarity messaging with the Revolution, as station announcers encouraged audience members to write and share reactions. P.O. Box 7026 became as well-known to their listeners as any other character in the revolutionary saga, a place where they could register excitement, sympathy, and occasionally discrepancy with Cuba's political project. But the communication did not end there. In its Department of Correspondence and International Relations, Radio Habana employed a fleet of workers—the station's largest bloc—to respond.[35] Among their most important tasks was selecting the messages that would be broadcast and later printed in Cuba's newspapers. The public airing of these private missives provided multimedia evidence of the Revolution's growing reach.

Radio Habana's first decade witnessed and amplified the Revolution's expanding international influence, as the Cuban government faced off against the United States in a variety of hemispheric and international struggles. Latin American governments engaged the two regional powers with a variety of aims and purposes yet rarely escaped this bipolar framework.[36] The contest for political loyalties was shaped by ideological prerogatives, with capitalism on one side and communism on the other. But a

If the Revolution's leaders and many Radio Habana Cuba announcers were men, the everyday work of forging transnational bonds was entrusted largely to women, as pictured here in the station's correspondence department. Francisco Pita Rodríguez, "Radio Habana Cuba: Nueve años llevando al mundo la verdad de Cuba," *Bohemia*, no. 21 (May 1970): 18. Photo by Rubén González.

long history of US imperialist intervention ran through such debates, triangulating the terms of the Cold War. For many, the Revolution's appeal derived from its defiance of a long-standing geopolitical order.[37]

In this contest for political allegiances, Radio Habana Cuba played a highly visible—or audible—role. The island's propaganda efforts, centered on such outlets as *Prensa Latina*, had accelerated considerably following the rupture of diplomatic relations with the United States in 1961.[38] But the US-led suspension of Cuba from the Organization of American States (OAS) in 1962 made the dissemination of print media increasingly difficult, as did the efforts of regional governments, often spurred by the United States, to confiscate such materials.[39] Radio thus took center place in the Revolution's media arsenal, as island leaders worked to route Operation Truth through a more accessible medium. Radio also provided a platform for kindred mobilizations across the hemisphere, ranging from deposed Guatemalan president Jacobo Árbenz to US civil rights activist Robert F. Williams. Over the airwaves, the juxtaposition of these causes served to render the Cuban Revolution in broad, even hemispheric terms, a rhetorical and political expansion that audience letters helped to cement. Sympathetic listeners offered evidence that Cuba's message could be heard well beyond its borders, in terms meaningful to them.

The cultivation of an international audience dated back to 1958, when, at the initiative of Ernesto "Che" Guevara, a radio transmitter was embedded in the sierra. 7RR debuted alongside the underground newspaper *El Cubano Libre* in February 1958, and its first broadcast featured, among other items, news of fallen comrades and recent engagements by Guevara's column. But the station's antennas did not facilitate close transmission, and so the broadcast could not be heard in Santiago. Nonetheless, as radio technician Eduardo Fernández recalled to veteran broadcaster Ricardo Martínez Victores, this early broadcast may have been audible in western Cuba. Fatefully, he adds, it could also be heard "perfectly" outside Cuba.[40]

As the station grew—and relocated to Castro's headquarters in La Plata—these international contacts, alongside a growing rebel radio network, served as the foundation of the Cadena de la Libertad (Liberty Network). According to participant Luis Buch, interviewed by Martínez Victores, it worked as follows: between 6 and 8 P.M., 7RR aired its program, which was then taped by "Indio Azul," the "official station of the 26th of July Movement." That recording was sent to Radio Continente in Venezuela, where it was edited and aired at 11 P.M., a broadcast that was aimed at Cuba and would therefore also reach Central America, the Caribbean, and the United States. Radio Caracol in turn targeted South America, as did La Voz de los Andes for the continent's Pacific coast.[41] The participation of Argentine journalist Jorge Ricardo Masetti (of later *Prensa Libre* fame) helped to grow 7RR's Latin American audience through interviews with revolutionary leaders such as Castro and Guevara. Other foreign journalists also sent in questions that were answered on the air.[42]

Che Guevara was inspired to establish 7RR by his conviction that radio propaganda was the most "effective" kind. In revolutionary contexts, he wrote, such messaging could "explain, teach, inflame."[43] This was the very mission that 7RR had taken on, with an emphasis on cultivating morale and sharing the "truth" about the movement with a Cuban and foreign audience. The station also served an important logistical function, as it was used to disseminate information about the failed April 1958 general strike and the Cero-Tres-Ce ("cero cine, cero compras, cero cabaret") campaign, in which

Cubans were urged to boycott theaters, stores, and the cabaret.[44] When Batista fled the country on January 1, 1959, 7RR broadcasting helped to avert a military coup and once again issued a call for a general strike, this time successfully.[45] Alongside commercial radio announcers, especially at the Santiago station Radio Oriente (CMKC), 7RR allowed anti-Batista forces to connect with each other, the civilian population, and a growing international constituency for the Revolution, transmitting strategic updates but also forging interpersonal connections.[46]

Like its successor Radio Habana, rebel radio thus took on not only informational but also communicative functions, as in the November 1958 letter from an "anonymous Cuban" read on the air by veteran actress Violeta Casals. "At night, at home . . . the hour known to all approaches," the author relates, "the entire family gathers around its short-wave radio and turns it on, but always carefully and quietly because an informant is near." Radio Rebelde, the letter declares, was that "invisible thread that unites the free territory of Cuba," such that the next morning everyone could expect the same conversation: "Did you listen to *Radio Rebelde* last night?"[47]

As we saw in chapter 2, the reliance of Cuban revolutionaries on radio dated to the impassioned broadcasts of Eduardo Chibás and the station seizures of groups like the Directorio Revolucionario Estudiantil. But in extending the medium's reach, 7RR transformed the political possibilities of radio. In this respect, internationalization represented both a quantitative and a qualitative change. Though Cuban radio had long depended on its connections to foreign partners and audiences, especially in the United States, only rarely had those connections served revolutionary ends.[48] Alejandra Bronfman argues that 7RR thus served to "[multiply the Revolution's] listening publics" within Cuba and beyond.[49]

The radicalization of Cuban radio accelerated in the aftermath of rebel victory. As had occurred with the written press and television, commercial radio stations were taken over by the revolutionary government and recast as vehicles for political consolidation. On January 12, 1959, this process began with the nationalization of the Circuito Nacional Cubano, in which Batista was the major shareholder, and it expanded in March 1960 with the creation of the Frente Independiente de Emisoras Libres (Independent Front of Free Broadcasters).[50] Not coincidentally, the acronym for the group— FIEL—signaled the affiliation of the sixty-one stations it brought together with the revolutionary project, also conveyed in its motto "Fiel a [Loyal to] Cuba, fiel a la Revolución."[51] By early 1961, media collectivization enabled the rebirth of the Cadena de la Libertad under the CMQ umbrella. The new

Cadena brought together all of Cuba's radio and television stations to work together in confronting an imminent US invasion.[52] This alliance served as an important precursor to Radio Habana Cuba.

In the face of an increasingly hostile North American press, Cuban leaders thus invested in the cultivation of an international, and especially Latin American, audience. Per Bronfman, radio represented a uniquely congenial vehicle given its very "invisibility," its ability to "reach across national boundaries."[53] This project expanded in concert with Cuba's forays into hemispheric politics, including covert missions to unseat Rafael Trujillo in the Dominican Republic, François Duvalier in Haiti, and Anastasio Somoza in Nicaragua. Bracketed by the Sino-Soviet split and Castro's frustration over the resolution of the 1962 Missile Crisis, the island government over the course of the 1960s increasingly charted its own hemispheric policy, centered on the promotion of rural guerrilla-style mobilization. Cuban leaders promoted that strategy in Venezuela and, most infamously, in Bolivia, where Guevara's 1966 mission concluded in failure and his own death. But the island's internationalist engagement also encompassed the recruitment of thousands of Latin Americans, who traveled to the island for political and military training.[54]

As Jonathan Brown has argued, Cuba's sponsorship of guerrilla struggle in Latin America proved largely unsuccessful but also, in many cases, counterproductive. Most of the island's missions were countered by US covert and paramilitary deployments, some of which led to the installation of governments far more repressive than those they unseated.[55] Even so, it is perhaps useful here to separate political outcomes—largely negative, even calamitous on balance—from their social and ideological effects. Cuba's leaders may not have been able to remake other Latin American countries in their image; in fact, the results of their efforts proved mostly antithetical to their stated aims. But military defeats in some cases spawned ideological victories. What survived these unsuccessful engagements was a conviction that, in the battle between the United States and Latin America, a counterweight had emerged in the form of the Cuban Revolution.[56] This in turn provoked a sentiment—solidarity—that would spawn a hemispheric movement.

Over the course of the 1960s and beyond, Radio Habana Cuba (RHC) played a critical role in amplifying revolutionary solidarity. On the one hand, RHC came to assume a strategic function, disseminating Cuba's example and, along with it, a variety of kindred causes. By 1963, the station was broadcasting over 180 hours per week in English, French, Arabic, Portuguese, Spanish, and Haitian Creole; Quechua and Guaraní were added soon after.[57] The station's messaging aligned closely with Cuba's hemispheric mission to promote armed struggle and anti-imperialist militancy. This earned RHC some high-placed enemies. In 1961, RHC's radio campaign against Venezuelan president Rómulo Betancourt was cited when the country broke diplomatic relations with Cuba.[58] Such antagonism extended to Anastasio Somoza, who in 1963 "expressed his indignation at the accusations made against him," which he claimed he could hear "in [his] home as if [Radio Habana] were installed in Managua."[59] The year before, the Dominican foreign minister had even submitted an official complaint to the OAS alleging that RHC was "attempting to destroy—by inciting to riot and murder—our beginning democracy."[60]

In fact, since the early 1960s, the Dominican Republic had received special attention on RHC, with shows run by Dominican exiles in Cuba and sonic battles against Trujillo's radio outlets.[61] Such programming provided a unique perch for those combating Trujillo and his allies while also cementing political affiliations for RHC listeners. In a July 1961 letter to the station, one listener from Peru related what he had heard the previous night, spanning "news of the '26th of July' celebrations, the visit of the world's first cosmonaut, Yuri Gagarin, the 'Playa Girón' Award that they gave him . . . ; followed at 8:45 P.M. by the program *Patria Libre* by the Movement for Dominican Liberation," and finally Fidel Castro's speech in the Plaza de la Revolución.[62] The juxtaposition of Cuban celebration, Soviet triumph, and Dominican liberation soldered all those causes together, establishing a translational political chain through which solidarity could be channeled.

Those connections would prove enduring. Famously, for over a month during the 1965 civil war in the Dominican Republic, RHC provided around-the-clock coverage of the conflict unleashed when the forces of Juan Bosch overthrew the government.[63] For this support, a Dominican listener convey his gratitude in an October 1965 letter, noting that the rebels had "acquired a strong will to continue the struggle when we heard the programs of support."[64] That uprising was thwarted by a US invasion—celebrated on Cuban exile broadcasts—but in its aftermath, RHC continued to promote the revolutionary Dominican cause. In August 1966, a Peruvian listener wrote to the station to express his appreciation for having learned through its broadcasts of the recently celebrated "Week of Dominican Solidarity."[65]

These efforts to forge Latin American and international solidarity accelerated in early 1966 with the landmark Tricontinental Conference. The meeting, which brought together hundreds of delegates from the Global

South, culminated in the establishment of the Organization of Solidarity with the Peoples of Asia, Africa and Latin America. Such mobilizations sought to project Cuba's cause outward and establish the Revolution as a political magnet, to which socialist and anti-imperialist struggles might in turn attach themselves. The hope was that Cuba's message would be magnified in turn, fortified as it was translated, literally and figuratively, into new languages and movements.[66] To that end, in the thick of the meeting, Radio Habana Cuba installed a new transmitter that enabled the station to reach Africa with its broadcasts.[67]

Significantly, this was also the moment at which *Granma* started publishing letters from RHC listeners. These communications provided evidence of, and instructional fodder for, the kind of multilateral connections Cuba's leaders sought to encourage. Above all, they celebrated the identification of RHC listeners with the Cuban cause. In October 1966, for example, a Brazilian listener wrote to explain the transformative impact of Fidel Castro's speeches: "One 'lives' the Cuban Revolution, one feels, as if part of the Cuban public, the identification between the people and its legitimate leaders, the total integration of individual and society." This letter recalls the experience of Cuban viewers confronting Castro's televised presence. Radio extended the possibilities for connection—and radicalization—over greater geographical distances. As this listener concluded, RHC broadcasts were responsible not only for the "awakening and development of his social consciousness" but also for his conviction that the only path forward for his own country was a "complete and true social revolution, like Cuba's."[68]

Launched in 1963, RHC listener competitions made concrete these different registers of identification. The best response to a prompt, submitted by mail, earned its author an all-expenses-paid trip to Cuba, including attendance as a special guest at the annual January or July anniversary celebrations.[69] The six winners of the 1966 competition, for example, included a "Colombian peasant, a Venezuelan teacher and student, a Chilean youth, a Mexican college student, a North American musician, and a Canadian specialist in urban planning." A jury composed of three survivors of the 1953 assault on the Moncada barracks, including Haydee Santamaría, Pedro Miret, and Melba Hernández, judged theirs to be the best treatments of the "vast historical significance and guiding example of 'History Will Absolve Me,'" Castro's famed self-defense in the trial following that attack.[70]

The 1967 competition, which invited participants to discuss "how to make most effective the support for Cuba proposed in the resolution of

RADIO HAVANA CUBA'S
NINETEENTH CONTEST

YOU CAN WIN AN ALL-EXPENSE
PAID TRIP TO CUBA...

THERE ARE FIVE TRIPS ALL
TOGETHER

Radio Havana Cuba announces its Nineteenth International Contest, in honor of the 29th anniversary of the attack on the Moncada Barracks, July 26th, 1982.

THE QUESTION:
Historically, what have relations been like between the United States and Latin America?

CONTEST RULES:

1. Only entries received in the city of Havana by April 30th, 1982 will be considered.

2. All Radio Havana Cuba listeners have the right to participate, regardless of political convictions, country of residence, religion, etc.

3. Applicants must fill in the attached form and send it along with their entry.

SPECIAL PRIZE FOR MEDIA ENTRY:

One of the five prizes will be awarded for the best journalistic work submitted. Length is unimportant. The item must have been published or broadcast. Authors of print items should send us three clippings of the published article. In the case of radio entries, a tape of the program must be included, along with a statement from the station manager certifying that the program was broadcast and giving the date of transmission.

TRIPS TO CUBA:

1. The five contest winners will be awarded all-expense-paid two week trips to Cuba on the 29th anniversary of the attack on the Moncada Barracks, July 26th, 1982.

2. Winners will visit farms, hospitals, factories, schools, tourist resorts and historical sites.

RADIO HAVANA CUBA
POST OFFICE BOX 7026
HAVANA, CUBA

Remember, the closing date for the contest is April 30th, 1982. We suggest you send us your entry as soon as possible, to guarantee eligibility.

Radio Habana Cuba's 1982 Annual Listener Contest invited its audience to reflect on historical relations between the United States and Latin America. The prompt likely spoke to renewed radio hostilities between the two countries during the presidency of Ronald Reagan, who oversaw a new media campaign against the Revolution, channeled with particular intensity through Radio Martí, established in 1985. Don L. Parrish Radio Collection, box 1, folder 2, Nellie Lee Benson Latin American Collection, LLILAS Benson Latin American Studies and Collections, University of Texas at Austin.

the Tricontinental Conference," encouraged perhaps the most overt expressions of listener camaraderie. The conference had received significant play on RHC, and the competition thus connected the experience of listening to expressions of Cuba solidarity to that of actualizing it. For the first time, the RHC contest also included a competition for international radio broadcasting, centered on "some aspect of Cuba's revolutionary struggle." First prize went to Radio Paris for its program *From the Bastille to Moncada*, which compared the founding moments of the two revolutions and was subsequently broadcast on RHC in Spanish. Yet the broadest listener participation greeted the RHC campaign by soliciting signatures around the world in support of the Cuban Revolution, collated in "albums of the International Campaign for Solidarity with Cuba." As of July 1967, the album recorded the impressive tally of 20,000 signatures.[71]

RHC listener contests bridged different media and platforms—radio, letters, travel—to encourage listeners to express and enact their solidarity with Cuba. In drafting responses to the station's prompts, participants not only registered their support for the Revolution but also initiated a process of revolutionary instruction. Much like the 1961 literacy campaign, which taught Cubans to read and write using the ideological lexicon of Revolution, RHC's far-flung listeners learned to apply that vocabulary. Writing essays about the Revolution was thus an act of political performance and fulfillment, which earned its most accomplished executors the opportunity to immerse themselves in Cuba's lived reality.

Not all Radio Habana listeners, of course, were sympathetic, though station representatives insisted that most letters were positive.[72] The most unfavorable tended to be sent from the United States, including two listeners in Colorado, who wrote in January 1966 to express their "regret that the people of the world allow you to insult their intelligence night after night."[73] Another listener from Staten Island, who identified as "pro-North American" and "center right" in his letter to the station, noted that he was a regular RHC listener and appreciated the absence of "shrill noises, screaming, and trash" in the broadcasts. Nonetheless, he concluded, "even with all of their trash," he "[preferred US] to [Cuban] stations given that they [operated] in an atmosphere of liberty."[74]

There were also more formal outlets for critical listeners, including the CIA-operated Foreign Broadcasting and Information Service, which drafted reports on international radio stations. An even more intriguing site for resistant listening was the Miami Radio Monitoring Service, which issued a "literal and objective transcription of the most important radio news of the day, just as it is transmitted, from Communist Cuba."[75] The nonprofit service did not shy away from the political implications of such work, which its emblem connected to "battling red tyranny in Cuba." And though the service mostly refrained from commenting on Cuban broadcasts, at times its staff could not resist the temptation, as when they lampooned the "gaffes" and "lapsus linguae" committed by island broadcasters. If the tongues of Cuban radio broadcasters were "trembling," they concluded, that could only mean that the "knees of the regime's bosses" were "shaking," too.[76]

Indeed, over the course of the 1960s, the most fervent engagement with Radio Habana—critical *and* enthusiastic—could often be found in the United States. Since its debut, RHC had targeted a North American audience with English-language programs hosted by, among others, Robert Taber, the director of a widely viewed documentary about Castro's troops in the sierra and later founder of the Fair Play for Cuba Committee (FPCC), and Barbara Collins (also known as "Beardless Barbara"), who had fled New Jersey "with her small daughter in hand" and become a citizen of Cuba.[77] In their RHC broadcasts, Frank and Libbie Park, longtime Leftist activists and authors from Canada, fielded questions from all over the world—Indonesia, Iraq, Japan, and beyond—about Cuba and the Revolution. The vast majority, however, came from the United States, with a notable volume from high school and college students. Some US listeners wrote to express their solidarity with Cuba; others, Libbie noted in a June 1962 broadcast, wrote to "debate with us on points of policy and politics."[78] Sometimes those interactions shifted mentalities. One listener from Skokie, Illinois, noted that he "[didn't agree with everything [they said]," but that his "idea of Cuba as a country existing in a state of chaos, on the brink of doom, [had] been completely changed."[79]

But the most influential English-language program on RHC was undoubtedly *Radio Free Dixie*, conceived and run from 1961 to 1965 by civil rights activist Robert F. Williams and his wife Mabel during their exile in Cuba. In 1961, the couple had fled the United States to escape bogus kidnapping charges brought against Williams.[80] As documented by Timothy Tyson, Williams had been impressed by the revolutionary government's stated commitment to racial equality and had even traveled to the island in 1960 to "see it for [himself]."[81] His experience during that trip and subsequent interactions with the Cuban leadership led him to collaborate with solidarity organizations such as the FPCC. The FPCC organizers, like their counterparts in the Cuban government, hoped that Williams would help build connections between the Revolution and the Black freedom struggle. Facing FBI persecution in the United States, he thus relocated his battle against racism to Cuban shores.[82]

Bolstered by the personal support of Fidel Castro, Williams pursued that mission on the airwaves. With his celebrated program *Radio Free Dixie*, Williams could amass a larger audience *within* the United States from outside it. "Formerly," he wrote to one fan of the show, "I could reach only a few people . . . with my Newsletter . . . and public speaking. From here, I am reaching the whole world."[83] Per Tom McEnaney, the Revolution thus enabled Williams to adapt an "imperial model"—the largely one-way flow of influence associated with cultural hegemony—and "[invert] it."[84] *Radio Free Dixie* quickly became an essential soundtrack to the civil rights struggle in the United States, thanks both to its denunciations of white supremacy and the Black music—especially jazz—that accompanied it (notably, at a time when such music was suppressed *within* Cuba).[85] At first three times a week and then daily, North American listeners could tune in to lessons on the past and present struggle against racism, as well as criticism of the Kennedy administration and the long arm of US imperialism.[86]

As Cristina Mislan has argued, *Radio Free Dixie* thus connected the civil rights struggle in the United States to the social and political project of the Cuban Revolution.[87] Even so, Williams and his collaborators fiercely guarded their independence, stressing that they did "not follow any political party lines," were not "an official part of Cuban propaganda," and were not subject to government oversight or censorship.[88] Letters to the station praised their autonomy from the "Communist line" even as fans and critics alike stressed the connections between *Radio Free Dixie* and the Revolution.[89] Some wrote to Williams hoping he might serve as a vehicle of education, bringing news about Cuba to a sympathetic US audience.[90] Meanwhile, an anonymous Spanish-speaking listener, who appears to have identified with the Ku Klux Klan, insisted that the revolutionary leadership had "bought" Williams to "spread hate between blacks and whites" and threatened Williams and his Cuban hosts with a public lynching.[91]

In the face of their common foes, Black American exiles and island officials cultivated solidarity, fusing the ideological and strategic goals of the US civil rights movement with the revolutionary project. For Black activists from the United States, Cuba offered (for some, for a time) a refuge from legal persecution, as well as a sympathetic ally willing to put resources at their disposal. For the revolutionary leadership, supporting the Black freedom struggle allowed them to broadcast their defiance of the United States while more selectively heeding the demands of Afro-Cuban intellectuals and activists at home. Yet the union between revolutionary socialism and Black justice was far from seamless.[92] We need only look, for example, to Carlos Moore, the only Cuban broadcaster involved with the show (fluent in English thanks to his Jamaican heritage). In 1963, Moore broke with the Cuban government over its reluctance to directly tackle racism.[93]

Moore's departure from Cuba foreshadowed Williams's own disenchantment with the Revolution. As the revolutionary leadership grew closer to the Soviet Union, Williams increasingly felt like he was reliving earlier battles with the US Communist Party, which was generally unsupportive of Black nationalism. Williams had little patience for those who insisted that the class struggle must come before the battle for racial justice, a position that had grown more prevalent on the island by the mid-1960s. In a 1968 interview, he put it thus: "I had a choice of remaining in Cuba, but I don't see any difference in being a socialist Uncle Tom than being an Uncle Tom in capitalist and racist America."[94] By the middle of the decade, this made China a more congenial destination for many civil rights activists. With Williams's departure to China in 1965, *Radio Free Dixie* went off the air.

Nonetheless, RHC outreach to North American audiences continued to expand in its wake. That included the launch of the English-language program *Voice of Vietnam*, which for nearly a decade (1968–76) sought to raise critical awareness about the Vietnam War.[95] A 1968 report commissioned by the US government insisted that "only the militants listen[ed] to these broadcasts." It also acknowledged, however, that they had "a large student following and notable political response . . . [serving] as a coordinating factor for the revolutionaries all over Latin America."[96] In fact, the popularity of Radio Habana Cuba had long worried listeners in the US government, who recognized that the broadcasts were not just preaching to the faithful.

Throughout the first decade of its existence, US-sponsored research teams consistently found that people across the hemisphere were listening—often enthusiastically—to RHC. In 1963, this included residents of Panama and most of the Central American capitals, where investigators reported that the "masses" and many "low income groups" tuned in on their "cheap transistor radios."[97] The station's audience extended to the "claypits of northeastern Brazil," where onetime RHC broadcaster Robert Taber found that "plantation workers" liked to "listen to the messages of the Cuban Revolution and learn about the struggle in Vietnam and Congo, about the riots in Panama and Harlem."[98] The 1969 *Rockefeller Report on the Americas* also documented a robust RHC audience, especially in Central America and the Caribbean, where the station filled the wee hours of the morning with "skillful communist propaganda." On the basis of that finding, Rockefeller urged President Nixon to double down on efforts to make Voice of America broadcasts "at least competitive with Radio Habana."[99]

Cita con Cuba: The Social Bonds of Exile Radio

When it came to Latin American listeners, Voice of America would never edge out its Cuban competition. On the island, however, VOA's *Cita con Cuba* (or *Cuban Hour*) consistently earned high marks for its informative broadcasts. This garnered it not only an underground following but also an appreciable volume of mail from the island. A 1963 memo noted that "an interesting book could be written based on letters received by the VOICE from its listeners," many "addressed to us, or addressed to non-existent individuals such as 'Jose Orozco, Washington, D.C.'" "Miraculously," the memo continued, "the Post Office sends them to us."[100] For "unhappy Cubans," such letters, it proposed, "[served] as escape valves," and for the "red Cubans" as well, who wrote to "[blow] off steam abusing us colorfully." The program's "ill wishers" even included some members of "Cuban official-dom," as evidenced by the critical responses delivered in the island press. But the overriding message that could be gleaned from this correspondence was also the most important one, rendered by the memo writer in all caps: "WE ARE HEARD."[101]

Voice of America, which director Henry Loomis once insisted ought not become the "Voice of the Administration," may have been the outlet that received the most attention from revolutionary leaders.[102] But it was just one of a mutually reinforcing network of stations and programs, many of which were far less restrained in their anti-Castro messaging. This included Radio Swan, resurrected, as we have seen, in the form of Radio Americas, and another CIA front organization, Free Cuba Radio (FCR), run by the "semi-notional" Cuban Freedom Committee (CFC).[103] The CFC had been established in the buildup to the Bay of Pigs and was directed by Mariada Arensberg, an American who moved to Cuba with her husband (a business-man) in 1946 and subsequently served as the headmaster of Ruston Academy, Havana's prestigious bilingual school. After leaving Cuba in 1961, Arensberg dedicated her enviable list of high-placed contacts to the work of organizing CFC activities.[104]

One of the organization's most important outlets was Free Cuba Radio, which largely transmitted using commercial stations and thus walked a delicate line around US laws restricting the broadcast of government propaganda to international audiences. As Arensberg pointed out, commercial transmission meant that a variety of audiences, especially in Latin America, "overheard" FCR programming, a phenomenon the organization actively encouraged through "listener groups" and the distribution of written materials. Yet broadcasters most hoped to reach island Cubans of the "lower and middle classes," who were less likely to own shortwave radios and were thus unable to access Voice of America.[105] Broadcasting to island Cubans was intended to hasten the fall of the government through operational and informational resistance.[106] Yet CFC representatives also treated communication as an inherently political activity, particularly in light of the Cuban government's efforts to jam its broadcasts and censor mail. Like Radio Habana Cuba, Free Cuba Radio and its counterparts set aside airtime for listener letters, particularly those that, despite the odds, reached them from Cuba.

Some exile programs mined these communications for intelligence in the fight against the revolutionary government. Tips from the island were prized by anti-Castro broadcasters, even if their collaborators in the US government raised doubts about their accuracy. Yet the value of such information was not limited to its strategic applications. Letters from Cuban listeners were scoured for intel inaccessible by other means and subsequently broadcast back to the island. This circular and often rumor-driven news flow positioned exile broadcasters as political intermediaries, helping Cubans on the island communicate secret or forbidden news to one another. By virtue of these exchanges, radio personalities, many of them already well known to Cubans, became trusted interlocutors to whom islanders could turn for information and, at times, material goods, particularly in the spartan conditions of the early and mid-1960s. Broadcasters were thus implicated in new social formations, which invested interpersonal relationships with political value.

Before and especially after the consolidation of state control over the media in the early 1960s, rumors (or "*bolas*," as they are known) occupied an outsized place in Cuban political and popular culture.[107] From their intentional dissemination as a political weapon, particularly at the hands of the CIA, to their denunciation by the government as a counterrevolutionary tool, popular gossip persistently collapsed the public and private spheres. Radio Bemba (lip radio) also bore countercultural implications. The term, if not the age-old medium, seems to date to the struggle against Batista, but its aims quickly shifted in the post-1959 period.[108] This was especially true for those self-proclaimed *gusanos* who fed it, thereby circumventing an increasingly closed press and sustaining a running commentary on political tensions and economic scarcity. In response, the government deputized ordinary Cubans, especially members of the Committees for the Defense of the Revolution, to combat not only the circulation of rumors but also the counterrevolutionary sentiment believed to have inspired them.[109]

One broadcaster who played a key role in forging those networks was Maria Josefa "Pepita" Riera Villafuerte, or Havana Rose, as she was dubbed for her work during Radio Swan's infamous Bay of Pigs performance.[110] Even before the invasion, however, Riera's personal story contained several novelistic turns. As a young woman in Cuba, she fled an engagement to join

PAREDON

PARA LOS
CONTRARREVOLU-
CIONARIOS QUE
PROPAGAN
FALSAS NOTICIAS

This leaflet condemns "counterrevolutionaries who disseminate fake news."

the Sacred Heart Order of nuns, but she left before taking her last vows to embark on a career as an author, sometimes mining her experiences as a lapsed nun in print, radio, and television. Her expanding media persona also shaped her entry into the anti-Batista resistance. Riera was an active member of the 26th of July Movement in Havana and was forced to flee to the Sierra Maestra. While there, she was made the director of the Rural Schools for Sierra Soldiers in the column of Huber Matos.[111]

With the revolutionary takeover of January 1959, Riera began work on a radio program that would memorialize the struggle against Batista. This became the popular *Tu vida y la mía* (Your life and mine), which aired in February 1959, and its various successors, including *Senderos de libertad* (Pathways to freedom), which gave dramatic—or melodramatic—form to recent events. The idea behind *Tu vida y la mía*, as Riera explained, was for the show to be "truthful," referring to individuals, whether partisans of Batista or the struggle against him, by their names.[112] These *radionovelas* became major, even international, hits and established an important precedent for her subsequent work.[113] Riera believed that the drama inherent to personalizing political battles promoted audience engagement and, potentially, affiliation.

But Riera's own identification with the revolutionary project did not last long. As she would later relate to Congress, "the end came when Castro sent two men to a phonograph-record factory owned by a relative of mine and ordered the production of two records within 24 hours. The records were Communist songs from Eastern Europe." When asked, she related, Castro "said the people were politically sterile, and he wanted to get started with their indoctrination."[114] By April 1959, she had joined the resistance to Castro's government. When the organization she had cofounded began to be targeted by revolutionary leaders, Riera sought asylum at the Brazilian embassy and fled to Miami in April 1960.[115]

Only three days later, Riera took to the air, first over Florida station WMIE and later Radio Americas. AMSHADY, as she was dubbed by the CIA, dedicated her radio broadcasts to exposing covert informants and members of the Cuban intelligence services. Her program depended on the collaboration of her listeners, who sent anonymous tips to her Coral Gables post office box or via clandestine radio broadcasts and anti-Castro couriers. Her targets included alleged agents, such as a "24-year-old medical student at the University of Havana," who gained confidence by "[buzzing] about the campus, [pushing] her pretty blonde head into any cluster of boys in sight," and then "[waiting] to catch their disclosures of some underground student meeting or some indiscreet remark against Castro."[116] By outing such individuals on the air, Riera claimed to have deactivated roughly 1,000 agents and 400 informers in 1965 and 1966 alone. This made her a target, including of at least one apparent assassination attempt.[117] Meanwhile, her fame continued to grow, thanks not only to her popular radio show but also to a published exposé, *Servicio de inteligencia de Cuba comunista* (1966), and a 1964 appearance on the US game show *To Tell the Truth*, where panelists grilled her about Cuban politics and offered their support and congratulations at the episode's end.

These different strains of Riera's work relied on the same approach she had once employed in her *radionovelas*. By sensationalizing and individualizing the battle against the revolutionary government, Riera elicited audience participation and mined it for strategic information. Veteran broadcaster Luis Conte Agüero would take such tactics to even larger audiences. Conte's previous fame in Cuba yielded an impressive volume of listener correspondence, totaling hundreds of letters from the island only a month after his WRUL debut. His CIA handlers quickly took notice.

According to a November 1962 *Newsweek* article, Conte's "private spy" work had begun a month earlier when he "invited a Washington official to his hotel to see a secret 'document,' . . . [which] turned out to be a suitcase jammed with letters bearing Cuban stamps." His visitor pronounced the haul the "most impressive collection of information about Cuba [he'd] ever seen."[118] That was the press-friendly version of the story—likely told by the broadcaster himself—as by that point Conte Agüero had been sharing letters with the CIA for months. Meanwhile, exasperated agency representatives struggled to convince Conte Agüero to keep his intel off the air.[119]

US government officials were not fully convinced of the "reliability" of those tips, but they put enough stock in the letters to research their contents.[120] Conte Agüero was even contacted by someone claiming to have information about the assassination of President John F. Kennedy. The theory presented by the letter writer, apparently a young Cuban Communist, featured a conspiracy among Fidel Castro, the Russian ambassador, Carlos Rafael Rodríguez, and "four people from Canada, plus one from Panama," to kill the presidents of Mexico and Panama. At the same meeting where the plan was hatched, the writer alleged, Kennedy's assassin, a "Mexican named DUGLAS," was also purportedly revealed. As a result of this tip, Conte Agüero became part of the Warren Commission hearings into Kennedy's death.[121]

But Conte Agüero valued Cuban correspondence not only for the information it provided but also for the relationships it established. Given his tempestuous history with leaders in the Cuban exile community, not to mention the US government, Conte Agüero turned to island fans to build an alternative web of anti-Castro resistance. In 1965, for example, he established the Sentinels of Liberty, described by the FBI as an "informal network of anti-Castro informants in Cuba who send him information, some of it exaggerated and unreliable, on excesses of the Castro regime."[122] Conte Agüero, however, regarded his sources as the vanguard of a more aggressive movement to overturn the revolutionary state. In cultivating them, he rejected the abandonment of offensive operations by the US government and their exile allies following the Bay of Pigs.

But Conte Agüero's audience was not always convinced of the advisability of his strategy. A 1962 letter from one listener, forwarded via a third party in Texas, admonished the recipient to "please tell Dr. Conte Aguero that what he wants is utterly impossible; to take to the streets when he says so. He should know that the G-2 Military Police and the Vigilance Committees are waiting for us with pieces of pipe and sticks."[123] In a similar vein, an anonymous survey respondent from Havana requested that Conte no longer "read the letters sent to him" on the air.[124] A newly arrived migrant echoed both sentiments, noting that "Conte Aguero calls too much on the underground to do something, but does not realize the conditions of it, and gives the actions away."[125] Evidently, some listeners agreed with the assessment of one of Conte Agüero's handlers that he was better at "saying what pleases his listeners than in actually giving them orientation."[126]

That gap between broadcaster intentions and listener reception was closely monitored by leaders at the CFC. This was not only a matter of growing the audience for Free Cuba Radio and other anti-Castro stations. Rather, the very success of their enterprise depended on the fluid transmission of information to and from the island. As a result, Mariada Arensberg and her collaborators placed great value on correspondence from Cuban listeners, even when letters from Latin American fans outnumbered them. They also developed other ways to feature the perspectives of their island compatriots, including interviews with Cubans who had recently arrived in the United States.

Indeed, far from a one-way barrage of anti-Castro programming, Free Cuba Radio is best imagined as a relay station, gathering news—or, just as often, rumors—from the island and beaming it back to those Cubans who might otherwise not be able to access it. In a similar spirit, FCR programs devoted airtime to countering the news presented in the Cuban media as well as the speeches of revolutionary officials. The chain, however, did not end there. Arensberg herself recirculated updates from the island to mainstream media outlets in the United States.[127] However modest its audience remained in absolute terms, the work of FCR thus shaped not only *what* was known about the Revolution, both on the island and beyond, but also—and perhaps more consequentially—*how* it was known, with personal testimony prized above all.

News from the ground occupied a central place in all FCR programs. Despite their diverse constituencies, these shows covered kindred themes, including food scarcity, medical breakdown, political repression, and popular resistance. Among the most popular was the *Women's Program* (or *Home Program*) in which hosts María Luisa and Rosa took up women's "emancipation," the "children killed by communism," but also "how to defeat communism" and the "stages of communist deceit."[128] Meanwhile, a typical 1966 episode on WGBS covered the arrest of two "patriots" by Cuban intelligence, the "terror, hunger and misery imposed by the regime on the Cuban people," prohibitions on street vendors, and other Cuban and Latin American news.[129]

In this, FCR programs tended to hit many of the same notes as their RHC counterparts, but in reverse. While *Radio Free Dixie* drew attention to violent segregation in the United States, broadcasters like George Volsky insisted that it was Castro who "[practiced] racial discrimination."[130] Another FCR program went so far as to air a *"Radio Free Dixie* script . . . translated into Spanish and broadcast back to Cuba to show what they are broadcasting to Negroes in the US in order to encourage the same agitation among the Cubans."[131] This point-counterpoint with Radio Habana Cuba took vivid form when FCR leaders decided to enter the 1966 RHC competition on the "History Will Absolve Me" speech while airing their responses alongside a dramatic reading by comedian Tito Hernández, well known for his Castro impersonation. The broadcast "[substituted] the original language of 'History Will Absolve Me' for words that better [matched] the . . . Communist regime in Cuba" and thus aimed to "counteract any effects the competition might have and create greater doubts in our Cuban and Latin American listeners."[132]

Alongside metacommentary on RHC, dialogue with Cuban listeners sat at the heart of FCR programming. In 1962, CFC representatives began to interview Cubans arriving in the United States and launched a survey about their radio listening habits. The interviews were among the most popular content on FCR shows, providing coverage of conditions in Cuba as well as the exile population. Potential participants in turn found opportunities for "venting," according to one fourteen-year-old listener, who bemoaned that he was not interviewed when he arrived in Miami and thus was left with a "bad feeling" inside.[133]

The value FCR ascribed to island testimony was even more evident in the central place afforded to listener letters. Most of these letters—some 14,203 between January 1961 and December 1965—were not from the island.[134] Even so, Cuban fan mail provided the CFC with the evidence it needed to justify its existence as well as much of the content for its programs. From rumors about political shake-ups to updates on material scarcity, letters presented a "very stark and realistic" picture of the Revolution, as Arensberg explained.[135] Island listeners in turn praised such programming as a counterbalance to the "rotten lies" of Cuban radio, per one correspondent, even as surveys continued to elicit frustration over unconfirmed or false reporting.[136]

The desire to inform and inspire required FCR personalities to walk a fine line between the kind of "hard news" many Cuban listeners demanded and the editorial commentary Arensberg felt they needed.[137] As she put it in a 1965 memo to FCR broadcasters, "Some of these headlines could cause anxiety among island Cubans, since they might think they indicate Communist victories, unless they are reported *extremely carefully and with commentary*."[138] But FCR efforts to promote the right kind of reporting went further, including a stock letter sent to Cubans who wrote in to the "Descarga" (complaint) section of the Havana newspaper *Revolución*, expressing sympathy for the economic and political conditions they faced and advising "resignation and patience." The letter concluded with a more careful acknowledgment that it might not be welcomed by the recipient, whom they hoped would not be "harmed" by it.[139]

Indeed, letters from Cuba were powerful precisely because they were illicit and rare, especially following the curtailment of direct mail service in 1963. As a 1962 letter from "Freedom" explained, "I can assure you that I know dozens of persons who listen to you daily, but as you will understand, all of us are afraid to write letters, as that might mean prison or disappearance in any moment if they catch you."[140] When letter volume was low or steadily declining (as occurred in the mid-1960s), station representatives explained it as evidence not of diminishing popularity but of intensifying censorship.[141] Another correspondent said as much in his 1967 letter to the station, in which he assured them: "If you don't receive more letters from Cuba it is because the people are afraid to write. Also, the censors destroy all letters reporting broadcasts."[142] Yet many who wrote nonetheless sought some kind of recognition, however oblique. As one New Orleans woman wrote of her island correspondents, expressing a common sentiment, "All of them get very excited when they listen to their letters on the air."[143]

Surreptitious engagement thus became a defining element of accessing Free Cuba Radio. The "defense committee," one listener informed WWL Radio, was "always spying on the persons that own short and long wave radio."[144] From Las Villas, another fan noted that the "militiamen and the 'informers' get close to the walls to listen," but he was confident that his "portable radio which I tune in at the lowest" wouldn't give him away.[145] Much like their predecessors who had followed Radio Rebelde, Cubans took "thousands of precautions" before listening, according to one letter writer, "tuning the radio as low as possible, closing all doors and windows, turning the radio off and hiding the connection to the antenna when danger seems possible."[146]

La Habana, martes 12 de febrero de 1963

SEÑORES

millares de personas en Cuba No son comunistas el pueblo mira la situación.

han sufrido tormentos hambre Doctrina comunista. Hoy en día las personas desean la ayuda de ustedes

todos los campesinos BEN con su propios ojos . El trabajo en los campos La falta zapatos camisa y pantalones

vestidos A los niños se les enseñar en las escuelas la doctrina del partido El país a

perdido todo lo que tenía. nuestro pueblo odia a LOS COMUNISTAS

hacen falta en el país Democracia. y libertad. Centenares de hombres luchadores por la libertad–

estan Viendo Las enfermedades que se sufren Los niños al país morirse de hambre hundir trasportes.

Rusia No Estados Unidos. SI

CUANDO llegara el camino de la libertad no hay que dejarse hundir Por los comunistas. SON

unos cobardes, «Estamos listos, guerra, A ellos Despierto y Alerta los

países de Latinoamérica ||los países socialistas

son Trabajo miseria y terror

Arriba Kennedy Cuba Apoya el fin de Fidel

Gloria?

This letter, pasted together in ransom-note style, sought to convey both the material and the political circumstances on the island and, through its construction, the risks of revealing those conditions. "Gloria" (Havana) to Free Cuba Radio, February 12, 1963, Cuban Freedom Committee Records, box 60, Hoover Institution Library & Archives.

Yet the dangers attached to such content also spawned opportunities for community. Throughout Latin America, FCR worked to establish listener groups, but in Cuba they emerged organically. A survey respondent from Havana noted that his "group of friends . . . gathered daily in a garage . . . to comment [on] daily news abroad, as well as the local ones."[147] According to another correspondent, some who hoped to access transmissions inaccessible in Havana hopped in their cars and traveled outside the city under the cover of night."[148] Arensberg herself expressed faith that their "audience [was] considerably multiplied by postbroadcast discussions and word-of-mouth circulation."[149] These new social formations implicated exile broadcasters as well.

One such host was Dr. Antonio Maceo y Mackle, who hosted *El médico y usted* (The doctor and you) on Radio Americas. Launched in 1963, the program ran continuously for the next two years and generated robust correspondence from all over the hemisphere. In daily ten-minute broadcasts, Dr. Maceo provided information about a wide variety of ailments and health practices, ranging from alcoholism to measles, osteoporosis, and nervous disorders. A distinguished generalist who had pursued his education in Paris and Havana, Maceo had worked as a medical practitioner and public health official in Cuba before leaving for exile in Miami. But Maceo was not just a physician, and his show reached well beyond medical concerns. As a prominent member of the exile community (and the grandson of the renowned Afro-Cuban patriot of the same name), Maceo had played a central role in Cold War politics and was even tapped to briefly lead the Cuban Revolutionary Council. *El médico y usted* thus formed part of US government efforts to wage cold war on the cultural front—in this case, through medicine.

The appeal of his program stemmed from the Cold War politicization of health. In early 1960s Cuba, drug scarcity had become a glaring effect of that politicization, as Castro's government moved to expand public health access across the island. Those plans quickly brought the revolutionary state into conflict with the US pharmaceutical industry. Before the Revolution, US medications had been a pervasive presence on the island's medical scene, and many middle- and upper-class Cubans were as attached to US brand names as their North American counterparts. With the intensification of bilateral hostilities, such pharmaceuticals disappeared suddenly from island shelves, replaced in some cases with generics from the Soviet bloc and other sources. But for some Cubans, those drugs were decidedly inferior to the ones they had known before.

Maceo took to the airwaves at the very moment that a public debate about drug scarcity—sustained in the same "Descarga" section of *Revolución*—began to close and as the public health system more broadly strained under the weight of a physician exodus.[150] In his shows, Maceo thus inscribed his political vision onto the individual body and its ailments, framing public health conditions on the island as failures of governance, along with the decline in sanitary conditions and food access. In late 1963, rumors of a gastroenteritis epidemic in Santiago and Havana allowed Maceo to bring these medical and political concerns together. The story provided fodder for several episodes of *El médico y usted*, in dialogue with letters received from Cuba. One writer, who claimed to be "nearly a relative" of Maceo, begged for information about gastroenteritis, "for here no one knows anything, but the situation is that the number of sick children and even adults, is truly terrifying."[151] A correspondent from Santiago de Cuba echoed this concern, informing Maceo that in that province, "something like 300" children had died. "My wife and I are devastated," he continued, "because beginning a week ago, our two children . . . began to get thinner every day, with many stools every day, sometimes vomiting often, and we're unable to feed them. We've tried to find medication, but those, like specialized physicians are very difficult to find."[152]

In response to these letters (Maceo noted on the air that he had received "hundreds"), the show dedicated a full episode to gastroenteritis. Casting blame at a "lack of attention, carelessness," and even "ignorance," Maceo presented gastroenteritis as a fundamentally political condition. Castro, he insisted, should be held responsible for poor sanitary conditions and impoverished medical services. But revolutionary sentiment, he alleged, was itself sickening: "Marxist-Leninist hate" had left the Cuban populace "weakened, sick, and febrile."[153] In the background of these indictments were Castro's own allegations that the US was waging bacteriological warfare against Cuba.[154] Maceo appropriated that logic to depict Communism as an agent of medical aggression.

In fulfilling his duties as a physician, Maceo proposed to "remain in touch over these radio waves and talk, offer advice."[155] But many fans sought more than advice, including autographed photos, flags, and even recordings of the Cuban national anthem.[156] Far more often, however, audience members, especially those from Cuba, sought medications they were unable to access, from cortisone to treat skin conditions to antibiotics for more serious conditions.[157] One listener from Camagüey, for example, wrote Maceo despairing over her diagnosis of progressive syphilis. The antibiotic she required was not available in Cuba, but she expressed "faith in you and in God, that you will consider my case, to send me as quickly as possible the necessary amount of medication to save once more a LIFE."[158]

These letters were so prevalent that Maceo tended to label them with the terse shorthand "*pide medicina*" (requests medication). Often, the expressed need was pressing enough that, despite the risks, letter writers provided their names and addresses. Others, however, exercised more caution. One Cuban wrote to Maceo from Florida on behalf of his epileptic nephew, reminding him of the need for quick action given that "nearly all of the transmissions of Radio [America] are blocked by Communist Radio in Cuba."[159] Another listener dared to write to Maceo directly from Havana to request information about colitis and appendicitis but indicated that, "for obvious reasons," Maceo should send it not to her but to a middleman.[160]

In Maceo's correspondence, one finds a complicated alchemy of solidarity and reciprocity. His Latin American listeners often led with expressions of political allegiance as grounds for requesting help. So common was this language of affective transaction that it assumed a generic quality, with denunciations of "Muscovite tyranny" transitioning seamlessly into entreaties for assistance. Only rarely did one find more ambivalent notes, such as the admission of one Mexican listener that he had often paired Radio Americas with Radio Havana, "to be able to form a clearer idea of the Cuban situation."[161]

But the letters of Maceo's Cuban correspondents are far more prosaic. In them we find an assumed logic of everyday solidarity, grounded in the new social codes of scarcity. "Even though you barely know me I'm practically a relative of yours," begins one letter from Santiago de Cuba. The author went on to remind Maceo that he had previously operated on his mother and offered news about the gastroenteritis outbreak. Finally, Maceo's correspondent closed by calling on God to deliver a "Cuba free of so many ills" and asking the physician to write to him at the "house of Cheché."[162] This letter presents and requests information, outlines a relationship as grounds for reciprocity, and openly seeks medication, establishing an illustrative framework in which Maceo occupied a position of privilege and, thus, obligation.

These emergent social formations closely mirror the Soviet concept of *blat*, which Alena Ledeneva defines as "a kind of barter based on personal relationships."[163] She explains that *blat* establishes "not a relationship for the sake of exchange but an exchange for the sake of a relationship."[164] If consumer scarcity invested material access with social value, it also entangled prized commodities in networks of giving and receiving, aligning citizens in a new kind of solidarity rooted in underground exchange.[165]

Defying the Cold War logic that inspired Radio Americas, *El médico y usted* thus achieved unexpected social effects. Island correspondents implicated the exile leader in a practice of everyday reciprocity—the Cuban notion of the *compromiso*, or mutual obligation. Transnational radio ties buttressed a system that Cubans would ironically baptize *sociolismo*—a play on words replacing the "socia" in "socialism" with "*socio*," a popular term for buddy or friend—getting by not by exhibiting exemplary political behavior but by drawing on one's well-placed *socios*, or friends. Scarcity, then, was not only a political language to be deployed but also a vehicle for forging new kinds of relationships.[166]

In the Latin America Cold War, all minds were potential recruits in an ideological war of global significance. Both in the United States and Cuba, this was the assumption that inspired massive investments in propaganda. But where CIA strategists and revolutionary officials proposed grand narratives of hemispheric (anti-)Communist collaboration, Maceo's audience presented something more mundane, even when dressed up in the terms of political identification. In response to the health politics of *El médico y usted*, some Cubans offered up their bodies for Maceo's politicizing consideration. Yet it was those same listeners that articulated a new ethos of solidarity, grounded in the terrain of everyday need. At the same time, the medium rendered Maceo's own body—notably, his race—imperceptible to his listeners. This represented a departure from the racialization of Maceo's family legacy as well as the racial politics that drove media crossfire across the Florida Straits.

From the denunciations of US racism on *Radio Free Dixie* to the denunciations of those denunciations on Free Cuba Radio, Cold War politics invited engagement with parallel battles while setting clear limits for their champions, as Robert F. Williams bemoaned. In this respect, radio channeled lateral solidarities while also entrenching a bilateral reluctance to afford precedence to *other* causes. But listeners continued to present unlikely equations, scrambling the presumed order of ideological priority. For many, the Revolution was indeed the most pressing framework in which they transacted their daily lives, whether they supported or opposed it. That did mean, however, that they always engaged Cuba's political project in the terms in which it was presented. From material scarcity to persistent racism, listeners pushed broadcasters on both sides to confront their shared subjectivity—the inevitable partiality of their perspective—thereby broadening (in however fleeting a way) the Subject of Revolution itself.

The Never-Ending Radio War

In 1968, radio enthusiast Tom Kneitel became one of the only US civilians to visit Radio Americas. In what he would later classify as a "strange and eerie excursion," Kneitel made the trek to Swan Island, where he met the two Cubans who handled the broadcasting, along with the diesel engineers, six "transmitter operators," and "10 Caymanian and Honduran laborers" who actually lived on the island.[167] Kneitel also found an answer to the question that had inspired his trip: "Was there a 50 kW clandestine CIA broadcaster on this strange little speck of rock? You betcha!"[168] But an equally intriguing mystery was the fact that he had been welcomed there at all. Kneitel speculated that it had something to do with the imminent closure of the station, which occurred "only a few months" after the visit, but brushed off speculations that his writings had hastened its end.[169] Rather, he proposed, Cubans themselves were no longer enthusiastic: "Cubans in Miami to whom I spoke in the Summer of 1967 said that RA had become something of a bore."[170] Similar pressures—and financial difficulties—influenced the 1967 shuttering of FCR.[171] By 1974, the VOA had also scaled back its Cuba broadcasting, even as RHC continued to air into the mid-1970s, albeit at a more muted volume.[172]

But the Cuba radio battles were far from over. In the early 1980s, amid a revived Cold War between Castro and President Ronald Reagan, political battles spilled over onto the airwaves once again as the two countries faced off in Central America, Grenada, and beyond. In South Florida, the emergence of secret anti-Castro broadcasters stoked indignation on the island as well as a series of complaints to the FCC, ultimately provoking a "major interagency battle" within the US government. Only the debut of legal anti-Castro broadcasting in the form of Radio Martí, established in 1985, finally reined in the phenomenon.[173] In response, RHC geared up to expand its programming across the Americas. This outreach was met—and amplified—by a familiar mode of response, as related by Howard Frederick. In the early 1980s, RHC vice director José Prado reported that the station continued to receive "thousands of letters . . . from the US each year," some of which were broadcast on a "twice-weekly program called *Post Office Box 7026*."[174]

As the US and Cuban governments continued to weaponize news and propagate rumors, combat over the airwaves established radio, like television, as an essential medium for constructing (or deconstructing) the Revolution. On both sides, the broadcasting of propaganda served to transact international relations and interpellate hemispheric subjects. The glue that bound them often took the form of solidarity: the experience of identification or kinship with political causes, near and far. Like television, radio thus connected the dissemination of information (true and false) to the cultivation of feeling.

Radio helped to shape what people across the world came to know about the Cuban Revolution but also how they adapted that knowledge to political practice. The very act of listening forged parasocial attachments but also new kinds of communities, local and transnational. Audience correspondence helped to cement these different registers of revolutionary and counterrevolutionary belonging. But listener letters did not merely echo the messaging of radio propaganda; they also rescripted ideological battles to accommodate their own contexts. This act of audience translation served to expand the meaning of revolution and counterrevolution from below, even if it did not alter their trajectory from above. The archive of that correspondence presents a key access point for contemporary understanding, a vehicle to engage and even breach the epistemological world the Revolution made.

· · · · · ·

If radio served as a vital medium for the consolidation of political affiliations, travel to Cuba represented an even more visible manifestation of solidarity, as generations of sympathizers sought to see the revolutionary experiment for themselves. Much like the Radio Habana listener competitions, such trips served a strategic function for Cuban leaders, who encouraged them in the interest of cultivating foreign allies. As chapter 4, however, such pilgrimages were made even more meaningful thanks to a framework of *restricted* travel. Curiously, this was another area in which revolutionary sympathizers found common cause with their political antagonists. Indeed, while US and Latin American officials worked to control the ability of their citizens to travel to the island, revolutionary officials in turn thwarted the ability of ordinary Cubans to leave it. In the process, travel bans made immobility a crucial way through which foreigners and islanders alike came to know the Revolution, sometimes inspiring them to mobilize on its behalf—and in other cases leading them to abandon it altogether.

4 Beyond the Sugar Curtain

· ·

"I want to meet Fidel," proclaimed Pedro, a thirteen-year-old Brazilian boy who had confronted the passengers on a May 1961 Havana-bound flight passing through his country. The flight crew, astonished but amused, quickly welcomed him on board. Upon arrival in Havana, Pedro was already famous: "He was the hero of the moment, the central subject for all the photographers, the 'note' in the papers for that day and all the following. The stowaway who escaped from Brazil to meet Fidel."[1] In a sign of his symbolic importance, the boy was even taken to stay in the home of Celia Sánchez, Castro's right-hand woman, while authorities sent a message to his family to reassure them that he was safe.[2]

In revolutionary Cuba, foreign travelers were prime subjects for celebrity. Many defied political and logistical obstacles to get to the island, but they did so with the conviction that travel promised access to knowledge that was otherwise out of reach. As Peter Hulme argues, the doubts raised about Western journalism and its reporting on the Revolution only enhanced the appeal of "seeing it for oneself."[3] From a thirteen-year-old Brazilian boy to New Left luminaries, sympathetic outsiders turned to travel to access the otherwise unavailable "truth" about Cuba. This turned travel into a key epistemological vehicle, through which knowledge about the Revolution was constructed by a variety of international observers, even as such journeys consolidated different interpretations of that truth, as shaped by one's identity and ideology.[4]

If much was made of foreign travel to Cuba, travel performed an equally important function *for* Cubans, from domestic tourism, which allowed many ordinary Cubans to travel around the island for the first time, to newly politicized routes of intraisland mobility. These included pilgrimages to the countryside, as in the 1961 Literacy Campaign, during which urbanites witnessed and were radicalized by the experiences of their rural counterparts. Revolutionary mobility also worked in reverse, extending to trips from rural areas to the capital (the Concentración Campesina of July 1960) or the expansion of Havana boarding schools.[5] The Revolution conveyed still others abroad for study and training, especially within the Soviet bloc. If well-heeled Habaneros had once favored sojourns to the United States for shopping, work, and school, revolutionary officials sought to reframe travel as a mode of political consciousness raising. For some, travel abetted both physical and social mobility.[6]

But there was also a darker face of revolutionary mobility, experienced by Cubans who were sent to labor camps or forced to relocate as a form of political punishment (for example, former rebels in the Escambray mountains, who were moved to Pinar del Río in 1971).[7] Most numerous, however, were those Cubans who elected or were compelled to leave the island altogether, totaling roughly half a million by 1973.[8] Many, not unlike their counterparts on the other side, assigned epistemological significance to exit, arguing that the truth about the Revolution could be apprehended only by living outside its borders.

The importance ascribed to travel within the Cuban Revolution thus stemmed from not only contested information flows but also the very politicization of mobility and immobility. Internationally, the Cold War brought these tensions to a head, unleashing forced and voluntary migration as well as new circuits of political tourism and solidarity travel.[9] Beginning with the first stirrings of superpower conflict on the Korean peninsula, political leaders turned to travel restriction as an arm of Cold War foreign policy. This was true even among those nations that had affirmed their commitment to Article 13 of the 1948 Universal Declaration of Human Rights, which stipulated that "everyone has the right to leave any country, including his own, and to return to his country."[10]

Restrictions on travel were often justified as a response to the bureaucratic challenges associated with political battles, yet they were patently invested with a prophylactic function as well. As governments claimed the prerogative to control their citizens' movement, they also asserted a right of de facto censorship, drawing the era's proliferating "curtains" on those contexts deemed dangerous.[11] Meanwhile, those same officials touted the mobility freedoms enjoyed by their citizens and contrasted them with the purported unfreedom imposed by their antagonists—hence, the particular significance attached to refugee resettlement, especially in the United States, as a symbolic enactment of that "openness."[12]

In this coalescing regime of global mobility control, revolutionary Cuba came to occupy a particularly conspicuous place. The most contested such restriction quickly became the US travel ban imposed in 1961. To isolate the Revolution and the presumed danger of its example, US policymakers went to extreme lengths to prevent anyone from traveling to the island.

Technically, they could apply such restrictions only to their own citizens, but behind the scenes, US officials exerted pressure on their counterparts throughout the hemisphere, spurring the creation of transnational networks of surveillance and control. But travel limitations were far from one-sided. Cuba's revolutionary government viewed mobility control as equally critical to its political goals. Travel restrictions on Cubans were felt most acutely in the form of the notorious exit permit, required to leave the country after 1961 and not eliminated until 2012. Though Fidel Castro periodically opened the gates to outmigration, the ability of Cubans to leave the island has remained circumscribed throughout the last six decades.

This chapter traces the history of travel restriction and the Cuban Revolution as a reflection of Cold War debates about the freedom of movement and information. In a context of politicized journalism and fractured objectivity, I argue that travel bans cemented, rather than undermined, the conviction that travel offered a unique path to political truth. Meanwhile, as both the US and Cuban governments decried the travel restrictions erected by their antagonists, *im*mobility became increasingly central to official and popular understandings of the Revolution. Throughout the 1960s, these debates evolved in an interactive way, with US and Cuban officials accusing each other of obstructing their citizens' freedom of movement while often improbably doing the same.

Here I focus on two signal moments in this history of politicized immobility. On the one hand, I trace the efforts of a group of Americans mobilized under the auspices of the Student Committee for Travel to Cuba (SCTC), which, through two trips to the island in 1963 and 1964, sought to force a legal reckoning on the US travel ban. Treated as suspect agitators in the United States, they were received as heroes on the island, where their legal tribulations were followed sympathetically for years to come. The SCTC travelers, many of them young people of non-elite backgrounds, thus found in the Revolution an opportunity to augment their agency. For these SCTC travelers, combating the travel ban not only served as a channel for revolutionary solidarity but also functioned as a means of political actualization, even as it led to new restrictions on their civil rights back in the United States.

Roughly a year after their second visit, battles over travel moved to the small port of Camarioca in Matanzas Province. In September 1965, Fidel Castro made a speech in which he invited Cubans in the United States to come pick up their relatives at Camarioca. The government thus sought to force US officials, who had denounced island mobility restrictions, to make good on their expressed willingness to receive refugees. This led to the Camarioca boatlift and eventually the so-called Freedom Flights (1965–73), the last major emigration wave of the early revolutionary period. The events at Camarioca prompted important changes to mobility regimes on both sides of the Florida Straits, while contributing to a coalescing vision of the revolutionary and exile subject inflected by race, gender, and class.

Both Camarioca and the SCTC trips (and their aftermath) came to shape what was known about Cuba, domestically and internationally, and, equally important, how it was known (and by whom). These events cemented the logic tying travel to knowledge *and* centered immobility and resistance to it in the transnational imaginary of the Cuban Revolution. Overall, the bilateral crossfire over travel restrictions only heightened the epistemological significance of peeking behind the sugar curtain. The Revolution was thus—and would continue to be—interpreted, championed, and contested in the name of immobility, while also defining its subjects in terms of their desire for, and access to, mobility within and beyond its world.

Drawing the Curtain

As sui generis as they sometimes seem, the mobility restrictions that came to define the Cuban Revolution were born of a broader Cold War context. The earliest US restrictions were issued against Hungary in 1949, and by 1955 US citizens were also prohibited from traveling to other socialist countries, including China, Albania, Poland, Rumania, Bulgaria, the Soviet Union, Czechoslovakia, North Korea, and North Vietnam.[13] By 1959, however, travel bans on Soviet bloc countries had been lifted, and by 1963 the Kennedy administration was debating an end to the prohibitions against China, North Vietnam, and North Korea.[14] What is striking about the Cuba travel restrictions, then, are their sheer longevity.

The travel ban as such first took form in Public Notice 179, issued by President Eisenhower in January 1961. This step immediately followed the severing of diplomatic relations between the two nations and was justified as a consequence of that measure.[15] The notice required that any traveler to Cuba seek a special endorsement for their passport from the Department of State; by 1963, the prohibition on Cuba travel was also printed inside every US passport. This ban was justified by reference to Section 215(b) of the Immigration and Nationality Act of 1952 (also known as the McCarran-Walter Act), which reframed racialized restrictions (on Asian immigrants, for example) and replaced them with national origins quotas inspired by Cold War politics. Section 215 spoke directly to these concerns, citing an emergency context in which the president might see fit to issue additional restrictions. Part (b) gave the president the authority to ban a US citizen from "depart[ing] from or enter[ing], or attempt[ing] to depart from or enter, the United States unless he bears a valid passport."[16]

This seemingly neutral language belied a more pointed goal: to control the mobility of suspected Communists. In 1952, the US Passport Office had begun to take on this function, empowered by new State Department regulations to deny passports to members of Communist organizations and, in other cases, revoke already-issued passports.[17] A 1958 Supreme Court challenge to this framing (*Kent v. Dulles*) affirmed, for the first time, a "constitutional right to travel," grounded in the Fifth, Fourth, and perhaps even First Amendments. Yet it was ultimately a narrower interpretation of the decision that guided subsequent government and judicial action. After *Kent v. Dulles*, US citizens did *not* enjoy the right to travel as a means of informing themselves about the world, but their right to international mobility could not be denied without due process.[18] For several decades to come, the Cuba travel ban would provide a key test case through which many of these arguments were revisited.

But even as the mobility of US citizens featured in public discussions of the Cuba travel ban, it was the hemispheric context—the professed need to set an example for Latin America—that took center stage behind closed doors. Leading up to the 1963 meeting of the Organization of American States in Managua, US officials pressured their Latin American counterparts to prevent their citizens from traveling to Cuba. In a February 1963 memo, President Kennedy expressed concern over the more than 1,200 "students," "labor leaders," and others who had traveled to Cuba in the previous year for "training and indoctrination."[19] Mobility controls had thus proven plainly *in*effective, but that did not stop US and Latin American officials from continuing to enforce them.[20]

Mexico quickly became the regional center of such efforts, given that, by the early 1960s, it was the only Latin American country operating regular passenger service to Havana. For this reason, CIA and State Department officials were particularly aggressive in their efforts to ensure Mexican collaboration, which, beginning in 1963, took the form of a new requirement that Cuba travelers "obtain transit visas from the Foreign Ministry in Mexico City."[21] Mexican surveillance, however, reached well beyond formal diplomatic procedures. Names, photos, and identifying information for Cuba travelers were passed on to other governments, including those in countries, such as Venezuela, where citizens enjoyed a constitutional right to travel.[22]

By 1965, this practice, a "relatively open secret" in the estimation of a US embassy official in Mexico, was nonetheless regarded as explosive enough that it should not be "publicize[d]."[23] Even those countries that did not issue a Cuba travel ban took pains to monitor their citizens' mobility. The Canadian government, which has never restricted travel to Cuba, kept tabs on those planning trips to the island, with an eye to surveilling not only Canadians who traveled in sympathy with the Revolution but also those planning to "[serve] in anti-Castro movements."[24]

While support for Cuba travel restrictions waxed and waned among hemispheric officials, few in the US government abandoned the regional calculus that had given the measure such urgency. Restricting the mobility of US citizens—their right to see and know Cuba—was the necessary price for maintaining order in the hemisphere, they concluded. That, in turn, justified restrictions on the mobility of Latin Americans, and their right to see and know Cuba. As a memo to President Lyndon B. Johnson explained in response to an intramural campaign to lift the prohibition on travel, "a relaxation of US restrictions would make it very difficult for us to prevent [Latin American] nationals from going to Cuba—where many would receive subversive training."[25] On that and all subsequent occasions, Johnson, like Kennedy before him, opted to retain the restrictions. That left it to ordinary citizens, together with a group of civil rights lawyers, to challenge the ban.

Defying the Ban

Almost as soon as the Cuba travel ban was issued, US citizens began mobilizing to challenge it, convinced that it would not stand up to constitutional scrunity. In this, they proved to be prescient in some respects and mistaken in others. Over the course of the 1960s, the travel ban as originally formulated was undoubtedly weakened, as daring escapades and legal maneuvering made it increasingly difficult, politically speaking, to uphold it. This, of course, did not bury the ban. But the very persistence of travel restrictions spurred continued resistance to them, making immobility the cardinal cause for generations of Cuba partisans.

At the center of this political maelstrom was a somewhat unlikely set of protagonists: a motley group of college students and activists who eventually came together as the Student Committee for Travel to Cuba. In the summers of 1963 and 1964, the SCTC successfully executed two Cuba trips, greeted by fanfare on the island and condemnation in the United States. Such publicity was indeed one of their principal objectives; organizers hoped to raise awareness of the travel ban and precipitate a legal fight. For many of the young people who participated in the trips, however, their goals were rather more modest: to see the forbidden island for themselves.

The SCTC emerged from a short-lived Ad Hoc Student Committee for Travel to Cuba, which had prepared to journey to the island in December 1962. The committee's efforts had been foiled thanks to a behind-the-scenes campaign by State Department officials, who convinced their Canadian colleagues to prevent a Cubana Airlines plane from picking up the group.[26] That action was opposed by some US officials, notably journalist Edward R. Murrow of the United States Information Agency, who cautioned Secretary of State Dean Rusk that the "right to travel" is "generally looked on as a basic right in the non-Communist world."[27] The cancellation also led to an unexpected invitation. Cuba's Federation of University Students (FEU) contacted leaders of the committee to propose that they organize a new trip for the summer of 1963 with the official sponsorship of the Cuban government.

Early on, the young people who spearheaded this campaign drew US attention for other reasons. Some were affiliated with Progressive Labor, a political group that had adopted a pro-China position at odds with that of the US Communist Party.[28] Though few trip participants openly identified as Communists, these links inspired government efforts to brand the SCTC as a red organization, extending to a July 1963 televised statement by President Kennedy himself. In their discussions of the trip, officials also expressed suspicion about the supposed student composition of the trip.[29] In fact, some of the trip participants had already graduated from college or taken leave from their university educations.

Yet the composition of the group was more heterogeneous than government messaging would suggest. Motivated by either simple curiosity or a commitment to the expressed ideals of the Revolution, most participants were unaware of the partisan affiliations of the group's leaders until the trip had already begun. But they were far from politically naive. Two such participants, John Coatsworth and his roommate Marty Nicolaus, made plans to join the trip when they were undergraduate students at Wesleyan University. Coatsworth's goals were broadly political, stemming from his involvement in the civil rights and peace movements in the United States and the "solidarity" those had awoken toward the goals of the Cuban Revolution.[30] Many in the group—which, per Nicolaus, included "conservatives, apolitical people, liberals, freedom riders, peaceniks, humanists, all shades of socialists, self-avowed marxist-leninists, Trotskyites, black nationalists and anarchists"—shared those sympathies in one form or another.[31]

Along with several dozen others, Coatsworth and Nicolaus were invited to join the trip after an in-person interview in New York City. What followed for those who enlisted had a distinctly cinematic flavor. Travelers were told to head to an address on the Upper West Side of New York, where the group was split into smaller units. From there, they began the long journey to Cuba via Europe, flying first to London, then Paris, and finally Prague. At each stop, they were met by US embassy representatives, who distributed a printed document alerting them to the consequences of violating the ban and urged them to turn back.[32] After being waylaid in Prague for three days due to mechanical issues with their plane, the young people finally set off for Havana, joined by a correspondent from the Cuban daily *Revolución*.[33] Two days later, they landed in Cuba after refueling stops in Shannon and Newfoundland.[34]

At the airport, the group was greeted by a delegation from the Cuban Institute of Friendship with the Peoples (ICAP), which had played an instrumental role in organizing the trip. Black activist Robert Williams, then living in exile in Cuba, was also on hand to meet them, as was the FEU president and Cuba's secretary minister of foreign affairs.[35] The warmth of that reception did not flag during the group's two-month stay in Cuba. During trips to farms, schools, factories, and workers' social clubs around the country, the young travelers were regularly met by the highest-ranking members of the Cuban government, including Fidel Castro himself.[36] By many accounts, however, it was an hour-long meeting with Ernesto "Che" Guevara, in which he sparred with students over Trotskyism and the salience of race in Cuban history, that made the deepest impression.[37] The SCTC travelers were also the "guests of honor" at the celebrations attending the July 26 anniversary of the *Granma* landing, where Castro lauded their "bravery."[38]

Behind the scenes, however, divisions within the student group, particularly along the lines of race and gender, proved fractious. The frustration that some Black and female members of the group felt with their fellow travelers, a sentiment that would only sharpen during the 1964 trip, reflected the very political heterogeneity that US officials had sought to elide. If they manifested different levels of commitment to the political battles that raged in the United States, however, nearly all participants were united by their excitement about Cuba.[39] Some pushed harder than others to bear witness

The Student Committee for Travel to Cuba received a warm welcome everywhere they traveled in Cuba, as documented here by one participant in the summer 1964 trip. Karen Brodkin Papers, box 2, folder 59, Brown University Library.

to revolutionary repression, asking to visit prisons and jails, for example. But for the most part, the young travelers were as convinced by the end of the trip of what group leader Levi Laub had proposed in a prepared statement upon their arrival: that they were "tired of canned reports, misleading synopses, garbled accounts, half-truths and no-truths."[40]

But as the group prepared to return and contest those "no-truths," US embassy officials throughout the Western Hemisphere collaborated to block them. The most obvious route—returning via Mexico City—was summarily closed off when Mexico's secretary of the interior refused to issue transit visas.[41] State personnel also convinced the Jamaican and Canadian governments to prevent any flight carrying the students from passing through their airports.[42] One month past their original departure date, Cuban officials finally booked the group on an Iberia flight to Madrid. The students took the place of fifty refugees who had been preparing to depart the island, a fact received none too warmly by Cuban exiles who confronted the group in Spain.[43] Finally, upon landing in New York, the students were met by Department of State agents, who promptly canceled their US passports.

This dramatic action was the result of a government plan months in the making, but it hardly caught the students unaware.[44] Before their trip, SCTC leaders had strategized about how to thwart eventual prosecution.[45] In Havana, several members of the group had also met with a senior partner in the firm of civil liberties attorney Leonard Boudin, who had defended accused Communists at the height of McCarthyism. By the early 1960s, Boudin was representing the Cuban and Czech governments in the United States, and he and his colleagues were thus uniquely positioned to assess the potential consequences of the students' trip. Boudin predicted that their passports would be confiscated but that the government's action would not hold up in court.[46]

Meanwhile, however, the attorney general had come to believe that group leaders could also be charged with travel to Cuba without a "properly validated passport" and conspiracy to violate the travel ban.[47] When the students returned to the United States, a grand jury subpoena (Eastern District of New York) was thus issued to twelve people, only three of whom had participated in the trip, while another group was summoned to appear before the House Un-American Activities Committee (HUAC).[48]

At the center of both sets of proceedings was an unlikely witness. Barry Hoffman, described variously as a Massachusetts-based appliance dealer and a real estate agent, had joined the trip at the behest of Gordon Hall, a Boston-based author focused on extremist movements.[49] Upon his return, Hoffman and Hall mobilized to impress their conclusion—that SCTC members were radicals with naive or suspicious intentions—on government officials, who, of course, already shared it.[50] By his own account, Hoffman dedicated his time on the island to spreading the "truth" to ordinary Cubans: that "most Americans supported our government, that we weren't all exploited, and that few people were breathlessly waiting for the revolution."[51]

Like Hoffman, the US government was also concerned about the public relations angle of the SCTC and closely monitored Cuban and Latin American media throughout the trip. Among other themes, one Foreign Broadcasting Information Service memo drew attention to the students' expressed goal to raise awareness about the Revolution after their return to the United States. According to Hoffman, the Cuban government had even produced a film chronicling the students' trip, which the students "were to combine . . . with lectures on Cuba to raise money for their defense."[52] Many group participants took on this informational mission with enthusiasm, organizing tours on college campuses throughout the United States. They did so not only to disseminate sympathetic accounts of the Revolution but also, per

Nicolaus, to "[help] to publicize and promote" a second trip, already in the works for summer 1964.[53]

And so, as grand jury proceedings and HUAC interrogations dragged on, SCTC geared up to recruit another group of travelers, larger and more diverse than the last. The head of ICAP had proposed such a trip to the 1963 group leaders, proposing that they could accommodate "several thousand" the next time while cautioning that it "might look better if . . . future delegations would pay their own way."[54] SCTC recruitment efforts evolved alongside a campaign to raise awareness about the FBI surveillance and legal consequences that many had experienced as a result of the first trip.[55] This effort generated exile protests throughout the country, including a demonstration at a Boston SCTC forum, where a three-year-old held a sign reading "Castro Bans Travel with Murder."[56] Cuban exiles also found opportunities to register private dissent. One even penned an anonymous letter to group spokesperson Vicki Ortiz in which they critiqued the Revolution and explained why they did "not wish to go to Cuba [that] summer."[57]

This was a cheeky reply to the application form that had begun to circulate for aspiring 1964 travelers, in which candidates were encouraged to describe their motivations for traveling to Cuba, the sites and people they hoped to see there, and their "understanding of the possible legal consequences of the trip."[58] From 1,000 applications and 400 interviews, a smaller contingent of 84 was chosen due to "practical problems in Cuba."[59] Despite previous admonitions, however, the Cuban government still paid most of the bill, clear evidence of the public relations value it ascribed to the trip.[60] In June 1964, a group that included SCTC veterans, actresses, professors, typists, mechanics, reporters, a cab driver, and students once again set off in a "cloak and dagger atmosphere."[61] A press statement before departure laid out their motivations: "We have come to realize that the fight against the travel ban is not only a fight to re-establish a basic civil liberty in our own country. . . . [It] is also a fight for the right of all Latin American students and people to be free of travel bans, to be free of the censorship which the travel ban creates, and to be free to make their own political choices."[62]

The travelers' itinerary in Cuba took them across the country and included familiar highlights, such as school tours and the yearly 26th of July celebration.[63] All but one of them also decided to donate their blood to Cuba in a vividly embodied act of solidarity; as one traveler put it, "My government is responsible for the loss of much Cuban blood and I want to give back to the Cuban people some of that lost blood."[64] Where their predecessors were treated to an hours-long table-tennis match with Fidel Castro, the summer 1964 group was invited to play baseball with him.[65] Joel Agee, who traveled to Cuba in the company of his half brother Stefan Uhse (both sons of writer James Agee), also chronicled memorable trips to the Camilo Cienfuegos vocational school in the Sierra Maestra, where, per Uhse's account, the American travelers acquitted themselves unattractively in front of the disciplined Cuban students, and to a housing complex for former sugar workers in Habana del Este, where they were greeted as the "heroic *Norteamericanos* who defied the US government to see the splendor of their new lives."[66]

Beyond the headlines, however, some participants distanced themselves from the more dogmatic items on their itinerary, including a prolonged film viewing at the Chinese embassy.[67] Meanwhile, political battles over race and gender again divided the group. For his part, Agee reported seeking refuge from such clashes (what he called "Politicus") in sexual pursuits, including with a fifteen-year-old Tropicana dancer. Such behavior, extending to masturbatory phone calls placed by men in the group to Cuban women they had just met, incited the protest of a recently formed "women's caucus." Members denounced the "white phallocentric neocolonialist American men who appeared to be using [the] trip as a pleasure-jaunt."[68]

Once again, however, the students remained largely united in their support for the Revolution. Asked why "American students should see Cuba," 1963 veteran Vicki Ortiz declared that the "process of education includes the questioning of all information."[69] And there was perhaps no greater galling evidence of "press distortion," Ortiz proposed, than the issue of "popular support for the Cuban Revolutionary Government."[70] Other participants privately recorded more ambivalent feelings about their experiences in Cuba. As one traveler wrote in a letter to her father, which he subsequently turned over to the FBI: "Some of the things I heard, were not entirely positive, or so it seemed to me. . . . One doesn't know what to believe." Yet despite that ambiguity, she held fast to the same principle that had brought her to Cuba to begin with. "We must have the *right* to see for ourselves," she concluded, "and if the government refuses us this right it is our *duty* to fight it."[71]

The Legal Fallout

In the thick of these events, a parallel debate had emerged within the Johnson administration as to the wisdom of the travel ban itself. In 1963,

Attorney General Robert Kennedy had come to oppose any legal impediments to Americans' freedom of movement, and Abba Schwartz, assistant secretary of state for security and consular affairs, had expressed sympathy for this position. Based on a sense that the Revolution represented an ongoing threat to US policy in Latin America, however, Schwartz generated a proposal to lift travel bans for all countries *except* Cuba. This measure was ultimately approved by Secretary of State Dean Rusk.[72]

On the eve of the second student trip to Cuba, a new effort to soften the travel ban made its way to President Johnson's desk. A memo prepared by National Security Adviser McGeorge Bundy laid out two possible positions for Johnson to adopt. The Department of Justice, Bundy noted, "[favored] relaxation of our controls on travel to Cuba" due to "our libertarian tradition and the difficulty of controlling travel to Cuba."[73] But US policy, he continued, emphasized the hemispheric importance of the ban in convincing "Latin American governments to prevent their nationals from going to Cuba."[74] In a handwritten note, Johnson declared that he was "of the *second* school, and so was JFK." He opted not to lift the ban.[75]

This decision meant that the 1964 group also faced legal consequences. Travelers' passports were withdrawn upon their arrival in New York, and a second HUAC subpoena was issued, soon followed by others. By September, grand jury proceedings against nine individuals, none of whom had traveled to Cuba that summer, had been initiated in Brooklyn on the charge of conspiracy.[76] Meanwhile, many trip participants continued to suffer extralegal consequences. According to Vicki Ortiz, "Several of the travelers lost their jobs, most of us experienced[,] at least once, violent physical confrontation with Cuban exiles, and all of us received piles of hate mail."[77]

But SCTC leaders were prepared for the ensuing legal battle. Since the previous summer, they had worked closely on the criminal indictments with Boudin and the Emergency Civil Liberties Committee, which boasted a long history of anti-McCarthyist activism. Soon the American Civil Liberties Union (ACLU) joined the fight, alongside a public relations campaign featuring such advocates as James Baldwin, Dr. Benjamin Spock, Ruth Benedict, Carleton Beals, Herbert Marcuse, and other academic luminaries, who signed a 1963 petition in support of the travelers.[78] In a widely circulated *New York Times* editorial, Amherst College professor Henry Steeler Commager insisted on the constitutional issues at stake: "What is important is the right to travel. What is important is the claim of the State Department to decide who may and who may not travel. What is important is the State Department assertion that travel is an instrument of foreign policy and that it alone should decide what is 'in the best interests of the United States.'"[79]

As the indictments against SCTC leaders proceeded, the grounds on which they would be decided remained an open question. Boudin and his colleagues encouraged individual travelers to appeal passport withdrawals by explaining their reasons for traveling to Cuba and renouncing any intention to return.[80] Before the first SCTC trip, the Justice Department had expressed reluctance to prosecute individual cases given the high evidentiary standard that would have to be met. It remained difficult, Assistant Attorney General J. Walter Yeagley noted, to establish entry and exit from Cuba, given that many people traveled via third countries. Even more challenging, a prosecutor would have to demonstrate that the individual acted "in willful defiance of the ban"; that is, it was necessary to establish intent to travel to Cuba *and* knowledge of the restrictions.[81] Hence, the Johnson administration largely adhered to a "policy of selective prosecution," per Lars Schoultz.[82]

Those targeted included prominent Black journalist William Worthy, who had previously lost his passport due to his travel to the Soviet bloc and China. Worthy had been sentenced to prison time by a Miami federal court for his 1961 trip to Cuba without a valid passport, but that judgment was subsequently overturned by a federal court of appeals in New Orleans. The ruling struck down the entry but not the exit restrictions attached to the McCarran-Walter Act—in other words, the court argued that Worthy could not be forcibly exiled from his home country—and thus had ambiguous legal implications for other such cases.[83]

Meanwhile, Helen Travis, frequently described in the press as a California "housewife," worked to overturn the $1,000 fine and six-month prison term (ultimately suspended) levied against her for two 1962 trips to Cuba without a validated passport. Her designation as a housewife was, one imagines, a strategic maneuver to draw attention away from her Communist Party membership and the explicit aim of her trip: to challenge what she regarded as an "unconstitutional" ban. Her political affiliations had previously inspired her to travel around the Soviet bloc and China, but those trips had only cost her a validated passport. As she argued in a statement published by the Southern California ACLU, the punitive judgment against her Cuba trips trampled over the vaunted US commitment to freedom of travel: "We who objected so righteously to the Berlin Wall could hardly build one of our own."[84]

Travis and her ACLU lawyers hoped to force a Supreme Court decision on the travel ban, but the case of peace activist Louis Zemel got there first.[85]

In 1962, Zemel requested passport validation to "satisfy [his] curiosity about the state of affairs in Cuba and to make [himself] a better informed citizen."[86] When the State Department refused his request, Zemel's challenge reached all the way to the Supreme Court. As their own fates remained uncertain, SCTC members watched the Zemel case closely, believing that it offered the best opportunity to establish whether it was constitutional for the executive branch to issue travel restrictions.[87]

In a 1965 decision (*Zemel v. Rusk*), the Supreme Court ruled 6–3 that the State Department did enjoy this power: that travel represented an "instrument of foreign policy . . . not subject to review by the courts."[88] In other words, as Schoultz explains, the "constitutional right to freedom of movement was not absolute."[89] This ruling also inspired the Johnson administration to issue Public Notice 257, which justified the mechanism of passport validation "in any case where travel 'would seriously impair the conduct of US foreign affairs.'"[90]

But this measure was also challenged by SCTC leaders and their lawyers. Their case turned on what the court had specifically declined to determine in the case of *Zemel v. Rusk*: whether travel in violation of the restriction represented a criminal act. In January 1967, the Supreme Court ruled on that issue when fielding the unique criminal conspiracy charge brought against the SCTC trip organizers.[91] As such, the court concluded that the *criminality* of Cuba travel was the only relevant issue raised by the SCTC case. The deliberations were consequently straightforward. "Crimes are not to be created by inference," reads the decision authored by Justice Fortas. "They may not be constructed nunc pro tunc."[92] Quite simply, given that there was no law criminalizing travel to Cuba, no criminal charges could be brought against travelers to Cuba. On this basis, the court also overturned Helen Travis's conviction.[93]

Yet the return of confiscated passports remained unsettled until a 1967 ruling by the US Court of Appeals in Washington, D.C., on cases brought by Staughton Lynd, a Yale professor and peace activist who had traveled to North Vietnam, and Jane Wittman, a former Antioch College student who had participated in the 1964 SCTC trip to Cuba. Both Lynd and Wittman hoped to challenge the State Department's refusal to return their passports when they would not forswear travel to prohibited areas. In its ruling, the court of appeals argued that, per *Zemel v. Rusk*, the right of the State Department to impose travel restrictions, refuse to issue a passport for travel to those sites, and revoke a passport remained undisputed. But what it could not do, the court found, was deny a passport request based on its suspicions that the individual intended to travel to a restricted area. In that case, the constitutional right to travel remained primary.

What did this mean for individual travelers? The court concluded that "the Secretary has authority to control the lawful travel of the *passport*, even though Congress has not given authority to control the travel of the *person*."[94] Though the legal implications of this decision remained opaque, many observers interpreted it as a loophole. As Vicki Ortiz put it, "The ruling states that no American may use his passport to travel to, in, or through Cuba or any of the other off-limit countries. In other words, you may go there if you *don't* use your passport to get there."[95] This legal back route to Cuba gave some legitimacy to the strategy SCTC leaders had relied on during their own trip and perhaps accounts for the long-standing reluctance of Cuban immigration officials to stamp US passports.

It also constituted the grounds on which many SCTC trip participants finally had their passports returned to them, including John Coatsworth, whose new wife and fellow Cuba traveler, Pat Sopiak, had been named and acquitted in the SCTC indictment. At the time of the judgment, Coatsworth and Sopiak were living in Mexico, where he was conducting dissertation research. Mexico had in fact been the only site to which he could travel without his passport, a contingency that shaped his subsequent career as a preeminent historian of Mexico. One day in 1969, while sitting in the Mexican National Archives, he was contacted by a US embassy official, who related the good news: the couple's passports were finally being reissued, six years later.[96]

This, however, was far from the end of Cuba travel restrictions. In fact, going back to the Kennedy administration, several presidents had reinforced the ban along parallel tracks, drawing on the 1917 Trading with the Enemy Act (TWEA), which gave the executive branch the power to restrict trade with "enemy" powers in wartime, updated in 1933 to apply in any declared "national emergency." The Cold War provided such an emergency as to become, in the case of Cuba, a permanent one. President Truman was the first to apply the TWEA to Cold War ends when he imposed sanctions on North Korea in 1950 (lifted in 2008). In 1963, President Kennedy drew on the same authority to target Cuba in the form of Regulation 201(b) and the Cuban Assets Control Regulations.[97] These sanctions, also known as the Cuban embargo, functioned for the next six decades as a de facto travel ban. In Schoultz's words, "Everyone understood that this was a simple legal legerdemain—the use of an antiquated law to achieve an end (a travel ban) that the courts would otherwise not permit under the Constitution—but it worked."[98]

Per a 1968 guide drafted by the Student Committee on Latin America at the University of California, Riverside, it also meant that aspiring Cuba travelers, limited by State Department policy to "those professionally engaged in furnishing the public information," had to navigate a complicated set of bureaucratic procedures. These included soliciting a visa to Cuba from its Mexican embassy (and thus transit visas to and from Mexico); requesting passport validation from the Passport Office, along with a letter testifying to the "bona fide public information purpose" of the trip; and requesting an Office of Foreign Assets Control license for travel-related expenses in Cuba. Yet the guide also suggested that the most serious hurdles awaited in Mexico City and specified which Cuban and Mexican officials to contact about travel permissions—and how aggressively one should push to see them.[99]

The obstacles attached to Cuba travel briefly ameliorated under President Carter, who in 1977 lifted the travel ban and revised the Cuban Assets Control Regulations.[100] The unprecedented wave of legal travel that followed was soon curtailed by President Reagan, who in 1982 reinstated restrictions but continued to permit travel and related expenses by specific categories of individuals, including government officials, journalists, scholars, and family members.[101] Across these shifts, US nationals, especially the politically motivated, continued to challenge travel restrictions, from the Venceremos Brigades beginning in the late 1960s to a first generation of Cuban American intellectuals and activists in the 1970s, once island officials permitted it.[102] Few have managed to force the legal reckonings precipitated by the SCTC, though some have experienced FBI surveillance or political harassment.[103] The cumulative effect of such efforts has been to establish island travel as a principal focus of solidarity politics while making mobility *and* immobility inescapable ways of knowing the Revolution.

The Camarioca Crucible

Over the course of these legal battles, the US travel ban was a regular subject in the Cuban press and official speeches. On the island, renegade travelers were feted as defenders of the Revolution and the stated, if not always honored, ideals of US political culture. Meanwhile, beginning in the early 1960s, opponents of the revolutionary government began to draw international attention to mobility restrictions—namely, those that Cuban officials had placed on their own citizens. While island coverage of the travel ban featured US aggression and international solidarity, it also sought to deflect allegations regarding the revolutionary curtailment of rights. These claims of constrained movement thereafter evolved in a kind of denunciatory counterpoint, with each side mining the other's obvious hypocrisy.

Over the course of the 1960s and '70s, revolutionary officials indeed issued several measures restricting Cubans' mobility. The first such law— Ley 2 (later modified by Ley 18)—was among the first passed in January 1959 and aimed to prevent "individuals entangled with the previous regime" as well as "common criminals" from leaving the country to "evade justice." It thus required any aspiring international traveler (with a valid passport) to seek a special authorization from the chief of the National Police.[104] By early 1961, following the rupture of diplomatic relations with the United States, foreigners were also required to seek a visa or permit for travel to Cuba (to be issued by the Czech embassy for US citizens).[105]

Later that year, rumors began to circulate that the ability of Cubans to leave would be eliminated entirely.[106] Ultimately, this took the form of the highly consequential exit permit requirement, later formalized in Ley 989. That measure, passed on December 6, 1961, affirmed the prerogative of security forces (recently consolidated in the Ministry of the Interior) to grant exit and return permits. Though Cubans who left the island early on assumed that their relocation would last only as long as Castro's (short-lived, they trusted) regime, the island government treated departures as permanent, converting migrants into de facto exiles.[107] This presumption also justified the provisions included in Ley 989 for confiscating the property of Cubans considered to have "abandoned" the country after over-staying a twenty-nine-day exit permit.[108] Here, as elsewhere, there was ample room for abuse, as in the case of Pepito Casal, a notorious Urban Reform official in Camagüey. Among residents, he was popularly known as Vulture Casal for confiscating and keeping the property of those who had applied to leave.[109]

Such mechanisms, legal and otherwise, proved essential to the enforcement of mobility restrictions. For example, the mandate that exit permits and flights be paid for in US dollars—when that currency had already been criminalized on the island—restricted legal exit to those with the ability to access money from abroad.[110] The measure was protested by at least a few Cubans in exile, who wrote to Pan American Airlines demanding that they accept pesos instead (and received no response).[111] Equally costly was the expectation that the bureaucratic wheels would need to be greased along the way through bribes to the police or customs officials.[112]

Despite the obstacles, 248,100 Cubans did leave the island during this period, first through direct flights to Miami (until the missile crisis of October 1962) and then at a much slower pace to Spain—the only country besides the United States where Cubans could remain—Mexico, and Venezuela.[113] This group, the so-called golden exile, consisted largely, though not exclusively, of upper- and middle-class white Cubans. Received as Cold War refugees from communism in the United States, Cubans, like Hungarians before them, gained access to preferential legal treatment, philanthropic aid, and public services. This, however, did not prevent them from experiencing racism and sometimes half-hearted official support.[114]

Over the course of the next decade, the sheer size of the exodus converted Cubans into prototypical refugees in the US political imaginary, at times virtually synonymous with the term "exile." As María de los Angeles Torres writes, the "idea of exile" in turn became the "thread that [held] together the political memory" of the Cuban diaspora.[115] This framing (and the distinction between "political" and "economic" migration) also anchored a racially and class-specific vision of the diasporic subject. The language of exile thus ennobled the experiences of some—those Cubans, many white, who had fled Spanish political persecution in the nineteenth century and dictatorial governments in the twentieth—and distinguished them, legally and politically, from others: African Americans, migrants from other sites, and the voluntary and involuntary migrants—many working-class and of African descent—who had long populated Cuba and its diaspora.[116]

The symbolic significance attached to Cuban migration endured long after the end of direct flights to the United States. Cubans who took their chances by leaving the country illegally received sympathetic attention in the US press in a symbolic parallel to the lionization of foreign visitors in Cuba.[117] Such accounts also served an instructional function on the island, where aspiring migrants "put them together in pamphlets and included letters from different people telling how they had escaped from Cuba."[118] But the circulation of that information could also have negative effects, according to one Radio Free Cuba listener, who bemoaned the outlet's coverage of clandestine escape routes. "Every time they make these declarations," he reported, "the Communist Government floods the location with guards, closing that escape path to other Cubans."[119]

Yet as the surreptitious out-migration continued, stoking island surveillance, an abrupt pivot loomed on the horizon. In September 1965, Castro gave a speech in which he ridiculed allegations that the Cuban government had restricted the ability of its citizens to leave the country. In seeking to instigate a "brain drain" (while also stemming Cuban migration overall), he further insisted that US officials had only "harmed themselves, because they rid this country of many *lumpen* and many lazy people." In fact, Castro proposed that the island government was "willing to open up a little port somewhere so anyone who has relatives here doesn't have to take any risks" in coming to fetch them.[120] In the following days, he returned repeatedly to these themes, calling on the United States to accept Cuban migrants and allow US citizens to travel to the island.

Castro's speech soon unleashed an exodus, the first of several occasions in which he would use migration to release political pressure at home. But the Camarioca boatlift of 1965, centered on a port in Matanzas Province, had caught US officials by surprise. On October 3, during a speech at the Statue of Liberty where he was scheduled to sign a new immigration bill, President Johnson made a hasty commitment to welcoming Cuban refugees. As Cuban exiles took to the water, US officials initially attempted to block them, while the island government provided lodging, fuel, and food.[121] Notably, they also extended a provisional welcome to a group of US journalists who had made their way to Cuba on the boats, though one UPI reporter was soon booted from the country for making "contact with counterrevolutionary elements" and disseminating a "false image of the Revolution."[122]

As Cuban journalists celebrated the hospitality of revolutionary officials at Camarioca, they also featured stories of people who refused to depart out of commitment to the Revolution. Many were women and children who spurned the efforts of male authority figures to reclaim them.[123] As one woman told a reporter, having decided to remain in Cuba with her two children, "I would never abandon my country. Every Cuban should feel proud to live in a country with a Revolution as beautiful as ours."[124] Seventeen-year-old Ester characterized her own decision to remain in Cuba as "painful" due to the "love and respect" she felt for her father, who had come to fetch her. "But that care and respect I have for him runs parallel to the love that I profess to my country and my Revolution," she affirmed to reporters.[125]

Even so, the Camarioca out-migration did include large numbers of women and children, with "students, housewives, and children" making up 63 percent of US arrivals.[126] In South Florida, some of those housewives entered the paid workforce for the first time, stoking racial tensions over employment exclusion.[127] Meanwhile, following the bilateral politicization of childhood in the Pedro Pan exodus (1960–62), Cuban authorities prohibited the departure of minors who expressed a "desire to remain" in Cuba and promised to care for any children or elderly people whose families had "abandoned" them.[128] This language resonated with the framing of migrants as those who had abandoned their country.

Portrayals of the Revolution as an alternative paterfamilias—and those who stayed as its grateful charges—also invoked racial cues. One article presents the story of a wife and two daughters who declined to leave the island through a picture of the seven-year-old Afro-Cuban daughter, who is identified as a "pionera," or member of Cuba's mass organization for children.[129] Migrants, on the other hand, were almost always pictured as white, even as Cuban coverage obliquely acknowledged the growing diversity of the exodus, which included not only "former landlords," "professionals and businessmen" but also "servants and some unskilled workers."[130]

Robert Williams himself traveled to Camarioca to shape interpretations of these dynamics. In contrast to the vision of the United States as a "paradise," Williams suggested that migrants would likely face "growing unemployment," worsening work conditions, and "competition with blacks for jobs" in the South.[131] He also noted "that he had communications from more than fifty white and black families in the United States, principally from California, who [were] awaiting the first opportunity to leave North American territory and come live in Cuba."[132] In fact, Williams concluded, "if we were to go to Mississippi or Alabama to pick up all of the discontented and persecuted . . . we'd need much bigger boats."[133]

The boatlift thus provided an opportunity to denounce not only the racialized curtailment of rights in the United States but also, most pointedly, US mobility restrictions. Daily updates on the exodus unfolded alongside headlines about the trial of SCTC organizers in the United States.[134] Revolutionary officials also seized on Camarioca to highlight both their disposition to let Cubans leave and US reluctance to receive them. Often directly interpolating material from US papers, reporters documented animosity in South Florida between Cubans and Black Americans, racial competition in the local labor market, and the pronouncement of one *Miami Herald* article that they were "up to here with the Cuban refugees."[135] Even as new mobility restrictions were established, including the requirement that young people (age 15 to 26) remain on the island to complete their recently established mandatory military service (Servicio Militar Obligatorio), the Cuban media countered with attention to the Vietnam draft in the United States.[136]

By early November, however, with the mediation of the Swiss embassy, Cuban and US officials finally came to an agreement. This took the form of the Freedom Flights, through which several thousand Cubans a month would be flown out of Varadero Airport at the US government's expense. In return, Cubans committed to halting the boat traffic out of Camarioca. Capping extensive coverage and politicization of family dynamics on both sides, the emphasis would be on family reunification, matching Cubans who wished to leave with relatives in the United States prepared to receive them.[137] Between 1965 and 1973, some 260,561 Cubans departed the island on these flights.[138] The majority (76 percent) were white, though Cubans of color were represented in larger numbers than in previous waves, and roughly half were identified as "working class" or "petit bourgeois."[139]

But as the Cuban government committed to regularizing migration, it also adopted mechanisms to impede it. In the early days of the boatlift, US journalist Lee Lockwood reported that outbound Habaneros expressed "no fear of reprisal," that "many families were openly making plans to go."[140] Soon, however, aspiring migrants began to lose their jobs.[141] By late 1965, workplaces across the country had witnessed mass firings, perhaps impacting even those who refused to renounce an intention to leave in the future.[142] Migrants also faced potential financial consequences, from the confiscation of bank accounts to demands that recent withdrawals be returned and threats of losing their ration books.[143]

Productive labor was perhaps the most notorious punishment applied to those seeking to leave, a practice that dovetailed with the 1965 establishment of the UMAP (Unidades Militares de Ayuda a la Producción, or Military Units to Aid Production) labor camps in Camagüey.[144] Islanders called up for military service were questioned about whether they hoped to leave the country; at least some who answered in the affirmative were sent to the camps.[145] One report even alleged that a special UMAP installation had been created for 120 people whose only "common feature" was the "possession of or an application for a Cuban passport, indicating an unexpressed desire to leave Cuba."[146] Across the country, meanwhile, those who applied to leave were required to work for minimal (or, by some accounts, no) compensation for several months at a time.[147]

These measures reflected and contributed to the hardening of the official position on migration. At first depicted in sympathetic, if depreciative, terms, migrants were increasingly treated as people "who couldn't make it in the new Cuba."[148] Even before the bilateral agreement was finalized, one article insisted that the "departure of the disgruntled, the unadaptable, the people who were morally and psychologically unfit for the tasks of a new society [had produced] a sensation of collective relief."[149] "No one has shed a tear for those who are leaving," another critical treatment noted, which characterized the migrants as being of "bad quality, owners of nightclubs, exploiters of women, small-time speculators and criminals," in addition to former landholders, blue-collar workers, and a variety of "middle-class" Cubans.[150]

That diversity reflected both the longtime association of exiles with the "old" Cuba as well as a tacit recognition that the dynamics of migration had begun to shift. The diversification of the migrant pool and the demonization of those leaving became enduring legacies of Camarioca. Long before the 1980 Mariel boatlift framed migrants as *lumpen* and *escoria* (scum), revolutionary officials used the Camarioca migration to fortify an archetype of the revolutionary subject. In the process, they placed those who sought to leave (some, according to this logic, in spite of their racial or class identities) outside Cuba's literal and figurative borders.

Revolutionary Borders

A November 1965 speech by Fidel Castro set the tone on this score. "Our borders," he announced, "are not geographical borders; they are class borders, revolutionary borders, ideological borders. That is why when this nation asks someone if he wants to leave, we do not prevent it. . . . This country does not lose a citizen."[151] Throughout the duration of the Freedom Flights, Fidel repeatedly returned to this theme, stressing that he would not "prevent" migration but rather counter its effects on revolutionary morale.[152] When US officials accused their island counterparts of thwarting the airlift, Castro countered that it was rather that there were no more Cubans who wanted to leave. A 1971 speech consolidated the sentiment he had expressed repeatedly over the course of the previous decade: that migrants were not "citizens" but *"gusanos"* (worms), with no *"patria"* (homeland) or "principles."[153] The following year, Raúl Castro referred to exiles as "apátridas," or people without a country, and decried their ideologically contaminating impact on Cuban society.[154]

In this respect and others, the political effects of Camarioca were long-lasting. In a confidential memo from December 1968, the British ambassador to Cuba noted that one of the principal causes of "discontent" among Cuban students was the "impossibility for most of them to travel abroad— and the difficulty even to travel in their own country."[155] Though Castro would clear the way for mass migrations on two more occasions—during the 1980 Mariel boatlift and the 1994 *balsero* crisis—the exit-permit requirement thereafter functioned as a brake on such aspirations. As formalized in the 1976 Migration Law, any Cuban wishing to depart the island would need both a valid passport and an exit permit, known informally by Cubans as the *tarjeta blanca*, or white card.[156] The requirement of government approval and the high price attached to the exit permit put it out of reach of most islanders, though that did not prevent many from seeking exit by other means. Between April 1973 and September 1978, for example, the Cuban Refugee Program processed 17,899 migrants who arrived on rafts or small boats or who migrated via third countries.[157] Cubans who took to the seas knew that such an action represented a violation for which they could be arrested and incarcerated.[158] In treating illicit emigration as an imprisonable offense, Cuban officials thus criminalized flight just as their critics had alleged.

Beginning in 1980, however, migrants had to contend not only with legal obstacles on the Cuban side but also with diminished political will to receive them in the United States. The 1966 Cuban Adjustment Act, passed in the thick of Camarioca, had created a fast path for Cubans to access a green card and, eventually, citizenship. As María de los Angeles Torres points out, the law essentially "'[legalized]' what the State Department had done 'illegally' in the early 1960s: issue hundreds of thousands of visa waivers to Cubans on the island."[159] The 1966 act has remained on the books through the present, but with important modifications. These include the designation of the Mariel migrants—whose arrival coincided with a mass out-migration of Haitians—as "Cuban-Haitian entrants" rather than "refugees," which left some in sustained legal limbo. In the thick of the 1994 *balsero* crisis unleashed by the fall of the Soviet Union (and another exodus from Haiti), President Bill Clinton established further limitations with the 1995 "wet foot, dry foot" policy, which required Cubans to reach US territory to access the customary rights. In both cases, though the precedence attached to Cuba migrants was eroded, they were still granted preferential (and often racialized) treatment vis-à-vis their Haitian counterparts, even as the 1980 and 1994 migrations reflected greater class and racial diversity than did previous waves.

On the Cuban side, major changes to migration policy would not be undertaken until Raúl Castro's tenure as prime minister. Most notably, in 2013 he eliminated the notorious exit permit, though the financial cost of international travel—along with the visa required to travel to the United States and many other sites—meant that it remained beyond the reach of most islanders. But Raúl took other consequential measures on this front, ending the 1961 policy that sanctioned the confiscation of a migrant's property. Cuban nationals could thus enjoy the benefits of "circular migration," traveling back and forth to take advantage of opportunities within and beyond Cuba as long as they did not spend more than two years outside the country at once. At the same time, however, the new migration regime allowed government officials to deny travel in cases where it would imperil "defense or national security," a measure repeatedly invoked to block the mobility of critics. That provision sometimes worked in tandem with Decree 217 (1997), which restricted movement within Cuba to relieve population pressures in Havana.[160] Meanwhile, taking to the seas, as has long been the practice for those who cannot afford to fly, remained illegal.

During the short window of diplomatic normalization initiated by Raúl Castro and US president Barack Obama (2015–16), greater freedom to travel was enjoyed by those with means, and even some without, on both sides. This has since been brought to a halt. Notably, however, one of Obama's final actions on Cuba policy was to revoke the "wet foot, dry foot" rule, ending the practice of automatically granting parole to any Cuban who entered the United States. This meant that under Obama and his successors, what represented freer travel for some entailed more restrictions for the growing numbers of Cubans who attempted to enter the US illegally. The "normalization" of their migration status meant they would be treated more like other migrants—that is, with *fewer* liberties—even as Cubans continue to have broader access to government resources upon arrival.[161] Meanwhile, those who have left the island in record numbers since 2021 find themselves again invoked in, but rarely invited into, debates about the island's present and future.

In the context of these shifts, there is one notable source of continuity: the Cuba travel ban remains in force in the United States, though different administrations have tightened or loosened the rules governing island travel and spending.[162] This attachment to ancient political hostilities strikes many observers as an anachronism at best. Yet the persistence of the travel ban also highlights something that Cubans across the political spectrum have long noted. Castro has seized as many opportunities as were afforded to him to force the hand of US politicians, but the perpetuation of the immobility attached to the Cuban Revolution was an interdependent and *unequal* affair. When it comes to bilateral mobility restrictions, the US government continues to hold many of the cards.

While acknowledging these asymmetries, this chapter has also highlighted the agency and responsibility of revolutionary officials in enacting their own mobility restrictions. Indeed, it is telling that nothing like the social history of US travel ban defiance can be charted on the Cuban side. When it came to resisting the forces that curtailed their freedom of movement, islanders' only recourse was often the surreptitious and dangerous path of exit. In response, leaders exceeded the conspicuous prosecutions of their US counterparts in their efforts to enforce "revolutionary borders." Critics have in turn demanded that they be held accountable for the casualties of such policies—namely, those who perished in the course of flight.

· · · · · ·

This chapter has lingered on the legal history of immobility in the Cuban Revolution in part because it has long remained so opaque. Debates among state officials, journalists, and ordinary citizens have shaped perspectives on mobility restrictions—and the politics transacted around them—as much as legal regimes. Mobility limits have in turn evolved in response to this politicization, as the SCTC trips and Camarioca would suggest. The dynamic interaction between politics and the law endowed mobility and immobility with a singular importance in the world of the Cuban Revolution.

Beginning in January 1959, travel to the island was centered on the quest of international observers to understand the Revolution. That attachment expanded in concert with political hostilities and polarized reporting. Travel to Cuba thus became a way of accessing hidden knowledge and performing sympathy with the Revolution. The more the US government worked to thwart the mobility of its citizens, along with that of many Latin Americans, the greater the stakes many attached to travel as a vehicle to understanding. Here, as elsewhere, epistemology and solidarity went hand in hand.

Meanwhile, travel was invested with an equally important function on the island. Officials promoted the identification of ordinary citizens with the revolutionary process and its international setting by facilitating mobility for work, study, and even play. Yet they simultaneously erected obstacles to other kinds of movement, notably emigration. For some, travel abetted the acquisition of revolutionary knowledge; for others, its impossibility stoked political opposition. In the process, the decision to stay or leave, along with the presumed racial and class coordinates of that stance, became a defining feature of the revolutionary (and exile) subject.

Despite legal shifts, the association between travel and knowledge has changed little in the past six decades. Government officials on both sides have repeatedly used mobility restrictions to block access to forbidden knowledge, and opponents of those policies have in turn stressed their right to movement and information. Rarely, however, has this promoted a sense of common cause. What has instead emerged is a curious silence enveloping the otherwise loud politics around travel—namely, the fact that both the US and Cuban governments have persistently treated their citizens' mobility as subject to curtailment, along with their freedom to know.

As people around the hemisphere came to frame their relationship to Cuba through mobility and immobility, aspiring Revolution experts established an even more direct relationship to travel. Actualizing their solidarity with—or at times, critique of—the Revolution's course depended on the evidence that only physical presence could provide, and they too encountered an initially warm reception on the island. As chapter 5 argues, however, seeing Cuba "for themselves" did not necessarily lead to straightforward political conclusions. Over the course of the 1960s, the dialogue between foreign experts and revolutionary officials turned increasingly acrimonious amid broader debates over Cuban socialism, revolutionary politics, and knowledge production. By the turn of 1970, the resulting debates over the place of expertise turned intellectual politics into a transnational measure of the merits or failings of the revolutionary project itself.

5 Experts in Revolution

· ·

Herminio Portell Vilá was a distinguished historian of Cuba and the United States with a formidable academic pedigree, including a Guggenheim Fellowship and prestigious visiting professorships in the United States. In Cuba his work also reached a broad audience through his publications in the press and his University of Havana classroom, where he taught several aspiring politicians—including, famously, Fidel Castro. According to Hugh Thomas, their contact did not end there: "In the early summer of 1953 . . . Portell Vila was sitting in a bar in Havana when a young ex-pupil . . . told him that he was planning an attack on the Moncada Barracks." The professor, Thomas relates, "tried to dissuade" him, unsuccessfully, as we know.[1]

As a scholar, Portell Vilá had long been a critic of US intervention in Cuba. It was not without some irony, then, that Castro's coming to power inspired not only his departure from Cuba but also an enduring relationship with the Voice of America. When on the air, he opined on matters as diverse as Che Guevara's management of the sugar industry, international relations, university politics, and the "veracity of statistics" under Communism.[2] But Portell Vilá's anti-Castro outreach was not confined to propaganda channels. In December 1964, the Cuban Freedom Committee reported that Portell Vilá had recently attended the annual meeting of the American Historical Association, where he "[distributed] several hundred of our pamphlets Cuba Hoy and Cuba Today."[3]

In academia and beyond, the Cold War produced more than one unlikely mise-en-scène. From the human sciences to engineering, and area studies to linguistics, the geopolitics of the era came to shape many fields of scholarly inquiry. As Andra Chastain and Timothy Lorek have argued, "The thorniest sociocultural problems posed by the Cold War—such as how to feed, shelter, and educate a rapidly growing population—seemed to offer a carte blanche for the intervention of a host of experts."[4] In many cases, governments eagerly sought their participation. In the battle for hearts, minds, and space, no topic was too arcane if officials saw in it the potential for application—or weaponization.[5]

Within this minefield of purposeful knowledge, the Cuban Revolution had an electric effect. On the island, revolutionary change inspired scholars and writers to rethink the country's intellectual traditions. Among the most impactful were those historians who recast subaltern historical actors—notably, enslaved Africans—as past (and future) subjects of revolution.[6] Government officials also called on experts to make their work responsive to the Revolution's goals, particularly the effort to stabilize the Cuban economy.[7] This endowed knowledge production with a relevance that many greeted with enthusiasm, even as others bemoaned its potentially censorial implications.

If experts helped to make the Revolution, the Revolution in turn minted experts, as scholars and intellectuals—located mostly outside the island—began to generate a self-referential corpus of knowledge *about* the Revolution. Cuba's deviations from Cold War truisms energized debates about geopolitics, developmental economics, and, above all, Marxist theory and its applications. This turned Cuba into a pole of attraction for anti-Soviet and anti-imperialist intellectuals seeking a socialist third way, while galvanizing critics in the political center and on the right concerned about the international implications of Cuban socialism. As experts on the left established partnerships with island officials, those in the center and on the right collaborated with Cuban exiles—who served as key interlocutors—and, at times, the US government. To study the Revolution was, inevitably, to take sides.

From public intellectuals, such as French agronomist René Dumont and US sociologist C. Wright Mills, to Cuban social scientists and self-made Cubanists in the US academy, scholars indelibly shaped the Revolution and knowledge about it. But the fragile peace between Cuba and its experts was not destined to last. By the late 1960s, private and public disagreements had surfaced in the relationships between revolutionary officials and some of their intellectual allies, among them Afro-Cuban artists and writers and heterodox Marxists who had sought to locate their critiques of racism and Soviet orthodoxies, respectively, within the revolutionary project. This reversal culminated in the international cause célèbre sparked by the 1971 imprisonment of poet Heberto Padilla. Padilla, who had chafed at an increasingly restrictive cultural environment, was forced to deliver a public self-criticism in which he repudiated, among others, high-profile Western experts, including Dumont and critical Marxist writer K. S. Karol. Many intellectuals formerly sympathetic to the revolutionary government distanced themselves in response.

To explain the rupture between the Revolution and affiliated intellectuals, scholars have often cited cultural policy, especially Fidel Castro's 1961

"Words to the Intellectuals" speech. Famously, Castro sanctioned cultural production that located itself "within the Revolution," thereafter justifying both state support for the arts and periodic censorship of its content.[8] By 1971, amid a broader repressive turn, he had consequentially reduced that foundational ambiguity, framing art as a "weapon of the Revolution" and an overt ideological instrument.[9] Here, however, I approach the evolving politics of culture through the prism of *economics*: notably, the engagement between foreign experts and revolutionary officials over the island's agricultural future. I propose that these interactions served as a touchstone for cultural politics writ large, as well as the subsequent explosion of Cuban studies as a field.

Throughout the 1960s, path-breaking scholars from Latin America, Europe, and the United States overcame political obstacles (not least the US travel ban) to witness, document, and influence the course of socialist change. Some hoped to help Cuba avoid the pitfalls that had stymied previous attempts at socialist transformation by conducting data-driven empirical research. Yet for many, being in Revolution—and even being part of it—was as important as their scholarly credentials. If previous chapters have highlighted the challenges of locating the truth about Cuba, the experts considered here are notable for their efforts to make the Revolution *knowable*, even as they remained attentive to the broader context of politicization. The exodus of many Cuban intellectuals and professionals earlier in the decade made their participation especially crucial, as did the privileges attached to foreignness. Foreign intellectuals, it was understood, were uniquely positioned to convey unpleasant facts and hard truths.

But allied experts quickly discovered that there were limits to what they could say. At times, island officials seemed to value such work less as a blueprint for revolutionary policy than as a medium for international publicity; in other cases, they repudiated it altogether. In several high-profile cases, scholars discovered that their attempts at critical engagement marked them not as friends of the Revolution but rather as political antagonists, and even (alleged) imperialist agents. As a result, the prospect that had attracted so many intellectuals to the island—that Cuban officials would prove less dogmatic and more open to critique than their Soviet predecessors—became a principal source of their alienation.

The interaction between the Revolution and its experts produced an enduring body of writing, through which generations of observers, especially those in the intellectual classes, have come to know the Revolution.

Arguably, it was on this front that such publications left their deepest epistemological mark. But over the course of its first decade, the Cuban Revolution also came to symbolize the clash between commitment and objectivity, values that the Cold War had raised to the level of political metanarrative.[10] As a result of the participation—and, in some cases, dissociation—of foreign experts, we share an understanding of the Revolution rooted in intellectual politics, from the early honeymoon between intellectuals and revolutionary officials to their public rupture by 1971, as well as the myriad relationships forged by critical observers with Cuban exiles or the US government.

The paradigm of betrayal runs through these different arenas of Revolution studies, connecting the content of this work to its context. Such language pervades the work of liberal observers who decried the socialist direction adopted by the revolutionary leadership as well as those Marxists who lamented the form that Cuban socialism had taken. Perhaps most enduringly, it also provided a rubric for the encounter between the Revolution and intellectuals themselves. If experts played a key role in producing knowledge about Cuba, and Cuba in turn shaped their worldviews, their fate came to propel enduring narratives regarding the value—or peril—of expertise in revolution.

Why Socialism

"The Cuban Revolution has given birth, among other less respectable things, to a new specialization: the Castrologists," wrote Andrés Valdespino, a former University of Havana law professor and a onetime revolutionary government official, in 1963. "With benedictine patience, the Castrologists . . . scrutinize the attitudes, reactions, and external manifestations of the 'Maximum Leader.'" The attention of Castro watchers, however, was not oriented solely to the present, or even the past. Rather, Valdespino noted, they also had their eyes trained on the future. This left them vulnerable to the same fate that had plagued the so-called Kremlinologists—namely, "the number of times . . . they had been proven wrong."[11]

The scholarly consensus was similarly harsh. "The few living US scholars who have written able studies of Cuban society," Dutch sociologist Harmannus Hoetink noted, "have wisely abstained from joining the off-tune and emotionally unstable chorus of Cuban 'experts.'"[12] Drawing on his own Latin America expertise, Canadian scholar John Harbron concluded that by the time of his writing in 1963, most of what had been written about the

Revolution "[displayed] unfortunate personal bias."[13] For his part, Ronald Hilton, founding director of the Institute of Hispanic American and Luso-Brazilian Studies at Stanford University and editor of the *Hispanic American Report*, proposed that fear had silenced potential US scholars of the Revolution. Many had thus chosen to ride the "anti-Communist wave" rather than face career "danger" if they dared to "say anything favorable about Castro."[14] Due to his own public position on Cuba, Hilton was pulled into a dispute with Stanford that ended in his resignation.[15]

Cold War politicization thus conditioned the birth of Revolution studies and continued to escalate alongside the Revolution's evolution from nationalism and humanism to avowed socialism by April 1961. Indeed, the question of *why* Cuba had turned to socialism drove some of the most heated polemics in the field.[16] That shift provoked the disaffection of many one-time liberal sympathizers as well as the more fervent adherence of some on the left. But if the radicalization of the Cuban Revolution had politically divisive effects, it also proved to be intellectually generative for an emergent corps of Revolution experts.

These observers included journalists whose engagement with Cuba had begun in the ranks of the sierra, most famously Herbert Matthews. Though marginalized from the reporting team at the *New York Times*, the veteran Cuba watcher nonetheless continued to publish on the Revolution, beginning with *The Cuban Story* (1961) and followed by a biography of Castro (1969) and *Revolution in Cuba: An Essay in Understanding* (1975). Antoni Kapcia notes that Matthews stood almost alone in maintaining a complicated sympathy for the revolution project, but from a "liberal perspective."[17] The critical verdict on his volumes was, perhaps predictably, mixed.

Other influential supporters included Waldo Frank, who was contracted by the Cuban government to write a book about the Revolution. As Rafael Rojas explains, *Cuba: Prophetic Island* (1961) depicts the "revolution itself . . . as a recovery of last national sovereignty."[18] Yet Frank's defense of Cuban self-determination stood alongside critiques of the government's reliance on Castro's charisma, the hasty pace of revolutionary change, and the looming threat of Marxist influence. Particularly following the 1961 Bay of Pigs invasion and the declaration of the Communist direction of the Revolution, Frank found himself with few allies in the United States, where his founding participation in the Fair Play for Cuba Committee rendered him suspect. In Cuba, meanwhile, his book was never published.[19]

Inspired by the example of Jean Paul Sartre, whose 1960 trip to the island with Simone de Beauvoir had culminated in a widely read volume, other members of the international Left saw in Cuba an opportunity to model their commitment to anticolonial struggle.[20] Among the most influential was sociologist C. Wright Mills, whose commitment, per Rojas, to "[destabilizing] the commonplaces of the Cold War binary mentality," led him to write *Listen Yankee* (1961).[21] The book was shallow in its treatment of Cuban history and culture, but it inspired many with its call for the United States to abandon its prejudices toward the Revolution. In the United States, it was among the most popular of all books about post-1959 Cuba, and it also became a bestseller in Mexico, where Mills's interest in Cuba had first been "awoken" by dialogues with prominent Mexican intellectuals.[22] *Escucha yanqui* subsequently circulated widely across Latin America and helped to galvanize a hemispheric "New Left," as Elisa Servín has observed.[23]

Especially in the United States, however, many more Revolution watchers stood on the other side of the political divide. As we have seen, Jules Dubois made several contributions to this genre, including *Fidel Castro: Rebel— Liberator or Dictator?* (1959). To this body of work, we might add Ruby Hart Phillips's *Cuba, Island of Paradox* (1959) and *The Cuban Dilemma* (1962), as well as other titles by those who had once served on the reporting front lines.[24] Further to the right, books such as *Red Star over Cuba* (1960) by Nathaniel Weyl, a former Communist Party member turned anti-Communist public intellectual, and *Cuba: The First Soviet Satellite in the Americas* (1961) by Daniel James, a freelance journalist with strong ties to Mexico, made explicit a theme present in many of these early titles—namely, that Fidel Castro was becoming—or had always been—a Communist.[25]

A small group of academics cast their lot with these writers on interpretive and political lines, including Columbia University historian and Mexico specialist Frank Tannenbaum, who had received Fidel Castro on campus during the leader's US goodwill tour in April 1959.[26] But Tannenbaum's enthusiasm faded quickly alongside Cuba's radicalization. In a 1962 article, the historian proposed that the Cuban Revolution "was legitimate and inevitable" in its opposition to "tyranny, base corruption and governmental indifference to the many needs of the populace." This did not, however, justify the "totalitarian dictatorship" that Castro had ultimately established, or the nationalizations and agrarian reform he had undertaken.[27]

Tannenbaum's stance on Cuba put him at odds with many of his Latin American counterparts. His declaration during a 1962 presentation at the Universidad de Concepción (Chile) that US empire "did not exist" generated public critique from such luminaries as Carlos Fuentes, Mario Benedetti, and Alejo Carpentier.[28] But Tannenbaum's Cuba politics also brought him into new organizational alignments. He was, for example, the most prominent scholar to join the Citizens Committee for a Free Cuba (CCFC), an advocacy group established by Daniel James, even as he privately shared concerns over the "accuracy" of information disseminated in the CCFC newsletter.[29]

The field of early Revolution studies came to include few scholars of Tannenbaum's stature and developed largely outside ivy-decked walls.[30] It was not, however, immune to government connections. In the aftermath of the Bay of Pigs invasion, the RAND Corporation completed its first reports about Cuba, and the army turned to the Foreign Areas Studies Division at American University to assemble operational information.[31] Through covert backing to organizations such as the Congress for Cultural Freedom, the CIA mobilized—with mixed success—to cultivate hemispheric intellectuals as anti-Communist allies.[32] Meanwhile, within and beyond Miami, which had become home to its most extensive operation by 1961, the agency also built a network of associated experts, a practice that continued for decades to come.[33]

Yet Miami was also the early seat of rigorous Revolution scholarship. The Cuban Economic Research Project, housed at the University of Miami (where the CIA maintained an office), brought together some of the exile community's most prominent specialists on the Cuban economy, including one of the field's few female doctorate recipients, Ofelia Tabares de Fernández Díaz. Many participants had collaborated with the revolutionary government in its early months but had become disaffected as a result of ideological radicalization and the sidelining of their expertise. The group's assessments of Cuba's economic and political policies were notably grim. Even so, its publications modeled closely documented, data-driven research, as well as a stated commitment to "[avoiding] . . . personal evaluations in an effort to achieve objectivity."[34]

In other cases, more direct ties of intellectual affinity connected Revolution observers to the US government. The United States Information Agency translated and circulated titles by Daniel James and Theodore Draper, among others, as part of its propaganda outreach to Latin America.[35] US officials thus turned such authors into vehicles for justifying their policies toward Cuba, expanding the audience for—and, in some cases, animosity toward—their work. In part because of these synergies, Draper quickly became among the most consequential *and* controversial of the early Revolution scholars.

Draper's interest in the Cuban Revolution stemmed from his evolution—shared by many first-generation American Jews of his generation—from

"Communist Party fellow traveler" to "liberal anticommunist."[36] During the 1930s, Draper had worked as a reporter for the Communist periodicals the *Daily Worker* and *New Masses* and even the Soviet news agency TASS. Over time, however, Draper bristled at growing Soviet rigidity, which had, among other things, foiled a planned reporting stint in Moscow.[37] Drafted late in World War II, he returned to a US political culture in the throes of a shift toward anti-Communism that, in some ways, mirrored his own. Draper was subsequently recruited into a team led by Cornell political scientist Clinton Rossiter, which was collaborating to write a complete history of the US Communist Party (CPUSA).[38] Drawing on his graduate training in history at Columbia University (he never finished his degree), he went on to publish two volumes in which he aimed to trace, "calmly and consecutively," the history of the CPUSA from its 1919 founding through the internecine struggles of the late 1920s.[39] The early history of the CPUSA, he concluded, reflected its "[transformation] from a new expression of American radicalism to the American appendage of a Russian revolutionary power."[40]

This work on Communism in the United States provided a relevant point of departure for Draper's next major research subject: the Cuban Revolution. Following a 1960 trip to the island, Draper published a series of articles in the liberal magazine the *New Leader*, many of them reprinted in the influential (and, as it was later revealed, CIA-funded) magazines *Encounter* and *Cuadernos*.[41] These works advanced what would prove to be an enduring interpretation of socialism as a betrayal of the revolutionary movement against Batista. They also turned Draper into the intellectual foe of a group of US and European intellectuals more sympathetic to the island's course.

The Draper school coheres around three principal arguments, the most foundational of which relates to the class character of the Revolution. Parting ways with those who had lionized a "peasant revolution" (Sartre) or a revolution led by intellectuals on behalf of peasants (Mills), Draper characterized the movement against Batista as a "rebellion by the sons and daughters of the middle class in the name of the workers and peasants."[42] This conclusion in turn bolstered Draper's assessment that socialism, for Fidel Castro especially, represented an expedient means to an alternative end. Months before socialism became the official revolutionary ideology, Draper anticipated its declaration as a vehicle for retaining power and dramatically "[changing] the social order."[43] Finally, Draper proposed that the radicalization toward socialism was a "betrayal" of the revolution Castro had promised.[44] From the postponement of elections to the neglect of Cuba's progressive 1940 constitution, the concentration of power in Castro's hands, and the growing influence of Communists in the revolutionary government, "Castro promised one kind of revolution and made another," Draper concluded.[45]

All three of these arguments inspired praise in some academic circles, where Draper was portrayed as the most scrupulous of the emergent Revolution scholars, and backlash among critics on the left. Particularly galling to many in the latter group was Draper's inattention to geopolitical factors—namely, the role of the US government—in explaining the origins and course of the Revolution. These critiques were not entirely fair, as Draper had not shied away from critiquing US intervention on the island, especially following the Bay of Pigs invasion.[46] But he did highlight Cuban forces and especially Castro's personal machinations in explaining the political vicissitudes of the Revolution. This approach aligned him not only with the Cuban exiles who served as his most important interlocutors but also with the US government itself.

Among the most prominent of Draper's critics on this score was diplomatic historian William Appleman Williams, who viewed Cuba's history as a crucible of US imperialism. Williams's work charted a long history of accumulated injustices through which Cuba's domestic concerns were inextricably linked to US interests. He in turn framed the Revolution as a necessary reaction against this past, arguing that "no Cuban could be a social revolutionary without being anti-American."[47] Williams and Draper agreed that the movement against Batista was bound up with a promise to actualize the 1940 constitution. But where Draper emphasized Castro's "betrayal" of that pledge, Williams maintained that US hostility "[accelerated] and [sustained] Castro's leftward movement to a position that made the socialist reading of the Constitution dependent upon Soviet aid and support."[48]

Yet the objections of Draper critics to the betrayal thesis went beyond analytical discrepancies. In his 1961 *In Defense of the Cuban Revolution*, Trotskyist journalist Joseph Hansen had also criticized Draper for ignoring the "role of American imperialism as a cause for the radicalization of the revolution."[49] More than scholarly oversight, however, Hansen saw sinister alliances at play. By the time of Draper's publications, Hansen observed, the discourse of betrayal was already a "well-gnawed theme in the Cuban counterrevolutionary press."[50] But he also pointed to a striking and, he proposed, telling coincidence. Draper's first reference to betrayal appeared in print on March 27, 1961. And on April 3, the State Department issued its own white paper echoing some of Draper's key points, including his critique of

Communist influence in the Revolution.[51] The Bay of Pigs invasion came shortly thereafter. The language of betrayal played directly into Washington's hands, Hansen contended, by "providing intellectuals with a perfect rationalization for abandoning any sympathy for the Castro regime."[52]

In published responses to his critics, Draper chafed at those "subtle and not-so-subtle allusions linking [him] to the State Department and Mr. Kennedy."[53] But his relationships with Cuban exiles, whom both Hansen and Williams identified as the intellectual authors of betrayal, were undeniably close. Draper's work depended on his ties to prominent members of that community—including Justo Carrillo, Max Lesnik, Joaquín Godoy, Raúl Martínez Aranas, Rufo López Fresquet, and Javier Pazos—many of whom had once belonged to the revolutionary government. Exile leaders represented the backbone of Draper's academic team, facilitating interviews, responding to questionnaires about their participation in recent events, and even connecting him to research assistants on the island. They thus became subjects and objects of the "human archive," as Carrillo once called it, on which Draper's research depended.[54] Draper in turn joked about "exploiting" his exile contacts, an insinuation they always rebuffed.[55]

In fact, these relationships modeled a great deal of reciprocity. Draper encouraged his interlocutors to publish about their experiences and even advocated with his publisher on behalf of Carrillo, a prominent businessman and revolutionary leader who in late 1959 resigned his position as the head of the National Bank for Agrarian and Industrial Development and left Cuba. Collaboration with exile leaders extended to the intellectual genesis of the betrayal thesis itself. Betrayal had indeed become an early, if not unambiguous, theme in critical responses to the Revolution, beginning on the island and extending into exile.[56] Letters from Draper's exile correspondents unsurprisingly reflect that prominence. Yet we might read something into the fact that Carrillo's book proposal, submitted to Praeger after close consultation with Draper, rendered the title of one section "The 'Betrayed Revolution,'" with quotation marks.[57] His punctuation seems to honor, obliquely, Draper's own contributions.

Many of Draper's correspondents had experienced revolutionary radicalization as personal and ideological betrayal. Though Communism was their target, they often concretized these two registers of treachery in the figure of Fidel Castro. Castro, they alleged, had disappointed expectations and broken bonds of trust. The discursive attachment to loyalty thus collapsed ideological battles into the microphysics of personal relationships.

The engagement of exile leaders with Draper was similarly invested with personal and political significance. In February 1964, Carrillo wrote to Orlando de Cárdenas, a longtime anti-Batista activist who had seen Castro off from Mexico in 1956, requesting his collaboration in Draper's research. He urged him to reinvest "his greatest loyalty—the same that you granted to 'Alejandro' [Fidel Castro's nom de guerre] without reciprocity—in someone you don't know but does merit it."[58] Like his Cuban interlocutors, Draper had experienced the disappointments of socialism firsthand. And for him, as for them, this was not a purely intellectual matter.[59]

Which Socialism

For some, the declaration of socialism represented an act of betrayal. Others, however, presented it as structurally necessary. This second group included political economist James O'Connor, whose 1964 Columbia dissertation, "The Political Economy of Pre-Revolutionary Cuba," drew on his several trips to Cuba, where he gathered economic data and interviewed government officials, such as Felipe Pazos and Che Guevara. O'Connor dismissed explanations for the rise of socialism based on US hostility or betrayal. Rather, he argued that radicalization, "accepted and supported by the majority of Cuban people," was "inevitable in the sense that it was necessary if the island was to be rescued from permanent economic stagnation, social backwardness and degradation, and political do-nothingism and corruption."[60]

The structural inevitability of Cuban socialism was also a major theme in the work of critical Marxist thinkers affiliated with the New York magazine *Monthly Review*, edited by Paul Sweezy and Leo Huberman. Among them were economist and Stanford professor Paul Baran, who traveled to the island for three weeks in 1960. In two articles, Baran proposed that socialism was Cuba's destiny, the natural progression from a project of national "liberation" to "political revolution" and finally "social [revolution]."[61] In a series of articles and an influential book, *Cuba: Anatomy of a Revolution* (1961), Sweezy and Huberman also insisted on the Revolution's socialist character even before it was formally declared. This early claim for Cuba's radicalism separated Huberman and Sweezy from many intellectuals of the international Left (and perhaps also inspired Cuban officials to translate and publish their book on the island), as Rafael Rojas notes.[62]

For sympathetic Marxists, however, the question was not only *if* but rather *which* socialism the Cuban Revolution would pursue. Revolutionary officials in turn approached foreign intellectuals as fellow travelers and potential interlocutors in its development.[63] The involvement of Marxist experts was particularly intense in the early 1960s, as island officials navigated a series of dramatic events, from agrarian reform (first in May 1959 and again in October 1963) to the nationalization of foreign businesses, the implementation of a US embargo, and economic rapprochement with the Soviet bloc. This rapidly shifting landscape provoked a series of swift reorientations in Cuba's economic model.

Carmelo Mesa-Lago has identified several stages in this evolution, from the "liquidation of capitalism and the erosion of the market" (1959–60), to the "attempt to introduce an Orthodox (Stalinist) model of central planning" (1961–63), and finally the so-called Great Debate (1963–64) in which the Soviet paradigm was pitted against alternative models, notably that championed by Che Guevara himself. Guevarism, which steered the Cuban economy for the rest of the decade, spurned the pragmatic turn in recent Soviet planning (which incorporated some capitalist elements within socialism) in favor of the quest to build socialism and communism simultaneously. The most famous symbol of that project was the much-touted "New Man," who would no longer require material incentives to work.[64] Running alongside these debates was the enduring problem of sugar. If the early 1960s had witnessed attempts to industrialize and diversify the Cuban economy away from sugar, the failure of that project by 1963 and closer economic relations with the Soviet bloc inspired a return to sugar and a campaign to produce a record 10-million-ton harvest in 1970.

Foreign experts were present for and implicated in every stage of this progression. Among them was US sociologist Maurice Zeitlin. As we saw in chapter 1, Zeitlin's support for the Revolution in the early 1960s extended to public activism against US policy. This cost him his first job as an instructor in sociology and anthropology at Princeton University in 1964.[65] Zeitlin soon found a more congenial home in the Sociology Department at UC Berkeley, where he completed his doctoral dissertation, later published as *Revolutionary Politics and the Cuban Working Class* (1967). Zeitlin's research drew on interviews he and his wife Marilyn conducted on the island with over 200 industrial workers to explore their attitudes toward the "ideology and social content of the revolution."[66]

Among other themes, Zeitlin analyzed the differentiation of the Cuban working class along generational lines, from their perspectives on Communists, to which older workers were the most sympathetic, to the Revolution itself, about which the youngest workers (age 21–27) expressed the least favorable views.[67] Notably, although Zeitlin did not include a formal question about race relations, many respondents "alluded spontaneously to the question."[68] Afro-Cuban interviewees were more likely to express support for the Revolution, but they, and especially the previously unemployed among them, were less likely to support Communism than their white counterparts.[69] These findings suggest that many Cubans of color understood the subject of Revolution as being fundamentally bound up with race, in concert with but also independent from its economic implications.[70]

Zeitlin's research in Cuba benefited from the direct support and sponsorship of Che Guevara, who professed a uniquely capacious view of the value of expertise in Revolution. In a similar spirit, he recruited Cuban psychologists and social scientists to help promote productivity and chronicle socialist transformation in real time.[71] International experts were perhaps most visible, however, in the work of economic planning. Their prominence stemmed from the early exodus of many Cuban professionals, as well as the dismissal of anti-Communist advisers from their posts.[72] That context endowed foreign voices with unique prominence and political sensitivity.

Though they sometimes parted ways on the specifics, foreign specialists were united by their conviction that expertise should guide economic planning. Behind the scenes, their engagement was grounded in constructive critique, steering revolutionary officials—especially Guevara, Fidel Castro, and writer, politician, and longtime Communist Party member Carlos Rafael Rodríguez, who served as the director of the Institute for Agrarian Reform (INRA) from 1962 to 1965—to time-tested methods for achieving their goals. Yet that mission proved more problematic in print, where experts tended not only to voice their support for socialist transformation in principle but also their concerns about its execution in practice.

Their publications helped to consolidate two contradictory perceptions of the Revolution on the international stage. On the one hand, the very presence of Western economists and agronomists on the front lines of the Revolution served to demonstrate openness to expert guidance. This served as an important mechanism to consolidate international support by recruiting informed witnesses to—but also sponsors of—revolutionary transformation. Yet the resistance with which Cuban officials often met their judgments cemented the opposite perception: that the Revolution was constitutionally hostile to expertise. Over the course of the 1960s, French agronomist René Dumont, among the most influential scholars invited to Cuba, would become a prominent symbol of that divergence.

But the Revolution's first expert allies emerged closer to home. An influential group of Latin American economists came to inform revolutionary economic planning thanks to their affiliation with the United Nations Economic Commission for Latin America (ECLA). ECLA was established in 1948 to promote economic development in the region with an emphasis on import-substitution industrialization. One of its founding members was Cuban economist Regino Boti, who later became the Revolution's first minister of the economy and broker of an ECLA commission sent to Cuba in 1959.[73] Participants—including Argentine economist Jorge Ahumada, Mexican economist Juan Noyola, and Chilean agronomist Jacques Chonchol—influenced early economic policy behind the scenes while also disseminating news of its achievements throughout the hemisphere. Both Chonchol and Noyola helped to orient the field toward expansive state reform as a response to US dominance. Latin American economic theory thus radicalized alongside the Revolution.[74]

Juan Noyola served as a particularly important architect of that shift. After graduating from Mexico's Escuela Nacional de Economía, Noyola began his career at the International Monetary Fund (IMF) in 1946. His work at the IMF reflects the structuralist approaches that would dominate within ECLA, framing inflation, for example, as a geopolitical rather than a monetary problem.[75] But Noyola's discomfort with IMF policies led him to return to Mexico in 1948, and soon thereafter he accepted a position with ECLA. That took him to Chile (1950), Mexico (1959), and finally Havana, where he led the organization's commission to the island government.[76] Noyola's encounter with Cuba represented a critical turning point in his career, leading him to resign from ECLA and integrate himself fully into the revolutionary project.[77]

In Cuba, Noyola helped to establish important institutions, such as the Junta de Planificación, a new body charged with central economic planning, and the Instituto de Economía at the University of Havana. Intellectually, Noyola provided structuralist weight for the argument that the island's economic problems, especially its external dependency and its chronic underutilization of resources, were the result of US imperialism.[78] In helping to draft the Revolution's first long-term economic plan, Noyola and Francisco García characterized its "*essential objective . . . [as repairing] the damages caused to our economy by imperialism* during more than a half century of domination."[79] Such far-reaching influence, Noyola argued, demanded an equally encompassing solution: rapid industrialization, the revision of property relations, and, most importantly, a "profound, radical" agrarian reform.[80] The next step, once those and other reforms had been achieved, was to initiate the "discipline of socialist planning."[81]

Progress toward a planned economy demanded international cooperation and outreach. Noyola was particularly committed to sharing Cuba's successes and challenges with the "revolutionary Latin American intellectuals" who sought to follow its path, especially in his native Mexico.[82] He publicly spurned "rose-colored glasses" in favor of "candor" in depicting Cuba's economic course.[83] As an adviser to the island government, Noyola took seriously the "great responsibility" thereby conferred on him not to "fill archives that no one consults" nor to "serenely wait for government officials to gain consciousness about the need to adopt urgent changes."[84] Yet that same urgency he cited demanded that experts approach critique carefully. In their discussion of the chaotic economic planning for 1962, Noyola and García noted that "errors were made and deficiencies and misunderstandings encountered" but suggested that the appropriate time to analyze them would be "some future day."[85]

For Noyola, however, that day never came. In November 1962, he died at the age of forty in a tragic plane explosion that also killed Raúl Cepero Bonilla, noted Marxist intellectual and president of Cuba's National Bank, and the Chilean economist Rodrigo Cabello, among others. Memorializing his service to the Revolution two decades later, Carlos Rafael Rodríguez praised Noyola as an apostle of intellectual militancy while also stressing the radicalizing influence of the Revolution, and especially "revolutionary Marxism," on his thought.[86] Noyola's commitment to developing Cuban socialism, Rodríguez proposed, was visible not only in his published work but also in his daily Cuban life, in which he "wore the uniform of a *miliciano*."[87] For this dedication, reflected in his son's decision to become an *alfabetizador* (literacy teacher), Noyola was posthumously named an honorary citizen of Cuba.[88] That loyalty also provoked criticism from another noted observer, Noyola's onetime IMF supervisor and former National Bank director Felipe Pazos, who alleged that the Mexican economist's "strong partisan emotion" had "[reduced] the rigor of his analysis."[89]

Noyola's ECLA colleague Jacques Chonchol, whose June 1959 to late 1961 stay in Cuba was dedicated to an assessment of agricultural policy, also highlighted the political complexity attached to their work. "There's little 'room' across the Continent for an attempt at an objective analysis of any aspect of what's happening today in Cuba," he lamented.[90] Chonchol himself would enter the political fray following his return to Chile, where he played a leading role in shaping agrarian reform undertaken by the Eduardo

Frei government and, following the consolidation of his own socialist convictions, as Salvador Allende's minister of agriculture.[91] But in Cuba Chonchol found himself, along with a handful of foreign advisers, participating in a fraught debate over the island's agricultural future.

From the vantage point of the early 1960s, Chonchol found much to praise in the way the Cuban government had undertaken agrarian reform, stressing its ability to maintain high levels of production while preserving the autonomy of small farmers.[92] Yet Chonchol raised concerns about the centralizing direction of agricultural policy. He was particularly critical of the so-called *granjas del pueblo* (farms of the people), which in early 1961 had replaced all cooperatives (except, for a time, those in the sugar sector) and directly administered properties with state-owned farms, tasked with supplying the country with essential foodstuffs and other goods. Crucially, compensation of workers on the state farms was not linked to their productivity. Chonchol noted the logistical challenges associated with the overdiversified *granjas*, especially in the absence of trained technicians who could administer them.[93] He also saw ominous signs in the expansion of consumption, which had quickly outstripped production, exacerbated by the US embargo on the one hand and the evaporation of Cuba's capital reserves on the other.[94]

In his 1963 "critical analysis" of revolutionary agrarian reform, Chonchol concluded with a warning wrapped in praise. Cuba, he posed, might yet achieve the "rapid development of its agriculture, at a growth rate not seen in recent years in any Latin American country." Yet this could only be accomplished if "'ideological dogmatisms' and 'political sectarianisms' did not impede the selection" of the production and organizational "forms most appropriate to achieve this goal, and in accordance with the concrete reality of the country." This depended, he concluded, on the willingness of Cuban officials to "efficiently utilize all of their useful men and not only those who think according to a predetermined ideological mold."[95]

The need to heed expertise was also professed by renowned agronomist René Dumont throughout his years of professional engagement with Cuba. Having worked in the socialist and developing world, including the Soviet bloc, China, and multiple African nations, Dumont dedicated his career as a public intellectual to promoting sustainable and equitable development, a mission that later inspired him to run for president of France. But in the early 1960s, Dumont was focused on the challenges of socialist development, particularly where they met the legacies of colonialism. Revolutionary Cuba offered an ideal target for his professional intervention.

He first traveled to the island in May 1960 and returned the following year and on multiple other occasions (in 1963 and 1968) at the invitation of Castro and Carlos Rafael Rodríguez. Dumont's research in Cuba served as the basis for private reports submitted to INRA as well as several widely read books on the island's socialist project.[96]

As early as his first writings about the Revolution, Dumont raised concerns about the precipitous pace at which the Cuban economy was being taken over by the state.[97] He also advocated for cooperatives over large state-owned farms; material incentives; and local initiative, direction, and management. Above all, however, he encouraged Cuban officials to respect the advice of experts and experienced technicians so that they might avoid past mistakes. This was particularly critical, he proposed, given that those steering the economy, apart from Dorticós and Rodríguez, had no economic experience or specialized expertise.[98]

Productive engagement necessarily demanded self-reflection, what Dumont frequently referred to as "constructive criticism." In 1961, he warned that such evaluation should not be "buried" but publicly disseminated as an educational exercise.[99] Moreover, the significance of self-assessment did not stop at the island's borders. Dumont intended for his publications to serve as a vehicle for all "young nations that are turning toward socialism."[100] Within and beyond Cuba, he hoped that his critiques might halt the "whole cycle of errors" in developing economies.[101]

Yet that professed openness was not greeted warmly by Cuban officials, most especially Castro himself. Dumont reported, for example, that on multiple occasions Fidel had proven "ill-disposed" toward his "warnings" against large state-owned farms.[102] Suspicion toward "unpleasant" advice was not limited to the revolutionary leadership, as Dumont discovered during a 1960 press conference: "I was asked if I would repeat these facts in France. I replied that I would, but that I would add other explanations, so that the objective causes of the situation would be better understood. They protested that criticism ought to be kept within the Revolution and be confined to the leaders, not set forth publicly." Castro had also bristled at this report, objecting that other "foreign friends that visit us have nothing but compliments for us, whereas all you seem to do is criticize."[103]

Dumont considered constructive criticism a vehicle to perform his "uncommitted [friendship]" toward the Revolution.[104] Yet other experts raised questions about this approach. One of them was Edward Boorstein, a US economist who had served in Cuba for over three years (May 1960–September 1963) as a "trouble-shooter for the Ministry of Foreign

Commerce . . . and the Vice Minister of Economy."[105] In a 1965 review of Dumont's book, Boorstein seconded the call for "humility before the facts," but wondered if Dumont had been carried away in their telling.[106] "The very fact that Dumont finds it necessary to criticize so many things, from the inefficiency of volunteer workers in the coffee harvest to the failure of students to study enough[,] should give him pause," he suggested.[107] Boorstein was more sympathetic, for example, to the decision to establish the *granjas del pueblo*, given that they aimed to equalize compensation among agricultural workers. He further noted that, in relating some missteps, Dumont was insufficiently attentive to what had come before, or ignored the fact that they had since been corrected.

In a 1968 book published by *Monthly Review*, Boorstein presented his own record of errors, especially in early attempts at planning and the sometimes rote contributions of Soviet bloc technicians to that process. Like Noyola before him, however, he was careful to stress context—namely, the influence of the United States. The Revolution, Boorstein argued, had necessarily tackled US interference head-on, making "economic independence" a principal goal.[108] Dumont had not been inattentive to that issue and regularly stressed Cuban sovereignty, but Boorstein made it the centerpiece of lecture tours across the United States and a pamphlet published by Students for a Democratic Society. Meanwhile, he urged observers to be wary of outsiders who, based on short visits, insisted that they "[saw] better what the Cuban people should do than the Cuban people themselves."[109]

A similarly delicate approach was adopted by the French Marxist economist Charles Bettelheim, who, as documented by Selma Díaz and Juan Valdés Paz, swiftly became one of the most influential foreign experts to shape the course of Cuban socialism.[110] Together with Michel Gutelman, a Belgian agronomist and sociologist who often served as his assistant, Bettelheim's contributions to the Cuban economic model stretched across most of the decade, from his first trip in 1960 to his last in 1968. At the time of his Cuban engagement, Bettelheim was a young but prominent voice in the field of economic development, who had published important work on central planning in the capitalist, socialist, and postcolonial world. On this basis, Sweezy and Huberman had personally recommended him to Cuban leaders.[111]

Intellectually, Bettelheim was largely in sync with other foreign experts. His first report to revolutionary officials was strongly influenced by Dumont and Chonchol, with whom he met in Havana, and translated into Spanish by Noyola, who greeted him at the airport. The document stressed Cuba's "impressive" economic achievements and its bright agricultural prospects, provided that "energetic and urgent planning measures" were applied.[112] On the basis of his observations, Boti and Guevara asked Bettelheim to return to the island as an "official advisor."[113] In subsequent trips (every year, sometimes multiple times a year), Bettelheim continued to highlight concerns his colleagues had already voiced: the importance of establishing reasonable goals, setting price scales and financial protocols to halt inflation, decentralizing economic management, and heeding the lessons of past attempts at socialist transformation.[114] Simultaneously, in his less technical writings, he highlighted the "political genius" of the Revolution's leaders in "always making decisions at the most opportune moments, the moment at which they truly match the aspirations of the masses."[115]

Bettelheim established particularly close partnerships with President Osvaldo Dorticós and Carlos Rafael Rodríguez, whom he, like his professional counterparts, found to be knowledgeable and receptive.[116] Yet it was his intellectually conflictive but warm relationship with Che Guevara that catapulted him to the center of the so-called Great Debate (1963–64). In their exchanges, Bettelheim raised doubts about Guevara's commitment to building a Cuban "New Man," stressing that "only new social relations [could] transform men."[117] He thus believed that a more pragmatic approach, like that being pursued in the Soviet Union, represented a more viable path to socialism.[118]

Notably, Bettelheim studiously avoided any intimation of conflict. From his carefully timed responses, intended to avoid any sign of a "polemical turn" to the debate, to his largely unpublished evaluations submitted to Cuban leaders, the French economist rooted his professional intervention in his underlying solidarity with the Revolution, most clearly evident in his role as president (1962–71) of the Association for Friendship between France and Cuba (Asociación de Amistad Francia-Cuba).[119] Bettelheim's political commitment also made him wary of airing critiques, as in his "warning," contained in a late 1962 report, "against the temptation to imitate forms of centralized and bureaucratic management that dominate in the Soviet Union."[120] The submission of that evaluation, which coincided with the Cuban missile crisis, inspired him to write to Cuban economist Jaime Barrios expressing his hope that its "total frankness" "wasn't too jarring, which I would never want."[121] He followed that up with a letter to Dorticós himself, stressing that "international solidarity ought not to be relaxed at any price."[122]

Throughout 1963 and 1964, the Great Debate kept Bettelheim closely involved in the Cuban economy. He even organized a parallel discussion at France's École pratique des hautes études with high-profile participants such as French philosopher Louis Althusser. But Bettelheim's report on "Problems of Development from the Perspective of the Cuban Economy," sent to Dorticós in late 1965, would be one of his last. After Guevara departed Cuba to wage guerrilla warfare abroad, Bettelheim fretted about increasingly delayed communications from revolutionary officials. His final report in 1967, which had recommended a "drastic overhaul in economic perspectives," received only a taciturn, belated response from Dorticós.[123] As Selma Díaz, Bettelheim's Cuban interpreter, has pointed out, "Having received this minimal and only courtesy acknowledgment, he must have understood what he had already intuited: that his opinions were not going to be discussed."[124] His official advisory role ceased soon thereafter.

Bettelheim's eclipse reflected not only the absence of his main interlocutor but also the dramatic reorientation of the Cuban economy. By the mid-1960s the island had settled into a state of economic duality, with Guevarist economics applied in industry and more pragmatic approaches largely guiding the agricultural sector. This shift coincided with a renewed emphasis on sugar, which many experts had advocated as a way to accumulate capital reserves. These measures allowed for a partial economic recovery after the challenges of the preceding years.[125]

In 1966, however, with Guevara gone and Carlos Rafael Rodríguez no longer leading INRA, Fidel Castro took over the reins. The result, Mesa-Lago relates, was a dramatic pivot to the Guevarist model, with ordinary Cubans "exhorted to work more, save more and accept the privations with revolutionary spirit."[126] Collectivization and nationalizations accelerated rapidly, encompassing nearly all land and private businesses; central economic planning was largely abandoned.[127] Henceforth, political leaders would take the lead on economic decisions. These included establishing the goal of a record 10-million-ton sugar harvest for 1970 to pay back Cuba's trade deficit with the Soviet Union and set it on the path to economic autonomy.[128]

The economic landscape had thus changed dramatically by the time René Dumont returned in 1969 as a "personal guest" of Fidel Castro.[129] Though Castro avoided discussing the agronomist's previous book about Cuba, the two men sustained, by Dumont's account, a "dramatic discussion" about "certain economic criticisms that inevitably touched on political matters.[130] Dumont also aired these misgivings in the French press and a 1970 book,

Cuba: Est-il socialiste?, which was greeted with avid surreptitious interest on the island.[131]

Cuba: Est-il socialiste? brought critical attention to the economic measures recently adopted by Cuban officials, as well as the concentration of political power in their hands, the curtailment of popular participation, and the "militarization" of the agricultural sector. Alongside economic rapprochement with the Soviet Union, Dumont also raised concerns about creeping "Stalinism," especially in the cultural realm.[132] The book provoked outrage among supporters of the Cuban government in France and beyond, as well as heated academic debate; sociologist James Petras denounced Dumont as "ill-informed," "arrogant," and effectively "racist."[133] But events on the island would soon implicate Dumont in a debate that concerned Cuba watchers of all political stripes. At stake was the future of critical inquiry itself.

Is Cuba Socialist? (The Great Schism)

Intertwined with the imprisonment of poet Heberto Padilla, the break between the Revolution and foreign intellectuals was a prominent front of what came to be known as the *quinquenio gris* (dated 1971–76, or sometimes 1968–76). "The five gray years" corresponded to a period of cultural repression on the island. It was set into motion with the so-called Revolutionary Offensive of 1968, which targeted anti-revolutionary sentiment and the remaining vestiges of capitalist activity, and capped by the failed ten-million-ton sugar harvest of 1970 and subsequent integration of Cuba into the Soviet economic bloc. Though many members of the international Left maintained a position of solidarity throughout this period, some of its most high-profile allies in France, Latin America, and the United States defected permanently from those ranks.

But was another path possible? The status of Cuban intellectuals within the revolutionary project remained an intermittently open question following Castro's 1961 "Words to the Intellectuals," as debates over intellectual responsibility and artistic freedom continued to simmer. By mid-decade, the relationship between intellectuals and revolutionary officials had reached a nadir due to the repressive management of long-standing members of the Popular Socialist Party (PSP) who had been charged with spearheading cultural policy. Beginning in 1965 but building on previous campaigns, many critical and gender and sexual nonconforming intellectuals were dismissed from their jobs; some were sent to the notorious UMAP work camps in

Camagüey. The dismissals helped to consolidate the official conflation of homosexuality with counterrevolutionary politics (per the emergent category of "ideological confusionism"), marking both as antithetical to revolutionary subjecthood.[134]

These events sparked outcry among artists and intellectuals within and beyond Cuba.[135] They also inspired a short-lived redirection in the Revolution's cultural course. By 1967, the unofficial "policy towards the intellectuals," as expressed in a CNC memorandum, was to "situate intellectuals in a revolutionary context and let the environment act on them." Cultural officials proposed to do this by "giving them tasks, listening to their problems, forming working groups, sending them to international events, situating them in centers of production . . . making them feel like they are trusted, that they are valued, that they are essential to the work of building a new society."[136] In this spirit, the same period also witnessed the 1968 Cultural Congress, the culmination of Cuban leaders' outreach to anti-imperialist, Leftist, and Global South intellectuals. The event brought together some 400 writers and artists from seventy countries to debate, among other topics, the political responsibilities of committed intellectuals.[137]

In this regard, the Cultural Congress reflected developments within the Cuban intellectual sphere as well. It coincided with a brief experimental period in which, Kepa Artaraz argues, island thinkers found space to "theorize the Revolution in original and specifically Cuban ways," often in dialogue with their foreign counterparts.[138] This current found its fullest expression in the pages of *Pensamiento Crítico* (inaugurated in 1967), which featured a "return to Marx's original writings in the hope of making Marxism relevant to an understanding of Cuba's recent history and in opposition to those who advocated the adoption of Soviet interpretations."[139] With an Althusserian accent, those affiliated with *Pensamiento Crítico*, many of them members of the philosophy department at the University of Havana, sought to establish themselves as both theorists and practitioners of Revolution.[140] Arguing that making Revolution and producing knowledge about the Revolution were essentially interdependent activities, their work established critique as not inimical but rather immanent to revolutionary process.[141] The vitality of these conversations was abetted by the appointment of University of Havana philosophy professor Rolando Rodríguez to the directorship of Cuba's Instituto del Libro, where he oversaw the Cuban publication of Gramsci and Althusser.[142]

But only a few years later, *Pensamiento Crítico* became another casualty of the gray years, dashing the hopes of many in Cuba's homegrown New

Left as well as their international interlocutors.[143] Behind the scenes, the Cultural Congress also reflected the tense engagement between revolutionary officials and Cuban intellectuals. Notably, leaders had restricted the participation of a group of Afro-Cuban artists and writers, including Rogelio Martínez Furé, Walterio Carbonell, Nancy Morejón, Sara Gómez, and Nicolas Guillén Landrián, who reportedly had planned to raise the issue of persistent racism at the event.[144] Several of them had previously been rebuked by Minister of Education José Llanusa Gobel in a meeting about their concerns, where, Carlos Moore relates, the minister "told the group they were being virtually 'seditious'" and that the "Revolution would allow no sort of activity that would 'divide' the people along racial lines."[145] In addition to experiencing censorship and professional marginalization, Carbonell and Guillén Landrián suffered more punitive consequences, including forced labor and psychiatric institutionalization. In the process, a critical rethinking of race in Cuba's past and present was prematurely silenced.[146]

Both of these shifts—an intellectual opening, followed by its precipitous shuttering—were registered by a first generation of professional Revolution scholars, who found in late 1960s Cuba a newly appealing destination for research. One of the most notable was Stanford political scientist Richard Fagen, a former colleague of Theodore Draper's at the Hoover Institution. Unique among US Revolution scholars, Fagen did not publicly identify or disidentify with the Revolution, though he praised those authors who helped to "elevate discussion about the Cuban Revolution to the level of reasonable and adult dialogue."[147] Instead, Fagen's enduring influence stemmed from the novel questions he posed, particularly his emphasis on political culture.

As an assistant professor in Stanford's Institute for Communication Research, Fagen made multiple attempts to travel to Cuba to advance that project.[148] But Fagen's efforts were impeded by the US travel ban and, on at least one occasion, by the revolutionary government as well. Undaunted, Fagen turned to high-placed allies in Cuba and the United States, especially journalist Lisa Howard, who, along with Ronald Hilton, promised to provide Fagen with a journalistic cover for the trip. While Fagen waited for approval to travel, his early work on the Revolution—dealing with Castro's leadership style, among other matters—was conducted long-distance.[149] The impediments to island research had in the meantime forced him to reimagine the project for which he had received funding from the Social Sciences Research Council, which became one of the first academic studies of the Cuban exile community, *Cubans in Exile: Disaffection and the Revolution*

(1968).[150] Soon thereafter, Fagen was finally authorized to travel to Cuba as a press representative in 1966 and then again in 1968.

In fact, in the late 1960s, US researchers were afforded a window of opportunity to travel to the island, giving rise to early talks between delegates from the newly established Latin American Studies Association (LASA) and Antonio Núñez Jiménez, president of the Cuban Academia de Ciencias. Beginning in 1967, the Ford Foundation also began to carefully promote the academic study of Cuba at Yale University, the University of Miami, and the University of Florida. Ford representatives recognized that there was political uncertainty attached to this work, including legal hurdles to travel as well as the question of "whether the Cubans would permit American scholars to work freely inside Cuba," or even those "Europeans and Latin Americans" who identified as "politically uncommitted." According to political scientist Kalman H. Silvert, who coordinated these efforts and served as the first president of LASA, success thus depended on avoiding "political chicanery."[151] Yet there were positive signs, including incipient conversations about bilateral academic outreach and the upcoming trips of several early career US scholars, including Marvin Leiner, an education professor at Queens College, and Bertram Silverman, an economist at Hofstra.[152]

For Fagen, it was also in the late 1960s that doors on the island seemed to finally open. This was in part because he, like C. Wright Mills before him, came to count René Vallejo, a physician and close sierra ally of Fidel Castro's, among his Cuban contacts.[153] The two men maintained an active correspondence following Fagen's first trip in 1966, from Vallejo's inquiries about US agricultural equipment and goods (forwarded through the Cuban Mission to the United Nations) to various publications, including Fagen's work on the Revolution and, at his request, a signed copy of Fidel Castro's "La historia me absolverá" speech.[154] Vallejo even reported having read one of Fagen's articles to Castro himself, who reportedly "found it very interesting and said [Fagen] had indeed grasped the essence of what [they were] trying to do."[155]

Fagen's trips to the island and the informal interviews he conducted there decisively shaped his 1969 book, *The Transformation of Political Culture in Cuba*. Fagen argued that revolutionary mobilizations (the 1961 literacy campaign) and institutions (the Schools of Revolutionary Instruction [Escuelas de Instrucción Revolucionaria] and the Committees for the Defense of the Revolution [Comités de Defensa de la Revolución]) had been central to constructing a new political culture, rooted in perpetual militancy. Though such language has since become second nature to scholars of post-1959 Cuba, Fagen was one of its pioneers, whose work helped to shift the emphasis of Latin American studies away from structuralist economic approaches, as Ernst Halperin has pointed out.[156]

The first two pages of *The Transformation of Political Culture in Cuba* notably include no references to Communism, supplanted by a more encompassing emphasis on "radicalism."[157] Economic and political radicalization along Marxist (or Leninist) lines was an important part of that process. But Fagen aimed to redirect attention from the *what* to the *how*, specifically the role ascribed to the masses in the island's emergent political culture. Where other observers had depicted Communism as the motor of revolutionary process, Fagen suggested that such changes were secondary to a more primary process: the "transformation of Cuban man into revolutionary man."[158]

Vallejo expressed enthusiasm about *The Transformation of Political Culture in Cuba*, which he expected would "be quite a book" and "cause a lot of controversy."[159] But they never had the opportunity to discuss it in person, due to the physician's untimely death at the age of forty-nine. When Fagen returned to the island in 1969, just in time to attend Vallejo's funeral, he discovered that the climate for academic exchange had worsened considerably. Despite fruitful meetings with Cuban social scientists—including psychologist Aníbal Rodríguez, sociologist Gilda Betancourt, and anthropologist Argeliers Leon at the University of Havana—Fagen predicted that it would soon be nearly impossible for "Yankee" scholars to conduct serious research on the island. This was due both to the "obvious political set of reasons" and the "shortage of resources" that had left island researchers struggling to access "pencils" and "paper."[160]

At that point, Oscar and Ruth Lewis's oral history project, an endeavor in sync with Fagen's work on political culture, was well underway. The Lewises had come to Cuba with Ford sponsorship and the personal backing of Fidel Castro, who admired Oscar's previous work on the "culture of poverty" in Mexico City and Puerto Rico.[161] Granted official support and assisted, but also overseen by, a ten-person team from the Union of Young Communists (UJC, Unión de Jóvenes Comunistas), the couple planned to spend several years conducting interviews with former slum residents in Havana. Their aim was to track the impact of revolutionary change on formerly marginalized citizens to determine, as Lillian Guerra writes, "whether the combination of socialism and the revolutionary government's demand for political participation had eliminated or reduced an array of socially deviant behaviors and values."[162] The result of their efforts was unprecedented documentation of the

Revolution from below, totaling "some 20,000 pages of transcripts."[163] For officials, Guerra argues, the interviews also served as a vehicle of surveillance, encompassing slum residents and the foreign researchers who proposed to study them.[164]

The convergence of Fidel Castro's political goals with the academic approach of the Lewises, as well as the couple's sympathy for the Revolution, certainly explains their unprecedented access.[165] But the Lewises were also affected by changing political circumstances. To the consternation of the UJC militants who worked alongside them, the researchers had uncovered perspectives that did not adhere to the narrative of "revolutionary redemption and rupture," prompting the official termination of the project.[166] Summoned to appear before Minister of Foreign Relations Raul Roa, they were accused of "subverting national security," while their Cuban informants met with more serious consequences, including "forced labor" and "house arrest" in at least one case.[167] As a result of the controversy, the Cuban government did not grant visas to any Americans in 1971, or for several years to come.[168]

Joining the Lewises in their fall from grace was Polish-born journalist K. S. Karol. Karol had a long and complicated track record with international Communism, stemming from his family's deportation from Poland to the Soviet Union in 1939. Years later, his disillusionment with Stalinism in Russia and his native Poland led him into exile in France. By 1954, Karol had become a correspondent for the British magazine the *New Statesman*, charged with covering "Communist affairs."[169] In that capacity, he undertook his first reporting trip to Cuba in 1961. Throughout the mid-1960s, Karol's attention turned to China, but he returned to Cuba for two extended research trips to Cuba in 1967 and '68, during which he—along with Huberman and Sweezy, Oscar Lewis, and others—awaited a much-deferred "meeting with the *jefe máximo*."[170]

When they finally sat down for a conversation at Castro's farm retreat, too much rum and Karol's halting Spanish impeded his ability to express the "critical observations" he wanted to share with Fidel.[171] But they would soon take published form in a 600-page book, *Les Guérilleros au pouvoir: L'itinéraire politique de la révolution cubaine* (1970). *Guerrillas in Power*, published in English the same year, chronicled the Revolution's first decade, as it navigated a variety of internal challenges and external threats. Karol found much to admire in the independent path charted by Cuban leaders, particularly in the face of US opposition. But he also expressed concerns about the form Cuban socialism had taken, including its top-heavy quality and the imitation of Soviet precedents. "The building of socialism cannot be the business of one man or of a single group of men, however well-intentioned," he wrote.[172]

In an August 1970 preface to the book, Karol declared that his work had been conducted "in a spirit of solidarity with the Cuban Revolution."[173] But Karol's discrepancies with revolutionary officials, especially Castro himself, were too substantial to be glossed over. *Guerrillas in Power* quickly became an international cause célèbre, prompting a publishing blockade at the Spanish press Siglo Veintiuno and furtive circulation on the island.[174] Meanwhile, Karol, who had once been told by Castro that he should "write what he [saw], critique," found himself at the center of an intellectual counteroffensive on the island spearheaded by Alfredo Guevara, the founding director of the Instituto Cubano del Arte e Industria Cinematográficos (Cuban Institute of Cinematographic Art and Industry).[175]

Without mentioning their names, Fidel Castro excoriated onetime allies like Karol and René Dumont in an April 1970 speech: "There are many who write about the Cuban Revolution," he observed. "Some of them don't even merit a response because they're obviously agents of Yankee imperialism." But there was another group, Castro posited, who had to be publicly debated: those "little writers on the Left [*escritorzuelos de izquierda*]" who, "from Rome or Paris, erect imaginary, hypothetical worlds."[176] Such false friends, he implied, were the most dangerous. A few months later, in an unprecedented public mea culpa, Fidel was forced to recognize that the 10-million-ton harvest projected for 1970 had fallen short of the mark, as Dumont and others had warned. This admission raised sensitive questions about the fallibility of revolutionary officials while also validating the critiques of foreign experts.[177] Yet even as Castro conceded that errors had been made, his words told a different story: "Our *enemies* say we have difficulties, and in that respect our *enemies* are right."[178]

The Padilla affair brought these tensions to a head. In the late 1960s, Padilla, once firmly integrated into the revolutionary cultural establishment, had begun to feel at odds with growing cultural repression. His protest took poetic form in the 1968 volume *Fuera del juego*, which had been awarded the top prize of Cuba's Union of Artists and Writers but published with a warning about its counterrevolutionary content. Padilla then became the object of a campaign against intellectual heterodoxy, waged from the pages of the military magazine *Verde Olivo*. Finally, on March 20, 1971, Padilla was imprisoned for his inconformity and, ostensibly, his efforts to publish critical work abroad. Two weeks later, he was forced to issue a public self-criticism as a condition of his release from prison, in which he implicated himself in the research of Karol and Dumont and denounced them as "counterrevolutionaries."[179] Raúl Alonso Olivé, the Cuban agronomist Castro had personally designated to work with Dumont, was also imprisoned for his critiques of the government. He subsequently appeared on TV and confessed to having collaborated with the CIA, accompanied by a dramatized sketch "representing the betrayal of the two men."[180]

Padilla's *auto-crítica* provoked indignation among writers in Europe and Latin America, many formerly supportive of the revolutionary government. In a public letter, cultural luminaries such as Gabriel García Márquez, Octavio Paz, and Jean-Paul Sartre warned that the "use of repressive measures against intellectuals and writers who have exercised their right to criticize from within the revolution can only have deeply negative repercussions among the anti-imperialist forces of the whole world."[181] Charles Bettelheim was also among those who permanently broke with the Revolution in a May 1971 letter to *Le Monde*. That statement prompted a rebuke from the Asociación de Amistad Francia-Cuba and the cancellation of a forthcoming book with Cuba's Editorial de Ciencias Sociales on the grounds that he had "[attacked] the Revolution."[182] Bettelheim responded by decrying the island's "campaign of defamation directed against honorable people, whom I know and whose work merits respect, even if I don't agree with everything they've said."[183] This became his last public declaration about Cuba.[184]

Castro and other revolutionary officials would revisit these battles for years to come. In August 1972, Osvaldo Dorticós told Herbert Matthews that Karol had "put words in his mouth that he never said; distorted a number of things he did say; and generally gave a false slant," while also "not telling him of his ideas and beliefs although there was no reason not to."[185] Carlos Rafael Rodríguez similarly bemoaned the "capricious distortions" of foreign "theorists," "sometimes in the name of a false friendship and at other times in the name of a true friendship, but always with a misunderstanding of our realities."[186] A few months earlier, the former Canadian ambassador to Cuba informed Matthews that Fidel had "become most suspicious of all foreign writers on Cuba."[187]

The feeling of betrayal was mutual. Leftist intellectuals around the world had flocked to the island because it seemed to provide a hospitable environment for critical inquiry, with *auto-crítica* the ostensible foundation of revolutionary praxis and governance alike. Even critics such as Dumont recognized that Cuban officials tended to be more open to their intervention than their counterparts elsewhere. Over the course of the 1960s, the berth for dialogic critique widened or narrowed in concert with the evolution of the revolutionary project and its economic trajectory. Yet it existed—until suddenly, it didn't.

Some observers found the disaffection of Leftist intellectuals to be, in a word, disingenuous. After all, the erosion of civil liberties in Cuba dated to the early 1960s, the point of rupture for many liberals and anti-Stalinists in the Draper camp. As Norman Podhoretz mused in the pages of *Commentary*, "If the imprisonment of Hubert Matos and so many thousands of others . . . could not arouse the libertarian ire of the radical intelligentsia of Paris and New York, why should the arrest of Heberto Padilla have done so?" His theory was that the controversy had "served these intellectuals as a convenient pretext for jettisoning Castro and the Cuban Revolution, not for the crime of Stalinism . . . but for the crime of failure."[188]

But whereas Podhoretz sees Padilla as a "pretext," we might instead view his case as an apotheosis. The revolutionary transformation of Cuba had drawn experts around the world energized by the opportunity to build a new kind of socialism, informed *by* expertise. The publications of foreign intellectuals sustained interest in and shaped opinions on that experiment. In many cases, they remain essential reading on the Revolution today.

Both in its domestic and global reverberations, however, the *quinquenio gris* turned the revolutionary romance with expertise toward confrontation. One after another, sympathetic intellectuals discovered that their criticisms had crossed a line, especially as the course of socialist transformation (which many had hoped to shape) began to falter by the late 1960s. The encounter between the island and its experts made the status of intellectual inquiry an international referendum on the Revolution itself, and irrevocably so. Thereafter, it would be impossible to produce knowledge about the Revolution without inheriting this political baggage. And so almost any publication about the Revolution has become a metatextual entry in this field, implicitly bound to the history that came before it and thus informed by the seeming impossibility of neutrality.

Cubanists/"Cubanologists"

It was in these improbable, seemingly unpropitious circumstances that Cuban studies was born. As the Revolution embarked on a decade of institutionalization and incorporation into the Soviet bloc, its US-based scholars, many of Cuban descent, began to organize across political lines. One of the pioneers of the field was economist Carmelo Mesa-Lago, who established its first journal, the *Cuban Studies Newsletter,* as a bibliographical reference, a mission that *Cuban Studies,* another recipient of Ford Foundation funding, would assume in 1975.[189] Jorge Domínguez explains that this focus was no accident: "Because it seemed so difficult to discuss Cuba without bitter polemics, the only resource on whose worth everyone agreed was bibliographic."[190] Even as the periodical expanded its scope, it maintained its founding commitment to airing "divergent ideologies and interpretations, provided that the work of those with opposing points of view is objective and scholarly," as Mesa-Lago put it.[191]

Cubanists, as they would be known, set Revolution studies on a newly rigorous intellectual footing, even as the "most prominent" remained hampered, in the estimation of the Ford Foundation, by their inability to do "field work" in Cuba.[192] This did not mean, however, that they abandoned the extramural advocacy of their predecessors. One of the most important sites for such work was the Instituto de Estudios Cubanos, established in 1969 under the direction of María Cristina Herrera, where "deep, serious, and respectful" conversations about Cuba were initiated among Cuban American researchers.[193] At the institute and more radical outlets like the magazine *Areíto,* a new Cuban American Left, galvanized by political struggles in the United States, prioritized dialogue with its island-based counterparts—and, to the extent possible, travel to Cuba—as both a political and intellectual mission.[194]

LASA also served as an important vehicle for such work, and the LASA presidencies of Fagen and Mesa-Lago, among others, helped to consolidate Cuba connections.[195] Scholarly exchange between the two countries thereafter evolved in concert with US-Cuban relations writ large, with an opening in the late 1970s (Carter) followed by an abrupt reversal (Reagan).[196] Whatever the state of Cuba policy, however, impediments to intellectual inquiry on the island have rarely featured prominently on LASA's agenda, as critics have charged. At the same time, per a handwritten note on a 1977 Ford memo, a conspicuous silence in Revolution scholarship persisted— namely, the voices of Cubans themselves.[197]

The Cubanists' commitment to objectivity, the unattainability of which many freely acknowledged, inspired criticism from all sides.[198] Some of the most vociferous continued to come from the island, where the "*cubanólogos*" (a sardonic reference to the Kremlinologists) were charged with embodying a "branch of bourgeois ideology, characterized by its essentially negative vision of the political, economic, and social evolution of the Cuban

Revolution."[199] Critic José Luis Rodríguez García further alleged that the ultimate aim of their work was to "demonstrate, beneath an academic cover and presumed scientific objectivity, the unviability of socialism in Cuba."[200] Yet their more fundamental sin, as one "top cultural official" privately told Mesa-Lago in 1978, may have been their inability to truly share the *vivencia* (experience) of the Revolution.[201]

· · · · · ·

As of 1969, according to one Cuban social scientist, a published account of the Revolution's first decade, grounded in that shared *vivencia*, remained a pending task on the Cuban side as well.[202] Behind the scenes, however, the research that might shape it was underway. Earlier in the decade, Cuban ethnographers, in collaboration with East German colleagues, had conducted an island-wide reconnaissance expedition. Their aim was to turn Cuban ethnography—traditionally focused on the "most exotic manifestations" of Afro-Cuban culture, per one account—into an instrument for tracing the "economic, social, and cultural transformations achieved by the Cuban Revolution."[203] To that end, they proposed to recruit ordinary Cubans, from *alfabetizadores* to peasant leaders, as agents and objects of their research.[204] Throughout the decade that followed, this mission became a staple of the social sciences in Cuba, as psychology, sociology, and anthropology came of age with the Revolution.[205] Fieldwork was in turn cast as a vehicle to document and facilitate revolutionary consolidation.[206]

At the center of their work, as chapters 6 and 7 explore, was the question of revolutionary integration. In putting the social sciences at the service of revolutionary governance, those drafted to represent the state in this capacity sought not only to excavate the impact of revolutionary socialism but also to identify and incorporate its subjects. Cultivating homegrown expertise in Revolution thus became a matter of seeing like—and seeing *through*—the state. The many Cubans so hailed became accustomed to seeing, and being seen by, the state. Some thus gained access to new forms of recognition and even exemplary subjecthood; others, meanwhile, worked to avoid the state's increasingly encompassing gaze.

6 The Revolutionary Work (of) Culture

· ·

Despite its heterodox foundations, the advent of Cuban socialism bore a strong Russian accent. As in the Soviet Union, and revolutionary France before it, the Cuban Revolution spurred linguistic transformation, disseminating a new vocabulary of Marxist application.[1] The 1960s and '70s thus saw the penetration of Russian into Cuban Spanish, countering its early twentieth-century "colonization" in the era of US occupation (though *jonrones* persisted).[2] But the implications of this shift were not solely semantic. Russianization channeled leaders' efforts to build communism by reshaping Cuba's human texture, perhaps even to "manipulate the thoughts of the 'new Cuban man,'" as linguist Oscar Pino contended, "by reforming the instrument [he] uses in his thinking."[3] Much as Soviet subjects had learned to "speak Bolshevik," so Cubans became fluent in socialism—with a distinct, though not exclusively, Soviet imprint.[4]

Can new words produce new mentalities? This chapter follows the course of two such terms—*superación* (roughly, "self-improvement") and *emulación* ("emulation," a socialist analogue to "competition")—that were enduringly recast in revolutionary Cuba. These concepts and the campaigns in which they took shape channeled official efforts to frame culture and work as crucibles of *conciencia*, or social commitment, rather than grounds for material compensation. Drawing on Soviet principles, both centered the cultivation of individual discipline in the quest to build communism. This was a fundamentally millenarian effort, with its emphasis on present-day exertion as the path to future utopia. Yet *superación* and *emulación* also survived the abandonment of that endeavor after the failed 10-million-ton sugar harvest of 1970, becoming, if anything, more pervasive in its aftermath. The words thus capture Cubans' translational engagement with transnational precedents, as the Revolution evolved from sui generis experimentalism in the 1960s to Soviet-style institutionalization in the 1970s.

Throughout these years, *superación* and *emulación* were cornerstones of the Cuban quest to forge new subjects: men and women who would work for the benefit of all without the incentive of financial reward. The institutions and mobilizations developed in the service of this goal, from the literacy campaign to popular militias to mass organizations, fundamentally changed the texture of everyday life. Whether *conciencia*—or communism—did (or, in the final analysis, did not) overtake the hearts and minds of ordinary Cubans, it nonetheless propelled the synergetic interaction between political activities and popular mentalities. In Richard Fagen's analysis, participation thus served as "motive and motor of the revolutionary effort."[5]

As island leaders constructed new socialist routines, they cultivated the work of, and work as, culture, in the Soviet spirit of "working on oneself."[6] Revolutionary initiatives of the 1960s sought to impart the discipline of work to the pursuit of culture and endow labor (especially of the productive variety) with cultural meaning. Such prescriptions drew on prerevolutionary precedents—from José Martí's canonical maxim that to be "cultured" was to be "free" to the long-standing politicization of agricultural labor—but expanded dramatically after 1959, gobbling up resources, energy, and time itself.

Throughout these years, Cubans were exhorted to allocate their few free hours to the pursuit of *superación*. The 1961 literacy campaign inaugurated what would become an enduring emphasis on the importance of education, extending to night classes, technical instruction, and Marxist schools. The value of such training bore an instrumentalist function, as officials worked to build cadres of revolutionary technicians, workers, and, ultimately, party members. But this was far from the only purpose ascribed to self-improvement. In the spirit of their Bolshevik predecessors, Cuban leaders theorized that the pursuit of culture would level social hierarchies and hasten the arrival of communism.

The socialization of culture served as both a horizontally equalizing force and a vertically integrating one, particularly when harnessed toward the political goals of the state. Here I foreground the so-called aficionado movement, which promoted cultural practice among historically marginalized and politically important constituencies, including workers, peasants, and students. There were tensions inherent to this project, including the elitist or folkloric definition of culture that at times drove and homogenized such efforts.[7] But the aficionado program could also be radical in its consequences, as Cubans who previously enjoyed little access to organized cultural activity began to reimagine themselves as artists and performers. In this they were guided by a new class of "arts instructors," some of them recruited from among their ranks. Theater thus entered the workplace, modern dance invaded state farms, and aficionados and instructors elaborated new artistic and political routines. Meanwhile, cultural officials promulgated a standardized repertoire that prompted aficionados to *perform* their incorporation into the state.

As ordinary Cubans entered the ranks of cultural performers, they were also drafted into campaigns of socialist emulation. Drawing on Leninist precedent, emulation encouraged workers to compete against one another (and themselves) to reach productive goals. Revolutionary officials thus sought to restructure work around collective aims and universalize its application. Socialist competition promoted new structures, values, and rhythms within and beyond the workplace. Over the course of the 1960s, emulation underscored a growing emphasis on nonmaterial compensation, while expanding the definition of "work" to include all militancy on behalf of the Revolution.

The economic payoff of emulation was clear: with the radicalization of the Cuban economic project over the course of the 1960s, it provided an instrument to promote agricultural, production, and political goals at a lower cost. But *emulación*, like *superación*, also bore utopian implications, namely the hope that it would forge communist subjects. By the mid-1960s, revolutionary officials exalted a new class of vanguard workers as avatars of that future. At the same time, emulation assumed an increasingly coercive edge with the expanding reach of uncompensated labor in the late 1960s and campaigns against absenteeism and "vagrancy" by the turn of the 1970s.

By then, revolutionary officials had come to terms with the fact that communism was not just around the corner. But as they worked to put socialism on a more stable footing, they did not abandon their commitment to the aficionado program on the one hand or socialist competition on the other. *Superación* and *emulación* endured, I propose, because of their continued importance in framing the relationship between the state and the populace. From the concert hall to the cane field, affiliated campaigns centered on discipline in the Foucauldian sense, spawning new mechanisms of oversight, assessment, and visibility. These efforts made the Revolution perceptible to ordinary Cubans, while constituting them as legible subjects of state power.

In this, discipline served as a reciprocal vehicle of knowledge production for revolutionary officials and subjects alike. As islanders were drawn into new socialist routines, these practices became important epistemological vehicles, rendering Marxist precedent in the complexity of revolutionary practice and facilitating both empowerment and repression. The work of culture thus channeled the paradoxes of building utopia one day at a time, as Cubans embarked on a seemingly perpetual apprenticeship to communism.

The School of Revolution

"The best book, our true textbook in matters of revolution," Fidel Castro declared in September 1967, "will be the revolutionary process itself."[8] In this, he and other Cuban officials sought to subordinate theory to practice, routing the Revolution away from rote Marxist application. Yet in opposing "books" to "process," Castro's words perhaps obscure the revolutionary investment in reading *as* practice. In fact, from the earliest days of the Revolution, literacy was imagined as a vehicle to promote political integration. Books thus served to both disseminate revolutionary theory and channel revolutionary process.

The September 1959 launch of the Festival del Libro Cubano (Cuban Book Festival), for example, sought to expand—and politicize—the island's reading public.[9] Featured works included selections from the Western canon but also touchstones in the island's political history, such as the largely disappeared work of student and Communist Party activist Julio Antonio Mella.[10] These efforts were accompanied by an explosion in domestic publishing. Featured titles included cheap paperback editions of *Don Quixote*, *Marco Polo*, and *Robinson Crusoe*, as well as a "biography of Simón Bolívar, and a history of the French Revolution."[11]

At the same time, the Biblioteca Nacional (National Library) in Havana began to expand its hours (including a night shift) and grow its roster of readers.[12] Yet one did not need to be physically present to access its holdings. The so-called Telephone Library made answers to any number of questions—including Fidel Castro's birthday, the meaning of "philosophical eclecticism," and a recipe for fish flan—just a quick dial away.[13] The Biblioteca Nacional also launched the island's first circulating collection, augmented by the establishment of traveling libraries, and the new Department of Library Extension. There, librarians collaborated with unions, workplaces, and mass organizations to bring books directly to workers, housewives, and other remote readers.[14]

The cornerstone of efforts to cultivate reading was the 1961 literacy campaign, in which armies of young volunteers fanned out across the country. The campaign came to incorporate some 271,000 volunteer teachers and 707,000 "new literates" (those who had achieved a first-grade level in reading and writing) and achieved a reported literacy rate of 96.1 percent by 1962.[15] But the importance of the initiative exceeded statistical outcomes. The military language attached to the campaign reflected the ideological significance with which the leadership had invested it, also evident in the politicized content of its textbooks and lesson plans. In this respect, the literacy campaign served above all as a vehicle of ideological instruction and social "fusion."[16]

The impetus for education did not end with the literacy campaign, nor did the linking of popular literacy to political goals. In its aftermath, a variety of initiatives sought to extend its effects, including the Program for Worker and Peasant Education, which developed a curriculum for Seguimiento (grades 1–3). A curriculum for Superación Obrera (grades 4–6) promoted the acquisition of math and Spanish skills and expanded into the so-called Battle for Sixth Grade, which by 1973 had seen some 500,000 adult graduates. New initiatives, such as the Escuelas de Superación de la Mujer (run by the Federación de Mujeres Cubanas), sought to bring school into the home, while others targeted the workplace, including a 1964 campaign spearheaded by the Confederation of Cuban Workers (CTC).[17]

As Cubans quickly discovered, the pursuit of education was a definitionally indefinite process. It spanned the Mínimo Técnico program, which promoted a "minimum technical understanding" among workers; polytechnic institutes; Facultades Preparatorias Obrero-Campesinas (Worker-Peasant Preparatory Schools); and new worker and peasant colleges in Havana, Santa Clara, and Santiago.[18] As one woman recalled of her young adulthood, in which she worked during the day and attended English classes after hours at the recently opened *facultad obrera* in her hometown, she was "almost always engaged in some kind of learning."[19] By the late 1960s, nearly one-third (27.6 percent) of the island's population was "getting some form of organized instruction."[20]

The goal, in the words of Raúl Ferrer, director of Worker-Farmer Education, was for "every worker to be a student, and every student to be a worker."[21] During their 1968 trip to the island, Leo Huberman and Paul Sweezy encountered one such worker-student, a molder at the Nícaro nickel plant, who had joined the plant with a third-grade education. Over the course of several years, night school had netted him a promotion (from a day laborer to a molder) and a raise. But the gains, Huberman and Sweezy proposed, were more consequential than this: "What began as a matter of principle for the revolutionary government—that it is unjust and morally wrong for education to be denied to all the people . . . has turned out . . . to be the key to the problem of revolutionizing Cuba."[22]

That conjoining of economic and ideological goals also inspired the founding of the Escuelas de Instrucción Revolucionaria (EIRs, Schools for Revolutionary Instruction), quietly opened in January 1961 before the so-

cialist character of the Revolution was publicly announced. Building on previous initiatives within the Ministry of Armed Forces, the EIRs aimed to
bring together the sometimes warring revolutionary factions "under the
philosophical umbrella of Marxism-Leninism."[23] With the April 1961 inauguration of the Escuelas Básicas de Instrucción Revolucionaria (EBIRs, Basic Schools of Revolutionary Instruction), this became a more far-reaching
enterprise, incorporating, as of July 1962, some 12,748 students, 76.4 percent
of them under the age of thirty-five.[24] Across the country, many more joined
study circles sponsored by Committees for the Defense of the Revolution,
unions, and other mass organizations, where they, like their counterparts
in the EBIRs, studied Fidel Castro's speeches and longtime Popular Socialist Party (PSP) militant Blas Roca's *Los fundamentos de socialismo en Cuba*,
the most published book in Cuba in 1962.[25]

Despite its political potential, Marxist education in Cuba suffered from
significant weaknesses, including nepotism in the selection of students and
the low educational levels of teachers and students alike.[26] By 1968, amid a
broader questioning of Soviet models and "manualism," the schools had
been shuttered, not to be reopened until the early 1970s.[27] But the campaign
for Marxist learning was not a wholesale failure. In this, as in other educational campaigns, Fagen contends that the objective was less Marxist conversion than revolutionary integration *through* socialism.[28]

Theoretical Marxism offered a curriculum, but the work of political
instruction sat at the nexus of book learning and practical application.
"The Schools," Fidel Castro proposed in 1961, were the "result of that
synthesis, in which, at last, theory and practice [marched] in lockstep."[29]
To hasten the arrival of communism, Cubans had to study (and study
Marxism), but they also had to practice it. Revolutionary practice was, in
turn, centered on work: hence, the omnipresent mantra of "work-study."
Whether in the literacy campaign (in which teachers worked side by side
with their students), the "school cities" opened for peasants, or the boarding schools established in 1966 for children entering the sixth grade and
above, pedagogical initiatives always extended beyond the classroom into
the fields.[30]

Throughout the 1960s and '70s, Cubans thus engaged in new routines of
socialist cultivation in which work and study, labor and culture, sat side by
side. These activities depended in turn on an underlying theory of *embodi-
ment*: the notion that mental states, even pathological ones, could be transformed through bodily practice. In this emerging repertoire, which included
military drills, mountain climbs, baseball, and the inescapable *fisiminuto*

with which Cubans were encouraged to begin their days, productive work undoubtedly occupied the most prominent place.[31] But cultural change was not a unidirectional process. If activity was envisioned as a means to transform mentalities, mentalities were also expected to act on bodily practice—to transform Cubans' relationship to the body itself, as in the official valorization of manual labor. This mode of socialist cultivation joined mind and body and propelled the theoretical (that is, dialectical) interaction between them, thus forging *conciencia*.

If such routines established an everyday praxis for building a utopian future, they also functioned as a mode of socialist discipline.[32] Here I draw on Michel Foucault's portrayal of discipline as the "specific technique of a power that regards individuals both as objects and as instruments of its exercise."[33] Through "hierarchical observation," "normalizing judgment," and "examination," discipline turns each individual into a "case," Foucault argues, bound up in the production of knowledge and the reproduction of power. Particularly relevant is his emphasis on "training": those practices, from military drills to school exams, which make individuals objects of power and subjects as a result, thus serving both productive and repressive ends.

Programs of *superación* and *emulación* implicated individuals in new power relations that made them revolutionary subjects—and sometimes outstanding representatives thereof. The campaign to forge collective consciousness thus relied on an expansive program of *individuation*. These efforts functioned as a vehicle to transmit revolutionary values, as we will see below, and to castigate those who lagged behind. But they also served as a relational structure through which Cubans were "seen" in the act of integrating themselves into new institutional structures (or refusing to do so). Significantly, social scientists enlisted by political officials to analyze the Revolution's advance increasingly foregrounded "integration" itself as the principal metric for assessing revolutionary adhesion.[34] As a result of the campaign for *conciencia*, all Cubans became objects of socialist discipline—and, in turn, subjects of the Revolution, willing or not.

Socializing Culture

A 1962 *Bohemia* report captures a group of artists in a moment of contemplation—and perhaps voyeurism. A contest launched by Havana's Provincial Council of Culture called for artists to submit drawings of the May 1 parade as well as fishermen and cane cutters at work. Cultural offi-

"The sea," this caption reads, "has always been a point of inspiration for the artist. But now it's not just the sails, the mast, and the reflection of the water that feature in his work. The painter is also moved by the unparalleled spectacle of man's work." Castillo, "Artistas con el pueblo," *Bohemia*, November 2, 1962, 96–97.

cials had hoped that having participants bear witness to labor and engage its relationship to artistic practice might "dissolve the wall of ice that capitalism had raised between artists and the people."[35] But this initiative also raised questions that would recur throughout the decade to come: Were artists workers? And how could workers, in turn, become artists?

These concerns would inspire revolutionary campaigns to "socialize" Cuban culture, bringing culture to the masses and the masses to culture. In these efforts, the working classes were a principal target, not only because they had long been excluded from the pursuit of high culture but also because they were seen as uniquely vulnerable to foreign media. From the beginning, expanding access to culture was thus linked to consolidating ideological authority, to eradicating, as one journalist put it, the "influence that imperialist ideology has achieved among us." He proposed that revolutionary officials had in turn assembled the "necessary weapons" for a "bloodless battle for the intellectual and artistic cultivation of our population."[36]

These included the Department of Theater Extension at Cuba's Teatro Nacional, which grew a popular audience by distributing free tickets in workplaces. It also took theater on the road with the famed Brigadas de Teatro Francisco Covarrubias, which traveled throughout the country staging works for workers and peasants.[37] In a kindred spirit, as of 1962 the Department of Film, Television, and Radio at the Consejo Nacional de Cultura (CNC, or National Culture Council) programmed film series and sent "mobile cinemas" into the island's most remote corners; inaugurated new television programs, such as the enduring *Pueblo y cultura*; opened a Popular Arts Market; and sponsored Popular Bookshelves, with public readings and workshops.[38] Building on previous efforts in the armed forces spearheaded by long-standing PSP members,[39] the department also curated a Revolutionary Film series, which it screened in "factories, student dorms, teacher training schools," and "centers for the rehabilitation of women and children." In the audience discussions that followed, "trained" moderators were charged with highlighting the "revolutionary quality of each work" as well as its "projections for our current national situation."[40]

The two missions that inspired such initiatives—promoting culture for the masses and disseminating revolutionary politics through culture—were also at the heart of the much-vaunted aficionado, or amateur arts, movement. As Robin Moore writes, the program, which built on earlier collaborations between the Department of Theater Extension, the CTC, and the Institute for Agrarian Reform (INRA), aimed to "challenge . . . the very concept of the artist in capitalist society," including the practice of compensation.[41] The program brought together otherwise unlikely allies, from historic PSP militants, who exercised significant influence on cultural policy in this period, to those who had long manifested a nonideological commitment to "cultural improvement," as Cary García Yero has explored.[42]

In fact, many activists at the Department of Theater Extension had participated in prerevolutionary campaigns to extend cultural access, from Paco Alfonso's CTC-sponsored Teatro Popular in Havana to the "cultural missions" of the Ministry of Education in the late 1940s and early '50s.[43] Some were also activists in the 26th of July Movement, which had centered cultural outreach in its early pronouncements, including a 1959 manifesto that proposed "to stimulate any [artistic work] that most appealed to the public, that was made by the public."[44] But cultural officials also turned to the Soviet Union for inspiration. During an early trip to the Eastern bloc, Carlos Franqui marveled over the "Culture Palaces," where workers could "become actors, musicians, and dancers."[45] The heterogeneous inspirations behind the aficionado movement likely reinforced the shared conviction that it would contribute to the public's "ideological education."[46]

At the First Provincial Festival of Aficionados, held at Havana's Payret Theater in September 1962, political integration was both the text and the subtext of the proceedings. Among the sixty theater and dance groups that participated, one of the most celebrated entries was a dramatized treatment of revolutionary transformation in the countryside, *Lo que va de ayer a hoy* (roughly, Yesterday and today). In one critic's estimation, the work—penned by Simón Pérez, a sixty-year-old farmer and lifelong aspiring writer— encouraged audience identification in its depiction of the "contrast be- tween the tears and exploitation" that characterized peasant life before 1959 and the "happiness that [was] now opening the path to fight that shameful past." The play, and the story of Pérez himself, offered layered testimony to revolutionary possibility, from the redemption of the countryside to the actualization of a frustrated writer, not to mention the "peasants and work- ers" of the theater group who had brought both to life. This message evi- dently resonated; following the festival, the work was staged three more times at the public's request.[47]

At the festival, political identification with the revolutionary project was performed on stage but also enacted behind the scenes. As José Garófalo, Havana's provincial coordinator, noted in a report delivered at the Novem- ber 1962 Plenaria de Cultura, most participants were "if not a *Federada* then a member of a Comité or if not a *Combatiente* or *Becado*," reflecting CNC outreach to mass organizations. Garófalo also expressed relief at the ab- sence of "strange, *amanerada* [loosely, 'queer']" people. But the aficionado movement did not just speak to the converted. It could also, he posed, serve as a "binding force" among those "elements" who remained politically "in- different."[48] Indeed, the aficionado movement would thereafter be incor- porated into the national "reeducation" program, in the hopes that cultural practice would "return *hombres nuevos* to society."[49]

In a notable departure from the Soviet model, some of the work of recruiting disaffected Cubans was performed by a new class of "arts in- structors." Early on, activists at the Department of Theater Extension had initiated such instruction spontaneously, as Fidel Castro discovered during a trip to cut cane at the onetime seat of the Hershey sugar complex. There, dramaturge Alfredo Pons had established a theater corps staffed by local peasants, who "[walked] half a league every night to attend classes after working all day." Employing an "experimental methodology" grounded in "conversation," Pons encouraged his pupils to speak about their past experiences, which the instructors transcribed. Then, the peasants would reenact the written "dialogues," turning themselves into theatrical objects and subjects—muses, characters, and actors—in a kind of performative dialectic.[50]

Some of Pons's students would soon matriculate in the official program to train arts instructors in Havana. The first Escuelas de Instructores de Arte (Schools for Arts Instructors) opened at Havana's Comodoro and Copacabana hotels in the thick of the April 1961 Bay of Pigs invasion. The inaugural class brought together 700 students from nearby cooperatives and *granjas del pueblo* to study theater, music, and popular dance.[51] The program, funded by INRA and soon taken over by the CNC, spanned three semesters of instruction, which included "primary education, rhythmic gymnastics, and art appreciation," in addition to "military instruction" and "ideological formation."[52] The initiative to train arts instructors, ostensibly devised by Fidel Castro himself, followed the model pioneered in the literacy campaign in joining educational to political goals. It also reflected official concerns that Cubans had begun the process of cultural socialization with less preparation than had their Soviet counterparts.[53] The goal was thus not to "forge artists, but [to forge] teachers," drawn from the popular classes, in the belief that they would be best positioned to extend cultural literacy to underserved areas.[54] But the effort to forge a new cadre of "intellectuals drawn from the . . . worker-peasant masses" also spoke to the tensions that had erupted between artists and CNC officials over the form and content of Cuban culture.[55]

Even so, the first students of the Escuelas de Instructores de Arte were a diverse group in terms of their backgrounds and cultural training. In the words of Rosa Ileana Boudet, a member of this class, "There were students from Havana or other important cities, with cultural preparation and interests . . . but there were also many students, mostly of peasant origin, who registered without knowing exactly what they were signing up for."[56] The curriculum was designed to bridge this gap, overseen by prominent cultural figures from Cuba and Latin America. Noelia González, another member of the first class, recalls that formal instruction at the theater school was supplemented by immersion in Havana's cultural scene, from classic film screenings to weekend trips to see live theater.[57]

As in the literacy campaign, the schools foregrounded political instruction, even offering classes in dialectical materialism (with a curriculum drawn from the EIRs and led, as of 1964, by graduates from party schools).[58] In the project of ideological cultivation, however, cultural officials placed the greatest emphasis on voluntary labor. In a 1962 address to the First National Congress of Culture, for example, Edith García Buchaca noted that during the recent coffee harvest, students had "disproved" the prevalent notion of a "certain half-heartedness among arts students for tasks requiring physical exertion."[59] At their 1963 graduation, the first class of 220 arts instructors in turn declared themselves "vigilant against lazy theorizers" and "free of the alienation attending the commoditization of art.[60] Behind the scenes, however, politicization could take more repressive forms. Tremendous learning opportunities—cultural, political, and otherwise—were accompanied by students' first experiences of "rejections and expulsions for ideological motives."[61] Indeed, it thereafter became an established norm that individuals with problematic political views or sexual identities could not work with the aficionados.[62]

Soon after graduation, the arts instructors fanned out across the country, tasked with carrying out three years of instruction. Boudet's first destination was the Isla de Pinos, where she, her husband, and two other instructors oversaw ten aficionado groups.[63] The isle had only recently acquired its first official library, and even newspapers were delivered irregularly.[64] Yet the arrival of the arts instructors—together with a variety of new institutions established by the local Consejo de Cultura, including cine móvil, cultural centers, and a music school—promised to transform the cultural scene.[65] The nighttime rehearsals of Boudet's groups, which came to include members of the "CTC, cowherders, grapefruit pickers, and even the unemployed workers at the Hotel Colony," provided training and "entertainment for the community."[66]

As a theater instructor in Camagüey, Noelia González experienced a similarly dynamic interplay between training performers and engaging audience members. She observes that theater groups fomented "cultural enrichment" and "arts appreciation," molding actors in the short term but also "habitual spectators of culture" in the long term. González recalls staging performances in libraries, prisons, and workplaces in surrounding municipalities, including a memorable rendition of Shakespeare's Othello in 1966. These shows were always followed by a discussion with audience members, "most, if not all, of whom had never seen a theater performance before."[67] As one participant recalled of his experience in another aficionado theater group, audience edification was far from their only goal; simply making people "laugh and have fun" was valuable enough.[68]

As aficionado artists and instructors sought to cultivate cultural appreciation and enjoyment, officials foregrounded the political benefits of such work. In the area of dance, for example, the CNC promoted the "inculcation of new political and artistic concepts . . . [through] works that reflected the life of the people and the very process of the Revolution."[69] The resulting performances, which took up such themes as the sugar harvest, agrarian reform, the literary campaign, and the Bay of Pigs, had an evidently "didactic" quality, though that did not necessarily overdetermine audience reception, as Elizabeth Schwall notes.[70] Sometimes the ideological charge of the aficionado repertoire developed spontaneously from below. Noelia González recalls working with a young repairman who had written a play centered on revolutionary change; it was enthusiastically received by her students and the audience for whom they performed it.[71]

The CNC also sponsored dramaturgical competitions to produce an aficionado repertoire attuned to "current national matters," such as Cuban opposition to the US embargo or imperialism.[72] Some entries were "politically on point" but "poetically mediocre," in the words of a reviewer.[73] In the first contest, one of the most lauded submissions was *Ahora es más dulce la caña* (The sugar is sweeter now), a play that featured the "situation of Cuban *macheteros* (sugar cutters) before and after the Revolution." A reviewer speculated that peasant audiences would "identify" with the play's central arc, which "[offered] them a retrospective vision of the shameful past of our land and the happy present that we all now enjoy."[74]

In deputizing ordinary Cubans to draft, reenact, and bear witness to the revolutionary epic, cultural officials thus ensured that it would be interpreted in politically correct and subjectively relevant terms. In the national aficionado festivals that would become a staple of the movement, such works figured prominently. These included *El santo milagroso* (The miraculous saint), a leading entry in the 1966 competition. One observer related that the play repudiated the "religious obscurantism in which most of our peasantry was submerged before the triumph of our Revolution" and "humorously" depicted their overcoming of it. It thus offered "proof" of "cultural development," not only in its narrative arc but also in the fact that it had been authored and performed *by* peasants.[75]

But the "official" aficionado repertoire, curated by CNC officials, did not always resonate as enduringly with grassroots participants. Boudet notes that she rarely drew on works such as *Como dijo Fidel* (As Fidel said), which dramatized a peasant couple's gradual embrace of agrarian reform, preferring to stage pieces from the universal repertoire or short satires by Cuban authors.[76] Noelia González also struggled to incorporate official works, but for a different reason: she could not access them. She recalls copying the plays that did make it to her "by hand," even as she drew criticism from local officials for staging a play penned by one of her actors, which featured revolutionary themes but was not part of the official repertoire.[77]

As a result of these and other challenges—supply shortages, poor housing, low compensation, and political tensions—many arts instructors did not remain long in their posts. By January 1971, 75 percent of the graduates of the Escuelas de Instructores de Arte were estimated to have left the program, even as the number of amateur artists continued to grow. In the early 1960s CNC officials had begun offering expedited training for "volunteer instructors" in response to high turnover; by 1966, the 600 "official instructors" who were still active were recruited to train more volunteers.[78] At the same time, CNC officials initiated a campaign to improve the quality of the aficionados' work through regular evaluations, completed by arts instructors and submitted to CNC officials. They also promoted the formation of *grupos selectivos* (selective groups), which were given the opportunity to perform in high-profile venues, including on the TV program *El pueblo en escena* (The people on stage).[79] With rising standards for the aficionados and declining standards for their instructors, the line between "professional" and "amateur" became increasingly hazy.[80]

By the mid-1960s, these forces contributed to the feeling that the aficionado movement had lost the "madness and poetry," as Boudet puts it, that had first drawn many instructors.[81] Yet their perception that official interest had waned also spoke to the changing course of the Revolution. As all of Cuba geared up for a record 10-million-ton sugar harvest, the imperative for artistic cultivation gave way to an island-wide mobilization in the fields. Resources, human and otherwise, were increasingly directed toward sugar, and the political and cultural course of the Revolution radicalized accordingly. Productive voluntary labor became the order of the day, uniformly prescribed for all Cubans. Where there had once been space to theorize culture as work, officials increasingly focused on promoting work *as* culture—an enterprise in which the revolutionary collective assumed precedence over the individuals (artists, workers) who composed it.

Socializing Work

In June 1961, a group of construction workers raised a flag in honor of an unparalleled achievement: they had earned first place in the *emulación* declared among participants in the reconstruction of Havana's Parque Maceo, one of ten pilot projects recently launched by the Ministry of Public Works.[82] Their win, for which they were awarded a "Vanguard Workers" flag in a public ceremony, coincided with the announcement of "magnificent" results in the island's first emulation in the sugar industry. In the assessment of one journalist, these successes proved that "socialist emulation" could "elevate productivity and perfect production," all while avoiding the destructive force of capitalist "competition."[83]

Though its form continued to evolve following the passage of the first formal regulations in 1962, emulation would quickly insinuate itself into nearly every corner of island life. For leaders, emulation represented a tool not only to improve the economy but also to cultivate new attitudes toward labor. The campaign to socialize work sought to supplant existing labor hierarchies, especially the divide between "mental" and "manual" labor, and institute new forms of achievement-based recognition. Emulation thus reinforced efforts to democratize and universalize productive labor in the buildup to the 10-million-ton harvest of 1970, making work the revolutionary duty of all Cubans and reframing political militancy as a form of work. In the 1960s, work thus became ubiquitous: a vehicle of distinction and integration, but also reeducation and correction.[84] Emulation became inescapable alongside it, enlisting Cubans to labor collectively in the service of their communist destiny.

Leaders theorized that emulation would serve as a key instrument in reaching that goal, but its institution required training in turn. Before 1959, campaigns of socialist competition were sporadic and almost exclusively sponsored by the PSP, following the model pioneered in the Soviet Union.[85] In their efforts to promote rapid industrialization, Lenin and other Soviet leaders had argued that some capitalist institutions, such as material incentives and wage inequality, could be refashioned to abet the transition to communism. Emulation represented one such instrument, which would allow the Soviets to "beat capitalism at its own game."[86] For workers, competing like socialists institutionalized new forms of discipline—a "regime of strict control . . . regulating the quantity, quality, and time of labor"—and public recognition, as with the famous Stakhanovites, named for a Russian miner who in one night "hewed 102 tons of coal, or fourteen times his quota."[87]

In early 1960s Cuba, emulation underwrote a parallel quest to stabilize the island's economy and bring its workers under state control. As the effects of the US embargo and diplomatic isolation began to be felt, exacerbated by industrial mismanagement and agricultural neglect, Cuban officials turned to workers to help shore up the island's economy. Yet they also raised doubts about their aptitude to do so. As Julie Bunck notes, Fidel Castro, Che Guevara, and others argued that "Spanish colonialism, Cuban slavery, and western capitalism" had fatally impaired the island's work culture, most notably shaping a widespread "disdain for manual labor."[88]

That attitude, they proposed, also manifested in the common practice of absenteeism. Island elites had long bemoaned workers' purported disinclination to work—sometimes drawing on racialized understandings of which Cubans were most apt for productive labor—even as the seasonal nature of sugar production had left cane cutters unemployed for months at a time. Such concerns had taken a new form in the early 1960s, as spending capacity and employment opportunities grew alongside material shortages. As Maurice Zeitlin observed, workers may have been "earning more (because they [were . . .] working more regularly)," but they had "little on which to spend their earnings," diminishing their incentive to show up.[89] To promote discipline and political adhesion, Cuban officials thus moved swiftly to assert control over traditional sites of worker autonomy, including unions.[90] They also passed laws establishing penalties for absenteeism, arriving late or leaving early, and poor performance.[91]

At the same time, leaders turned to emulation to cultivate new attitudes toward labor, grounded in their "belief that workers should perform out of a moral obligation to revolutionary goals."[92] But early emulation programs, which relied largely on "honorary awards" (such as the title of "labor hero"), inspired little popular enthusiasm, so officials established "material stimuli," including (partially) funded vacations and houses, in the first regulations passed in 1962.[93] By late 1962, over 1,000 workers had earned trips to the Soviet Union, among other prizes, where many laid offerings at Lenin's tomb.[94] By that point, officials had issued new regulations to promote popular participation.[95] In the next year, some 11,456 work centers and 721,952 workers—9 percent of whom would be awarded the status of vanguard workers— formally signed up to emulate, even as officials continued to lament that workers had not been sufficiently involved in their development.[96]

Though the specifics changed over time, a core set of principles defined the essence of "vanguard" work. Emulating laborers signed contracts (*convenios*) indicating their intention to go to work regularly and punctually, exceed their daily production norms, ensure quality in production and the parsimonious use of resources, and make productive use of their nonworking time, namely through *superación* and, as of 1964, "voluntary" labor.[97] The formalization of this requirement spoke to persistent labor shortages, especially in the sugar and coffee sectors, but also ideological imperatives. As one account of the 1964 regulations posed, volunteer work was "equivalent to a veritable school of communism."[98]

Assessment methods also changed over time, but all the emulation codes outlined means for ensuring compliance. Per the 1964 regulations, emulation commissions were established in each workplace and staffed by representatives from the relevant economic and union sectors and the Communist Party (at that point, the Partido Unido de la Revolución Socialista de Cuba). These groups were charged with evaluating workers' performance and forwarding the results to regional and provincial emulation commissions, overseen by a national commission run by the Ministry of Work.[99] This weblike oversight framework channeled both visibility and discipline.

Workers who exceeded their emulation standards gained access to a variety of material and moral rewards, whose value was augmented by the publicity attached to them. One of these workers was Victor Rojas, a trash collector featured in a 1964 documentary who proudly displayed his certificate of socialist emulation and a "Vanguard Worker" banner hanging in his modest house. "A trash collector," he proclaimed, "is not a dog," as he touted his family's contributions to the Revolution.[100] Thus, in some cases, work allowed Cubans to leave behind a marginalized past and enter the pantheon of revolutionary "heroes."[101]

Anecdotal evidence suggests that Afro-Cubans figured prominently among them, given their historical overrepresentation in agricultural labor. One of them was Tomás Torres, a resident of rural Matanzas who lived with his wife and two children in a leaking house with no running water. But Torres was also a seasoned cane cutter, who had joined the Brigada Camilo Cienfuegos to contribute to the historic *zafra*. He quickly distinguished himself in its ranks, reaching the status of *"decimillionario"* (applied to those individuals who had cut 100,000 *arrobas*—roughly 4,000 pounds—of sugar cane). That made him eligible for membership in the touring Delegation of Outstanding Young People and for a new house, built and furnished in record time.[102]

Perhaps the most famous vanguard worker of the decade was Reinaldo Castro, a cane cutter from Matanzas who was declared a National Labor Hero in 1963 and 1964. Castro, who reportedly cut an average of 1,200 *arrobas* of sugar cane a day, was celebrated as an example for all workers to follow, not only for his productive achievements but also for his willingness to commit himself to *superación* (at Fidel Castro's personal urging) and his adherence to the revolutionary project.[103] This conjoining of physical and political achievements mirrored those embodied by Fidel Castro himself, who in 1965 became, by one account, the "country's most renowned vanguard worker." After a week in which he claimed to best his previous cane haul day after day, Castro proclaimed that he would thereafter "emulate against himself" and encouraged other workers to learn from his achievements, notably the "samurai method" he claimed to have invented.[104]

As photos of outstanding workers lined the walls of workplaces across the country, they were joined by images of workers and managers who had fallen short of expectations.[105] "Behind the prizes," Carmelo Mesa-Lago and Roberto Hernández Morales write, loomed the "ever-present threat of punishment."[106] In a 1964 television appearance, Labor Minister Augusto Martínez Sánchez presented the recently passed Labor Justice Law, which inaugurated new "disciplinary measures" (docking wages, being sent to work) as a necessary response to those "undisciplined" workers who had yet to "take the revolutionary leap."[107] Indeed, emulation implicated all workers in a system of vigilance, including in the fulfillment of uncompensated labor. According to one account, beginning in the 1963 sugar harvest, CTC leaders required weekly reports on voluntary work battalions; by the following year, this extended to the formation of disciplinary councils, soon brought under party authority.[108] Emulation commissions thus required their members to serve as de facto "informants" on their coworkers.[109]

Unsurprisingly, these measures did not inspire popular enthusiasm. A study carried out by César Escalante in October 1964 found that in fifty-five Havana workplaces only 30 percent of the 70–80 percent of workers who signed emulation contracts were actually meeting their goals; few were attending the prescribed emulation assemblies.[110] Cuban officials were dismayed by workers' apathy; as one privately told a reporter in 1965, "I don't understand these people. . . . At the time of the Bay of Pigs invasion, these peasants took up their guns and enthusiastically hurried to their posts, ready to lay down their lives. . . . A few months later, I saw them dozing in the fields, shirking work. Why, I ask myself, are they ready to die for the Revolution, but not to work for it?"[111]

Opposition groups seized on this gap between official expectations and popular response. Over the course of the next year, the Cuban Freedom Committee responded to worker discontent by peppering their broadcasts with inversions of revolutionary slogans, such as "*Zafra*, what for?" and "Work, what for?"[112] According to a report by an exile workers' organization, prior to 1959, Cubans harbored resentment toward those workers known as "pushers" (*empujadores*), who "dedicated themselves to producing in excess with the sole objective of gaining the sympathy and favor of their bosses."[113] Other critics depicted emulation norms as outright slavery; in the words of one island letter writer, "Here we have to work more than ever, and now we do it as slaves."[114] Echoing this framing, an oppositional poster characterized *metas* (goals) as an "instrument of slave labor." Such rhetoric displayed little sensitivity to Cuba's long history of racialized bondage. In using such language, opposition groups failed to address the different resonances such analogies might have had for Afro-Cuban workers. Indeed, all the laborers depicted in this poster series, housed in the Theodore Draper Papers, are white.

Yet some workers did experience emulation as exploitative. In 1964, *New York Times* reporter Juan de Onís encountered one such group in the thick of an emulation at a Santiago dam project. The construction workers had been informed of the norms, determined based on the "best work done in each category" that day, and "asked to endorse them." According to one laborer, those norms had "raised the minimum pace of drillers," as enforced by a "section of clerical workers." On these grounds, a "confused comrade" had complained of "exploitation." Onís relates that the worker "was taken in hand by the party representative and union delegate. . . . At the next meeting he said he had recognized his 'error.'" Meanwhile, none of the cane cutters at a plantation Onís visited in Santiago were able to identify the *machetero* hero, Reinaldo Castro. When asked, they all "denied that any man could cut 10 tons of cane a day."[115]

Having failed to galvanize worker enthusiasm, officials passed a new set of emulation regulations in 1966. Moving away from bureaucratic forms of assessment, including the contract, the new code reflected the Guevarist radicalization of the revolutionary project, which marginalized material incentives and celebrated "vanguard workers."[116] The newly launched Movimiento de Avanzada (Advanced Workers' Movement), for example, brought together those Cubans who displayed the most outstanding attitudes toward labor within and beyond the workplace.[117] By early 1969, 235,000 Cubans— or 18 percent of organized workers—had earned "advanced" status, nomi-

"Las metas: Instrumento de trabajo esclavo en Cuba
Comunista," Theodore Draper Papers, box 1, folder 3,
Hoover Institution Library & Archives.

nated by their coworkers in assemblies that coincided with the new Historic
Date Emulation program (July 26, May 1, and so on). In addition to exceeding
production norms, "advanced" workers were expected to dedicate themselves
to "cultural, technical, and ideological" improvement, "have and maintain
correct social conduct, within and beyond the workplace," "participate actively in volunteer work," and be "active militant[s] in revolutionary tasks."[118]

With cash prizes no longer on the table, only 1.7 percent of workers in
the 1966 sugar harvest received material rewards.[119] By 1969, they were

encouraged to "waive bonuses, overtime pay, and historical wages" as well.[120] As revolutionary leaders sought to marginalize financial incentives, the Movimiento de Avanzada channeled their efforts to reorganize labor around revolutionary militancy. Emulation thus became a "mass movement," in Roberto Bernardo's words, "emphasizing group solidarity and minimal bureaucratic forms."[121] Dovetailing with the 1968 Revolutionary Offensive, the reorganization of socialist competition reinforced what Lillian Guerra describes as the "'rallification' of everyday life," which "politicized the most mundane aspects of daily tasks and linked them to the broader national drama taking place in the sugarcane fields."[122]

The new emulation standards were also applied to those workers who did not meet productivity and political expectations. In 1969, another confidential party study of a railroad factory in Camagüey had turned up evidence of worker dissatisfaction. Since railroads bore strategic importance in transporting raw cane to mills, Armando Hart and other leaders decided to overhaul the factory's emulation program. Acknowledging complaints about poor work conditions (shortages of food, clothing, and supplies)—the conditions that had stoked discontent—they nonetheless directed their attention to ideological solutions: "It was necessary to turn every administrative measure into a political activity, that is, a mass activity, and only the Party could do that."[123]

Leaders thus decided to foreground the work of "political assurance" (*aseguramiento político*), a mission that the Central Committee's Commission of Revolutionary Orientation had already undertaken in sugar mills.[124] Commissions tasked with *aseguramiento político* sought to impart the accepted practice and politics of work to ordinary laborers. Printed pamphlets, "often crafted with a sense of humor, in color and simple language," spelled out "essential principles so that each worker [could] learn to do their job efficiently." Such interventions often included the screening of a 1969 documentary titled *Productividad* (dir. Luis Felipe Bernaza), which depicted the "work of the most outstanding cane cutters, crane operators, and other workers" to show "why they've been the best."[125]

In the case of the Camagüey railroad factory, officials reported having achieved impressive results, including a 75 percent reduction in absenteeism and a 65 percent increase in voluntary labor. As one "advanced" worker and soldier told reporters, "Emulation is the driving motor of work. . . . No one wants to lose!" He credited, above all, the "political work" undertaken in the factory, including the establishment of the Partido Comunista de Cuba (PCC, or Communist Party of Cuba) and the Unión de Jóvenes Comunistas

(Union of Young Communists).[126] Indeed, in many cases, vanguard workers and party leaders were one and the same, such that "membership in the Union of Young Communists was often awarded conjointly with Vanguard Worker status."[127] By the late 1960s, vanguard workers had effectively supplanted Cuba's unions, just as the party had become aligned with management in enforcing productivity and promoting political goals.[128]

In the lead-up to the record sugar harvest projected for 1970, vanguard workers thus came to play an increasingly important role. As a British diplomat noted in a September 1969 cable, a "dedicated minority" was "carrying the rest of the country on their backs. There is no doubt that the militants are responding well to the challenge of the ten million tons. But the majority of workers are just not interested in becoming 'Heroes of Moncada' . . . and their level of productivity bears a close relationship to the general standard of living."[129] In a context of consumer scarcity—but state rationing of food and goods—there was little incentive for individual workers to exert themselves, no matter how enthusiastically or forcefully they were encouraged to do so.

Revolutionary officials responded in kind. By the late 1960s, noncompliant workers were subject to an expanding regime of visibility and discipline. These included more severe penalties for vagrancy (work camps or incarceration) and the establishment of a new "labor file" and ID card to catalog each worker's "merits and demerits."[130] According to Lowry Nelson, those cards became a civic currency that could be confiscated as a form of punishment. He reports that "during the 1970 harvest in Matanzas province some persistently absent workers had their names read over the radio and finally had their labor cards taken from them."[131] These corrective measures were curiously inattentive to the structural conditions that agricultural workers had long faced. After witnessing the penalties meted out in the popular courts, which had expanded dramatically in this period, Luis Salas wrote: "Teaching a sugar worker who is accustomed to being unemployed during the cultivation period that this is now vagrancy is difficult enough, but making him understand that vagrancy is counterrevolutionary is even more difficult."[132]

The disappointing results of the 10-million-ton harvest brought these tensions to a head. Even as Fidel Castro publicly assumed responsibility for the outcome, ordinary Cubans also faced the fallout behind the scenes. Jorge Domínguez has argued that workers responded to these pressures by launching an "apparently uncoordinated" strike. Given the official prohibition on striking, this action—which encompassed some "20 precent of the work

A DARLO TODO POR LOS 10 MILLONES

FORJADORES DE LA
CONCIENCIA COMUNISTA
CREADORES DE LA RIQUEZA
CON CONCIENCIA

Para construir el Comunismo simultáneamente con la base material, hay que hacer al hombre nuevo.

CHE

Si queremos expresar cómo deben ser nuestros obreros.

Debemos decir: Que sean cómo el CHE.

FIDEL

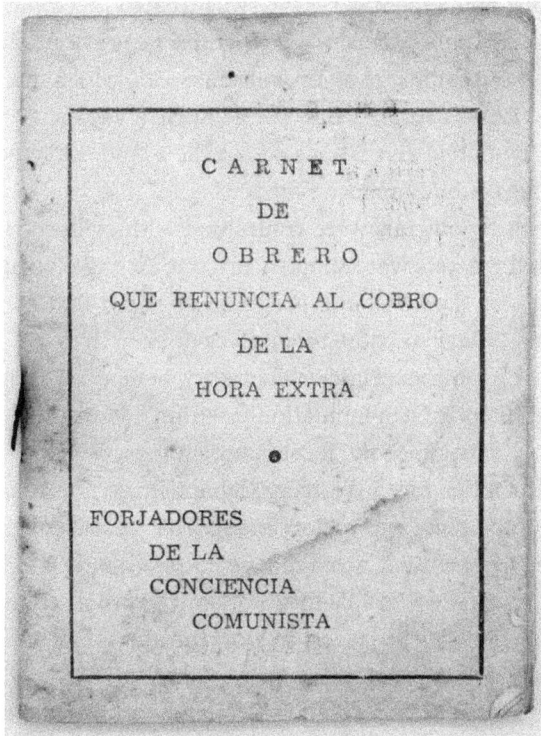

CARNET
DE
OBRERO
QUE RENUNCIA AL COBRO
DE LA
HORA EXTRA

FORJADORES
DE LA
CONCIENCIA
COMUNISTA

A booklet cataloging the hourly contributions of those workers who had agreed to give up their overtime pay for the 10-million-ton harvest of 1970 presents them as "forgers of Communist consciousness" and exemplars of the "hombre nuevo." Yet the choice of Afro-Cuban labor activist and politician Jesús Menéndez to convey this message is an interesting one. In 1946, Menéndez had lobbied successfully to impose higher sugar prices on the United States—and extra compensation for sugar workers—when export prices rose, a measure known as the "sugar differential." Menéndez was assassinated two years later when the Grau San Martín government ordered him detained.

force" in August and September 1970—was treated by revolutionary leaders as "large-scale absenteeism."[133] In response, revolutionary officials launched an all-out campaign against absenteeism, which finally took legal form in the 1971 Anti-vagrancy Law (Ley contra la Vagancia). The measure was preceded by public discussions across the island, targeted to building (and performing) public support.

In these debates, officials were confronted with evidence that even the most committed workers were simply worn out. At a twelve-hour 1970 provincial meeting of the CTC, one port worker noted that at many docks, laborers had no "water to bathe themselves or even to drink." Meanwhile, an employee at a pharmaceutical laboratory bemoaned that "[voluntary labor] and the Historic Date Emulation program had resulted in the physical wear and exhaustion of the most conscientious workers." Others highlighted the difficulties faced by many Cubans in getting to work. Yet the driving spirit of the event was to promote stricter measures against workers who continued to be absent, from a cane cutter who demanded a "law to really punish *ausentistas*" to a factory worker who proposed that the names of habitual offenders be "broadcast in local theaters." Indeed, even as Fidel Castro proclaimed that "slavery" no longer existed (implicitly rebuking exile critics) and that *conciencia* could solve many problems, he nonetheless proposed that some Cubans "might require a grade of coercion."[134]

These discussions intensified in late 1970, as a draft proposal of what would become the Anti-vagrancy Law began to circulate in workplaces and mass organizations. A full-scale publicity campaign accompanied it. *Granma*, for example, ran a comic strip about the misadventures of Mogollón, the Lazy Bird, "who regularly received warnings and threats from diligent fellow workers." The press in turn reported on "rallies and demonstrations" in which "effigies of Mogollón . . . were burned."[135] Officials reported that most workers not only supported the measure but also demanded harsher sanctions for repeat offenders. Ian McColl Kennedy, present in Cuba during the campaign, has concluded that "it would not be difficult to persuade [workers] that it [was] wrong for others to sit back in idleness and partake of that which they have produced."[136] Julie Bunck, in contrast, has argued that there is little evidence that Cuban workers were concerned about absenteeism or supportive of serious penalties.[137]

The final version of the Anti-vagrancy Law defined *vagancia* as a crime equivalent to "robbery" and framed work as an individual "duty." Those who did not fulfill it ("physically and mentally able" men aged seventeen to sixty), identified for the first time in the 1970 census, would thereafter be subject to disciplinary measures.[138] In almost all cases, this included compulsory productive work, whether completed in a reeducation camp or under house arrest. Those targeted were identified on a spectrum ranging from "pre-criminals," including laborers who had been absent from their workplace for more than two weeks, to habitual "loafers," who had been punished before. As officials established a new network of "labor councils" to enforce the measure, they nonetheless hoped that the passage of the law would serve as sufficient motivation. In fact, in the four months between the circulation of the draft and the publication of the law, over 100,000 men joined the labor force, half for the first time. In the same period, 1,000 workers were tried in the new labor courts for the crime of *vagancia* (15 percent of whom had previous criminal records), though the number of cases prosecuted beyond individual workplaces remained low.[139]

Yet the infrequency of formal prosecution does not necessarily signify the absence of correction. After finishing his compulsory military service, Jorge Luis González Suárez was cited to visit his local Dirección de Trabajo y Seguridad Social. There, he was told that he could either work in agriculture or catch crocodiles in the Ciénaga de Zapata. He opted for the former and was sent to pick squash and then tobacco and corn under strict disciplinary conditions; only with time were he and other workers allowed to return home after the workday. Following the completion of his sentence, there was no formal record of the punishment: "In that period, which lasted for more than two years, I was the worker who never existed."[140]

Based on these results, Lowry Nelson argued that the "main thrust" of the vagrancy law had been to decentralize labor enforcement "from the government and the party to the local workers' councils in the factories and fields." In this, they were aided by campaigns to revitalize unions after an extended period of forced dormancy.[141] Alongside efforts to stabilize socialism, this period saw a growing emphasis on "democratizing" the labor sector, with the first real elections for union leadership held in the aftermath of the 1973 CTC Congress.[142] Marifeli Pérez-Stable has argued that these and other measures recast unions as mass organizations with the capacity to represent workers, though still subordinate to the authority of the Communist Party.[143] In the next few years, salaries rose and overtime pay was restored (in principle if not always in practice).[144]

The decade that followed brought more opportunities for participation and compensation, including the reintroduction of material incentives, but also the expanding reach of norms.[145] In fact, emulation programs were dramatically scaled up over the course of the 1970s, with 1972 declared the official "Year of Emulation." In 1973, a new emulation code introduced contracts grounded in five points, including "output quotas," "conservation of resources," "work discipline," adult education, and volunteer labor.[146] By 1976, 88 percent of Cuban laborers were emulating "on at least one point," and 38 percent had been granted the status of "vanguard worker."[147] Crucially, emulation once again became a vehicle to access consumer goods, including appliances, apartments, and vacations.[148] The focus of such programs continued to evolve over time, with a reorientation toward moral incentives in the mid-1980s, but what remained constant was emulation itself.[149]

That continuity might seem surprising, given that emulation largely failed to meet its stated goals. In 1970, Carmelo Mesa-Lago concluded that "four sets of regulations for socialist emulation, more than five years of Marxist-Leninist education, rigorous and strict control of state administrations, and the constant pressure of the government, the Party, the trade unions, and other mass organizations" had "all . . . failed to elevate the socialist conscience of the Cuban worker."[150] Equally suggestive was the assessment delivered in a 1978 report for the Ford Foundation that, due to a "lack of flexibility and creativity in their enterprises," Cubans "[did] not take a great deal of pride on [sic] their work."[151] Writing two decades later, Julie Bunck reached the same basic conclusion: that "Cuba's labor culture in the early 1990s bore little, if any, resemblance to the ideal 'socialist' culture that the government had long sought to create."[152]

Yet emulation programs have undoubtedly shaped generations of Cubans, if not in the ways revolutionary officials had imagined. By implicating workers in a new culture of work, emulation occupied, above all, their *time*. Miriam Leiva speculates that young people today "can't imagine all of the useless effort expended on work that was neither productive nor voluntary," the "nights of insomnia spent on neighborhood watch," or the "hours-long meetings to assess the completion of one's obligations, where things of vital importance were decided, such as the right to buy a television, a fridge, a tiny plastic Soviet fan, or even spend a few days in a hotel."[153]

By virtue of the imperative to compete, emulation encouraged Cubans to imagine all kinds of activities—in mass organizations, schools, and the workplace itself—as political and cultural labor and the stuff of daily life. One woman, who embarked on her professional career in the 1970s, remembers collectively peering in on the meetings of her workplace's emulation commission, a neat inversion of the apparatus of visibility in which emulation had implicated them. Yet when I asked her whether they thought of emulation as a good thing or a bad thing, she paused and responded that it was neither. It simply was.[154]

Theater of Popular Participation

In the early 1970s, the forces that propelled the revitalization of emulation—institutionalization, economic stabilization—also sparked renewed attention to aficionados. At the 1971 Congress of Art and Culture, officials called for the revival of the program, which had fallen to the wayside in the lead-up to the 1970 sugar harvest. The growth that followed was dramatic: from 14,872 participants (or 0.2 percent of the population) in 1965 to 193,376 (2.1 percent) nearly a decade later (1974). Though formal enrollment remained a minority phenomenon, many more Cubans came to participate as audience members.[155] By the late 1970s and early '80s, Soviet-style *casas de cultura* promoted not only a growth in aficionado numbers but also the intensification—and "massification"—of cultural outreach across the island.[156]

The revival of the aficionado program catalyzed new discussions about its political importance. Overseen by Luis Pavón, the infamous CNC president who spearheaded the repression of the *quinquenio gris* (including the Padilla affair), the movement was framed as "political work."[157] In the context of unparalleled tensions between Cuban officials and artists, aficionados (and their instructors) were once again imagined as a political counterweight. The ideological importance of the aficionados also demanded renewed scrutiny of their qualifications. Cultural officials wrote of the need to purge participants who manifested less than an "exemplary attitude toward work and national defense" or "feminine attributes or moral problems."[158] But recruiting the teachers who would guide them remained an obstacle; by 1974, the number of *instructores de arte* (603) still ranked below the high point reached in 1965 (615), leading officials to open two new schools in Havana and Camagüey.[159] On these grounds, a Soviet consultant noted that culture workers sometimes needed a "little more" than "thanks," whether "orders and medals," "money," or "personalized watches."[160]

The place of money in the pursuit of culture remained a fraught subject into the 1970s, even as material incentives reentered the picture. One of the issues was that the best aficionado groups expected to be paid for their work. As one arts instructor discovered, in his hometown of Guanajay, many groups "only performed in Cabarets, dances and other lucrative places," having been promised by local officials that they could do so when they were first "captured" for the movement.[161] For years to come, cultural officials bemoaned the "illegal hiring of [aficionado] cultural groups," while some aficionados became famous performers in their own right.[162] The program thus continued to reflect and further muddy the ambiguous line between "amateur" and "professional."[163] Despite its stated goals, the program at times pitted professionals and aficionados against each other in competing for status and access to resources.[164]

At issue, however, was also the question of being *seen* by the state, as noted in a 1974 letter by Vienbenido Cárdenas, a member of the Conjunto Ritmo Social Campesino. Despite his group's high level and punishing performance schedule, they had not yet been acknowledged by cultural officials in Santa Clara. In fact, though there was an evident need for more than one official "peasant group" in their city, a representative of the Frente Campesino Provincial had refused to recognize their group and instead "invented another Conjunto," even attempting to poach some of their members. "We believe," Cárdenas concluded, "that we have a right to form part of the great Family of the Peasant Front of the CNC."[165]

But was being seen by the state equivalent to being heard? To answer this question, we might turn to a mobilization that emerged alongside the aficionado movement, what would come to be known as *teatro nuevo* (new theater) or, in one of its more influential variants, the *teatro de participación popular* (theater of popular participation). In November 1968, a group of twelve actors, led by *Memorias del subdesarrollo* (1967) star Sergio Corrieri and his mother Gilda Hernández, left Havana for the Escambray mountains of Trinidad. There, they proposed to put theater at the service of the Revolution and the "public . . . that was making it: peasants, workers."[166] The choice of Escambray was not incidental; the actors viewed it as an area "rich in contradictions," having served as the seat for the Segundo Frente (Second Front), a breakaway revolutionary group, and, from 1961 to 1965, the site of a peasant uprising officially known as the Lucha contra Bandidos (Battle against Bandits).[167] Historically isolated from the state and the arts, the inhabitants of this area would benefit from their presence in a cultural and political sense, group members theorized. Local party officials agreed.

The Grupo Teatro Escambray (GTE), as it would come to be known, thus began to "get to know" that public, a mission that would later be formalized in collaboration with a University of Havana research team.[168] As they lived and worked among the intended members of their new audience, GTE actors began to perform plays taking up the region's history of political unrest, most notably Jesús Díaz's *Unos hombres y otros*, which dramatized the recent peasant insurgency. Each performance was followed by a discussion with audience members. In 1969, the GTE also initiated a collaboration with the Manuel Ascunce Teachers' School in Topes de Collantes, drafting its students as both viewers and future actors.[169]

On the basis of their success, Fidel Castro himself traveled to Topes in 1969 to attend a GTE performance, which, at his request, continued into the wee hours of the morning.[170] Castro seems to have recognized that the GTE promised what the aficionado movement had attempted but not yet achieved: turning Cubans into artists, workers, *and* revolutionaries. In short, as Corrieri explained, they sought to "[achieve] . . . the [public's] organic participation in the course of revolutionary development."[171] In the 1970s, GTE and other *teatro nuevo* groups thus mobilized theater as an "ideological weapon," per Gilda Hernández, revolutionizing the medium and their message in the process.[172]

Based on their research, GTE members concluded that one of the most significant political obstacles in the area was the long-standing influence of the Jehovah's Witnesses, who had discouraged peasants from working and joining revolutionary organizations.[173] Several GTE works thus featured critiques of the Witnesses, including Corrieri's *Y si fuera así* (And if it were so). The play adapted Bertolt Brecht's *Señora Carrar's Rifles*, set during the Spanish Civil War, to Cuba amid a mercenary invasion. It dramatizes the political evolution of a Cuban mother who, grieving the loss of her husband, comes under the influence of a Jehovah's Witness. He encourages her to isolate her son from military engagement, but her son chooses not to heed her and is ultimately killed during a US invasion. His death realigns the mother's loyalties. Her closing words cement her renunciation of the Witnesses and loyalty to her country: "If there is a God who condemns [fighting for the nation], then that God isn't worth anything at all."[174] Audience interviews conducted after one performance suggest that they identified with her change of heart.[175]

But persuading Escambray's peasants was not just a matter of ideology in the abstract. In encouraging peasants to abstain from revolutionary integration, the Witnesses imperiled a signal economic and political mission: that of transforming the region's peasants into proletarians. That change of mentality was viewed as particularly essential to the so-called *plan genético*, launched in the municipality of Mataguá. In the context of a nationwide milk shortage, Castro had determined that it would be an ideal site to develop Cuba's cattle industry. Yet the project would require extensive plots of land, to be acquired by leasing (*arrendamiento*) roughly 321,000 acres held by some

10,000 local peasants, for whom a new town known as La Yaya was to be built.[176] The initiative stoked tensions stemming from the first agrarian reform, in which many peasants had first gained rights to their land. Convincing them to relinquish the plots over which the Revolution had formalized their ownership would thus demand psychological work, observers theorized, highlighting the benefits of living in a "modern" town and developing a new *conciencia* among those who were "bound to the possession of land."[177]

At the invitation of Nicolás Chao, PCC secretary-general in Escambray, the GTE turned to culture to, quite literally, *create workers*. Group members undertook a monthlong investigation, an enterprise that would later incorporate University of Havana students and faculty affiliated with the new Grupo Desarrollo de Comunidades. On the basis of more than 100 interviews, they concluded that a contradictory mindset prevailed among many peasants.[178] In the past, they had been "willing to serve the Revolution" and were "conscious of the material benefits" that would derive from their incorporation.[179] Nonetheless, investigators noted, they clung to their land, the "historical objective of their classist aspirations and the sustaining base of their illusory individual liberty." It thus fell to the GTE to "show the peasant a contradictory image of himself."[180]

La vitrina (The showcase), written by Albio Paz, served as the theatrical vehicle for that "autocrítica."[181] The play tells the story of a peasant couple, Pancho and Ana, who received a plot of land and a chance for a better life thanks to the agrarian reform. They and other members of their community were thus chagrined by the prospect of relinquishing their land to join a new town. Confronting that prospect, Pancho suddenly falls ill and dies, leading Ana to resist *arrendamiento*. Her insistence on burying him on a plot designated for the *plan lechero*, per Fidel Castro's previous promise, provokes a debate within the community over the merits of incorporation. In keeping with the group's methodology, the actors planned to continue the debate with audience members at the play's end.

The first performance of *La vitrina* provoked a discussion as robust and conflicted as the one staged within the play, coming to focus on one spectator's critique of the peasants' *egoísmo* (selfishness). In the wide-ranging conversation that followed, things got so heated that the moderator proposed to stage the work again the following night. During another consequential performance, a farmer in the audience interrupted the play to challenge an actor representing a peasant's hesitancy about the move.[182] Meanwhile, other audience members, notably agricultural laborers and small landholders, assumed some of the persuasive work the play had set into motion. In the words of a *pequeño agricultor,* "I've worked the land and no one can say I'm lazy. . . . And I'll keep working; but now I'll work for everyone, not just for me."[183]

Increasingly emphasizing "participation" along the lines of Umberto Eco's "open theater," as Rine Leal has charted, these experiences led GTE members to "bury the idea of a blank audience."[184] The results of their engagement in La Yaya were so impressive that Castro himself came to view *La vitrina* many times, including at the 1971 inauguration of the new town and again at the 4th Congress of the Asociación Nacional de Agricultores Pequeños (National Association of Small Farmers), where the work was presented live at his request.[185] Meanwhile, both the text and the context of the work continued to evolve in response to the move.[186] Gilda Hernández relates that having adjusted to life in La Yaya, the peasants "would laugh at how they used to be." Albio Paz was also surprised by this detachment: "They didn't recognize themselves in those characters at all."[187] The final version of the play, drafted in 1978, memorialized the town's founding and its residents' change of heart; per Alma Villegas: "In the middle of the performance, the town residents remember their past—how afraid they were to move to the new town and how they conquered that fear."[188]

For decades to come, the GTE, operating from a permanent seat in La Macagua, would continue to build support for revolutionary initiatives, often in collaboration with the Communist Party. The theater of popular participation, as coined by two former GTE actors, in turn incorporated ordinary Cubans as actors. These efforts provided for the individuation of historically marginalized constituencies, whose voices were thereby heard—and sometimes staged.[189] On this basis, Laurie Frederik has proposed that the group's method provided a "feeling of dialogic empowerment."[190]

At the same time, dramaturgically and politically, theater integrated audience members and actors alike as subjects of the Revolution. Popular participation was essential, and the script was thus malleable, but the core message remained consistent with revolutionary ideology. Yet Rosa Ileana Boudet, who became one of the most prolific chroniclers of the GTE, has proposed that its work was not official but "counterculture," promoting "debate and discrepancy."[191] When I asked her to expand on this, she noted, "Those who dismiss it never saw it, and theater can be studied in texts and reviews, but you must live it. And if not, read it with respect."[192]

· · · · · ·

How, then, should we read the revolutionary work (of) culture: as a channel for popular recognition, political extension, or, simultaneously, both? In preparing for a socialist future, Cuban leaders turned to culture and work as instruments of ideological instruction, yet with an eye to promoting incorporation from below. This was the mission at the heart of socialist discipline, which brought new groups—peasants and workers among them—into state view and made them political subjects in both senses of the word.

From above and from below, this interaction had epistemological effects. On the one hand, revolutionary leaders turned culture and work into mediums of official knowing: ways to assess, and monitor, politically important constituents. They also mobilized to shift the historical meanings attached to culture and work, refashioning culture as a kind of work and establishing work as the cornerstone of culture. This fusion served as a vehicle for state projection and a crucible of popular understandings. And those, whether mimetic or resistant, often framed work *and* culture as the essence of living in Revolution.

In chapter 7, I argue that leisure has also enduringly connected state extension to popular interpretation. In laying claim to time away from work, political leaders and cultural officials sought to embed revolutionary ideology in a field long viewed as politically suspect due to its connections to US capital and audiences. This context made pop culture political, birthing new forms of sociability and forbidden pleasures. Yet such efforts to politicize the popular demanded that officials apprehend what *was* popular. Over the course of several decades, this quest generated actionable knowledge for the state while informing perspectives about the state for the many Cubans so implicated.

The Politics of the Popular

· ·

In July 1967, National Cultural Council (CNC) vice president Lisandro Otero issued a novel request to the national director of the aficionado program. "I think we should establish some kind of survey to regularly assess the cultural tastes of the Cuban people," he mused. "We often say that 'the people like this' or 'the people don't like this.' But do we really know what the people do and don't like?"[1] As Cuban officials sought to reshape the island's culture of work, often mobilizing the work of culture, this question bore clear political implications. Popular taste represented a real-time referendum on the project of revolutionary extension.

Island leaders were far from the first to assign ideological significance to popular culture. Building on the foundational writings of Frankfurt school theorists Theodor Adorno and Max Horkheimer, Marxist critics had long drawn attention to capitalist influences on cultural preferences. In this respect, they tended to frame mass culture as a site of alienation and valorized those forms—from high culture to folk—that evaded marketization.[2] But what happens when the culture industries are state directed? Can popular culture shed its commercial trappings, even channel socialist values?

Like their Soviet counterparts before them, Cuban officials answered these questions decisively in the affirmative. The Revolution, they proposed, should celebrate the folk and marginalize the foreign, combat commercialism, and elevate true artists. "Folklore," wrote ethnographer Rogelio Martínez Furé in 1973, "is assumed to be the most authentic creation of the masses, the refuge of some of the best traditions of popular struggle in the face of the . . . foreignizing cultural penetration promoted by the national oligarchies."[3] Though revolutionary leaders privileged "high" culture (notably ballet) as a site of revolutionary achievement, they also directed state support to vernacular, especially Afro-descendant, traditions, which they rescripted in secular and sometimes primitivizing terms.[4] Indeed, the distinction between high and popular was far from absolute in practice, thanks in part to the aficionado program.[5]

Yet the creation of a new popular culture did not occur on a blank slate. Revolutionary officials inherited a highly developed culture industry, which not only had introduced Western and especially US content to island media but also conveyed Cuban music and dance forms around the world. The turn to "state-sponsored" or "organized" popular culture thus required not only the establishment of new structures and institutions but also the disarticulation of an entire cultural apparatus, from binational record companies to an internationally renowned leisure landscape.[6]

Over the course of the 1960s, as the US embargo obstructed the transnational flows that had once powered the Cuban culture industry, island officials nationalized record companies, intervened cabarets and clubs, assumed control over the contracting of performers, and abolished artistic royalties. They also established new organisms to manage popular culture, including the CNC (later the Ministry of Culture), the Cuban Institute of Cinematographic Art and Industry (ICAIC), the Instituto Nacional de la Industria Turística (INIT, later INTUR, which directed cabarets, clubs, and festivals), the Instituto Cubano de Radiodifusión (ICR, later ICRT, under the jurisdiction of the Ministry of Communications), and EGREM (the national music label, as of 1964).[7] This plurality meant that cultural officials did not always interpret revolutionary directives in uniform ways.[8] In principle, however, they all answered to official priorities, channeled by the mid-1960s through the Communist Party's Commission on Revolutionary Orientation (COR).[9]

The significance of these changes was not merely infrastructural. Beginning in the 1920s, coalescing anti-imperialist sentiment had affirmed popular culture as a site for articulating national identity. But celebrating what was distinctly Cuban had also foregrounded the cultural influence of Blackness. From danzón to son, most Cuban genres had been influenced by African percussive traditions, often blended with European instrumentation and vocal styles. Though some sought alternatives grounded in Cuba's Spanish, peasant, or Indigenous traditions, this search for origins ultimately served to "nationalize" Blackness, as Robin Moore has argued. The centering of Black culture inevitably aroused racist concerns, promoting variegated distribution and persistent prohibitions. By the 1940s and '50s, however, "Cuban culture," as it was understood on a national and international stage, prominently featured performers of color. The transculturative interaction between African, European, and US cultural influences in turn shaped how foreign observers perceived Cuba, as well as how Cubans understood themselves. In significant ways, culture came to define what it meant to be Cuban.[10]

The Revolution inherited this fraught dialectic and made it a matter of state politics. As popular culture was subsumed into revolutionary process, its international projection slowed considerably. Yet isolation only raised the stakes on popular culture. Lauding the island's cultural heritage as an antidote to imperialism, political officials boosted content previously marginalized from island media and denounced trends they viewed as a threat to such traditions, especially those that were international in inspiration. Drawing on radio, television, the written press, and film, their efforts to revolutionize popular culture sparked debates about mass media, (im)mobility, the place of intellectuals, and the work of culture. Over the course of the 1960s, popular culture became a vehicle for revolutionary integration and (self-)definition alike.

In engaging culture as a vehicle for ideological work, officials raised—and at times effaced—the very question of "the popular." On the one hand, leaders celebrated the populace as the reservoir of authentic traditions, affording some Cubans new visibility and even acclaim within the state cultural apparatus. On the other, they worried about Cubans' vulnerability to foreign temptations, spurring efforts to improve popular taste. The politicization of popular culture in turn shaped how ordinary Cubans understood the Revolution. For some, it channeled incorporation and identification; for others, it spurred disconnection and alienation.

As this book has charted across a variety of mediums, revolutionary officials aimed to incorporate popular culture into revolutionary politics, thus binding the subject to the "Subject" of Revolution. Cubans have in turn come to regard culture in highly political but not always identical terms. Over the course of six decades, this has made popular culture both an ideological battleground and an enduring platform for subject formation, neither autonomous from nor fully contained by the Revolution itself.

Integrating Culture

From the stage to the field, chapter 6 traced how integration became a measure of revolutionary consolidation. Those efforts at once referenced and rebranded an older, overtly racialized touchstone in Cuban political culture. The value of integration was championed by nineteenth-century patriot José Martí, who promoted "racelessness" as the foundation of the Cuban nation in the struggle for independence from Spain. Throughout the decades that followed, the notion underwrote critiques of both racism and racial separatism, as in the 1912 massacre of the Partido Independiente de Color.[11] As a result, prominent Afro-Cuban intellectuals at times questioned whether integration was a viable platform for anti-racist politics. In the late 1950s, Juan René Betancourt, president of the National Federation of Black Clubs, argued that, taken to extremes, it might even abet the "collective suicide of a race."[12]

The counterpoint between the silencing of race on the one hand and Afro-Cuban assertion on the other was revived following a March 1959 speech, in which Fidel Castro formally committed the Revolution to a campaign against racial discrimination. The path he outlined was, unsurprisingly, one of integration, to be enacted and overseen by the state. Castro identified workplace discrimination as the foremost target of the government's efforts. Yet he also promised to eliminate educational and recreational segregation, evoking an image of a Black child and a white child playing together as the foundation of revolutionary society.[13]

Even these modest goals prompted backlash among some white Cubans, amid "rumors . . . that Castro intended black men to invade elite social clubs and dance with white women."[14] Revolutionary officials responded to such concerns with denial and euphemism, employing a "language of class rather than race."[15] Their aim, they insisted, was to abolish discriminatory structures, not foment interracial sociability. As Castro declared in a televised press conference, it "would be absurd" to "force blacks and whites to dance together." Everyone could dance with whomever they wanted, he clarified, as long as everyone danced "with the Revolution."[16]

Yet the imperative for integration did turn popular culture into an enduring object of political attention, as officials worked to refashion cultural institutions, forms, and content along racially inclusive and ideologically uniform lines. State intervention thus facilitated the projection of revolutionary values, framing racial differentiation as a social and political obstacle to be overcome. But Cubans quickly discovered that the two faces of revolutionary integration were not necessarily consonant in practice. This was especially true when ideological prerogatives curtailed the potential radicalism of racial integration, or even racial assertion.[17]

Beginning in early 1959, ordinary Cubans mobilized with mixed success to challenge racial divisions in cultural spaces. At the student newspaper *Combate*, writers denounced the distribution of pamphlets advertising a "white only" dance to be held in Pinar del Río in honor of revolutionary combatants. Meanwhile, in Guanajay, activists affiliated with a local Afro-Cuban club were rebuffed in their attempts to shut down the city's all-white *comparsa* group, told by the local government that they did not want to be seen as "giving in to the pressure of Blacks."[18] Local officials in rural areas also targeted the popular *paseos*, or public strolls, that had long been segregated along racial lines. But they, too, largely chose to avoid conflicts, often "remodeling" the parks so as "not to confront embedded racial habits," as Alejandro de la Fuente notes.[19]

This combination of discursive daring and strategic circumspection extended to early efforts to establish "beaches for the people."[20] The immediate target of the campaign was the most famous waterfront real estate on the outskirts of Havana, but by the summer, Operación Playas Populares had expanded to include fifty-seven beaches across the island.[21] Behind these efforts lurked what W. E. B. Du Bois once called the "color problem of summer."[22] With the island's most desirable beaches accessible only to those with means, many could identify with the experience related by one journalist, whose student group had been turned away from a Havana beach because "there were several Black students among" them.[23]

As dramatized in the ICAIC short *Playas del pueblo* (1960), outright exclusion, and the poor condition of many public beaches, had long forced working-class and Afro-Cuban beachgoers to frequent Havana's Malecón or other unclaimed beachfront areas. With a nod to Castro's March speech, the film personifies the beach problem in two children, one white and one Black. When they are barred from entering a private beach, the boys go to the "only place that remain[s] to them: the reefs," where the Afro-Cuban boy struggles to swim and drowns. The film concludes in the revolutionary period, with an image of his white friend joining the fun at a newly integrated beach. There, he befriends a similarly shy, notably Black, child. "What had once been stolen, [is] now returned," the film concludes.[24]

Expanding beach access soon became linked to a new program of popular tourism. As hostilities with the US government escalated throughout 1959–60, INIT officials strategized about how to preserve one of the island's most important economic sectors. Before 1959, the Cuban tourism industry had largely catered to foreigners, with disfiguring effects on the island's reputation.[25] At the same time, even as Batista-era programs encouraged Cubans to "Travel Cuba first," middle- and upper-class Cubans had largely favored foreign destinations.[26] In attempting to revive the industry, revolutionary officials sought to enlist a new class of politically sympathetic travelers, including Cubans themselves.[27]

Beginning in summer 1960, INIT initiated a campaign to turn "Every Cuban into a Visitor," establishing payment plans so that even the "most humble" could finance their own vacations.[28] In the first half of 1961, over 32,000 *excursionistas* accessed the new program of popular tourism, exploring national parks, beach towns, and picturesque settings across the island.[29]

Soon, workers could also vacation at Varadero's famous beaches through passes distributed in unions and *emulaciones,* as CTC officials promoted tourism as an antidote to the "vice of alcohol, the principal cause of absenteeism."[30] As one emulation winner explained, entering this previously inaccessible territory evoked a time when he, a sugar mill worker, and his daughters had been invited to a party at the plantation owner's home but had been told that, due to their skin color, they would have to enter through the kitchen. Such discrimination, he declared, was a matter of the past: "There are no blacks or whites here. We're all one family."[31]

In this respect, the integration of popular culture was perhaps most dramatically realized in Cuba's private recreational clubs. Dating back in some cases to the late nineteenth century, Havana's beachfront clubs had long channeled Americanization, especially for middle- and upper-class Cubans.[32] Membership in turn served as a vehicle of distinction and often discrimination. The most exclusive clubs, Havana's so-called Big Five, maintained informal but consequential racial bans, with even President Fulgencio Batista turned away from the Habana Yacht Club.[33]

Since the late nineteenth century, however, Cubans of color had organized their own clubs, drawing on precedents stretching back to the era of slavery. The most prominent responded to racism by mobilizing against discrimination. At times, however, they adapted their own forms of exclusion by promoting "civilization" and distancing themselves from "African" influences.[34] Class and racial hierarchies also prevailed within these walls, with elite clubs largely restricted to light-skinned and professional members. But in the early decades of the twentieth century, these clubs, along with their white counterparts, underwent a process of "popularization."[35]

If recreational clubs had previously facilitated racial inclusion and exclusion, officials proposed to enact integration within their walls. They began with the most potent symbol of republican distinction, reopening the Biltmore Country Club as Cubanacán, the island's first Workers Social Club (Círculos Sociales Obrero, or CSO). By fall 1960, four more CSOs were under construction in Havana, and leaders had announced a nationwide "chain" of some 300 CSOs, overseen by the CTC and sustained through modest monthly dues.[36] With ambitious plans for developing libraries, sporting facilities, and cultural activities, the idea was not simply to equalize recreational access but also to reorganize popular sociability around class identification rather than racial separatism.[37]

The CSOs were formally inaugurated on May 1, 1961, in honor of International Workers' Day, but it was an event several weeks later that symboli-

As with other signature recreational initiatives, revolutionary leaders frequently stressed the values of decency and high moral quality when discussing CSOs. As this cartoon suggests, their use was also to be restricted to Cubans who worked. Political cartoon, "Círculo Social Obrero," *Palante*, no. 44 (August 25–27, 1962), 6. Courtesy of the Cuban Heritage Collection, University of Miami Libraries, Coral Gables, Florida.

cally captured their significance. On May 20, ordinary Cubans breached the "fortresses" of the capital's most exclusive clubs, in what Jaime Sarusky described as a "happy assault on the bastilles of Havana." He also recorded a *conguita* improvised for the occasion: "We have the sand, we have the sea, which thanks to the Revolution, we can finally see."[38] Meanwhile, in a symbolic affirmation of integration, the walls formerly separating Havana's most exclusive clubs from each other and the public were torn down, greeted by thunderous applause.[39]

If revolutionary officials focused their denunciations on the most exclusive clubs, these were not the only targets of their integrating efforts. Members of Afro-Cuban clubs also received notice that such institutions were considered "incompatible" with the Revolution.[40] Amid internal battles over the merits of racial separatism, Afro-Cuban clubs began to close in 1960, with few surviving into the mid-1960s. Some Black and mixed-race Cubans celebrated recreational integration as an affirmation of their newfound political importance. Others, meanwhile, quietly bemoaned the impoverishment of their social and political prospects, as de la Fuente and Devyn Spence Benson have proposed.[41]

The campaign to integrate social clubs also had cultural implications. For decades, Afro-Cuban clubs had incubated the most innovative currents in Cuban music, hosting trailblazing acts (from Pérez Prado and Celia Cruz to Cachao) and shaping the evolution of dance styles, including danzón, mambo, and cha-cha. Rosa Marquetti Torres has argued that they thus served as "authentic musical laboratories," where performers and dancers engaged face-to-face.[42] At the time, many Afro-Cuban performers were unable to perform in the island's exclusive recreational destinations; as Benny Moré exclaimed during a 1963 visit to the famed Casino Español: "Can you imagine if those *gallegos* saw me sitting here now!"[43] Such exclusions only magnified the creative importance attached to Afro-Cuban clubs.

If discrimination at times restricted opportunities for Afro-Cuban performers in the 1930s, '40s, and '50s, Cuban culture was nonetheless increasingly defined by their contributions. Robin Moore proposes that Afro-Cuban influence pushed Cuban dance and musical forms "away from the strophic, sectional, European-derived music and toward cyclic, improvisational, African-derived forms."[44] The resulting innovations drew on the generative environment of the social clubs, a public to whom the most famous performers remained responsive. They also received international acclaim, thanks to the rapid growth of the island's recording industry (and radio infrastructure), inventive engagement with international trends, and the opportunity to perform for foreign and especially US audiences, both at home and abroad.[45]

The impact of Afro-Cuban performers extended even to those clubs they were not allowed to join. One of them was the Casino Deportivo, established by senator and businessman Alfredo Hornedo Suárez when he was barred from the Habana Yacht Club due to his mixed-race (mestizo) heritage. That inspired him to establish his own club, which in turn maintained an unofficial ban on Afro-Cuban members.[46] But it was within the walls of the Casino Deportivo where a new dance style began to develop in the mid-1950s at the intersection of son, cha-cha, and American rock. "Casino," as it came to be known, was characterized by its "interdependent" quality, with multiple couples dancing in stylized collaboration.[47] It also channeled a kind of racial alchemy. According to Jesús Díaz, whose classic *Los iniciales de la tierra* takes place within the walls of the Casino Deportivo, racial "imitation" by the club's white dancers gradually gave way to appropriation and transculturation: "They began to invent a way of dancing that wasn't . . . as free or spontaneous or fresh as that of Black dancers at the *verbenas* of La Tropical, but that was also beautiful, a little spectacular, choreographed, ordered, and charming, sensual, and tasty in its own way."[48]

On the eve of the Revolution, casino represented a prized but still subcultural dance style. According to Juanito Gómez, a lifelong casino booster and cofounder of the legendary aficionado band Grupo Moncada, in 1959 there were perhaps several dozen *casineros*, almost all of them affiliated with the Casino Deportivo, soon to become the CSO Cristino Naranjo. Yet casino soon invaded other CSOs, including the Círculo Patricio Lumumba (formerly the Miramar Yacht Club), as the Revolution "nationalized" casino. Cubans from the provinces who came to Havana to study brought casino back home with them, and Habaneros traveling to the countryside for voluntary labor did the same. Yet casino did not remain static but continued to incorporate other, often Afro-descendant, influences, including changüí and rumba.[49]

Indeed, in the early 1960s, popular dance was nearly inescapable and served, like political rallies, as a site of sociability across racial lines. As one observer noted, "Who could have imagined that in the old Havana-Hilton, blacks and whites, Cubans all, could have gotten together to celebrate a fiesta like this one?"[50] The inauguration of the new CSOs in May 1961, which marked not only the first socialist Workers' Day but also the recent defeat of the Bay of Pigs invasion, represented a dramatic case in point, spawning "unprecedented massive popular fiestas," as Adriana Orejuela Martínez writes.[51] Like their prerevolutionary counterparts, the CSOs became vital venues for Cuba's most beloved artists to perform in, and for ordinary Cubans to channel the euphoria of integration. As captured in the iconic final dance scene of *Nosotros la música* (dir. Rogelio París, 1964), featuring the acclaimed Afro-Cuban performers Silvio and Ada, that meant literally dancing their way across a landscape—in this case, the Miramar Yacht Club— that formerly barred their entry.[52]

The turn to "state-sponsored popular culture," per Gleb Tsipursky, was a direct response to the disintegration of Havana's legendary nightlife.[53] As popular artists left the country and clubs were closed or nationalized, officials worked to reimagine recreation on revolutionary terms. Elizabeth Schwall has noted that in doing so they were often torn between the uninhibited *pachanga* of the Revolution, to use Carlos Franqui's memorable framing and ideological imperatives, including a creeping moralism.[54] In the early 1960s, however, some leaders (Franqui among them) promoted popular culture as a channel for revolutionary celebration *and* integration—in both senses of the term.

At the most basic, officials opened new venues to replace those that had been shuttered, including the CSOs and Salón Mambí, located outside the iconic Tropicana. Like the Afro-Cuban clubs, Salón Mambí, which drew thousands of people for weekend dances, served as a testing ground for pop innovations, a veritable "temple," as one journalist described it, "of good dance music."[55] Some musical hits were even promoted by the state. These included the pilón, developed by Pacho Alonso and drummer Enrique Bonne in imitation of the movements associated with grinding coffee. In 1962, Bonne's fifty-person percussion ensemble undertook an unparalleled government-sponsored tour, bringing his blend of Afro-Cuban and international sounds to audiences across the island.[56]

Another drummer, Pedro Izquierdo, better known by his stage name, Pello el Afrokán, became the face of the mozambique, perhaps the most famous fad to sweep the island's airwaves and dance floors. The dance, set to charging horns and fast-paced percussion, featured an up-and-down choreography that the performer had devised, accessible to even the most flat-footed dancers.[57] But Izquierdo, who came from the working-class Havana neighborhood of Jesús María, was also an Abakuá practitioner, who incorporated rhythmic elements from Afro-Cuban religious music into his performances. Moore explains that the very name of the dance was chosen to "emphasize [Izquierdo's] own African heritage and the contributions of Africa to Cuban culture."[58]

Alongside officials associated with the CTC, Fidel Castro, who notoriously took little "personal interest in music," displayed public enthusiasm for the group, even encouraging them to help promote the upcoming sugar harvest.[59] Notably, at a time when leaders had carefully portrayed integration in structural rather than interpersonal terms, Pello el Afrokán and his nearly all-Black ensemble defied that circumspection "by inviting white women into his troupe as dancers and by interacting with them onstage," Moore observes.[60] As the highest-paid performer of the period and one of the few allowed to tour abroad, Izquierdo represents the power of state sponsorship for Black popular culture.[61] Greeted with enthusiasm across the island, he was given his own TV platform, *Ritmo de juventud*, and received, by his estimation, 55,000 fan letters in the two weeks following its debut.[62]

At the same time, state officials began to sponsor Afro-Cuban sacred culture, channeled through new institutions such as the Department of Folklore at the Teatro Nacional and the Instituto de Etnología y Folklore. With the collaboration of ethnographers Rogelio Martínez Furé, Argeliers León, Odilio Urfé, and others, the period saw a "dramatic expansion of public drumming" as well as media visibility for dance and music associated with the practice of Santería and Abakuá.[63] At the first and second Festivales de Música Popular Cubana, organized by Urfé, the island's African heritage, along with its rural and peasant forms, moved to center stage. Such performances served as an expression, as participant Benny Moré put it, of the "flavor of the people."[64] These incorporative gestures sought to establish Afro-Cuban culture as having "developed, evolved, according to the logic of our people, in our people, and by our people," in the words of Argeliers León.[65]

These efforts were not without precedent in the recent past. Many organizers were students of or affiliated with Fernando Ortiz, who, since the 1920s and '30s, had promoted Afro-Cuban vernacular culture with an integrationist bent. Though such efforts had provoked racist backlash, a turning point was reached with a 1937 public performance of batá drumming by Pablo Roche, Águedo Morales, and Jesús Pérez. In its aftermath, ballet and cabaret choreographers began to incorporate elements from Black sacred culture—often transposed, Elizabeth Schwall notes, onto white bodies for "outsider consumption"—while composers like Gilberto Valdés folded batá drumming into orchestra compositions.[66] At the same time, Afro-Cuban "religious pop" brought a sacred vocabulary and musical elements to popular culture writ large.[67]

After 1959, Afro-Cuban vernacular expressions gained even broader public exposure, including in the many aficionado groups who began to take them up.[68] Such promotion spoke to strategic efforts to cultivate Afro-Cuban support as well as the prerogatives of secular-minded ethnographers, who, following Ortiz, highlighted the dialectical—that is, integrative—aims of revolutionary folklore. But the expanded visibility of Afro-Cuban ritual culture also reflected the mobilization of Afro-Cuban intellectuals such as Walterio Carbonell, who presented Africa as the singular foundation of Cuban culture, and the collaboration of many ordinary Cubans, who brought their own religious and artistic imperatives to this work.[69]

Of course, these visions were not necessarily synchronous in practice. The Conjunto Folklórico Nacional (CFN), founded in 1962 by Furé and Mexican choreographer Rodolfo Reyes Cortés, offers a notable case in point. The CFN—which began as an aficionado group but by the end of the decade had achieved national recognition and, eventually, the status of "full-time" (paid) performers—represented a unique effort to bring Afro-Cuban sacred culture to a broader audience.[70] It did so by drawing on the expertise of group members, who were presented as "informants" and "living libraries."[71] Such language was consistent with the anthropological perspective of cultural officials and bore desacralizing implications, reflecting other tensions behind the scenes.

Indeed, the CFN's unprecedented visibility did not translate into generous compensation, media promotion, or popular acclaim. Though audience reactions tended to cleave along racial lines, practitioners who did not object to the public staging of sacred culture tended to prefer more "authentic" renderings to the group's "stylized" interpretations.[72] Yet despite the "indoctrinating" aims of their interlocutors, Elizabeth Schwall suggests that the group maintained an "overwhelming identification with blackness," thereby threading "sacred wisdom" into their rendition of "revolutionary culture."[73]

The question of whether cultural promotion would facilitate racial integration (and vice versa) thus remained an open one. As one journalist had written in April 1959, the "race problem," understood as a "matter of national integration," was "easier to consider and overcome." Far thornier, he proposed, was the problem of "discrimination," viewed as a "mental phenomenon."[74] Revolutionary officials had focused accordingly on physical geographies—workplaces, beaches, and clubs—rather than psychological states. But tackling the economic and social base of racism did not necessarily ameliorate its social and cultural forms. As an official dispatched to integrate a Havana Carnival group wrote in 1962, that work required interpersonal engagement. She cited the case of one mother, who at first opposed the selection of a dark-skinned dance partner for her daughter, even as she insisted that she was not "racist." After the pairing was upheld, however, the mother "ceased to put up a fight."[75]

And so, despite Fidel's stated intentions, dancing across the color line became, as with Pello el Afrokán's performances, a defining assertion of revolutionary values. Yet even as Izquierdo featured white women onstage, footage of his performances, from Salon Mambí to Havana's Carnival, shows that many audience members were Afro-Cuban. Meanwhile, for supporters and opponents alike, revolutionary popular culture became marked as implicitly if not explicitly Black.[76] Indeed, despite the integrationist efforts of the revolutionary government, the early to mid-1960s witnessed the persistence and at times intensification of cultural differentiation along racial lines.

These shifts had consequences for musical creation *and* consumption. Throughout the hemisphere, the emergence of a youth generation with lei-

This suggestive image accompanied Eugenio Pedraza Ginori's 1966 report on the Salón Mambí. The picture shows that the Mambí's crowd was predominantly but not exclusively Afro-Cuban. In addition, this and other photos suggest that dancing couples were primarily formed within rather than across racial groups. Eugenio Pedraza Ginori, "Salón Mambí," *Cuba*, April 1966, 30. Photos by Carlos Núñez, courtesy of the Cuban Heritage Collection, University of Miami Libraries, Coral Gables, Florida.

sure time and consumer capacity had relocated music from the background of popular recreation to the foreground of subject formation. It played a particularly important role in the political awakenings of the 1960s, as taste became a vehicle to mark not only subcultural identification but also ideological affiliation.[77] Yet the consolidation of youth cultures in the Americas was not, in most cases, a racially integrating phenomenon. Even though Black performers shaped many innovations of the period, their adoption—or cooptation—into white youth culture rarely fomented interracial sociability. In fact, for decades to come, musical tastes and fan communities cleaved largely along racial lines.[78]

These trends had their counterpart in Cuba, particularly in the interactions between the so-called *pepillos* and *guapos*. Beginning in the 1950s, the term "*pepillo*," whose Cuban antecedents stretched back decades, was applied to those "young people—generally from the middle and upper classes—who dressed in the most current fashions and listened to foreign music," per Orejuela Martínez.[79] But in the face of intensifying political hostilities, in the early 1960s, listening to US and British rock music marked not only adherence to what was internationally au courant but also discrepancy from what was locally promoted. In that spirit, the *pepillos* depicted Cuban music in general as *cheo*, or unhip, especially the dance music favored by the *guapos*, so named for their macho behavior and flashy dress. While the *pepillos* furtively listened to the Monkees and the Beatles, the *guapos* danced casino—and, for a time, mozambique—at the CSO Lumumba and Salón Mambí.[80]

Such differences might have been left to smolder in the realm of youth sociability were it not for the fact of government intervention. In the early 1960s, the *pepillos*' enthusiasm for foreign music began an ideological problem for which revolutionary leaders worked to devise a political solution. Meanwhile, even as many Afro-Cubans remained more aligned with the revolutionary government, their cultural preferences did not escape scrutiny. As officials sought to organize culture along revolutionary lines, their interventions made culture inescapably political, a fact that could serve the project of integration in both of its registers, or promote resistance to it.

Banning the Beatles

In 2007, the ghosts of the Revolution's past came back to haunt its present when Luis Pavón, the infamous former CNC president, suddenly appeared on television screens across the country. As he was treated to a largely celebratory interview, Pavón's reappearance provoked indignation among island intellectuals, culminating in the so-called *guerra de los emails*. The resulting exchanges amounted to an extraordinary public reckoning with the experience of *parametración*, or dismissal from the ranks of the state cultural apparatus, suffered by many in the late 1960s and early '70s.[81] But Pavón was not the only ghost to be exorcized. Several weeks earlier, two other figures had been treated to a televised resurrection: Armando Quesada, who once headed the theater and dance department at the CNC, and Jorge "Papito" Serguera, director of the Instituto Cubano de Radiodifusión between 1967 and 1974. Uniquely, Serguera was remembered not only for his censorial tenure at the ICR but also for its broader pop-cultural implications, for Serguera, many have alleged, was the man who banned the Beatles in Cuba.

If battles over culture were a universal effect of the Cold War, in Cuba they were perhaps uniquely pitched. In light of the proximity (and allure) of capitalist media, island leaders viewed popular culture as a latent threat to revolutionary authority. The persistence of US efforts to overturn the Revolution—often channeled, as we have seen, through cultural mediums—only raised the stakes on combating "imperialist" influence. Culture, however, was rarely imagined as an end in itself. Officials conflated taste with physical appearance, gender identity, and, by extension, political loyalty.[82] Policing popular culture was thus a matter of safeguarding revolutionary hegemony.

From the earliest moments, political scrutiny of popular culture was undertaken in the name of nationalism. In April 1959, the Comisión Revisora de Película, an institution inherited from the Batista government, sent a representative to the Hotel Flamingo to "occupy" the script of a British adaptation of *Our Man in Havana*, citing the fact that it "[made] Cuba look like a country full of vices and social blemishes that have now been completely eliminated by the Revolution."[83] By early 1960, the Communist youth magazine *Mella* had begun to publish film reviews critiquing those that were "pornographic" or "ill intentioned," including in the second category "newsreels filmed in capitalist countries."[84]

Meanwhile, in a December 1960 speech, Fidel Castro critiqued Hollywood for producing the "most savage movies, the most inhumane movies, movies full of scenes of killing of Indians by white men; killing of Africans by white men."[85] By 1962, many of those films could no longer be viewed on island screens, in part because of the US embargo and the nationalization of most movie theaters. But the island's collection of some 200 US films made before 1960—which, one columnist noted, continued to "attract large audiences"—was also subject to new rules.[86] Western, gangster, and horror films were banned, and any US film had to be presented as a "second feature" to a film from a Communist country.[87]

Foreign films were not alone in drawing political attention. The most notorious act of censorship was perhaps that applied to the 1961 short *P.M.*, directed by Orlando Jiménez Leal and Sabá Cabrera. Filmed in the lead-up to an expected US invasion, *P.M.* set out to document Havana's nightlife in a free cinema style. In the directors' depiction, however, Havana after dark featured plenty of dancing and drinking and little in the way of military preparation. After several closed-door screenings, the film raised alarms among cultural authorities and sparked a series of debates about its content and form. These discussions culminated in Castro's famous "Words to the Intellectuals."[88]

The participants in these exchanges may have been intellectuals and bureaucrats, but the people were never absent from the picture. Notable are the words of Edith García Buchaca, influential CNC vice president, as captured by Abel Sierra Madero at the distance of several decades: "It was a moment of great tension . . . and this young man makes a short. . . . [And it made it seem like] Havana at night was two or three Black people [*negros*] in the port playing drums and dancing and drinking rum."[89] García Buchaca's description epitomizes the judgments on which cultural policy increasingly rested: that, in a context of imperialist threat, popular taste, especially when grounded in embodied pleasures, could bleed into political heterodoxy. It is not incidental that this denunciation was rendered in racialized terms.[90]

Rosa Marquetti has observed that the fate of *P.M.* also reflected official attitudes toward the small and sometimes unsavory clubs that dotted the coastline of Marianao. Those sites, made legendary in the pages of Cuban and foreign literature alike, had long provided space for "any Habanero" to "blow off steam" after hours. Arguably, they were also the stars of the film, where they played host, Marquetti points out, to the legendary Afro-Cuban drummer Silvano Shueg Hechavarría, popularly known as "el Chori." Though el Chori had previously been the subject of a laudatory edition of the *Noticiero ICAIC Latinoamericano*, the "*cabaretuchos*" that had provided a platform for his talent would not survive the controversy over *P.M.* In July 1963, many were closed as a result of INIT's Plan for the Sanitation of the Playa of Marianao.[91]

The censorship of *P.M.* thus also highlights the political stakes assigned to music. As an early CNC document put it, music was, "of all of the arts, the one that most directly reached the people," making management even more pressing. The same document notes that the Revolution had, "for the first time," established the "conditions so our popular music [could] express itself in all its force . . . free of all of the foreign elements that had tried to disfigure it."[92] The form of this sentence belies a familiar anxiety. For decades, intellectuals and performers had raised concerns about external influences on Cuban music, held up since the late nineteenth century as a site of national distinction. After 1959, combating Western and especially US influence acquired renewed urgency, premised on a fundamentally top-down (and thus often misdirected) notion of how musical taste was formed.

Yet this focus did not eliminate the ambivalence attached to Blackness, as we have seen. Rock was a foundationally Afro-diasporic form, even though its popularity in Cuba was largely channeled through white performers. As would occur elsewhere, the uproar it generated invoked racial cues, dating to its island debut in 1956.[93] Indeed, the first prohibitions on rock were enacted not by the revolutionary government but by Fulgencio Batista's Ministry of Communications, which in 1957 issued a short-lived ban on television programs that featured the "frantic" (*agitado*) and "frankly immoral" dancing associated with rock.[94] The ban was soon reversed in response to protests, though regulations regarding dancing and dress remained on the books.[95] According to Yeidy Rivero, the measure formed part of an expanding project of policing "indecency" on TV, including "anything that digressed from European languages, religious traditions, and norms of sexual conduct," such as Afro-Cuban dance and music or men in drag.[96]

The vilification of rock was thus far from unprecedented in Cuba, but after 1959 it acquired new political force, extending to an outright ban between 1964 and 1966.[97] The effects of that prohibition persisted for at least a decade thereafter, echoing parallel campaigns in the Soviet bloc and Mexico, where rock and jazz were decried as instruments of imperialist penetration and discouraged or, in some cases, translated and co-opted.[98] Yet accounts of musical censorship in revolutionary Cuba have long been plagued by ambiguity. During a 1997 colloquium organized by Cuba's leading Beatles historian, Ernesto Juan Castellanos, a former radio host and fan of the group argued that it had been reasonable to limit the "diffusion" of Beatles music in the context of US aggression. But given that he and many others continued to listen to the group throughout this period, he concluded that he could not "affirm as a fact the prohibition on the Beatles in Cuba in keeping with the general understanding of the term 'prohibited.'"[99] On the other side, Castellanos contended that censorship was a reality, even as he noted that "there was never a law or official norm that prohibited listening to or disseminating" Beatles music.[100] As he has written, however, this does not absolve censors from blame: "Even though 'no one' prohibited anything, 'no one' did anything to stop it either."[101]

In fact, revolutionary efforts to contain Western popular music predated (and extended beyond) the 1964 British Invasion. Much like their Batista-era counterparts, early campaigns targeted rock in the spirit of Elvis and his Cuban interpreters, citing concerns about indecency as well as the genre's purported connections to imperialism and homosexuality. Following a *Mella* exposé alleging that rock records (and pornography) had been introduced to the island through the West German embassy, an April 1963 radio report bemoaned that rock had mobilized "a whole series of parasitical, vice-ridden, and homosexual elements . . . with the evident intention of catching young people in their web."[102] Soon, similar language began to surface in the press and the pronouncements of revolutionary leaders. Most famously, in a March 1964 speech, Fidel Castro derided "Elvis Presley fans" (elvispreslianos) and their "jeans and long hair."[103] That message was broadcast across the country and taken up in local campaigns, as in Puerto Padre, where a cafeteria was covered with signs featuring his words. All the rock records were subsequently removed from its jukebox collection.[104]

But it was the Instituto Cubano de Radiodifusión that would play the leading role in curating and policing popular music. As suggested in a 1966 report on music policy, it was one of the organization's founding principle. Rock, however, was not its first target. While purging unpalatable language, characters (the chuchero, or "stupid and illiterate peasant"), and storylines ("the maid tricked by the man of the house"), the ICR also targeted music "in which one could still find vestiges of the so-called 'victrola numbers.'"[105] In jukebox roundups of the preceding years, boleros and filín (feeling) music had also been criticized for their "pessimistic" tone and purportedly North American roots.[106] Tellingly, such efforts did not diminish the music's popularity; Los Zafiros, one of the few blockbuster groups to emerge in the early 1960s, were renowned and beloved for their blend of American doo-wop, calypso, and bossa nova.[107]

But in 1963, in response to "growing interest," rock and, to a lesser degree, jazz became the focus of the ICR's energies. Popular enthusiasm for rock, jazz, and the twist had spawned new radio programs and attracted new fans, not only "unintegrated young people" but also "revolutionary youth," including members of the Unión de Jóvenes Comunistas (UJC), who celebrated jazz as the soundtrack to the US civil rights movement. Meanwhile, the out-migration of many performers—whose music was thereafter "removed . . . from the airwaves"—had left a vacuum that foreign genres quickly filled. An international agreement on music royalties, to which Cuba was a signatory, had raised the problem of exile songwriters, forcing the ICR to shelve much of their music as well. The result, the report notes, was a full-fledged "crisis" for Cuban music.[108]

In response, the ICR moved to purge rock and disseminate more acceptable content. On the one hand, it began to promote Cuban music and especially homegrown dance genres, including the pacá, pilón, dengue, cuba-ya, melao, changüi, and, most famously, the mozambique.[109] Throughout the mid-1960s, the mozambique was virtually inescapable as a result of this policy and, by many accounts, overstayed its welcome among fans.[110] As island media boosted his music, Izquierdo took on the role of defending Cuban music against foreign influence, declaring that "as long as there was Cuban music[,] no twist or anything like it would get in."[111]

As they promoted national music, ICR officials also worked to suppress rock and the twist. These efforts were imperiled from the start. Live performances were almost impossible to police, and artists took advantage of the "veil" of calypso or bossa nova to perform rock. Aficionado groups presented an even greater challenge, given the recent importation of electric guitars for their use; through the program, rock and twist had "reached the large masses who, in the past, would hardly have had access to such rhythms."[112] The ban was also combated in the press. Cultural critic Orlando Quiroga was so committed to rock that he personally distributed Beatles records to radio stations across the country. For this advocacy, he paid a price, as he related in an interview with Ernesto Juan Castellanos: "I was called by a *compañero* from the COR [Commission of Revolutionary Orientation] . . . and he told me I couldn't speak about those British mop-tops (*melenudos*). . . . When I asked him why, he pounded the desk and shouted: Because the Beatles are *maricones*, man!"[113] Quiroga was later suspended from writing in *Bohemia* for several months, as was a Bayamo producer who played a record he had received from him.[114]

Even so, Cubans who studied or served in diplomatic capacities abroad continued to serve, alongside the merchant marine, as agents of rock dissemination, as did the mass organizations and "official organisms" that contracted performers to play at their events.[115] At the same time, Cubans accessed rock and other international music by tuning into US and British radio stations, though doing so was not without its risks, as documented by Humberto Manduley López.[116] In short, for all practical purposes, the rock ban not only failed but earned the ICR a great deal of notoriety. By its own account, it was "censured by some sectors for intellectual narrowness, sectarianism, musical illiteracy," even as others accused it of serving as the "chief propagandist for foreign music." The author of the 1966 report chafed at this latter accusation, noting that the ICR had promoted only "Cuban arrangements" of popular foreign songs, such as Raphael's "Yo soy aquel." Songs such as these could not reasonably be ignored, the writer proposed, if Cuba was "not to give in to the pressure of Rock and the Twist."[117]

The only logical path forward, the document concludes, was to establish a coordinated policy toward rock, authored by the Communist Party and applied across all agencies. The problem was not just one of shaping musical taste but also of combating the "external appearances," from "long hair" to clothing and "gestures," that came along with it.[118] We can intuit what kinds of behind-the-scenes decisions were made in response to this report. In 1966, rock music began to be cautiously introduced into radio programming and would soon play a starring role on such legendary programs as *Nocturno* and *Sorpresa musical*.[119] As of September 1967, eleven of the fourteen most requested songs on *Nocturno* were by foreign artists, including the Rolling Stones and the Mamas and the Papas.[120]

Yet this did not signal full-fledged acceptance. Instead, the mid-1960s witnessed the halting assimilation of genres previously treated as taboo. On the one hand, Spanish covers were inescapable, so much so that critics have skewered the Spanish wave they engendered. Meanwhile, consistent with previous efforts to cultivate Cuban music as an alternative to the foreign, in 1967 the Orquesta Cubana de Música Moderna, along with its six provincial offshoots, was established to assimilate those genres, especially jazz, grouped under the euphemism of "modern music."[121] At the same time, a homegrown protest-song movement, which drew on Latin American and US sources of inspiration, established a precarious niche under the protection of Haydée Santamaría at Casa de las Américas.

These tentative gestures of incorporation would not last. By 1968, revolutionary leaders had renewed their attacks on youthful cultural tastes. They also unleashed police repression, as in the notorious Operation Hippie, which, Anna Veltfort recalls, ensnared not only "homosexuals but all long-haired 'enfermitos'—young men who wore jeans, tight *tubito* pants, or sandals & girls who wore miniskirts. They were known to listen to forbidden music on the 'W' stations, like WQAM, transmitting from Miami."[122] The 1968 Revolutionary Offensive and the unofficial Ley Seca in turn aimed to "defeat . . . cabaret culture" altogether.[123] The campaign also led to the definitive closure of many signature Havana venues, in what Leonardo Acosta has characterized as an "irreparable" blow.[124]

By 1967, the ICR was also under new leadership.[125] A lawyer by training, Jorge "Papito" Serguera had earned political trust thanks to his role in defending survivors of the 1956 *Granma* landing and in the 1966 prosecution of six men accused of CIA collaboration. By the time he assumed the ICR directorship, Serguera had also served as Cuba's ambassador to Algeria and the Congo.[126] He took over the ICR directorship promising to target *caudillismo*, nepotism, and sexual harassment.[127] His strategy, by producer Eugenio Pedraza Ginori's account, was to bring in "bureaucrats, members of the old Stalinist PSP, ex-combatants," and others, who helped to establish "radio and television . . . as simple platforms . . . for disseminating political messages."[128] What followed became the stuff of history and, to some degree, legend.

Serguera has earned enduring ignominy for canning *Mientras tanto*, a televised platform for Cuban protest music and singer Silvio Rodríguez. Though the cast and production faced pressure (and, in one case, being sent to the cane fields) for featuring long hair or miniskirts on-screen, the real trouble began when Rodríguez praised the Beatles during a live transmission. Serguera responded with indignation: "If he was there to play his guitar and sing his songs, why did he have to get me in trouble over the Beatles?!"[129] Rodríguez has presented the controversy in similar terms: "For me it was . . . some *dirigente* or something like that, who saw the program and called Papito: "Listen, that boy there is talking about and publicizing the Beatles!" Rodríguez was subsequently dismissed from the ICR and incorporated into the ICAIC Grupo de Experimentación Sonora (GES), which served as a refuge for many musicians, including director Leo Brouwer, whose interest in "modern" music had gotten them in trouble. Rodríguez continued to experience regular police harassment until he and the genre of protest music were officially rehabilitated in the form of "nueva trova" in the early 1970s.[130]

In an interview with Castellanos, Serguera bemoaned that he had been blamed for the Beatles ban despite his own passion for their music. He even insinuated that he had "opposed those measures" in "letters written to high officials of this country." Yet Serguera offered few consistent explanations for the censorship that transpired during his tenure, asserting that neither "directives [n]or governmental resolutions" nor the Commission on Revolutionary Orientation shaped ICR policy. Later, however, he suggested that the "problem became law, directive, perhaps originating in the COR or the Communist Party," which led to actual "sanctions for young people, and even people removed from the UJC and PCC."[131]

Here, Serguera seems to reference the intensification of censorship following the 1971 Congreso de Educación y Cultura and the campaign against ideological diversionism unleashed in the same period. In a 1972 speech, Raúl Castro denounced the role of radio in US-sponsored "diversionist campaigns" that "incited young people to acquire extravagant lifestyles and abstain from the revolutionary process."[132] With "imperialist" music, including rock, newly associated with political transgression, English-language music was again suppressed on Cuban radio and TV in 1973.[133]

Meanwhile, drawing on the work of theorists such as Theodor Adorno, Cuban musicologists and their Latin American colleagues analyzed "cultural colonization" in its diverse manifestations, from imposition and commercialization to more subtle means of co-optation. As Olavo Alén argued, these included the conscription of Latin American artists to disseminate US values, among them José Feliciano, a vehicle for "pacifist ideas" and "conformism" with respect to the "colonization of Puerto Rico," and Carlos Santana, with his "underground" style and drug use.[134] As many Cubans recall, for a time Feliciano's music disappeared from island media under opaque circumstances.[135]

A 1973 letter to Luis Pavón, CNC president, offers a window into the enactment of these prohibitions. The recent appearance of Soviet singer Edita Pieha on Cuban television had raised alarms due to the long hair sported by several members of her band. In response, Serguera had called a meeting in which he informed ICR department heads that "until that moment it had been permitted to use 'foreign hairdos' on television," but no longer. This represented a problem for the CNC, which was sponsoring upcoming concerts by Italian singer Settimelli, Spanish singer Joan Manuel Serrat, and the Hungarian group Estudio 11, who all sported problematic hairstyles. The institutional discrepancy between sartorial policies was one of the issues to which the letter writer sought to draw attention, along with the fact that the ICR's "music problem" continued to "drive commentary in the street. "It's believed," he noted, "that the decision that was made *did not come originally from that organism.*"[136]

This language echoes the reference to a "received orientation" in the 1966 ICR document, as well as Serguera's exculpatory explanations to Castellanos. Even as he insisted that neither "Fidel nor Raul ever interfered" in his work as ICR director, he nonetheless acknowledged that they sometimes "raised certain concerns" with him, including "that famous thing, ideological diversionism," as it applied to "modern music." Serguera proposed that censorship was largely executed by ICR employees hindered by "pseudoculture," even as he maintained that "we still don't know who was responsible."[137] In this, Serguera coincides with Fidel Castro, who was asked about the Beatles ban when a John Lennon statue was inaugurated in Havana in 2000. "I ask myself the same question," he replied. "It's very possible it could have been a case of extremism, for different reasons." Castro's tone, however, quickly changed to the defensive: "But don't look at me as if I were responsible for it!" Indeed, Castro insisted that he had only learned of the ban in the days before the statue's debut.[138]

Nonetheless, the 1966 report states that the "leadership of the Government and the Party" were briefed by ICR representatives before they implemented the first systematic prohibitions on rock in 1963. Based on that report and following a "personal conversation with the Co. President of the Republic [Osvaldo Dorticós]," the decision was made to "contain the divulgation of that music on Radio and TV."[139] Though Castro may not have been party to this conversation, he undoubtedly was involved in the decision-making, as his subsequent public denunciations would suggest. Yet the same document repeatedly stresses the need for a more consistent policy elaborated by the PCC, requesting, in effect, the same grounds for exoneration claimed by Serguera and Castro himself.

In 1974, Serguera was removed from the ICR directorship for unclear reasons.[140] The ban on English-language music was lifted, never to be imposed again.[141] But the everyday practice of censorship changed little as a result. Arguably, the most consequential instrument remained the act of proscription, what employees referred to as "blacklists." As to who ended up there, Pedraza Ginori relates that it could include anyone who left the country or intended to, those "disaffected from the political system or not sufficiently integrated into revolutionary activities," as well as gender- and sexual-nonconforming individuals and those with "questionable friends" or "strange" hair. He further notes that those included on the lists, which went largely unwritten, were often left to guess at their absence from the airwaves.[142]

The blacklist included mostly Cuban artists, yet international performers continued to generate significant controversy within and beyond ICR walls. Even as the ban on English-language music was reversed, new prohibitions targeted popular Spanish and Latin American singers such as Julio Iglesias, Roberto Carlos, Camilo Sesto, Raphael, and José Luis Rodríguez (El Puma). The presumed reason for the ban was that all of them had participated in the Festival Internacional de la Canción de Viña del Mar, a Chilean music competition, following Augusto Pinochet's 1973 coup. Some of the artists subsequently banned in Cuba were indeed supporters of Pinochet. But Iglesias, a conservative with strong familial connections to Spanish fascism, seems to have made no public statements on the matter, though he did participate in Viña del Mar multiple times between 1973 and 1981.[143]

On the island, however, no formal justification was given for Iglesias's disappearance from the airwaves, and it was left to Radio Bemba to fill in the gaps.[144] When two students and I asked Cubans about their memories of cultural censorship, many of them pointed to the Beatles, but nearly all of them cited Julio Iglesias, who was then at the peak of his Cuban popularity following the unprecedented island-wide screening of his film *La vida sigue igual* (dir. Eugenio Martín, 1969) in 1972. The film, which depicts Iglesias's life story from the car accident that ended his career as a soccer player to the competition that launched him as a singer, was a watershed event in Cuban cultural history and became, by Joel del Río's estimation, the "most popular film of the year . . . , the decade, and perhaps of all time."[145] *La vida sigue igual* made Iglesias into a Cuban icon and heartthrob, generating devotion and one-upmanship among fans, who boasted of having seen it dozens of times.[146] In fact, the film became so popular that ICAIC would periodically dig it out and reprogram it across the island when theater attendance was down. Del Río proposes that *La vida sigue igual* gave Cubans the opportunity to put a personal story—in this case, a heroic and inspiring one—to a performer's music.[147] It thus furnished them with one of the first international pop icons in revolutionary times.

In this regard, it is interesting to note that one of producer Pedraza Ginori's own songs had been censored at the ICR due to its reference to a *galán,* the term historically used to describe—and "glorify"—male television stars.[148] Since the early 1960s, such representations had been subject to withering criticism in the revolutionary press, where they were denounced as "archaic, corny, stupid," and "unbearable."[149] By the mid-1970s, a Marxist critique had also been brought to bear on pop idols, who, as one critic argued, misdirected the "latent or actual rebelliousness" of young people toward "generational conflict" rather than "class struggle."[150]

Whatever the reasons, Iglesias's disappearance from the airwaves was keenly felt, even as his songs were rereleased as Cuban covers or listened to surreptitiously by fans.[151] Yet for many, it was the unexplained nature of his proscription that proved most impactful. Though popular rumor filled in the gaps, often invoking "political" concerns, expressions such as "nadie sabe por qué," "no sé por qué," and "nunca supe por qué" are most prevalent in popular accounts of the Iglesias ban.[152] In contrast to the rock ban, in which Cubans encountered a constant stream of official denunciation— linking rock to homosexuality, counterrevolutionary attitudes, and ideological diversionism—the very absence of a justification for the Iglesias ban conveyed a different, perhaps unanticipated, message: that no artist was too beloved to end up on the chopping block and that, in that circumstance, the public was owed no explanation.

In late 1974, a new committee was established to regulate music on Cuban media. An internal account from the time identified musical dissemination—including the balance between national and foreign artists—as a pressing matter under investigation at the ICR and within the party.[153] Another document from the following year recounts efforts to rein in the "massive and indiscriminate use of Western music" and its associated fashions, including "hairstyles and clothes coming from capitalist countries and some manifestations of Blackness [*negritud*]."[154] Much as Beatles fans were chided for their long hair and tight pants, sartorial displays of racial pride were treated as imitative of US examples and antithetical to the official discourse of integration. These restrictions—enacted amid continued high-profile engagement with Angela Davis and other US Black activists, as well as the Cuban government's own expanding forays into African liberation struggles—marked yet another disjunction between the Revolution's domestic and international projection.[155]

Meanwhile, by the mid-1960s, a shift toward scientific atheism had prompted a harsher attitude toward Afro-Cuban sacred culture. This brought greater scrutiny for practitioners, who once again had to request official approval to hold *toques de santo*.[156] The official classification of such practices as "superstitious" or "primitive" also had cultural implications. Even as aficionado groups continued to present "religious folklore" for local publics, vernacular Afro-Cuban music and dance were absent from the island's music schools through most of the following decade and subject to "strict limits" on radio and TV, as documented by Robin Moore.[157]

From the Beatles to Black Power, such bans reflected the concern that popular culture could catalyze political disaffection. Censorship took certain artists off the air, and some were never known as a result. Yet ordinary Cubans understood that bans were happening, and at times they openly flouted them. In this respect, it is tempting to regard the censorship of popular music as an enterprise doomed to failure. Even as the state deputized its institutions to police culture, it remained almost impossible to banish an artist or genre given the many underground outlets through which it could be accessed. Often, the fact of persistence forced cultural bureaucrats to reverse course: to incorporate rather than proscribe.

But when it comes to fans, the story of musical censorship is perhaps one of unintended—even counterproductive—success. The global Cold War made the political increasingly personal (and vice versa), as popular culture was reframed in ideological terms. In Cuba, as in the Soviet Union, this interaction was distinctly intense. Thus, while island officials worked to re-signify musical taste as a matter of political consequence, the bans they enacted convinced fans of the importance attached to their cultural choices. Sometimes this endowed musical taste with samizdat and subcultural value, the dangers of consumption only magnifying its dissident appeal.[158] In other cases, however, censorship bred resentment toward politicization. Fandom could thus serve as a mode of escaping or even rejecting the insinuation of state power in the cultural realm: an insistence that some pleasures should not be beholden to ideological concerns.

Recovering the Popular

From the doldrums of the *quinquenio gris*, a cultural phenomenon emerged, attached not to forbidden foreign pleasures but to homegrown musical innovation. In the late 1960s, Juan Formell, a young bass player who had delivered an injection of pop to Elio Revé's *changüí* style, set out on a mis-sion to "make Cuban music modern."[159] The effects of that experiment proved electrifying for young fans and quickly established Formell as the "songwriter with the greatest hold on the populace." He soon started his own band, Los Van Van, whose name honored a slogan associated with the projected 10-million-ton harvest of that year. Indeed, Formell located his efforts to revitalize Cuban dance music firmly within the revolutionary project, which he presented as having given "meaning to his life."[160]

Los Van Van's early sound was rooted in the fertile interplay between foreign music, especially rock, and Cuba's traditional dance genres. This cross-fertilization was at the heart of "songo," described by one observer as a mix of "Yoruba and beat music with *son*."[161] For years to come, that fu-sion enshrined Los Van Van as "one of the few [groups] . . . making music that appealed to young people." Yet this did not make Los Van Van either a critical darling or an international success. Amid ongoing battles over for-eign music, Formell frequently bemoaned that cultural officials continued to privilege Cuba's musical traditions over its potential future. As he told an interviewer: "Why keep fooling ourselves and returning, demagogically, to that music that belongs to the historical past?"[162]

In the same period, official ambivalence greeted the appearance of an-other pioneering musical outlet. Irakere, founded by pianist Chucho Valdés and composed of many former members of the Orquesta de Música Mod-erna, debuted in 1972 with a sound spanning jazz, rock (especially in the horns-driven style of Blood, Sweat, and Tears), and Afro-Cuban percussion.[163] The group's use of the batá and chekére established bridges between international and Yoruba trends, even as Valdés pushed his musicians to make their music genuinely popular, extending to trial-by-fire performances at the Salón Mambí. Yet as cultural bureaucrats dragged their feet in authorizing the group—a serious obstacle, given that professional performers had become state employees in 1968—Irakere, like Los Van Van, was largely marginalized from Cuba's musical circuits.[164] Not until an international tour in 1977 and a celebrated performance at the Newport Jazz Festival the following year—culminating in a record deal with CBS and a Grammy—was the group officially embraced.[165] In the meantime, both Los Van Van and Irakere faced sporadic censorship for "innocuous" lyrics and continued doubts as to whether they were "Cuban" enough.[166]

Cultural officials instead threw their support behind traditional music, with the Orquesta Aragón and other such groups representing Cuba abroad, and the Movimiento de la Nueva Trova (MNT). Sponsored by the UJC, the MNT had been founded in 1972 with the signing of a manifesto at the foot of the Sierra Maestra. The very name served to nationalize the genre, linking it to a long tradition of Cuban and Latin American popular song (trova) rather than the Western rock from which it had also drawn inspiration. Whereas artists like Silvio Rodríguez and Pablo Milanés had once incarnated a countercultural spirit for which they had faced punitive consequences (including, in Milanés's case, internment in the UMAP camps), in the early 1970s the MNT located itself firmly within revolutionary culture.[167]

Lillian Guerra proposes that MNT musicians executed this shift by making propaganda "beautiful," with love songs that "seduced listeners into believing that the love they described was romantic or familial when, in fact, it was entirely political." *Trovadores* thus assumed the mission of turning art into a "weapon of the Revolution" by championing and personalizing its values.[168] At the 1979 MNT festival, performers, some of whom had once been accused of "foreign-izing" (*extranjerizantes*) influences, pledged to "work to expand the musical culture of [their] people, so that it might serve as a weapon against cultural colonialism."[169] Though associated artists continued to bemoan the "plebeian" (*populacho*) tastes of TV and radio producers, they soon became the standard bearers for an "official" popular culture, both in island media and abroad.[170]

Thanks to the resources afforded to the MNT, it may have indeed achieved mass proportions, if measured by the number of Cubans who picked up guitars in response.[171] But was nueva trova actually *popular*? By the mid-1970s, this was the kind of question on the minds of cultural bureaucrats and political leaders alike. Earlier in the decade, integration into the Soviet bloc had spurred the reintroduction of market mechanisms into the Cuban economy. As leaders reoriented production to material incentives and wage differentials, new institutions such as the Instituto Cubano de Investigación y Orientación de la Demanda Interior (ICIODI, or Cuban Institute of Research and Orientation of Internal Demand) spearheaded a kindred process of rationalization. From yogurt to shoes, toys to television, the consumer tastes of ordinary Cubans newly became a matter of economic and political interest.[172] In the cultural realm, this shift was abetted by decentralizing currents in both cultural and state politics, with the liberalizing presidency of Armando Hart at the Ministry of Culture and the Poder Popular system of local governance, launched in the mid-1970s under the authority of the Communist Party.[173] Popular perspectives sat at the discursive, if not necessarily structural, center of these innovations.[174]

Occasional efforts to assess popular taste had been initiated in the preceding years, often undertaken by the Commission of Revolutionary Orientation or in the state-academic collaborations discussed in previous chapters.[175] Yet this research was largely classified and rarely informed cultural policy.[176] As a result, film became the most accessible means to assess popular tastes, given that box-office records—not to mention the length of lines outside theaters—could be used to determine what audiences liked, from the Cuban film *Lucía* (dir. Humberto Solás, 1968) to a pirated Chilean copy of *The Godfather* (1973).[177] Indeed, in spite of efforts to center socialist fare in Cuban theaters, part of what made movie viewing so *visibly* popular, in addition to its accessibility, was the relative frequency with which Western content continued to appear on island screens.[178]

By the early 1970s, however, officials began to sponsor systematic polling about popular habits. The ICIODI, for example, undertook island-wide surveys on a variety of issues, especially the use Cubans were making of their leisure time.[179] So, too, did the Communist Party's Department of Revolutionary Orientation, which sponsored a 1975 survey about radio and television. This shift responded to the fact that Cuban social scientists, like their Soviet counterparts, had discovered that contrary to the official imperative for *superación*, Cubans were not making very "productive" use of their free time.[180] As readers of the youth magazine *Somos Jóvenes* bemoaned, this was not for lack of trying. Many correspondents, especially outside Havana, insisted that their real problem was not the failure of productivity but the paucity of opportunities.[181]

In fact, as surveys revealed, Cubans spent quite a lot of time working, but they dedicated most of their free time to watching TV (urban respondents) and listening to the radio (rural respondents).[182] Musical programs, including *Nocturno*, ranked among the most popular fare, reflecting and continuing to spark debates over the correct balance of Cuban and international content. But when it came to TV, the highest-ranked program was *San Nicolás del Peladero*, a comedy that had been on the air for over a decade at that point and had largely evaded ICR censors by setting its satire of political corruption in the island's republican past.[183]

And so, in dialogue with the historic First Congress of the Cuban Communist Party in 1975, leaders once again turned to mass media to chart the island's future. Public declarations affirmed the ideological and pedagogical significance of radio, television, film, and the press, while calling for the cultivation of "active" consumers. This would demand not only opportunities for the populace to "express their judgments, suggestion, and complaints," as a 1976 resolution from the Department of Revolutionary Orientation proposed, but also the incorporation of popular "tastes and preferences" into island media.[184] In short, leaders wanted entertainment to transmit revolutionary values—but they also wanted Cubans to like it.

Officials at the Instituto Cubano de Radio y Televisión (ICRT, as of 1976) thus focused their attention on those programs with the greatest "political and ideological significance" as well as the "largest audience[s]," while working to develop "programs with popular participation." Meanwhile, the ICRT also pledged to refresh Cuban radio and "develop an intelligent policy in defense of our music."[185] In the years to come, these goals underwrote new TV shows centered on spy intrigue, including *En silencio ha tenido que ser* (a joint production with the Ministry of the Interior) and *Julito el pescador*, both of which garnered broad popularity while lionizing Cuban intelligence forces.[186] In fact, Michael Bustamante proposes that the 1970s proliferation of "revolutionary action stories" turned the Revolution itself into a "source of entertainment."[187]

But revisionist currents did not run in exclusively politicizing directions. *Para bailar* (1978–83), conceived and directed by Eduardo Cáceres Mansó, was a televised dance competition that required couples to perform to the most cutting-edge international sounds as well as classic Cuban music. With an appealing cast of nonprofessional hosts, live performances from Cuba's top bands, and, above all, outstanding dancing, *Para bailar* became required viewing for every Cuban on Sunday afternoons. As documented by Enrique del Risco, it also became a mass phenomenon, in some cases prompting a revival of *bailes masivos* not seen since the early 1960s.[188] Bolstered by the recent establishment of the Casas de Cultura, this period in fact witnessed the "massification" of dance, with some 98 percent of Cubans ages thirteen to eighteen reporting that they knew how to dance, compared to less than half of the generation that grew up in the 1960s.[189]

Indeed, *Para bailar* spoke directly to young people, and this was among its most celebrated effects.[190] As the show's first lead host Salvador Blanco has explained, the show achieved a "reconquest of Cuban music via American music."[191] That reconquest bore racial implications. One fan cited the show's integrative power, especially for those young (mostly white) Cubans who had been fans of the Beatles and Silvio Rodríguez. For them, engaging with Cuban music meant thrilling to *Afro*-Cuban music, perhaps for the first time.[192] Yet the fact that *Para bailar* achieved what officials had long called for did not spare it from scrutiny. As Cáceres has explained, production was required to "give three months' notice of all possible winners so they could be investigated. They decided who won and who didn't."[193] The show's cast was also affected by political surveillance, and infighting—driven by allegations of collaboration—followed two of the lead hosts into exile.

Despite these circumstances, the show survived for a time, perhaps thanks to support from an unexpected source. Carlos Rafael Rodríguez, a longtime Communist Party member and close Castro ally, wrote Cáceres in 1978 to congratulate him on the show's success, especially among young people. Rodríguez noted that he had long thought it "absurd to present modern music, and above all North American music, as an example 'of decadence,'" given its roots in Black culture. He also claimed to have opposed the repression enacted in this area, even though he had, a decade earlier, critiqued the "servile imitation of fashions that [originated] in the worst circles of capitalist decadence."[194] Rodríguez thus encouraged Cáceres to avoid politicization: "If the program is used to support cane-cutting, voluntary labor or other similar things, [it] . . . could perish."[195] Ultimately, however, Rodríguez's admonitions did not spare the show from political blowback. ICRT officials regularly expressed doubts about the director's "ideological trustworthiness" and made multiple efforts to replace him until he finally left the show, leading to its precipitous decline.[196]

Yet the lessons of *Para bailar* would not soon be forgotten. The late 1970s and early '80s saw halting efforts to identify what was popular and, in some cases, make it accessible to mass audiences.[197] In 1979, *Opina*, an innovative magazine launched by the ICIODI, was perhaps the most visible symbol of that initiative. Like the ICIODI, *Opina* was under the oversight of the Consejo de Estado (Council of State) and thus was not subject to the control of the Department of Revolutionary Orientation, as founding co-editor and cultural journalist Armando López explains. He recalls that the magazine was intended to function as a "capitalist" vehicle, with a thick section devoted to classified ads.[198] In the spirit of Fidel Castro's recent recognition of "deficiencies" and "difficulties" in Cuban socialism, *Opina* focused on consumer-oriented reporting that drew attention to problems in national industries, even sending undercover journalists to state restaurants.[199] Many of the writers brought in to execute this sensitive enterprise had been dismissed from other institutions and found *Opina* to be a desirable place to work, thanks to its atmosphere of editorial freedom and the compensation it provided for freelance reporting.[200]

The magazine, which also covered pop culture, became a runaway success, drawing record crowds to newsstands and quickly expanding its initial run from 5,000 to 300,000 copies.[201] It was not an oppositional outlet; one article, for example, skewered the "American Gay of Life," while a cartoon published in the thick of the 1980 Mariel boatlift advertised a "special offer" for cleaning up Mariel "escoria."[202] But official backing did not prevent ordinary Cubans from perceiving *Opina* as "critical."[203] In part, that sense was bolstered by the prominence afforded to reader perspectives. *Opina* asked its readers to send feedback about topical issues, from their opinions about Cuban television—*Para bailar* was an unsurprising top choice, though 73 percent of readers classified Cuban TV as "leaving much to desire"—to how they planned to spend their vacations (overwhelmingly: on the beach). Notably, most responses came from young people, ages fourteen to twenty-nine.[204]

Beginning in 1980, *Opina* editors debuted an amplified version of these surveys, which would thereafter be known as the Encuesta de la Popularidad. The Encuesta was based on a published questionnaire, which invited readers to submit their responses by mail. By 1982, survey winners were being awarded metal sunflower trophies (the Girasoles) in a televised ceremony, which featured a performance of an original Los Van Van song celebrating *Opina* as a magazine with "traction."[205] Two years later, 510,724 mail respondents, together with 155,000 households polled by ICIODI interviewers, selected Los Van Van as their favorite musical group, Antonio Núñez Jiménez's *En marcha con Fidel* as their top literary work, *Nocturno* as their preferred radio program, and the Brazilian telenovela *La esclava* as the best international TV show.[206]

Yet the Encuesta—and the Girasoles—also provoked renewed debate over the very definition of "popular." One observer, for example, cited Armando Hart's recent call to "distinguish . . . between what truly penetrates in the essences of the *pueblo* . . . [from] what has become generalized in the population, often in a transitory fashion and at times motivated by promotion." This, the writer pointed out, would better be described as "pseudopopularity," arguing that such phenomena impeded the development of a more "coherent" cultural policy set by the Communist Party.[207]

But some critical appraisals of the Girasoles had a more specific target in mind—namely, the fact that despite continued efforts to frame nueva trova as genuinely "popular" culture, Silvio Rodríguez and Pablo Milanés had made a relatively poor showing in early surveys, with Silvio garnering only a nod for songwriting in 1984.[208] Amid continued tensions, ICIODI head Eugenio Balari determined that the best path forward would be a compromise. Beginning in 1985, the magazine debuted a new award, the Girasoles de Cristal, to be decided not by popular vote but by an expert panel; Silvio Rodríguez and Pablo Milanés were among the first awardees.[209] This nod, however, did not satisfy Rodríguez, who, when asked about his win, critiqued the Girasoles for not "[taking] into account the criteria of specialists." "In questions as delicate as these," Rodríguez proposed, "sometimes the people make mistakes."[210]

Asked about the recognition of Los Van Van as Cuba's favorite group following the success of their 1982 album *El baile del buey cansao*, Juan Formell struck a different note. "I'm troubled and disappointed," he told *Opina*'s culture editor, "that the music that is truly popular . . . is disparaged by some sectors of the national culture." Noting the opportunities for international exposure enjoyed by the MNT, he bemoaned the fact that groups like Los Van Van were sent on tour "without even a note in the press," to encounter audiences largely ignorant of their music. When asked about the exacerbating role of the US embargo, Formell laid blame principally at the feet of Cuba's cultural bureaucracy.[211]

Indeed, just a year earlier, Pablo Milanés had been feted at a high-profile album release in Madrid, the fruit of a novel *convenio* between EGREM and the Spanish firm Ariola (of the BBC).[212] In contrast, artists like Los Van Van continued to face critics at home, who decried Formell's efforts to incorporate popular vocabulary into his songs as "vulgar," "populist," and "apolitical." Yet Formell rejected the notion that his songs were remote from political concerns. "It's premeditated that there's no direct political message in my songs," he maintained. "But, at a time when the penetration of foreign music is huge, what could be more political than making young people dance to Cuban music?"[213]

· · · · · ·

In spite of these battles, the mid-1980s likely represented the zenith of efforts to explore and even embrace the popular. The most notable innovations, from *Para bailar* to the Girasoles, owed their genesis to the innovative energies of individual performers and producers, whose institutional backing was always fragile. Yet attention to the popular was more than political lip service. A 1985 working document from the ICRT, for example, once again called for the "formation of an active listener or viewer," insisting that the "tastes of the public" should always be at the forefront of its efforts. This was necessary, it concluded, if only to prevent consumers from drifting toward "populism, expediency [*facilismo*], the enemy, who takes advantage of that breach to offer 'what the people want,' that to which they've already been conditioned." And so, much as officials once promoted the mozambique to lure young people away from rock, they now proposed to focus on *what Cubans like* to the same end.[214] Even Julio Iglesias made his way back on to the radio, though he continued to be critiqued for his ties to the exile community.[215]

In 1984, *New York Times* columnist Joseph B. Treaster noted recent changes in Cuban media, from more "lively" television broadcasts to "invigorated" radio programming. A new station, Rebel Radio New Style, featured "old Latin favorites" alongside "popular American and British tunes," while US movies were featured more prominently on island TV. Foreign observers also noted the expanded visibility of popular perspectives in island media, including "criticism of things that don't work as they should." Treaster cited "Western diplomats" who argued that these changes were a result of escalating tensions between Castro and Reagan, including the imminent launch of Radio Martí. Cuban officials countered that the changes were "part of an evolutionary process that [had] been in the works for years."[216]

Since the mid-1970s, liberalizing currents in island politics had indeed made it possible to reimagine the place of the popular in Cuban culture. A decade later, Reagan-era hard-liners and island fears over the contaminating effects of glasnost and perestroika would fuel another reversal. In 1986, Fidel Castro launched the Campaign for the Rectification of Errors and

Negative Tendencies, which rolled back incipient experiments with private enterprise and resurrected the Guevarist economic vision of the late 1960s. In the cultural realm, this produced renewed battles in and over media, efforts to combat foreign influence, and intensified censorship, contributing to the final demise of *Opina* and the Girasoles by 1990.[217]

What no one imagined was that bigger changes loomed on the horizon. The 1990 dissolution of the Soviet Union catapulted Cuba into an existential crisis, prompting Fidel Castro and later his brother Raúl to introduce capitalizing measures with major consequences for popular culture. Notably, the resurgence of tourism inspired investments in new cultural enterprises as well as expanded efforts to monetize Cuban culture abroad.

Yet intervention along these lines tended to follow a familiar pattern. Cuban rap, which emerged in the 1990s as a vehicle for grassroots Afro-Cuban protest, was belatedly incorporated into the state cultural apparatus, much like nueva trova before it. Some critics have argued that it was defanged in the process, though an underground and critical rap scene continued to draw fans. The contemporaneous emergence of *timba*—a fast-paced, heavy metal dance music innovated by former members of Irakere and Los Van Van, among others—sparked years of censure and censorship before it was tepidly accepted as a potential moneymaking vehicle. With its makeshift soundscape, embrace of capitalist values, and overtly sexualized lyrics, *reggaetón* has not achieved even that degree of toleration.[218] Each of these shifts has been accompanied by renewed criticism of the contaminating effects of foreign and especially US culture, even after Abel Prieto, a long-haired, Beatles-loving intellectual was appointed minister of culture in 1997 (a position in which he served until 2012, and then again from 2016 to 2018).

In the 1960s and '70s, through both promotion and repression, Cuban officials had enduringly politicized popular culture. Though their efforts enduringly changed island culture, they did not rescript the popular in the Revolution's image. State intervention could even bear contrary effects, threading political and cultural alienation together. But if political and popular culture never became fully identified, it is also because ordinary Cubans defied the homogeneity ascribed to the Subject of Revolution. Indeed, as cultural officials and their allies discovered time and again, when it comes to popular culture, it has always been—and remains—impossible to speak of "subjects" in the singular.

Conclusion

. . . .

¿Sabes quién es Gente de Zona? ¿Sabes?

¿Sabes que tienes que hacer para ser como Gente de Zona? (¿Sabes?)

Es imposible (Seguro)

Porque simplemente tienes que saber qué es la calle (Claro)

Tienes que tener conocimiento de lo que es vivir en un barrio humilde

Tienes que aprender a relacionarte con la gente (Claro)

Y tener presente que *nosotros mismos* somos la gente

[Do you know who Gente de Zone is? Do you?

Do you know what you have to do to be like Gente de Zona? (Do you?)

It's impossible (Clearly)

Because you simply have to know what the street is (Clearly)

You have to know what it means to live in a poor neighborhood

You have to know how to get along with people (Clearly)

And you have to remember that *we* are the people]

—"El Animal," Gente de Zona (2008)

All movements require messages, but some of the most consequential have also acquired soundtracks: songs that raise consciousness, vanquish fear, and propel feet into the street. Where ideology falls short and censorship inhibits connection, popular music has served as a medium to mobilize and unify. From the US civil rights movement to the fall of the Soviet Union, the "wind of change" has often left a political *and* melodic mark.[1]

In February 2021, a unique contribution to the musical repertoire of resistance debuted on YouTube and immediately went viral, seeding its message and melody throughout the Cuban mediasphere. "Patria y Vida" brought some of the most well-known artists in Cuba's musical diaspora (Gente de Zona, Yotuel, Descember Bueno) together with outspoken rappers and opposition activists on the island (Maykel Osorbo, El Funky). The song was rooted in a simple but memorable rejoinder to Fidel Castro's famous slogan, *Patria o muerte* (Fatherland or death). The performers instead championed *"patria* and life," rejecting a vision of patriotism grounded in existential choice. The song quickly set familiar dynamics into motion. High-profile members of the exile community celebrated it as an anthem of freedom, while it was denounced in the Cuban media as a front for exile or CIA manipulation.[2] In the coming months, "Patria y Vida" inspired both imitations and homages, as well as rebuttals, musical and otherwise, from the island.[3] These extended to the appropriation of the song's axiomatic paradigm (#patriayvida) by Miguel Díaz Canel, president of Cuba since 2019.[4]

Yet what no one could have predicted was the role the song would play in the unprecedented grassroots mobilization soon to appear on the horizon. Spurred by the toll of the second wave of the COVID-19 pandemic, the process of economic restructuring undertaken by Díaz Canel, and the intensification of US sanctions under President Donald Trump, in July 2021 ordinary Cubans took to the streets to protest material shortages, power outages, and a general sense of economic and political crisis. Alongside the ongoing resistance spearheaded by the Movimiento San Isidro, among other artistic constituencies, some also decried restrictions on their cultural and political freedoms. But in a powerful encapsulation of these diverse grievances, many demonstrators demanded simply "patria y vida." Though one could sketch a long genealogy of protest music located within and outside the Revolution, "Patria y Vida" has become the first entry in that tradition to both accompany and spur popular dissent.[5]

What made it so galvanizing? The song channels the political power of the prosaic, juxtaposing the "drums and cymbals" that marked Havana's 500th anniversary with "empty pots" in people's houses, or the luxurious tourist "paradise" at Varadero with mothers' despair over their children's departure. It thus spoke through and to the grievances of ordinary Cubans, who were thereby connected to the high-profile resistance led by artists and intellectuals since the passage of the notorious Decree 349 (2018). That measure imposed restrictions on artistic activities occurring outside the purview of the official cultural bureaucracy as well as any expression deemed anti-patriotic, "sexist, vulgar, or obscene," or "harmful to ethical and cultural values."[6] The law thus connected historic tensions between cultural officials and independent artists on the one hand and *reggaetoneros* on the other, whose music was at one point the object of direct state suppression.[7]

In this respect, the mediums for this message were highly suggestive. Many observers have highlighted the central role played by the Afro-Cuban artists and performers associated with the Movimiento San Isidro, including not only El Funky and Maykel Osorbo but also performance artist Luis Manuel Alcantará, all of whom have faced punitive consequences for their opposition to the government. Lillian Guerra argues that "Patria y Vida" thus reflects the increasingly defiant articulation of "Black consciousness" among island artists and intellectuals, which has been greeted by escalating repression.[8] December Bueno, a trained classical and jazz performer, founding member of Yerba Buena, and celebrated songwriter, and Yotuel, formerly an independent rapper in Cuba and later cofounder of the Grammy-winning Orishas, can similarly boast artistic credibility and critical acclaim, especially outside Cuba.

Arguably, though, the most significant participants were Alexander Delgado and Randy Malcolm of the *reggaetón* duo Gente de Zona. For decades, Gente de Zona has been one of the most popular groups on either side of the Florida Straits. Thanks to a 2014 collaboration with Enrique Iglesias (penned by Iglesias and December Bueno, who also appears on the track), they also became one of the first mass crossover successes since the Revolution. The fact that they had long faced censure in the exile community for their reluctance to openly criticize the island government magnified the political impact of their participation, rendering them a neat stand-in for those island Cubans who were expressing dissent for the first time. In them, Cubans found two performers whom they not only knew but could identify with.[9]

In this respect, "Patria y Vida" speaks on behalf of ordinary Cubans ("llora mi pueblo y siento yo su voz"), represented here by an entirely Afro-Cuban group of performers. As Coco Fusco has proposed, it thus reflects the "power of popular music to evoke the experience of Cuba's vast Black underclass."[10] Throughout the video, Yotuel even presents his body as a canvas for the reimagining of "patria" in terms of "vida."

That imagery circulated widely and inspired a flood of admiring memes, as well as racialized and homophobic derision in the Cuban media.[11] Significantly, the song also prompted a high-profile repudiation from one island journalist, who asserted that José Martí, Che, and Fidel—as well as "Silvio [Rodríguez]" and "Israel [Rojas, of the pro-government duo Buena Fe]"—"represented" him, and not the song's performers, whom the author referred to as "rats" and "zombies."[12]

The song's power is thus grounded in part in its messengers, who recast the Cuban subject in distinctly embodied and implicitly racialized terms. Yet this also raises the question of *to whom* the song is addressed. In the

Still from "Patria y Vida" (dir. Asiel Babstro, 2021), accessed at YouTube, www.youtube.com/watch?v=pP9Bto5lOEQ.

opening lines, the singer hails an unnamed siren who carries away his sorrows but causes him pain, even from afar. One senses that, following a long cultural tradition, he is invoking Cuba itself. As the song proceeds, however, its addressee becomes more ambivalent, and not necessarily more concrete: a purveyor of useless ideals in the face of devastation in Cuba's *solares*, the destroyer of what was once and continues to be dreamed in the name of freedom.

One might conclude that the singers are hailing the revolutionary leadership, especially Díaz Canel himself, who was also implicated in the popular protest slogan "Díaz Canel *singao*" (Díaz Canel, asshole). Yet the decision not to explicitly name an addressee also seems significant. This is perhaps best reflected in the song's enigmatic dominoes imagery, specifically the juxtaposition of "your 59" with "my double two's" (the latter often taken as a reference to the anticipated outbreak of popular resistance to come). "Patria y Vida" indeed marks a generational divide, notably its assertion of an "abyss" that lies "between you and me." Yet the song also makes a case for finality—"it's over" (*se acabó*)—and thus stages a declaration of independence: not from Díaz Canel, or even Raúl or Fidel Castro, but perhaps from the Subject of Revolution itself.

The Truth about Cuba

In this respect, recent events mark a decisive turning point in the relationship between the subjects and Subject of Revolution. Yet they are also squarely rooted in the forces and fault lines described in this book, from the fertile and contentious interface of political and popular culture to enduring battles over the truth about Cuba. Most directly, the original July 2021 protests (11J) as well as many follow-up mobilizations have sparked bilateral allegations of "fake news," driven by social media, a novel and volatile medium of interpretive engagement.[13] The seeming instability of representation has in turn shaped competing narratives over how to understand Cuba. Island voices have condemned an external "media war," waged by the US government, exile leadership, and corporate interests, while others within and outside Cuba have cited government censorship—especially internet blackouts—as the principal obstacle to information.[14] All of this is wrapped up in an epistemological (and, more consequentially, political) problem that the Cuban state has faced for decades, as detailed in several chapters of this book. Namely, in the absence of open governance and meaningful forums for popular representation, island leaders have manifested a sometimes bewildering disconnect from the needs and desires of "the people," in all their heterogeneity.

At the same time, the dramatic events of 11J have galvanized a diverse network of transnational observers, who, to put it mildly, do not always agree on their significance or necessary consequences. As some exile constituencies called for military intervention and even "airstrikes," high-profile writers associated with the Cuban government demanded renewed attention to the embargo, US imperialism, and, in a notable echo of early 1960s psyops, solidarity in the face of "cognitive war."[15] Long-standing divisions in the Revolution's international reception have also surfaced on other fronts. Notably, when a July 14 statement from the Black Lives Matter Foundation overlooked the protests and emphasized resistance to the US embargo, the organization entered a heated debate over the significance of race in understanding 11J, as well as the long fraught relationship between racial justice and (counter-)revolutionary solidarity.[16]

Meanwhile, scholarship on the Revolution's past, present, and future has developed significantly in the last decade, thanks in part to expanded (if uneven) archival access. Yet academic work remains deeply imbricated in current events and political battles. Almost any historical treatment of the Revolution will inevitably be read as a commentary on Cuba's contemporary reality—and any discussion of Cuba's present a verdict, implicit or explicit, on its past. The very urgency of current events endows scholarship with obvious relevance in the public sphere, while historians work to ground their interpretations in an increasingly robust and diverse source base. Indeed, it seems notable that some recent work, including this book, aims less to resolve than to historicize the fact of competing (and often irreconcilable) interpretations.[17]

As has long been the case, events in Cuba have shaped transnational framings that sometimes intersect with but just as often depart from the multiple and incommensurate scripts crafted by Cubans themselves. Notably, and thanks in part to the very medium (social media) that has inspired transnational battles over Cuba's truth, the perspectives of ordinary Cubans are increasingly accessible: not only to external observers seeking to understand from afar but also to those who seek to mobilize on their basis. This includes Cubans on and off the island who have harnessed social media messaging to various political ends, sometimes amenable but other times contrary to the intentions of the creator(s). Such politicization has in turn made social media platforms vulnerable to critical scrutiny, whether grounded in the potential mechanics of media manipulation or in questions of representativeness. In short, the promise and peril of subjectivity continues to shape the ways in which many across the hemisphere access—and understand—the Revolution itself.

Revolutionary Subjects

From the battle against Batista to the protests of today, this book has traced how Cuban subjects, along with their hemispheric counterparts, became connected to the Subject of Revolution. Whatever their ideological leanings, few were those, especially on the island, who lived beyond the Revolution's definitional—and self-definitional—grasp. Yet this argument for coarticulation similarly implicates the Subject of Revolution. Ordinary Cubans rarely determined the course of macropolitical or economic events, but they nonetheless exercised interpretive power, however self-referential, over the construct of "the Revolution." The subjects and Subject of Revolution thus evolved in epistemological concert, channeling power through the production of knowledge and generating knowledge through the circulation of power. In this sense, knowing the Revolution became intimately connected to being in Revolution, and vice versa.

From France to the Soviet Union, Mexico, and beyond, several generations of scholars have engaged the questions raised by this conjunction, exploring when the course of revolutionary process has veered toward popular acceptance or rejection, conformity or agency (or conformity *as* agency). These debates have often been grounded in considerations of hegemony—the boundaries of revolutionary inclusion and exclusion, the reach of popular incorporation and co-optation—but also, particularly in a post-Foucauldian era, in considerations of subjectivity. Such work has further probed whether political subjectivity should be considered an effect of power or, in fact, constitutive thereof.[18]

In entering a long-standing and perhaps exhausted interpretive field, I have sought less to revive a scholarly stalemate than to shift the terms of the conversation.[19] Throughout this book, I have only occasionally broached the issue of how or if Cubans were remade as "new men" (or women), as distinct from revolutionary subjects. In part, this is because I cannot help but partake of the retrospective circumspection that has guided previous observers in this respect, rooted in the suspicion that humans tend to be less malleable than utopian theories would predict.[20] Instead, I have approached this question, like many others, as *implicated* in revolutionary politics—one of the many sites of knowledge production that runs straight through revolutionary governance—and thus one we would be wise not to tackle without interrogating the terms in which it has traditionally been presented.

In contrast, I have sought to understand how the context of Revolution spawned new ways of thinking and interpreting reality, from both above and below. Engaging but also historicizing the fraught question of whether most Cubans tilted toward acceptance or rejection (and how political boundaries shifted, as they inevitably did, over time), I have centered interpretation as a unifying activity, whether directed toward political affirmation or opposition, neither of the two, or (at times) both. In short, I have sought to redefine the subject of Revolution as anchored less in ideological identification (Communist or anti-Communist, "new men" or "old") than in the fact of epistemological intention. Do subjects, in short, make revolutions, or do revolutions make subjects? The obvious answer is, of course, both.[21] Yet I have also reframed this question to propose that, over the course of six decades, the very fact of interaction has forged something that extends beyond but is ultimately unimaginable without those subjects: namely, "the Subject of Revolution."

After Revolution

Recent events have highlighted the fragility of this constitutive bond. Yet its weakening dates back several decades to the fall of the Soviet Union, the Special Period of the 1990s, and the corresponding reframing of the state-populace compact. Two generations of Cubans have now come of age in the aftermath of that halting pivot away from what had once defined the Revolution in the economic realm, with the revival of tourism and new joint state ventures with foreign companies, along with their social and political consequences. Much to the consternation of some who remember the "before," new values have supplanted a long-standing if often conflicted emphasis on collectivism, anti-imperialism, and self-abnegation. Once cherished figureheads long ago lost their luster, and few new idols have emerged to replace them. In the harsh light of severe economic crisis (and shrinking state support), rapidly shifting international relations, and the aftermath of a global pandemic, the Subject of Revolution, as traditionally understood, has become increasingly amorphous, hollow, or perhaps, as some have argued, extinct.[22]

What does this mean, in turn, for the subjects of Revolution? The fact that recent years have witnessed the island's largest outmigration since 1959 suggests that many have ceased to identify in any obvious way with that category, even as mobility and immobility continue to define both the "subjects" and "Subject" of Revolution. Those who remain, meanwhile, face the question of how to define themselves as political subjects in a context in which economic hardship resulting from Cuban and US policy remains acute and dissent criminalized. As of summer 2021, this penalization extends, per Decree 35 and Resolution 105, to online and social media activity deemed false, "offensive," or harmful to the country's "prestige."[23] Decree 35 also outlines enforcement mechanisms, though the government's most efficient recourse remains cutting off internet service, which it deployed multiple times during and after that summer's protests.

Yet despite its control over telecommunications access, the government has not been able to curtail online criticism. We do not have to partake of the technological determinism that has greeted the past decade's internet-driven uprisings to recognize that the medium—notably, the expanded wireless access (3G and 4G) debuted in the context of Obama-era normalization and mobilized to political ends well before the July 2021 protests—presents its own irrepressible message.[24] As this book has argued, that message is consistent with a long-established framing of revolutionary political culture as transacted in and through popular culture, both from above and from below. From letters to the editor to amateur theater, popular dance, and *Opina* polls, Cubans of all persuasions have turned to the cultural mediums at their disposal to both understand and respond to the political context they inhabit. All evidence suggests they will continue to do so in imagining a future Cuban subject of—or after—Revolution.

Notes

Abbreviations in the Notes

AMMP   Antonio Maceo and Mackle Papers
CNC   Archivo General del Ministerio de Cultura
BNJM   Biblioteca Nacional José Martí
ICRT   Centro de Documentación, Instituto Cubano de Radio y Televisión
CFCR   Cuban Freedom Committee Records
CHC   Cuban Heritage Collection
DM   *Diario de la Marina*
FFR   Ford Foundation Records
FCR   Free Cuba Radio
HMP   Herbert Lionel Matthews Papers
AARC   John F. Kennedy Assassination Archives and Research Center
JFK   John F. Kennedy Presidential Library
LAC   Library and Archives Canada
LBJ   Lyndon B. Johnson Library
MM   Museo de la Música
NYT   *New York Times*
NH   *Noticias de Hoy*
RFP   Richard Fagen Papers
RFWP   Robert F. Williams Papers
TDP   Theodore Draper Papers
VOP   Victoria Ortiz Papers

Introduction

1. Dirección de Cultura, Ministerio de Educación, "Cortometraje para anuncio del concurso para un argumento cinematográfico de la Dirección de Cultura del Ministerio de Educación y el Instituto Cubano del Arte e Industria Cinematográficos," May 1961, folder NO C4 Concursos ICAIC Correspondencia, 1961–62, 16/1, CNC.

2. MINED, "Relación de argumentos recibidos en la Sección de Cine, Televisión y Radio que con esta fecha se remiten al Dr. Alfredo Guevara, Director del ICAIC," Havana, August 28, 1961, folder NO C4 Concursos ICAIC Correspondencia, 1961–62, 16/1, CNC.

3. Díaz Castañón, *Ideología y Revolución*, 8. See also Hunt, *Politics, Culture, and Class in the French Revolution*; K. M. Baker, *Inventing the French Revolution*;

Trouillot, *Silencing the Past*; Joseph and Nugent, *Everyday Forms of State Formation*; Kotkin, *Magnetic Mountain*; Sewell, *Capitalism and the Emergence of Civic Equality in Eighteenth-Century France*.

4. For relevant theoretical reflections on this process, see Díaz Castañón, *Ideología y Revolución*, 37–94.

5. See Anderson, *Imagined Communities*; Warner, "Publics and Counterpublics," 63.

6. Guerra, *Visions of Power in Cuba*, 12.

7. See, among others, Gosse, *Where the Boys Are*; Artaraz, *Cuba and Western Intellectuals since 1959*; Gronbeck-Tedesco, *Cuba, the United States, and Cultures of the Transnational Left*; Brown, *Cuba's Revolutionary World*; Rojas, *Fighting over Fidel*.

8. Sontag, "Some Thoughts on the Right Way (for Us) to Love the Cuban Revolution," 6–19.

9. Not to mention universal; "every individual," Díaz Castañón suggests, "contributes to the theoretical thought of an era." *Ideología y Revolución*, 69.

10. On related themes, see Yurchak, *Everything Was Forever, until It Was No More*.

11. Edward Hunter, "Anatomy of a Film: Analysis of *Three Faces of Cuba*," in *An Exposé of the Insidious Film "Three Faces of Cuba,"* by Truth about Cuba Committee, Inc. (Miami, 1965), 16, Truth about Cuba Committee, Inc. Records, CHC.

12. Bernhard, *U.S. Television News and Cold War Propaganda*, 1–2, 7.

13. On the broader political and cultural context, see Menand, *The Free World*.

14. See Díaz-Briquets and Pérez, "Cuba," 26–27 (year ending June 30). In the United States, the legal designation of "refugee" was a product of the Cold War, mobilized in ad hoc measures throughout the 1950s and formalized in the 1965 Immigration and Nationality Act. See Bon Tempo, *Americans at the Gate*.

15. Daston, "Objectivity and the Escape from Perspective."

16. See Lambe, "Revolution's Fourth Face on the Fourth Network."

17. Scott, "The Evidence of Experience."

18. On related concerns, see Novick, *That Noble Dream*.

19. Polanyi, "Knowing and Being," 468, 465.

20. See de la Fuente, *A Nation for All*, 259–344; Ayorinde, *Afro-Cuban Religiosity, Revolution, and National Identity*; Quiza, "Sujetos olvidados"; Hamilton, *Sexual Revolutions in Cuba*; Guerra, *Visions of Power in Cuba*; Chase, *Revolution within the Revolution*; Benson, *Antiracism in Cuba*; Hynson, *Laboring for the State*; Bustamante, *Cuban Memory Wars*; Sierra Madero, *El cuerpo nunca olvida*.

21. For relevant (and heterogeneous) touchstones on the interplay between revolutionary ideology and mythologies, see Pérez-Stable, *Cuban Revolution*; Díaz Castañón, *Ideología y revolución*; Farber, *Origins of the Cuban Revolution Reconsidered*; López Rivero, *El viejo traje de la revolución*; Guanche, *El continente de lo posible*; Guerra, *Visions of Power in Cuba*; Rojas, *Historia mínima de la Revolución Cubana*; Lambe and Bustamante, "Cuba's Revolution from Within"; Kapcia, *Short History of Revolutionary Cuba*; Bustamante, *Cuban Memory Wars*; Guerra, *Patriots and Traitors in Revolutionary Cuba*.

22. As summarized in Luis Agüero, "¡Vikingos!" *Cuba*, no. 9 (September 1967): 62.

23. Omar, email message to author, May 6, 2015.

24. Cited in Agüero, "¡Vikingos!," 62.

25. Omar, email message to author, May 6, 2015. On contemporaneous tensions regarding the proper role and organizational autonomy of the CDR, see Domínguez, *Cuba: Order and Revolution*, 263–64.

26. Memo, Chief of Operations, Operation Mongoose (Lansdale), to the Special Group (Augmented), August 14, 1962, https://history.state.gov/historicaldocuments /frus1961-63v10/d374. See also D. Díaz, "¿Gusanos?"; Guerra, *Visions of Power in Cuba*, 198–227.

27. John Bland, "'Gusano' New Nickname for Anti-Castro Cubans," *Montreal Star*, April 12, 1962, 19.

28. Woodard, "Intimate Enemies," 149–51.

29. As in Kotkin, *Magnetic Mountain*; Siegelbaum and Sokolov, *Stalinism as a Way of Life*. See also Díaz Castañón, *Ideología y Revolución*; Guerra, *Visions of Power*.

30. In addition to works on the Soviet Union cited throughout, my thinking has been shaped by Joseph and Nugent, *Everyday Forms of State Formation*; Joseph, Rubenstein, and Zolov, *Fragments of a Golden Age*; M. K. Vaughan, *Eagle and the Virgin*; R. A. López, *Crafting Mexico*.

31. See Hernandez, "Filmmaking and Politics"; Chanan, *Cuban Cinema*; Castillo, *Conquistando la utopía*; Malitsky, *Post-Revolution Nonfiction Film*.

32. Quiroga, *Cuban Palimpsests*, 95. On poster art, see Desnoes, "Los carteles de la Revolución Cubana."

33. For a helpful survey, see Bustamante, "Cultural Politics and Political Cultures of the Cuban Revolution."

34. See J. Franco, *Decline and Fall of the Lettered City*; Iber, *Neither Peace nor Freedom*.

35. For exceptions, see R. D. Moore, *Music and Revolution*; Orejuela Martínez, *El son no se fue de Cuba*; Vazquez, *Listening in Detail*; Porbén, *La revolución deseada*; Guerra, *Visions of Power in Cuba*; Y. Rivero, *Broadcasting Modernity*; Bronfman, *Isles of Noise*; Marquetti Torres, *Desmemoriados*; Lam, *Esta es la música cubana*; Bustamante, *Cuban Memory Wars*. For illustrative perspectives on these questions in the post-1991 context, see Fernandes, *Cuba Represent!*; Hernández-Reguant, *Cuba in the Special Period*. On contemporary popular culture in exile, see Laguna, *Diversión*.

36. On the terms of early Cuban debates, see Urfé, "Factores que integran la música cubana." On revolutionary political culture, see Fagen, *Transformation of Political Culture in Cuba*; Valdés, "Cuban Political Culture"; Guerra, *Visions of Power in Cuba*; Guerra, *Patriots and Traitors in Revolutionary Cuba*. In framing the inter-action between political and popular culture, I follow the lead of Hall, "Notes on Deconstructing the Popular"; J. Franco, "What's in a Name?"

37. Joseph and Nugent, "Popular Culture and State Formation in Revolutionary Mexico," 22.

38. See Hall, "Encoding/Decoding."

39. See Smith and Padula, *Sex and Revolution*; M. K. Vaughan, *Cultural Politics in Revolution*; Vaughan et al., *Sex in Revolution*; Chase, *Revolution within the Revolution*.

40. In addition to works cited in chapters 1, 3, 4, and 5, see Ribadero and Domenech Hernández, "Presentación del Dossier."

41. See Guerra, *Visions of Power in Cuba*; García Yero, "State within the Arts"; Schwall, *Dancing with the Revolution*.

42. In the interest of preserving anonymity, all interviewees who participated in this project are identified using pseudonyms.

43. See Ferrer, *Insurgent Cuba*; Guridy, *Forging Diaspora*; Roa, *Bufa subversiva*; Gronbeck-Tedesco, *Cuba, the United States, and Cultures of the Transnational Left*; Bronfman, "'Batista Is Dead'"; Guerra, "Searching for the Messiah."

44. For relevant literature on Latin America not already cited here, see Zolov, *Refried Elvis*; Dunn, *Brutality Garden*; Green, "'Who Is the Macho Who Wants to Kill Me?'"; Manzano, *Age of Youth in Argentina*; Cowan, *Securing Sex*.

45. See Domínguez, *Cuba: Order and Revolution*; Pérez-Stable, *Cuban Revolution*; Guerra, *Visions of Power in Cuba*. Many of these efforts were in turn reversed in the Campaign for the Rectification of Errors and Negative Tendencies, launched in 1986.

46. See Kapcia, *Havana*; Gallardo, *El martillo y el espejo*; Fornet, *El 71*; Gordon-Nesbitt, *To Defend the Revolution Is to Defend Culture*; Grenier, *Culture and the Cuban State*; Bustamante, "Cultural Politics and Political Cultures of the Cuban Revolution." Only in 1976, with the liberalizing directorship of Armando Hart at the newly integrated Ministerio de Cultura, did this counterpoint between popular integration and ideological repression abate, if not fully recede. Roger Reed has argued that the post-1976 period did not witness a significant decline in cultural repression; see Reed, *Cultural Revolution in Cuba*, 143–60.

47. See, for example, Lambe and Bustamante, "Cuba's Revolution from Within."

48. For more on this argument, see Lambe, "Cuban Leaders Have Long Relied on Anti-Imperialist Anger."

Chapter 1

1. Joseph Hansen, "The Truth about Cuba," *Militant* (May 9–August 22, 1960), www.walterlippmann.com/hansen-truth-about-cuba.html.

2. Truth about Cuba Committee, "¿Qué es el Comité La Verdad Sobre Cuba?" (1972), box no. 128, folder no. 68, The Truth about Cuba Committee, Inc. Records, 1961–1975, series 4, CHC, https://digitalcollections.library.miami.edu/digital/collection/chc0193/id/1479/rec/2.

3. Truth about Cuba Committee, Background on "The Truth about Cuba" (1961), The Truth about Cuba Committee, Inc. Records, series 4, CHC, https://digitalcollections.library.miami.edu/digital/collection/chc0193/id/1528/rec/13.

4. Fidel Castro (speech, Presidential Palace, January 21, 1959), www.cuba.cu/gobierno/discursos/1959/esp/f210159e.html.

5. On relevant contexts, see Cane, *Fourth Enemy*; Feinberg, *Curtain of Lies*; Freije, *Citizens of Scandal*; Smith, *Mexican Press and Civil Society*.

6. See Díaz Castañón, *Prensa y revolución*; Guerra, *Visions of Power in Cuba*; Fernández, *La imposición del silencio*; Bustamante, *Cuban Memory Wars*.

7. See Marrero, *Dos siglos de periodismo en Cuba*, 126–42; Pérez, *War of 1898*; Hoganson, *Fighting for American Manhood*.

8. See Gronbeck-Tedesco, *Cuba, the United States, and Cultures of the Transnational Left*.

9. See Gosse, *Where the Boys Are*.

10. Letter to "Ted" and "Manny," January 22, 1958, box 2, folder 9, HMP. See also DePalma, *Man Who Invented Fidel*; Teel, *Reporting the Cuban Revolution*.

11. See González, "Percepciones de la Sierra Maestra"; González, "Enrique Meneses, un periodista español en Sierra Maestra."

12. Teel, *Reporting the Cuban Revolution*, 5.

13. Mallin, *Adventures in Journalism*, 74.

14. Teel, *Reporting the Cuban Revolution*, 4–10, 34–35.

15. "Dos periodistas a quienes el pueblo de Cuba, rinde emocionado tributo," *Bohemia*, January 11, 1959, 74.

16. Teel, *Reporting the Cuban Revolution*, 3–4.

17. See St. George, "A Revolution Gone Wrong"; Guerra, "Searching for the Messiah," 67–95.

18. Mallin, *Adventures in Journalism*, 120.

19. Chapelle, *What's a Woman Doing Here?*; Webb, "Radical Portrayals."

20. Quoted in Webb, "Radical Portrayals," 197.

21. Webb, 203.

22. "Report from Cuba: The Yankees-Going-Home," pp. 12–14, Mss 87AF, box 10, folder 3, Pt. 1, Dickey Chapelle Papers.

23. Philip Bonsal, Joint Weeka, No. 33, August 18, 1959, Cuba109 Correspondence DOS 2005-11-23 Grafeld-JHL Release part3, AARC, www.maryferrell.org/showDoc .html?docId=146885. Unless otherwise noted, all documents in this series are from the US embassy in Havana.

24. Teel, *Reporting the Cuban Revolution*, 101.

25. Teel, *Reporting the Cuban Revolution*, 100.

26. "La prensa norteamericana perdona su ingerencismo," *NH*, January 7, 1959, 1; "¡Ese Mr. Dubois que echara Venezuela!" *NH*, January 10, 1959, 1.

27. See Hadley, *Rising Clamor*.

28. Dubois, *Freedom Is My Beat*, 157.

29. Dubois, *Freedom Is My Beat*, 146, 210.

30. Dubois, *Freedom Is My Beat*, 190–91.

31. "¿Dubois vs. Cuba?" *Combate*, April 28, 1959, 2.

32. Dubois, *Freedom Is My Beat*, 275–76.

33. On this event, see chapter 2 of this book.

34. "Jules Dubois será declarado persona no grata en Cuba," *NH*, August 1, 1959, 1.

35. "Repudia la C.T.C. al agente Dubois," *NH*, September 17, 1959, 1.

36. Daniel M. Braddock, Amembassy Habana, Joint Weeka, No. 37, September 16, 1959, p. 8, Cuba109 Correspondence DOS 2005-11-23 Grafeld-JHL Release part3, AARC, www.maryferrell.org/showDoc.html?docId=146885.

37. Fidel Castro, "Mass Demonstration," October 26, 1959, Foreign Service Despatch, FBIS, Report Date: November, 12, 1959, from AmEmbassy Habana, to the Department of State, http://lanic.utexas.edu/project/castro/db/1959/19591026-2.html.

38. Ortega, *La coletilla*, 89.

39. "Condenan los periodistas a 'Time' y 'Life'" acusadas de dar pretextos para la invasión," *NH*, August 2, 1959, 1; Philip Bonsal, Joint Weeka, No. 32, August 11, 1959, p. 8, Cuba109 Correspondence DOS 2007-11-07 Grafeld-JHL Release, AARC; Philip Bonsal, Joint Weeka, No. 33, August 18, 1959, p. 8.

40. See Philip Bonsal, Joint Weeka, No. 32, August 11, 1959, p. 9, Cuba109 Correspondence DOS 2007-11-07 Grafeld-JHL Release, AARC, www.maryferrell.org /showDoc.html?docId=146860.

41. "*Time* and *US News and World Report*, o la técnica de la difamación," *Revolución*, April 19, 1960, 2.

42. Jacinto Torres, "Una información contra Cuba 'Made in USA,'" *NH*, September 3, 1959, 1, 7.

43. Samuel Feijóo, "La A.P. y la U.P.I. en el rencor," *Revolución*, December 10, 1959, 2.

44. Daniel M. Braddock, Joint Weeka, No. 14, April 7, 1959, Cuba109 Correspondence DOS 2003-02-25 Grafeld-JHL Release part3, AARC, www.maryferrell.org /showDoc.html?docId=146840; letter to Carlos Todd from Horacio Bas Maristany, January 12, 1960, box 1, Carlos Todd Newspaper Articles.

45. Keller, "Revolution Will Be Teletyped," 95–96.

46. Keller, 97–108. In 1968, Castro shut down AP and UPI services in Cuba, leaving Agence France-Presse and Reuters as the only Western wire agencies on the island. Matthews, *Revolution in Cuba*, 3.

47. Zeitlin and Scheer, *Cuba*, 284.

48. Zeitlin and Scheer, 288, 296–99.

49. Zeitlin and Scheer, 293–94.

50. Zeitlin and Scheer, 302.

51. John H. Sengstacke, "Castro Abolishes Race Bias in Cuba," *Chicago Defender*, January 23, 1960, 1.

52. Benson, *Antiracism in Cuba*, 159.

53. Matthews, *Revolution in Cuba*, 2.

54. DePalma, *Man Who Invented Fidel*.

55. Rojas, *Fighting over Fidel*, 32.

56. Francis, "U.S. Press and Castro," 265.

57. Francis, 260.

58. Francis, 265–66.

59. Francis, 264.

60. Anthony DePalma, "Ronald Hilton, 95, Scholar of Latin America Dies," *NYT*, February 24, 2007, www.nytimes.com/2007/02/24/us/24hilton.html. See also Aldrich, "American Journalism and the Landscape of Secrecy."

61. "US Curbing Cuban News," *Baltimore Sun*, April 21, 1961, 13; David Wise, "How Much Should the Public Know?" *New York Herald Tribune*, May 2, 1961, 24.

62. Tim Weiner, "C.I.A. Had Ability to Plant Bay of Pigs News, Document Show," *NYT*, March 24, 2001, A7, www.nytimes.com/2001/03/24/world/cia-had-ability-to -plant-bay-of-pigs-news-document-shows.html.

63. Houghton, "Cuban Invasion of 1961 and the U.S. Press," 429–30.

64. Schudson, *Discovering the News*, 172–73.

65. See United Press International, "US Reporters Jailed in Cuba," *Washington Post*, April 20, 1961, A15; "Cuba Frees A.P. Reporter," *NYT*, May 14, 1961, 22; Ruby Hart Phillips, "Castro's Cuba Described as Isle of Fear and Hate," *NYT*, May 20, 1961, 1, 5; Jules Dubois, "52 Americans Freed by Cuba Return to US," *Chicago Daily Tribune*, May 20, 1961, S3; Robert Berrellez, "Reporter's Story of 25 Days in Cuba Prison Filth," *Chicago Daily Tribune*, May 21, 1961, 4; Robert Berrellez, "Underground Men Call Cuba Invaders Traitors," *Los Angeles Times*, May 24, 1961, 2, 7.

66. Mallin, *Adventures in Journalism*, 120–30. Some of these outlets later sent new correspondents.

67. Letter from Robert Taber to Herbert Matthews, March 16, 1964, box 2, folder 5, HMP; Lyle Stuart, "Diary of a Visit to Cuba with Thirty-Five American Reporters," *Independent* Issue 147 (September 1964): 1, in box 1, folder 3, Jay Mallin Papers, CHC.

68. For more, see chapter 4 in this book.

69. See also Cubillas, "6 periodistas de países capitalistas visitan a Cuba," 4–7, 111.

70. *Attempts of Pro-Castro Forces to Pervert the American Press: Hearing before the Subcommittee to Investigate the Administration of the Internal Security Act and Other Internal Security Laws of the Committee on the Judiciary*, 87th Cong. 14 (1962) (statement of Carlos Todd).

71. "Cuba—1966–32–33," box 12, folder 1, HMP.

72. See Lazo, *Writing to Cuba*; Luis-Brown, *Waves of Decolonization*; Muller, *Cuban Émigrés and Independence in the Nineteenth-Century Gulf World*.

73. See Salwen, *Radio and Television in Cuba*; Marrero, *Dos siglos de periodismo en Cuba*.

74. Salwen, *Radio and Television in Cuba*, 101.

75. Salwen, 105.

76. See, for example, Guerra, "Searching for the Messiah."

77. Guerra, *Visions of Power in Cuba*, 42.

78. Marrero, *Dos siglos de periodismo en Cuba*, 228.

79. Guerra, *Visions of Power in Cuba*, 44.

80. Park F. Wollam, AmConsulate, Santiago de Cuba, to Department of State, Washington, "Foreign Service Despatch," #104, Apr. 9, 1959, p. 3, Cuba109 Correspondence DOS 2003-02-25 Grafeld-JHL Release part3, AARC. See also Benson, *Antiracism in Cuba*.

81. Díaz Castañón, "'We Demand, We Demand . . . ,'" 108.

82. Salwen, *Radio and Television in Cuba*, 107, 127.

83. Quintana Suárez, *Recuerdos no olvidados*, 22–24.

84. Ortega, *La coletilla*, 29.

85. Ortega, 28.

86. Salwen, *Radio and Television in Cuba*, 127–28, 130.

87. "Tele-Radiolandia. El caso Pumarejo," *Bohemia*, June 14, 1959, 58–62; Ortega, *La coletilla*, 37; Salwen, *Radio and Television in Cuba*, 135–36.

88. Ortega, *La coletilla*, 37.

89. Marrero, *Dos siglos de periodismo en Cuba*, 244.

90. Marrero, 232–33.

91. Rodríguez Gómez, "Diario de la Marina," 142.

92. See Bustamante, *Cuban Memory Wars*, 25–62.

93. Nerey Obregón, "Hoy," 265.

94. Bustamante, *Cuban Memory Wars*, 40–58.

95. Díaz Castañón, "Revolución," 160.

96. See Bustamante, *Cuban Memory Wars*.

97. Philip W. Bonsal, Joint Weeka, No. 12, March 24, 1959, pp. 10–11, Cuba109 Correspondence DOS 2003-02-25 Grafeld-JHL Release part3, AARC.

98. Philip Bonsal, Joint Weeka, No. 15, April 14, 1959, p. 8, Cuba109 Correspondence DOS 2003-02-25 Grafeld-JHL Release part3, AARC.

99. Fidel Castro (speech, Céspedes Park, Santiago de Cuba, January 1, 1959), www.cuba.cu/gobierno/discursos/1959/esp/f010159e.html.

100. Fidel Castro (speech, Plaza de la Ciudad de Camagüey, January 4, 1959), www.cuba.cu/gobierno/discursos/1959/esp/f040159e.html.

101. Carlos Todd, "Let's Look at Today," *Times of Havana*, February 9, 1959, 8, box 1, Carlos Todd Newspaper Articles. For a full analysis of the cartoon, see Bustamante, *Cuban Memory Wars*, 49–51.

102. "'Hay libertad de prensa en Cuba,' dijo J. Quintana," *NH*, June 9, 1959, 1; Philip Bonsal, Joint Weeka, No. 23, June 9, 1959, p. 8, Cuba109 Correspondence DOS 2005-11-23 Grafeld-JHL Release part3, AARC.

103. "Al Gobierno que restauró en Cuba las libertades públicas," *DM*, June 23, 1959, 1; "Admiten obreros madereros haber amenazado al diario," *DM*, June 26, 1959, 1.

104. Carlos Rafael Rodriguez, "El cielo está firme," *NH*, June 24, 1959, 1; Carlos Rafael Rodriguez, "¿Amnesia o cinismo?" *NH*, June 25, 1959, 1; Carlos Rafael Rodriguez, "¡Toda la verdad, señores del Diario," *NH*, June 26, 1959, 1.

105. Dr. Pastor, "El derecho de asilo y la libertad de prensa," *Revolución*, January 21, 1959, 4.

106. Angel Cuiña Fernández, "Libertad de prensa, oportunismo y depuración," *Revolución*, January 23, 1959, 2.

107. "Revolucionarias," *Combate*, June 10, 1959, 3.

108. Carlos Rafael Rodríguez, "La libertad de prensa," *NH*, June 10, 1959, 7.

109. See Cane, *Fourth Enemy*.

110. Carlos Rafael Rodríguez, "La libertad de prensa," *NH*, June 10, 1959, 1.

111. Dubois, *Freedom Is My Beat*, 138.

112. Carlos Rafael Rodriguez, "Ayer y hoy de la SIP," *NH*, October 10, 1959, 1; Dubois, 138; Ortega, *La coletilla*, 47–48.

113. Tony Delahoza and Carlos M. Castañeda, "¿Hay en Cuba libertad de prensa?," *Bohemia*, August 2, 1959, 80; also discussed in Fernández, *La imposición del silencio*.

114. "Desmienten periodistas a la 'UPI,'" *NH*, July 23, 1959, 1; Philip W. Bonsal, Joint Weeka No. 30, July 28, 1959, p. 9, Cuba109 Correspondence DOS 2007-11-07 Grafeld-JHL Release, AARC.

115. United Press International. "Declina Bartholomew la invitación," *DM*, July 23, 1959, 2-A.

116. Delahoza and Castañeda, "¿Hay en Cuba libertad de prensa?," 80–81.

117. Delahoza and Castañeda, 83–84.

118. "Felicitación a los periodistas cubanos demanda de la SIP el decano del CNP," *NH*, September 30, 1959, 1.

119. Jose I. Rivero, "Hablemos claro," *DM*, September 29, 1959, 1-A.

120. Jose I. Rivero. See also Jose I. Rivero, "La libertad de expresión," *DM*, October 2, 1959, 1-A; Jose I. Rivero, "Mensaje de nuestro Director a la SIP," *DM*, October 3, 1959, 1-A.

121. Associated Press. "Debe considerar la 'S.I.P.' caso especial la situación cubana," *DM*, October 4, 1959, 2-A.

122. "Mueve Dubois sus peones en la SIP para atacar a Cuba," *NH*, October 5, 1959, 1, 8; Blas Roca, "¿Cuál libertad de prensa?," *NH*, October 4, 1959, 1, 11; "Pretende la SIP imponer censura suya a Fidel Castro," *NH*, October 6, 1959, 1, 7; Carlos Rafael Rodriguez, "La SIP muestra la cara," *NH*, October 9, 1959, 1, 7; Carlos Rafael Rodriguez, "Ayer y hoy de la SIP," *NH*, October 10, 1959, 1.

123. "Subraya la SIP su ataque a Cuba: premia a Prensa Libre," *NH*, October 7, 1959, 1; Ortega, *La coletilla*, 76.

124. "La Asamblea General de los Periodistas de La Habana, decidió condenar a la SIP," *NH*, October 13, 1959, 1; Philip Bonsal, Joint Weeka, No. 41, October 13, 1959, Cuba109 Correspondence DOS 2007-11-07 Grafeld-JHL Release, AARC; R. Seoane, "La SIP está al servicio del Imperialismo Yanqui," *NH*, October 16, 1959, 2.

125. Euclides Vázquez Candela, "Sobre la libertad de Prensa," *Revolución*, October 10, 1959, 18.

126. Philip W. Bonsal, Joint Weeka, No. 44, November 3, 1959, p. 10, Cuba109 Correspondence DOS 2003-02-25 Grafeld-JHL Release part3, AARC; Philip W. Bonsal, Joint Weeka, No. 45, November 10, 1959, Cuba109 Correspondence DOS 2003-02-25 Grafeld-JHL Release part3, AARC.

127. Philip W. Bonsal, Joint Weeka, No. 47, November 24, 1959, p. 7, Cuba109 Correspondence DOS 2003-02-25 Grafeld-JHL Release part3, AARC.

128. Daniel M. Braddock, Joint Weeka, No. 50, December 15, 1959, p. 7, Cuba109 Correspondence DOS 2007-09-13 Grafeld-JHL Release part3, AARC, www.mary ferrell.org/showDoc.html?docId=146859.

129. J. I. Rivero, *Contra viento y marea*, 161.

130. "El sepelio de los libelos," *NH*, December 23, 1959, 1, 4.

131. Not all the targeted papers were associated with counterrevolutionary views. According to Armando A. Machado, publisher of the Santa Clara daily *El Villareño*, a February 1960 burning there had also targeted *Hoy*, *Bohemia*, and his own paper. See Pflaum, *Tragic Island*, 66.

132. On this context, see Guerra, *Visions of Power in Cuba*, 107–9.

133. "Comparencia de Fidel Castro en televisión," *NH*, February 20, 1960, 11, quoted in Fernández, *La imposición del silencio*, 43.

134. Ortega, *La coletilla*, VII.

135. Fernández, *La imposición del silencio*, 66.

136. "Protesta la prensa por el incidente de 'Información,'" *DM*, January 17, 1960, 1-A & 2-A; on these battles, see also Ortega, *La coletilla*; Guerra, *Visions of Power in Cuba*, 122–25; Fernández, *La imposición del silencio*.

137. See "Cuba Denounces: What the *Miami Herald* and the *Miami News* Did Not Publish," Public Relations Department, Ministry of Foreign Affairs. Cuba, February 1960, FBI Cuba 109-12-210—Volume 40—Serials 1801–1838, www.maryferrell .org/php/showlist.php?docset=1957.

138. Ortega, *La coletilla*, 158–70.

139. Mesa, "Respaldan al Gobierno Revolucionario los trabajadores de periódicos," *NH*, January 20, 1960, 4.

140. "Los colegas de 'Información,'" *Combate*, January 17, 1959, 1.

141. See also Fernández, *La imposición del silencio*, 74.

142. J. I. Rivero, *Contra viento y marea*, 217, 172.

143. Carlos Robreño, "Algo más sobre las 'coletillas,'" *Prensa libre*, March 17, 1960, 2.

144. Robreño, "Algo más sobre las 'coletillas,'" 2.

145. Robreño, 2.

146. Carlos Robreño, "Acusación injustificada," *Prensa libre*, March 19, 1960, 2.

147. Daniel M. Braddock, Joint Weeka, No. 22, May 31, 1960, Cuba109 Correspondence DOS 2007-04-18 Grafeld-JHL Release part3, AARC, www.maryferrell.org /showDoc.html?docId=146858.

148. Guerra, *Visions of Power in Cuba*, 132.

149. "The Press in Cuba," *NYT*, May 12, 1960, 34.

150. Miller, *90 Miles from Home*, 25.

151. See "No se leen periódicos en el 40% de los hogares de Cuba," *Revolución*, February 20, 1961, 8, 11; *Cuban Information Service* 1, no. 19 (March 1961): 9.

152. "Señala la SIP a Castro como Traidor," *Avance Criollo*, March 24, 1961, 17.

153. De la Fuente, *Nation for All*, 280.

154. See Benson, *Antiracism in Cuba*, 231–40.

155. Pedro Revuelta, "Tachuelitas," *Prensa Libre*, March 25, 1960, 2.

156. Wilfredo Cancio, "En el Centenario de la República de Cuba," *Memorias del Porvenir: La restauración del espacio público* (Miami: Ediciones Universal, 2002), 709, cited in Fernández, *La imposición del silencio*, 135. For relevant Soviet parallels, see Lenoe, *Closer to the Masses*.

157. See Salado, *Censura de prensa en la revolución cubana*.

158. Kahl, *A Cuban Diary*, 34–35.

159. *Attempts of Pro-Castro Forces to Pervert the American Press: Hearing before the Subcommittee to Investigate the Administration of the Internal Security Act and Other Internal Security Laws of the Committee on the Judiciary*, 87th Cong. 110 (1962)

(statement of Hendrik J. Berns; Exhibit B: WGBS Feature Report—Miami, Fla. June 26, 1962).

160. On the history of the right to reply, see Salwen, *Radio and Television in Cuba*, 73.

161. *Gaceta Oficial*, July 29, 1960, 18, 259–262, cited in Ortega, *La coletilla*, 217–18.

162. "La juventud opina: Sobre 'la coletilla,'" *Combate*, May 11, 1960, 4.

163. On one such exchange, see Lambe, "Drug Wars."

164. Dimitrov, "Functions of Letters to the Editor in Reform-Era Cuba," 2–3. On the political function of "letting off steam," see also Bengelsdorf, *Problem of Democracy in Cuba*; Baldacci, "Consumer Culture and Everyday Life in Revolutionary Cuba."

165. Roberta, interview with author, January 2022.

166. Dimitrov, "Functions of Letters to the Editor in Reform-Era Cuba," 6.

167. Roberta" interview with author.

168. Ahmed, *Complaint!*, 10.

Chapter 2

1. Jean Ziegler, "How Castro Rules by TV Marathon," *Washington Post*, February 29, 1960.

2. Kennedy invited cameras into the White House, pioneered televised addresses to the nation, and, on more than one occasion, used television to circumvent the traditional channels of policymaking. See Watson, *Expanding Vista*.

3. Given the absence of accessible televisual archives in Cuba, I rely on transcripts of Castro's TV appearances that appeared in island newspapers and US intelligence reports. The challenges of ephemeral TV archives are not unique to Cuba; see Spigel, "Our TV Heritage."

4. Boorstin, *Image*, 11.

5. Boorstin, 30.

6. Boorstin, "Television," 30, 37.

7. See González de Bustamante, *"Muy Buenas Noches"*; Y. Rivero, *Broadcasting Modernity*; Almeida, "Soul of a Modern Nation"; Gumbert, *Envisioning Socialism*; Doherty, *Cold War, Cool Medium*; Imre, *TV Socialism*; Spigel and Curtin, *Revolution Wasn't Televised*; Watson, *Expanding Vista*; Spigel, *Make Room for TV*; Mickelson, *Electric Mirror*.

8. Y. Rivero, *Broadcasting Modernity*, 6.

9. See Y. Rivero, 75–101. For a relevant parallel, see Almeida, "Soul of a Modern Nation."

10. Pérez, *On Becoming Cuban*, 334.

11. Bronfman, *Isles of Noise*, 137–40.

12. Pérez, *On Becoming Cuban*, 334.

13. Maritza, interview by Eileen Artigas, January 2018.

14. The Orthodox Party emerged in response to the corruption of Cuba's post-1933 politics. For more, see Ehrlich, *Eduardo Chibás*.

15. See Ehrlich, *Eduardo Chibás*; Casuso, *Cuba and Castro*, 98.

16. Bronfman, "'Batista Is Dead.'"

17. Porbén, *La revolución deseada*, 15.

18. See Porbén, 34–72; Phillips, *The Cuban Dilemma*, 25–26; Guerra, *Visions of Power in Cuba*, 42–44; Guede, *Cuba*, 184–218, 272–80.

19. Guerra, *Visions of Power in Cuba*, 350–51.

20. See Chanan, *Cuban Cinema*; Castillo, *Conquistando la utopía*.

21. Hall, "Encoding/Decoding."

22. See Corner, "Performing the Real."

23. Max Weber (1864–1920) outlined three types of "legitimate" authority: "traditional," "rational-legal," and "charismatic." In his conception of the charismatic leader, he drew on early Christian (via Greek) notions of someone possessing a "certain quality of an individual personality by virtue of which he is set apart from ordinary men and treated as endowed with supernatural, superhuman, or at least specifically exceptional powers or qualities." Weber, *Theory of Social and Economic Organization*, 358.

24. See, for example, Shils, "Charisma, Order, and Status"; Friedrich, "Political Leadership and the Problem of the Charismatic Power"; Downton, *Rebel Leadership*; Horowitz, *Party Charisma*.

25. With respect to Cuba, see Miller, "Religious Symbolism in Cuban Political Performance"; Routon, *Hidden Powers of State in the Cuban Imagination*; Guerra, *Visions of Power in Cuba*.

26. Valdés, "Revolutionary and Political Content of Fidel Castro's Charismatic Authority." For other scholarly accounts, see Fagen, "Calculation and Emotion in Foreign Policy"; Fagen, "Charismatic Authority and the Leadership of Fidel Castro"; Pérez-Stable, "Charismatic Authority, Vanguard Party Politics, and Popular Mobilizations"; Morton, *Castro as Charismatic Hero*; Hoffmann, "Charismatic Authority and Leadership Change."

27. See Richard Fagen, "Comment on 'Charismatic Authority and the Leadership of Fidel Castro,'" April 1973, box 16, folder 2, RFP. For a sample of recent studies taking up this question (with varied responses), see Pérez-Stable, *Cuban Revolution*; Sweig, *Inside the Cuban Revolution*; Díaz Castañón, *Ideología y revolución*; Farber, *Origins of the Cuban Revolution Reconsidered*; López Rivero, *El viejo traje de la revolución*; Guerra, *Visions of Power in Cuba*; Guerra, *Patriots and Traitors*.

28. See, for example, de la Fuente, *Nation for All*; Ayorinde, *Afro-Cuban Religiosity, Revolution, and National Identity*; Quiza, "Sujetos olvidados"; Chase, *Revolution within the Revolution*; Benson, *Antiracism in Cuba*.

29. On the history of public-opinion polling, see Fried, *Pathways to Polling*; Cordero, *La sociedad de la opinión*; Herbst, *Numbered Voices*. On public-opinion polling in Cuba, see Romay, *La opinión pública en el ocaso de la neocolonia cubana*. On Cold War connections, see Simpson, *Science of Coercion*. On fidelity in the world of Caribbean radio, see Bronfman, *Isles of Noise*, 126–30. On the relationship between advertising and Revolution, see Quiroga, *Cuban Palimpsests*, 94–97; Guede, *Cuba*, 184–218, 272–80.

30. See A. Rodríguez, *Transitando por la psicología*. *Bohemia* magazine was an important forum for this genre and often sponsored its own surveys, including one with the US public.

31. The last public survey, carried out in June 1959, registered a drop from a February high of 91.85 percent support to 78.31 percent. See López Fresquet, *My Fourteen Months with Castro*, 56. Castro was reportedly unperturbed, assuring his ministers that they were "still doing fine."

32. Pedraza Ginori, *Memorias Cubanas*, 1:71. Public opinion ceased to be a debatable matter in Cuba, but domestic and foreign studies in this vein did not cease; on this context, see chapter 5.

33. Free, *Attitudes of the Cuban People toward the Castro Regime in the Late Spring of 1960*, 2.

34. Free regarded these findings as so important that he repeatedly submitted them to the National Security Council. Tragically, according to one account, Free's report "was not read by President John F. Kennedy's principal advisers until after the Bay of Pigs fiasco." See Robert McG. Thomas Jr., "Lloyd A. Free, 88, Is Dead; Revealed Political Paradox," *New York Times*, November 14, 1996, www.nytimes.com/1996/11/14/us/lloyd-a-free-88-is-dead-revealed political-paradox.html.

35. Free, *Attitudes of the Cuban People toward the Castro Regime in the Late Spring of 1960*, 6.

36. Reproduced in Bonachea and Valdés, *Cuba in Revolution*, 169.

37. Willner, *Spellbinders*, 152.

38. Published in McLuhan, *Understanding Media*, 45.

39. McLuhan, 337.

40. On this front, the Communist paper *Noticias de Hoy* waged a particularly critical campaign; see, for example, Aldo Guasch, "Hoy en escena, audio y video," *NH*, May 8, 1959, 6; Aldo Guasch, "Hoy en audio y video," *NH*, May 27, 1959, 6; Aldo Guasch, "Hoy en audio y video," *NH*, June 5, 1959, 6.

41. Alberto Giro, "¿Hay exceso de tele-novelas en la televisión actual?" *DM*, April 17, 1959, 15-A; Dani Suarez, "Radio y televisión," *NH*, July 15, 1959, 6; Dani Suarez, "Radio y televisión," *NH*, July 24, 1959; Gil, "Tele-Calle," *La Calle*, January 15, 1960, 3; "BAZAR de la vida breve. ¿El final de los novelones?" *La Calle*, May 7, 1960, 2; "Puntillazos," *Mella*, June 1960, 52.

42. Rey, *¿Adónde va la televisión cubana?*, 5.

43. Y. Rivero, *Broadcasting Modernity*, 134.

44. The rebel paper *Revolución* was the only exception. See Dubois, *Fidel Castro*, 350. In a 1957 interview with Raúl Chibás—a close ally of Castro—Dubois also discovered that Castro had kept a television set in his sierra "headquarters" (175).

45. Alberto Giro, "Se anota un éxito CMQ-TV con la entrevista a Fidel Castro," *DM*, January 6, 1959, 10-A; Alberto Giro, "Ofrecieron Canal 12 y CMQ-TV el recibimiento a Castro," *DM*, January 9, 1959, 6-A; Phillips, *The Cuban Dilemma*, 13; Y. Rivero, *Broadcasting Modernity*, 134–43; Carlos Todd, "Let's Look at Today," *Havana Times*, January 8, 1959, box 1, folder 7, Carlos Todd Newspaper Articles.

46. I am grateful to Thamyris Almeida for encouraging me to consider this possibility.

47. Alberto Giro, "Reanudan emisoras de radio y TV sus programas habituales," *DM*, January 7, 1959, 12-A; "Reaparece esta noche, 'Frente a la Calle' por CMQ-TV," *DM*, January 10, 1959, 20-A. Critics also pushed networks to bring their programming closer in line with the new order. See, for example, Aldo Guasch, "La televisión: Fusión social y artística," *NH*, May 22, 1959, 6.

48. Noticias de televisión, *DM*, February 5, 1959, 15-A; Alberto Giro, "Gran labor de González Rubio en Lidia Sandoval, CMQ-TV," *DM*, March 20, 1959, 14-A; "Realiza el Canal 12 de TV otro telemaratón a favor del pueblo," *DM*, November 1, 1959, 5-B; Noticias de televisión, *DM*, November 3, 1959, 16-A; Noticias de televisión, *DM*, November 5, 1959, 10-A.

49. Franqui, *Family Portrait with Fidel*, 18. See also Alberto Giro, "Gran transmisión de CMQ-TV desde el 'Coliseo Deportivo,'" *DM*, January 22, 1959, 14-A; Guerra, *Visions of Power in Cuba*, 46–49; Chase, "Trials."

50. Franqui, *Family Portrait with Fidel*, 14.

51. Szulc, "Cuban Television's One-Man Show," 198.

52. See Guerra, *Visions of Power in Cuba*, 46. On this, she cites Santiago Cardoso Arias, "Guanahacabibes: Leyenda y realidad de una península," *INRA*, no. 2 (February 1960): 60.

53. See Ziegler, "How Castro Rules by TV Marathon."

54. R. Hart Phillips, "Castro Reaches 95% of Cubans with Radio-TV Exhortations," *NYT*, August 6, 1959, 9.

55. R. Hart Phillips, "Cuban TV: The Fidel Show," *NYT*, July 23, 1961, 12.

56. Alberto Giro, "Brillante esfuerzo de la TV cubana se ofreció el domingo," *DM*, April 21, 1959, 12-A. On Castro's appearances on US TV, see Y. Rivero, *Broadcasting Modernity*, 150–55.

57. Alberto Giro, "Gran labor de R. Revuelta y Coega en La Novela de las 10," *DM*, April 30, 1959, 12-A.

58. Alberto Giro, "La televisión, vehículo de solidaridad social por excelencia," *DM*, May 10, 1959, 8-B.

59. See, for example, "Televisión Revolución," *Mella*, no. 177 (June 1960): 53–54.

60. Szulc, "Cuban Television's One-Man Show," 197.

61. Quoted in Matthews, *Revolution in Cuba*, 127. Earlier, in 1959, he had informed a reporter: "If I do not speak to the people at least every ten days they become confused." See Phillips, "Castro Reaches 95% of Cubans."

62. Lockwood, *Castro's Cuba, Cuba's Fidel*, 72.

63. Matthews, *Revolution in Cuba*, 126.

64. V. Franco, *Morning After*, 43, 46. Those in the US Foreign Service charged with recording his appearances tended to agree; one transcriber noted that he could not in words "capture the atmosphere of the program." See Foreign Service, "4 Hour TV Appearance," March 13, 1959, Castro Speech Data Base, LANIC, http://lanic.utexas.edu/project/castro/db/1959/19590313.html.

65. James N. Wallace, "Themes and Variations: Castro on Camera," *Wall Street Journal*, November 17, 1960, 16.

66. V. Franco, *Morning After*, 191.

67. Y. Rivero, *Broadcasting Modernity*, 145–47.

68. For classic accounts of the gendering of mass culture, see Radway, *Reading the Romance*; Modleski, "Femininity as Mas(s)querade."

69. See Guerra, "Gender Policing, Homosexuality and the New Patriarchy"; Chase, *Revolution within the Revolution*; Hynson, *Laboring for the State*.

70. Szulc, "Cuban Television's One-Man Show," 197.

71. Wallace, "Themes and Variations."

72. See Daniel M. Braddock (Minister-Counselor) to US Ambassador, "Excerpts from the Appearance of Fidel Castro before the Press (CMQ Television Program) on February 19, 1959," Castro Speech Data Base, LANIC, http://lanic.utexas.edu/project /castro/db/1959/19590219-1.html.

73. Matthews, *Revolution in Cuba*, 126.

74. United Press International, "Critica el periodista Dubois al gobierno de Fidel Castro," *DM*, October 11, 1959, 1-A.

75. Szulc, "Cuban Television's One-Man Show," 200.

76. On these dynamics, see Dayan and Katz, *Media Events*.

77. James, *Cuba*, 193.

78. Innovative programming, including interviews with ordinary Cubans about unfolding events, also greeted the occasion. See Dani Suárez, "Radio y televisión," *NH*, July 21, 1959, 6; "16 horas que conmovieron a Cuba," *Bohemia*, July 26, 1959, 72. On the broadcast in general, see "En la televisión se hizo historia," *Bohemia* (supplement), July 26, 1959, 74–75; Dani Suárez, "Radio y televisión," *NH*, July 24, 1959, 6.

79. According to Abel Mestre, Raúl Castro had approached him earlier in the afternoon to arrange the broadcast and remained at the CMQ studio with 250 soldiers to help coordinate the evening's events. See James, *Cuba*, 195.

80. "16 horas que conmovieron a Cuba," 77. See also López Fresquet, *My Fourteen Months with Castro*, 124–26.

81. "16 horas que conmovieron a Cuba," 78.

82. "16 horas que conmovieron a Cuba," 79. Urrutia, Carlos Franqui relates, had sat down to that broadcast "fully expecting to see Fidel accuse his brother Raúl of being a Communist" and was surprised to instead find himself the target. Franqui, *Family Portrait with Fidel*, 43. He had apparently toyed with delivering a televised response to the attack—preparations were even made to initiate a broadcast from the palace—but CMQ workers refused to bring the equipment. See James, *Cuba*, 192–96. See also Y. Rivero, *Broadcasting Modernity*, 148.

83. "16 horas que conmovieron a Cuba," 80.

84. Guerra, *Visions of Power in Cuba*, 68–69.

85. On denunciation as a political "speech genre," see Derby, "In the Shadow of the State."

86. Phillips, *The Cuban Dilemma*, 148.

87. "Text of Castro Television Interview," *Telemundo pregunta*, January 20, 1960, Castro Speech Data Base, LANIC, http://lanic.utexas.edu/project/castro/db/1960 /19600120.html.

88. Phillips, *The Cuban Dilemma*, 148.

89. "Text of Castro Television Interview," *Telemundo pregunta*, January 20, 1960.

90. "El deplorable incidente de *Telemundo*," *DM*, January 22, 1960, 1-A; "Parte el embajador Lojendio; llega el Dr. J. Miró," *DM*, January 22, 1960, 1-A & 12-A.

91. Williams, *Television*, 81, 88.

92. Y. Rivero, *Broadcasting Modernity*, 156.

93. Feuer, "Concept of Live Television."

94. See also Y. Rivero, *Broadcasting Modernity*, 147.

95. "Fidel ante la prensa," *Revolución*, May 15, 1959, 11.

96. "Cuba no aceptará nada que merme su soberanía," *Revolución*, July 4, 1959, 20.

97. "Fidel ante la prensa," *Revolución*, May 15, 1959, 14.

98. Che Guevara, "Socialism and Man in Cuba," March 1965, www.marxists.org /archive/guevara/1965/03/man-socialism.htm.

99. See Green, Brock, and Kaufman, "Understanding Media Enjoyment," 312, 317.

100. The classic account is Habermas, *Structural Transformation of the Public Sphere*. See also Piccato, *Tyranny of Opinion*.

101. See, for example, Welch, *Propaganda, Power and Persuasion*.

102. For a helpful survey of these debates, see Soules, *Media, Persuasion and Propaganda*. Notably, the negative cast of "propaganda" is less pronounced in Spanish.

103. The first television station to be nationalized in early 1959 was Channel 12, which became the new revolutionary channel Tele-Rebelde; the last was CMQ-TV (September 1960). See Y. Rivero, *Broadcasting Modernity*, 165.

104. The show, first launched in 1951, had become embroiled in Batista's on-again, off-again censorship efforts and had, in June 1957, mounted a valiant response when it aired *El estudio vacío* (The empty studio), which "depicted an empty studio and used a narration to tackle the importance of freedom of expression." See Y. Rivero, *Broadcasting Modernity*, 108.

105. Among this group, for example, was Carlos Robreño of *El Mundo*, who asked all interview subjects if they were Communists. See Carlos Todd, "Let's Look at Today," *Havana Times*, June 18, 1959, 8, box 1, folder 7, Carlos Todd Newspaper Articles.

106. "Fidel ante la prensa," *Revolución*, May 15, 1959, 8.

107. "Fidel ante la prensa," 8.

108. Jorge Mañach, "Relieves. Una puntualización necesaria," *DM*, June 2, 1959, 4-A. This was not a uniform stance, however; Guillermo Martínez Márquez, another newspaper director, had been previously afforded televised time to reply to Castro's allegations against him. See Carlos Todd, "Monday's Picadillo," *Havana Times*, May 18, 1959, box 1, folder 6, Carlos Todd Newspaper Articles.

109. "Concentrará Fidel Castro un millón de personas frente al Palacio el próximo lunes día 26," *DM*, October 23, 1959, 6-A.

110. See, for example, Joalo, "Televisando," *El Crisol*, August 21, 1959, 6; Conte Agüero, *Héroes y mártires*.

111. Monahan and Gilmore, *Great Deception*, 94.

112. Phillips, *The Cuban Dilemma*, 183.

113. "Quieren los comunistas hacer de Cuba la Hungría de América dice Conte Agüero al Premier," *DM*, March 26, 1960, 1-A; "'La porra comunista me impidió leer la carta a Fidel'—Conte," *DM*, March 27, 1960, A-1. On the relevance of these events for student politics, see Guerra, *Visions of Power in Cuba*, 128–30.

114. "'¡Intrusismo comunista, no!' reitera Luis Conte Agüero," *DM*, March 30, 1960, 1-A; "Fidel in Diatribe against Conte Agüero," March 30, 1960, Castro Speech Data Base, LANIC, http://lanic.utexas.edu/project/castro/db/1960/19600330.html.

115. This section also relies on Phillips, *The Cuban Dilemma*, 183–83; Monahan and Gilmore, *Great Deception*, 93–96; Szulc, "Cuban Television's One-Man Show," 203; James, *Cuba*, 261–65; Guerra, *Visions of Power in Cuba*, 128–30; Salwen, *Radio and Television in Cuba*, 152–59.

116. James, *Cuba*, 265.

117. See also Sirvén, *El rey de la TV*, 99–108.

118. Meyer and Szulc, *Cuban Invasion*, 144.

119. See *Playa Girón*, 4:31.

120. *Playa Girón*, 4:24.

121. See *Playa Girón*, 4:54, 66, 77, 128, 262, 304, 412.

122. See *Playa Girón*, 4:439, 466, 484,

123. See Bustamante, *Cuban Memory Wars*, 108–16.

124. *Playa Girón*, 4:467; Bustamante, *Cuban Memory Wars*, 108–16.

125. *Playa Girón*, 4:527.

126. See "Cuba and American Television: The Missile Crisis and Beyond," pt. 1 (panel discussion), October 22, 2002, Museum of Television and Radio, New York, video recording.

127. On the formation of audience practices, see Bronfman, *"El naciente público oyente."*

128. Lueck, *Cuba TV*, 9.

129. Pedraza Ginori, "Entre pueblo y gobierno: Teléfono directo," *Cuba*, October 1967, 8.

130. Ginori, "Entre pueblo y gobierno, 9."

131. Ginori, 9. See also "El Pueblo Pregunta en *Granma*," *Granma*, November 21, 1967, 3.

132. Ginori, "Entre pueblo y gobierno," 8.

133. Foreign Broadcast Information Service—Daily Report 1967–1968, "Questions Answered on Havana Cultural Congress," Havana Domestic Television Service in Spanish, 0316 GMT 30 December 67 P [El Pueblo Pregunta program on Havana Cultural Congress], box 12, folder 4, RFP.

134. Eugenio Pedraza Ginori, "'El pueblo pregunta,' una farsa para vender humo," June 2, 2020, *El blog de Pedraza Ginori*, http://elblogdepedrazaginori.blogspot.com/2020/06/el-pueblo-pregunta-una-farsa-para.html.

Chapter 3

1. Sirvén, *El rey de la TV*.

2. Memo, Edwal Jones (Deputy Director of Security, Personnel Security and Investigations) to C/OPS/OSC/OC, December 16, 1975, reel 4, folder J: Conte Aguero, Luis, NARA Record Number: 104-10165-10185, HSCA Segregated CIA Collection (Microfilm), Central Intelligence Agency, AARC, www.maryferrell.org/php/showlist .php?docset=1093.

3. Jules Dubois, "Exiled Press to Broadcast News to Cuba," *Chicago Daily Tribune*, September 18, 1960, 9.

4. Keller, "Fan Mail to Fidel," 10.

5. See citations in this and chapter 4.

6. Somerville, *Radio Propaganda and the Broadcasting of Hatred*, 33–152.

7. Bergmeier and Lotz, *Hitler's Airwaves*; Horten, *Radio Goes to War*.

8. Frederick, *Cuban-American Radio Wars*, 16.

9. See, for example, Hess, *Representing the Good Neighbor*.

10. Nelson, *War of the Black Heavens*.

11. Johnson, *Radio Free Europe and Radio Liberty*, 5.

12. Johnson, 5.

13. See also Mickelson, *America's Other Voice*; Puddington, *Broadcasting Freedom*; Cummings, *Cold War Radio*; Schlosser, *Cold War on the Airwaves*.

14. See Joseph, "What We Now Know and Should Know."

15. See Gleijeses, *Shattered Hope*; Schlesinger and Kinzer, *Bitter Fruit*; Cullather, *Secret History*.

16. Elliston, *Psywar on Cuba*, 15.

17. Elliston, 20.

18. Elliston, 28.

19. Memo, Henry Loomis (VOA) to Edward Murrow (USIA), February 10, 1961, "Broadcasting to Cuba," 1, reprinted in Elliston, *Psywar on Cuba*, 32–34.

20. Loomis to Murrow, 3.

21. Loomis to Murrow, 3.

22. Loomis to Murrow, 3.

23. Quoted in Valdés-Dapena, *Piratas en el éter*, 42.

24. Soley and Nichols, *Clandestine Radio Broadcasting*, 178.

25. Castro quoted in Pérez Salomón, *Estrellas en la frente*, 71; see also Loomis to Murrow, 3.

26. Frederick, *Cuban-American Radio Wars*, 7.

27. Frederick, 7–8.

28. Elliston, *Psywar on Cuba*, 47.

29. Quoted in Elliston, 47.

30. Elliston, 47; Hinckle and Turner, *Fish Is Red*, 87.

31. Wise and Ross, *The Invisible Government*, 334.

32. Quintero García, *La hegemonía mediática contra Cuba*; "Historia de la radio y la televisión cubana" (1979), Centro de Documentación, ICRT.

33. Wise and Ross, *The Invisible Government*, 335.

34. Radio Habana Cuba, *¡Cuba estamos contigo!*, 3, 5.

35. Santiago Cardosa Arias, "Radio Habana Cuba: Una voz que recorre el mundo," I, *Granma*, January 12, 1966, 2.

36. See Brown, *Cuba's Revolutionary World*.

37. See Keller, "Fan Mail to Fidel"; Pettinà, *Historia mínima de la guerra fría en América Latina*; Field, Krepp, and Pettinà, *Latin America and the Global Cold War*.

38. American University, *Special Warfare Area Handbook for Cuba*, 485.

39. United States Information Agency, *Cuba*, 10.

40. Martínez Victores, *7RR*, 105–7.

41. Martínez Victores, 182.

42. Martínez Victores, 141, 180.

43. Quoted in Martínez Victores, 222.

44. See Guede, *Cuba*, 184–218.

45. Martínez Victores, *7RR*, 287.

46. As related in Martínez Victores, 33, 50.

47. Quoted in Martínez Victores, 2–3.

48. See O. L. López, *La radio en Cuba*; McEnaney, *Acoustic Properties*.

49. Bronfman, *Isles of Noise*, 138.

50. O. L. López, *La radio en Cuba*, 447.

51. Ortega, *La coletilla*, 177; O. L. López, *La radio en Cuba*, 447.

52. Ortega, *La coletilla*, 251–55. See also Salwen, *Radio and Television in Cuba*.

53. Bronfman, *Isles of Noise*, 143.

54. See Brown, *Cuba's Revolutionary World*.

55. Brown, 228.

56. Brown, 453.

57. "Cuba as a Base for Subversion," 1963, General Counsel's Files, Record No. 198-10001-10009, Office of the Secretary of Defense, OSA, AARC, www.maryferrell.org/php/showlist.php?docset=1990.

58. Per Jules Dubois, cited in Cozean, *Cuban Guerrilla Training Centers and Radio Havana*, 26.

59. *XV Annyversary of Radio Havana Cuba*, 9.

60. "Voice of Castro," *Time*, August 10, 1962, http://content.time.com/time/subscriber/article/0,33009,873690,00.html.

61. "Cuba as a Base for Subversion," 1963, General Counsel's Files, Record No. 198-10001-10009, Office of the Secretary of Defense, OSA, AARC, www.maryferrell.org/php/showlist.php?docset=1990.

62. Radio Habana Cuba, *¡Cuba estamos contigo!*, 45.

63. *XV Annyversary of Radio Havana Cuba*, 10.

64. "Radio Habana Cuba: Correos Internacionales," *Granma*, January 20, 1966, 2.

65. "Radio Habana Cuba: Correo Internacional," *Granma*, August 6, 1966, 2.

66. See Seidman, "Venceremos Means We Shall Overcome"; Gronbeck-Tedesco, *Cuba, the United States, and Cultures of the Transnational Left*, 198–235; Mahler, *From the Tricontinental to the Global South*.

67. Cardosa Arias, "Radio Habana Cuba: Una voz que recorre el mundo," I, *Granma*, January 12, 1966, 2.

68. "Radio Habana Cuba: Correo Internacional," *Granma*, October 7, 1966, 2.

69. Francisco Pita Rodríguez, "Radio Habana Cuba: Nueve años llevando al mundo la verdad de Cuba," *Bohemia* no. 21 (May 21, 1970): 18.

70. "Vendrán a Cuba para el 2 de enero seis oyentes de Radio Habana Cuba," *Granma*, December 12, 1966, 2.

71. "Solidaridad con Cuba: Ganan 8 oyentes en 20 concursos de Radio Habana Cuba," *Granma*, July 29, 1967, 6.

72. Cardosa Arias, "Radio Habana Cuba: Una voz que recorre el mundo (Final)," January 13, 1966, 2.

73. "Radio Habana Cuba: Correos Internacionales," *Granma*, January 20, 1966.

74. Cardosa Arias, "Radio Habana Cuba. Una voz que recorre el mundo (Final)," January 13, 1966, 2.

75. See bound edition of MRMS transcripts in box 21, folder 169, Bernardo Benes Papers, CHC.

76. "Comentarios de los monitores: A los locutores les tiembla la lengua," March 28, 1963, box 21, folder 169, Bernardo Benes Papers, CHC.

77. "Voice of Castro."

78. *Post Office Box 7026*, June 10, 1962 [I-3], p. 2, Frank and Libbie Park Fonds, MG31-K9, vol. 25, Manuscript Division, LAC.

79. *Post Office Box 7026*, June 24, 1962 [I-5], p. 1, Frank and Libbie Park Fonds, MG31-K9, vol. 25.

80. Tyson, *Radio Free Dixie*, 262–86.

81. Tyson, 224.

82. Tyson, 220–44.

83. Robert F. Williams to Mr. J. A. L. (Galesburg, IL), January 30, 1964, box 7, RFWP. In this and subsequent letter citations, I have redacted personal information.

84. McEnaney, *Acoustic Properties*, 147.

85. See Kane, "*Radio Free Dixie* Playlists."

86. Robert F. Williams, "*Radio Free Dixie*," *Crusader* 4, no. 6 (February 1963): 1–8, http://freedomarchives.org/Documents/Finder/DOC513_scans/Robert_F_Williams/513.RobertFWilliams.Crusader.Feb.1963.pdf.

87. Mislan, "Transnationalism, Revolution and Race"; Mislan, "'In the Spirit of '76 Venceremos!'"

88. Robert F. Williams to Mr. J. A. L. (Galesburg, IL), January 30, 1964, box 7, RFWP.

89. (Miss) Jo Salas to E. T. P. (Key West), January 30, 1964, box 7, RFWP.

90. T. T. (Kalamazoo) to *Radio Free Dixie*, February 17, 1964, box 7, RFWP.

91. Anonymous (signed with a cross) to *Radio Free Dixie*, August 21, 1965, box 7, RFWP.

92. See Seidman, "Tricontinental Routes of Solidarity"; Seidman, "Venceremos Means We Shall Overcome"; Benson, *Antiracism in Cuba*; Mahler, *From the Tricontinental to the Global South*; Guerra, "Poder Negro in Revolutionary Cuba"; Seidman, "Angela Davis in Cuba as Symbol and Subject."

93. On Moore's complicated engagement with the revolutionary project, see C. Moore, *Pichón*.

94. Quoted in Tyson, *"Radio Free Dixie,"* 294.

95. *XV Annyversary of Radio Havana Cuba*, 11.

96. Cozean, *Cuban Guerrilla Training Centers and Radio Havana*, 25.

97. "Report of the Interdepartmental Team on Counter Subversive Measures in Central America and Panama," 1963, folder: Cuba: Security, 1963, JFKPOF-115-005-p0074, Papers of John F. Kennedy, Presidential Papers, JFK, www.jfklibrary .org/asset-viewer/archives/JFKPOF/115/JFKPOF-115-005.

98. Robert Taber, *War of the Flea: The Classic Study of Guerrilla Warfare* (New York: L. Stuart, 1965), quoted in *XV Annyversary of Radio Havana Cuba*, 14.

99. Rockefeller, *Rockefeller Report on the Americas*, 138–39.

100. Memo, Homer Gayne to Mr. Karst, IBS/RL, "Evidence of Effectiveness: THE CUBAN HOUR," October 1, 1963, box 37, CFCR.

101. Memo, Homer Gayne to Mr. Karst, IBS/RL, "Evidence of Effectiveness: THE CUBAN HOUR," October 1, 1963.

102. US Information Agency, "Address by Henry Loomis, Director, Voice of America, before the National Press Club, Washington, D.C., Wednesday, February 21, 1962," box 37, CFCR; Elio E. Constantin, "La 'voz' yanqui. Cita contra Cuba," *Granma*, November 13, 1968, 7.

103. David R. McLean, "Excerpts from History: *Western Hemisphere Division, 1946–1965*," vol. 1, Historical Staff, Central Intelligence Agency (1973), 281, www .archives.gov/files/research/jfk/releases/2018/104-10301-10001.pdf.

104. "Mariada Bourgin; Began Anti-Castro Radio," *Washington Post*, November 18, 2005, www.washingtonpost.com/wp-dyn/content/article/2005/11/17/AR 2005111701922.html?nav=E8

105. House Committee on Foreign Affairs, *Winning the Cold War*, 571.

106. FCR, "Fact Sheet," September 1965, box 37, CFCR.

107. The following paragraph is drawn from Lambe, "Communist Closet."

108. Comisión de Orientación Revolucionaria del Comité Central del PCC, "La bola o rumor, la provocación" (n.d.), 5, BNJM; Guerra, *Visions of Power in Cuba*, 204–5.

109. Guerra, *Visions of Power in Cuba*, 201–6.

110. On the figure of Tokyo Rose, who inspired Riera's nickname, see Shibusawa, "Femininity, Race and Treachery."

111. "Tele-Radiolandia," *Bohemia*, February 15, 1959, 52; Joseph Newman, "Castro and the Ex-Nun," *Baltimore Sun*, January 30, 1966, 16.

112. "Tele-Radiolandia," *Bohemia*, 52 (my emphasis). See also Alberto Giro, "'Tu vida y la mía,' una obra inspirada en la gesta cubana," *DM*, February 10, 1959, A18.

113. See "'Senderos de Libertad' conmueve a la radioaudiencia por la 'CMQ,'" *DM*, May 31, 1959, 12-A; Aldo Guasch, "HOY en audio y video," *NH*, June 10, 1959, 6.

114. "Castro Betrayed Our Country" (condensed from Latin American report by Joseph P. Blank), cited in 107 Cong. Rec. S6943 (daily ed. May 1, 1961), www.congress .gov/87/crecb/1961/05/01/GPO-CRECB-1961-pt6-1-1.pdf.

115. Riera, "Datos sobre autora."

116. Newman, "Castro and the Ex-Nun," 5.

117. Newman, 16.

118. "Cuba: Private Spies," *Newsweek*, November 24, 1962, 34 [?], LCA, www .maryferrell.org/showDoc.html?docId=52116#relPageId=44.

119. Dispatch, Chief of Station, JMWave, to Chief, Task Force W, Subject: Forwarding Tapes of [Redacted] Broadcasts, June 16, 1962, LCA, www.maryferrell .org/showDoc.html?docId=52116#relPageId=96.

120. "Correlation Summary," FBI file no. 105–86025, Subject: Luis Ernesto Conte Aguero, June 1, 1972, NARA record no. 124-10287-10053, AARC, FBI—HSCA Subject Files, Luis Conte Aguero, www.maryferrell.org/php/showlist.php?docset =1553.

121. Report of James J. O'Connor, March 27, 1964, Warren Commission Hearings, vol. 26, Commission exhibit no. 2950, Warren Commission Hearings and Exhibits, www.maryferrell.org/showDoc.html?docId=1142#relPageId=456.

122. "Correlation Summary," FBI file no. 105–86025, Subject: Luis Ernesto Conte Aguero, June 1, 1972.

123. Letter from "A R 6L" (Cuba) to [Redacted], to be forwarded to WWL, September 9, 1962, p. 2, box 50, CFCR.

124. Cuban Freedom Committee Survey #1, box 38, CFCR.

125. Cuban Freedom Committee Survey #5, box 38, CFCR.

126. Dispatch [Redacted] 3142 A, January 24, 1962, Subject: Evaluations on Members of the Revolutionary Council, LCA, www.maryferrell.org/showDoc.html ?docId=52116#relPageId=120.

127. Mariada C. Arensberg, "Free Cuba Radio Activities," box 42, CFCR.

128. Maria Luisa y Rosa (Women's Program), September 30–October 30, and "Monthly Report" (February 1964), box 43, CFCR.

129. "Reporte de Programa," July 14 and 15, 1966, WGBS, Radio Miami, box 40, CFCR.

130. "Scripts (Sr. G. Volsky), Mayo/67," box 42, CFCR.

131. Robert R. Mullen & Company, Report for Cuban Freedom Committee, July 1–December 31, 1965, pp. 2–3, box 42, CFCR.

132. Memo, Mrs. Mariada C. Arensberg to Sres. Locutores de Radio Cuba Libre, July 12, 1966, and July 21, 1966, box 39, CFCR.

133. Radio Cuba Libre, "Carta remitida a nuestro programa por la WWL, por un muchacho de 14 años, . . . con fecha 22 de noviembre (recibida en Dic. 7)," box 54, CFCR.

134. FCR, "Total Number of Letters Received from Our Listeners, Groups and Collaborators, from January 1st. 1961 to May 31, 1966," box 42, CFCR.

135. Report, September–December 1966, box 42, CFCR.

136. Radio Cuba Libre, "Párrafos de carta de Santiago de Cuba, recibida en Enero 5, 1967, firmada por 'El Caballero Blanco,' remitido a nuestro programa por la WGBS, Miami, a traves de un oyente en Hialeah, Fla," box 53; Cuban Freedom Committee Survey #3, box 38, CFCR.

137. Report, September–December 1966, box 42, CFCR.

138. Memo, Mrs. Mariada C. Arensberg to Sres. Locutores de Radio Cuba Libre, May 26, 1965, p. 1, box 39, CFCR.

139. Sample "Carta a Cuba," box 60, CFCR.

140. "Freedom" to WGBS (Miami) . . . , February 9, 1962, box 50, CFCR.

141. FCR, "Programming," October 1966, box 37, CFCR.

142. FCR, "Excerpts from letter rcvd. on Feb. 8, 1967, signed by R.L.P., A Cuban refugee now living in Washington, D.C.," box 53, CFCR.

143. FCR, "Excerpts from letter dated Oct. 17, 1966," box 54, CFCR.

144. Listener, El Campo, TX, to WWL Radio (New Orleans), January 20, 1962, box 50, CFCR.

145. Anonymous (Santa Clara, Las Villas) to WGBS, February 15, 1962, box 50, CFCR.

146. Anonymous to WRUL (New York), January 20, 1962 (translated July 1961), box 50, CFCR.

147. Cuban Freedom Committee Survey #5, box 38, CFCR.

148. Juan de Dios, reception report to Mariada C. Arensberg % Mario J. Rodriguez (Miami, FL), March 14, 1963, box 54, CFCR.

149. House Committee on Foreign Affairs and Subcommittee on International Organizations and Movements, *Winning the Cold War*, 572.

150. The following material regarding Maceo was originally published in Lambe, "Drug Wars."

151. Anonymous to Antonio Maceo, October 8, 1963, box 40, folder 3, AMMP.

152. JS to Antonio Maceo, n.d., box 4, folder 3, AMMP.

153. "Gastroenteritis," n.d., box 4, folder 3, AMMP.

154. MCSN to Antonio Maceo, June 11, 1964, box 4, folder 37, AMMP.

155. Show #380, August 6, 1965, box 5, folder 1, AMMP.

156. EDV to Antonio Maceo, June 9, 1964, box 4, folder 37; AHO to Antonio Maceo, n.d., box 4, folder 37, AMMP.

157. FV to Antonio Maceo, n.d., box 4, folder 37, AMMP.

158. LP to Antonio Maceo, September 17, 1964, box 4, folder 38, AMMP.

159. DU to Antonio Maceo, February 2, 1965, box 4, folder 38, AMMP.

160. GR to Antonio Maceo, July 16, 1965, box 4, folder 38, AMMP.

161. AHO to Antonio Maceo, n.d., box 4, folder 37, AMMP.

162. Anonymous to Antonio Maceo, October 8, 1963, box 4, folder 3, AMMP.

163. Ledeneva, "Between Gift and Commodity," 45.

164. Ledeneva, 46.

165. Ledeneva, 47.

166. See, for example, Rosendahl, *Inside the Revolution*, 28–51; Guerra, *Visions of Power in Cuba*, 294.

167. Kneitel, "Inside the CIA's Secret Radio Paradise," pt. 1, 20; Kneitel, "Inside the CIA's Secret Radio Paradise," pt. 2, 21.

168. Kneitel, "Inside the CIA's Secret Radio Paradise," pt. 1, 20.

169. Kneitel, pt. 1, 22.

170. Kneitel, pt. 1, 19.

171. Ray Cromley, "Lack of Funds Closes Free Cuba Radio," *Washington Daily News*, August 16, 1967, box 17, CFCR.

172. Soley and Nichols, *Clandestine Radio Broadcasting*, 183.

173. Soley and Nichols, 185.

174. Frederick, *Cuban-American Radio Wars*, 14. On related dynamics, see also Hernández-Reguant, "Radio Taino and the Globalization of the Cuban Culture Industries."

Chapter 4

1. Bernhard and Etcheparo, *Reportaje a Cuba*, 61–62.
2. "Quería conocer a Fidel," *Revolución*, May 15, 1961, 1.
3. Hulme, "Seeing for Themselves," 203.
4. See Lekus, "Queer Harvests"; Benson, *Antiracism in Cuba*, 153–97.
5. Guerra, *Visions of Power in Cuba*, 67–75.
6. Berg, "'La Lenin Is My Passport.'"
7. Guerra, *Visions of Power in Cuba*, 186.
8. Duany, "Cuban Migration."
9. See Gorsuch and Koenker, *Turizm*; Gorsuch and Koenker, *Socialist Sixties*; Hollander, *Political Pilgrims*; Kami, *Diplomacy Meets Migration*; Zhou, *Migration in the Time of Revolution*.
10. "Universal Declaration of Human Rights," December 1948, www.un.org/en /about-us/universal-declaration-of-human-rights#:~:text=Article%2013,to%20 return%20to%20his%20country.
11. The most infamous example remains the Berlin Wall; see, for example, Merritt and Merritt, *Living with the Wall*; Major, *Behind the Berlin Wall*. See also Light, "What Does It Mean to Control Migration?"; Czaika, Haas, and Villares Varela, "Global Evolution of Travel Visa Regimes."
12. See Bon Tempo, *Americans at the Gate*; Oyen, *Diplomacy of Migration*; Marinari, Hsu, and García, *Nation of Immigrants Reconsidered*.
13. Restrictions on Egypt, Israel, Jordan, and Syria briefly followed from 1956 to 1957. Abram Chayas and Abba P. Schwartz to the Secretary, "Regulations on Travel Control of U.S. Citizens," June 28, 1963, folder: Travel restrictions, Papers of John F. Kennedy, Presidential Papers, JFK, www.jfklibrary.org/asset-viewer /archives/JFKNSF/310/JFKNSF-310-005?image_identifier=JFKNSF-310-005 -p0018. I am grateful to Craig Daigle for his guidance in navigating these and related records.
14. This would not happen until 1971 for China and 1991 for North Vietnam. The US travel ban to North Korea has since been reactivated.
15. Telegram, Department of State to All American Diplomatic and Consular Posts, Circular 1057, January 19, 1961, box 45, folder: Traveling Misc., Papers of John F. Kennedy, Presidential Papers, JFK.
16. Immigration and Nationality Act, Pub. L. No. 82–414, 66 Stat. 163 (1952).
17. D. A. Farber, "National Security, the Right to Travel, and the Court," 266. This reflected a new understanding of the passport as a legal prerequisite for foreign travel whose use could be curtailed by the government. For relevant parallels in the Soviet passport system, see Baiburin, *Soviet Passport*.
18. R. C. James, "Right to Travel Abroad," 842–43. On relevant precedents, see Boudin, "Constitutional Right to Travel," 47–75.

19. Memo, John F. Kennedy to Secretary of State, Defense, and Director of CIA, February 15, 1963, box 45, folder: Traveling Misc., Papers of John F. Kennedy, Presidential Papers, JFK. As of March 1963, officials in Argentina, Chile, Colombia, Costa Rica, the Dominican Republic, El Salvador, Guatemala, Honduras, Jamaica, Panama, Paraguay, Uruguay, and Venezuela had either begun to monitor and dissuade such travel or expressed a willingness to do so. See Victor Krulak (Major General, USMC), "First Progress Report, Committee on Cuban Subversion," to ICCCA, March 30, 1963, box 4, folder 18, Califano Papers, 198-10007-10018, www.archives .gov/files/research/jfk/releases/198-10007-10018.pdf. As of March 1965, passports in Paraguay, Peru, and Nicaragua carried prohibitions on travel to Cuba and other Communist countries, but enforcement there and elsewhere in Latin America remained largely unofficial. See telegram, Siracusa (AmEmbassy, Lima) to Department of State, March 2, 1965; telegram, Snow (AmEmbassy, Asunción) to Department of State, March 2, 1965; telegram, Smith (AmEmbassy, Panama) to Department of State, March 2, 1965; telegram, Brown (AmEmbassy, Managuay) to Department of State, March 2, 1965; and telegram, Brown (AmEmbassy, Managuay) to Department of State, March 2, 1965, all in box 32, Travel to Cuba, vol. 2, 12/63–7/65, LBJ.

20. On the tactics deployed by Latin American travelers to evade these controls, see Daniel James, "Cuban Airline Carries Little Cargo, Many Agents," MSS 69, series 2, box 28, Daniel James Papers, Holt-Atherton Special Collections and Archives, University of the Pacific, Stockton, CA.

21. Memo, Gordon Chase to McGeorge Bundy, August 9, 1963, "Louis Lomax—Difficulties in Returning from Cuba," box 45, folder: Traveling Misc., Papers of John F. Kennedy, Presidential Papers, JFK.

22. See telegram, AmEmbassy Caracas to Department of State, March 3, 1965, box 32, Travel to Cuba, vol. 2, 12/63–7/65, LBJ.

23. Telegram, Freeman (AmEmbassy, Mexico) to Department of State, March 2, 1965, box 32, Travel to Cuba, vol. 2, 12/63–7/65, LBJ.

24. See memo, Deputy Passport Officer, Department of External Affairs, to Admin Staff and Examiners, Passport Office, July 17, 1962, "Information on Travellers to Cuba," RG 25, vol. 5611, file 12992-6-6-40, LAC; memo, Fulgence Charpentier, Passport Officer, to Consular Division, January 4, 1961, "Recruitment of Anti-Castro Forces in Canada," RG 25, vol. 5611, file 12992-6-6-40 05, LAC.

25. Memo, McGeorge Bundy to the president, Student Travel to Cuba, May 21, 1964, box 32, Travel to Cuba, vol. 2, 12/63–7/65, LBJ. See also Brown, *Cuba's Revolutionary World*.

26. State Department memo, attachment in memo from Bromley Smith to Ben Clifton, n.d., box 45, folder: Students, 7.63, Papers of John F. Kennedy, Presidential Papers, JFK.

27. Memo, Edward Murrow to Dean Rusk, "US Student Travel to Cuba," December 18, 1962, box 45, folder: Traveling Misc., Papers of John F. Kennedy, Presidential Papers, JFK.

28. For more on Progressive Labor, see Umezaki, "Breaking through the Cane-Curtain."

29. Memo, J. Walter Yeagley to White House, "Student Travel to Cuba (President's Press Conference)," July 31, 1963, box 45, folder: Students, 7.63, Papers of John F. Kennedy, Presidential Papers, JFK.

30. John Coatsworth, phone interview by author, July 30, 2019.

31. Document in "1963 Trip—Martin Nicolaus photo and text exhibit first 22 pages," p. 4, RL.00979, VOP.

32. Airgram, Department of State, AmEmbassy (Paris), to Department of State, July 4, 1963, "US Students to Cuba via Prague," box 45, folder: Students, 7.63, Papers of John F. Kennedy, Presidential Papers, JFK.

33. Tomás Toledo and Vicente Cubillas, "Llegó un grupo de 59 estudiantes de EE.UU.," *Revolución*, July 2, 1963, 1, 4, VOP.

34. Coatsworth, interview by author.

35. United Press International, "59 Students Start a Visit to Cuba, Defying Washington," *New York Times*, July 1, 1963, box 45, folder: Students, 7.63, Presidential Papers, JFK.

36. Coatsworth, interview by author; dispatch, George Kidd (Amb.) of Canadian Embassy (Havana) to Secretary of State for External Affairs (Ottawa), "Visit to Cuba of the 59 United States University Students," no. 395, July 15, 1963, box 45, folder: Students, 7.63, Papers of John F. Kennedy, Presidential Papers, JFK.

37. José Vázquez, "Reunión de Guevara con estudiantes de E.U.," *Revolución*, August 2, 1963, VOP.

38. Dispatch, George Kidd (Amb.) of Canadian Embassy (Havana) to Secretary of State for External Affairs (Ottawa), "Visit to Cuba of the 59 United States University Students," no. 395, July 15, 1963; Hoffman and Tunley, "Red Junket to Cuba"; Susana Lee López, "A través de Cuba con los estudiantes norteamericanos," *Hoy Domingo*, August 4, 1963, VOP.

39. Interview with Coatsworth; Hoffman and Tunley, "Red Junket to Cuba." On a similar dynamic, see Lekus, "Queer Harvests"; Latner, *Cuban Revolution in America*, 27–75.

40. United Press International, "59 Students Start a Visit to Cuba, Defying Washington," *New York Times*, July 1, 1963.

41. Telegram, Mexico City [Mann] to Secretary of State, no. 252, July 29, 1963, 8 P.M., and telegram, Mexico City [Mann] to Secretary of State, no. 378, August 9, 1963, 5 P.M., box 45, folder: Cables 6/15/63-10/15/63, Papers of John F. Kennedy, Presidential Papers, JFK.

42. Telegram, Kingston [Klosson] to Secretary of State, no. 71, August 20, 1963, 2 P.M., and telegram, Ottawa [Butterworth] to Secretary of State, no. 280, August 23, 1963, 11 A.M., box 45, folder: Cables 6/15/63-10/15/63, Papers of John F. Kennedy, Presidential Papers, JFK.

43. Telegram, AmEmbassy Madrid to Department of State, "54 American Students Arrive in Madrid from Cuba," August 28, 1963, box 45, folder: Cables 6/15/63–10/15/63, Papers of John F. Kennedy, Presidential Papers, JFK.

44. Memo, Gordon Chase to Mr. Bundy, "American Students Returning from Cuba—Handling at Idlewild," August 28, 1963, box 45, folder: Students, 8.63, Papers of John F. Kennedy, Presidential Papers, JFK.

45. Laub, for example, had apparently advised the travelers "not to show their passports to any Cuban official when they arrived in Cuba." United States Congress, House Committee on Un-American Activities, *Violations of State Department Regulations*, 653.

46. Coatsworth, interview by author.

47. Memo, J. Walter Yeagley to White House, "Student Travel to Cuba (President's Press Conference)," July 31, 1963, box 45, folder: Students, 7.63, Papers of John F. Kennedy, Presidential Papers, JFK.

48. Memo, Gordon Chase to Mr. Bundy, "American Students," September 9, 1963, box 45, folder: Students 9.63, Papers of John F. Kennedy, Presidential Papers, JFK.

49. "Cuba Student Was Counterspy," *Washington Daily New*, August 27, 1963, and Associated Press, "With Madrid-Students," August 27, 1963, box 45, folder: Students, 8.63, Papers of John F. Kennedy, Presidential Papers, JFK. For more on Hall, see Ernest, "Snapshot of the 'Radical Middle.'"

50. Associated Press, "With Madrid-Students"; Hoffman and Tunley, "Red Junket to Cuba," 26; United States Congress, House Committee on Un-American Activities, *Violations of State Department Regulations*, 653; memo, Gordon Chase to Mr. Bundy, "American Students," September 9, 1963, box 45, folder: Students 9.63, Papers of John F. Kennedy, Presidential Papers, JFK.

51. Hoffman and Tunley, "Red Junket to Cuba," 28.

52. United States Congress, House Committee on Un-American Activities, *Violations of State Department Regulations*, 655.

53. Martin Nicolaus, "Cuba 1963," https://nicolaus.com/my-life/cuba-1963/ (site discontinued).

54. United States Congress, House Committee on Un-American Activities, *Violations of State Department Regulations*, 656–67.

55. Nicolaus, "Cuba 1963." Memo, Benjamin Read to McGeorge Bundy, "Report on Students' Plans to Travel to Cuba in Violation of Travel Restrictions," May 7, 1964, box 32, Travel to Cuba, 12/63–9/64, LBJ. The New York and Philadelphia offices of the FBI had several dozen informants reporting to them about SCTC plans; they also put a mail cover on the SCTC post office box in New York. See memo by Special Agent in Charge, Federal Bureau of Investigations, New York, "Student Committee for Travel to Cuba," May 18, 1964, obtained under the FOIA from the FBI.

56. SCTC newsletter, September 27, 1963, file: 1963 Trip—Student Committee for Travel to Cuba, VOP; "Travel Ban Defiance Protested. Cubans Picket Ford Hall," *Boston Record American*, April 27, 1964, file: 1963 Trip—US Press, related materials, VOP.

57. Anonymous to Vicki Ortiz, n.d., file: 1963 Trip—Student Committee for Travel to Cuba, VOP.

58. Application for summer 1964 trip, MS 76, box S-61, folder 312C:43, Hall-Hoag Collection, John Hay Library, Brown University.

59. "75 Americans on Visit to Cuba Show Wide Variety of Motives," *New York Times*, June 15, 1964, 14, MS 2010.007, box 2, folder 64, Karen Brodkin Papers, John Hay Library, Brown University; Roger Taus, SCTC newsletter, n.d., file: 1963 Trip—US Press, related materials, VOP.

60. Pieter Romayn Clark, "I Saw Cuba—My Impressions," 7.

61. "25 Young Americans Land in Paris on Way to Cuba," *New York Times*, June 10, 1964, box 2, folder 24, Karen Brodkin Papers, John Hay Library, Brown University; Clark, "I Saw Cuba."

62. "A Press Statement on the Announcement of the Second US Student Trip to Cuba," May 20, 1964, box S-61, folder 18413:98, Hall-Hoag Collection, John Hay Library, Brown University.

63. Max Beagerie, "Who Went and How Did We Get There," 45.

64. Special Agent John W. Robinson, New York Office, Federal Bureau of Investigation, "Student Committee for Travel to Cuba," July 15, 1964, p. 54, NY 100–150205, obtained under the FOIA from the FBI. My thanks to Lily Hartmann for sharing her thoughts on this act.

65. Beagarie, "Who Went and How Did We Get There," 45.

66. Agee, *In the House of My Fear*, 83, 94–95.

67. Agee, 91.

68. Agee, 91.

69. "Another Visit to Cuba. Students Will Defy Cuba Travel Ban This Summer," *Columbia Owl*, March 11, 1964, 2–3, in John W. Robinson, "Student Committee for Travel to Cuba," May 15, 1964, Federal Bureau of Investigation, New York field office file no.: 100–150205, bureau file no.: 100–439769, box 32, Travel to Cuba, 12/63–9/64, LBJ.

70. "Another Visit to Cuba," 3.

71. [Redacted] to her father, June 22, 1964, pp. 11–12, in memo by Special Agent W. Rulon Paxman, Federal Bureau of Investigation, Salt Lake City, "Student Committee for Travel to Cuba," July 6, 1964, obtained under the FOIA from the FBI.

72. On Schwartz's vision and work, see Schwartz, *The Open Society*.

73. Memo, McGeorge Bundy to the president, Student Travel to Cuba, May 21, 1964, box 32, Travel to Cuba, vol. 2, 12/63–7/65, LBJ.

74. Memo, McGeorge Bundy to the president, Student Travel to Cuba, May 21, 1964.

75. Memo, McGeorge Bundy to the president, Student Travel to Cuba, May 21, 1964. Also cited in Schoultz, *That Infernal Little Cuban Republic*, 299.

76. Memo, Gordon Chase to McGeorge Bundy, "Travel to Cuba," September 17, 1964, box 32, Travel to Cuba, 12/63–9/64, LBJ.

77. Vicki Ortiz, "Part One: Travel . . . Right or Privilege? Cuba," *Info* [Elizabeth Irwin High School], 26, no. 3 (January 1964[?]), file: 1963 Trip—US Press, related materials, VOP.

78. Petition in support of students and against travel ban, 1963, file: 1963 Trip—Student Committee for Travel to Cuba, VOP.

79. Henry Steeler Commager, "Passport Barrier: 'It Must Come Down,'" *New York Times*, 1963, reprinted by SCTC, box S-61, folder 545, Hall-Hoag Collection, John Hay Library, Brown University.

80. See correspondence between William and Karen [Brodkin] Sacks and Rabinowitz & Boudin in box 2, folder 27, Karen Brodkin Papers, John Hay Library, Brown University.

81. J. Walter Yeagley to attorney general, cc: White House, April 2, 1963, box 45, folder: Traveling Miscellaneous, Papers of John F. Kennedy, Presidential Papers, JFK.

82. Schoultz, *That Infernal Little Cuban Republic*, 299.

83. "Max," S.C.T.C. News, n.d., folder: 1963 Trip—Student Committee for Travel to Cuba, VOP. See also Lovelace, "William Worthy's Passport"; Latner, *Cuban Revolution in America*, 86. On other inconclusive precedents, see Levi Lee Laub, "Recent Decisions on Travel," *Rights* 11, no. 2–3 (April–June 1964): 17.

84. Helen Travis, "The Right to Travel: A Personal Statement, *Open Forum* 43, no. 4 (April 1966), in "Ephemeral materials, 1966–," Helen Simon Travis Papers.

85. L.W., "Lawsuit Made Legal History," *Hartford Courant*, May 2, 2005, www .courant.com/news/connecticut/hc-xpm-2005-05-02-0505020021-story.html.

86. "Twenty Years in Jail for Traveling to Cuba!" A May 2nd Movement Pamphlet, p. 2, "Travel ban, [ca. 1963–64])," VOP.

87. "Max," S.C.T.C. News, n.d., "1963 Trip—Student Committee for Travel to Cuba," VOP.

88. "Twenty Years in Jail," p. 2.

89. Schoultz, *That Infernal Little Cuban Republic*, 298.

90. Schoultz, 299.

91. Laub et al. v. United States, 385 U.S. 475 (1967).

92. Laub et al. v. United States, 385 U.S. 475 (1967).

93. Travis v. United States, 385 U.S. 491 (1967).

94. Lynd and Wittman v. Secretary of State, 389 F. 2d 940 (D.C. Cir. 1967) (italics mine). In accordance with this ruling, Lynd had his passport returned to him, given his assurances that he would not use it to travel to restricted areas, and Wittman, having refused to affirm that, did not.

95. Vicki Ortiz, "Cuba," n.d., "1963 Trip—US Press, related materials," VOP.

96. Coatsworth, interview by author.

97. The Office of Foreign Assets Control (OFAC) was first set up in 1950 to execute sanctions against China.

98. Schoultz, *That Infernal Little Cuban Republic*, 301.

99. State Department Student Committee on Latin America (University of California, Riverside), "Procedure for Travel to Cuba," Report No. 1 (October 1968).

100. Schoultz, *That Infernal Little Cuban Republic*, 301–2.

101. Mark P. Sullivan, "Cuba: US Restrictions on Travel and Legislative Initiatives," *Congressional Research Service*, RL31139, p. 19, updated November 2018, https://fas.org/sgp/crs/row/RL31139.pdf.

102. Latner, *Cuban Revolution in America*, 27–75.

103. Latner, 75–123. One of the few cases resulted in a 1984 Supreme Court ruling affirming that the government could "impose travel restrictions for national security reasons." See Sullivan, "Cuba: US Restrictions on Travel and Legislative Initiatives," 19.

104. *Folletos de divulgación legislative: Proclamas y Leyes del Gobierno Provisional de la Revolución*, vol. 1, January 1–31, 1959 (Havana: Editorial Lex, 1959), 20, https://dloc.com/fr/AA00063775/00001/images.

105. A June 1961 law placed additional restrictions on foreign travelers, especially their personal goods and financial activities on the island. In response, the Canadian ambassador bemoaned that "the regulations [had] now become so complex that it scarcely [seemed] possible for Canadian authorities in Ottawa to attempt to give information on this subject to any potential travellers to Cuba who might request it." Numbered letter from T. C. Hammond, the Canadian Embassy, Havana, to Under-Secretary of State for External Affairs, Ottawa, No. L-392, "Travel to Cuba," June 14, 1961, RG 25, vol. 5611, file 12992-6-6-40 05, LAC.

106. *Servicio Cubano de Información* 1, no. 46 (September 23, 1961): 7; *Cuban Information Service* 1, no. 52 (November 4, 1961): 8.

107. On this context, see Torres, *In the Land of Mirrors*, 22–41.

108. "Fijan normas para poder salir y regresar al país," *Revolución*, December 6, 1961, 2. See also Castellanos and Henken, "Migration and Diaspora."

109. "Un habanero de paseo por Camagüey" to WGBS, June 3, 1962, box 50, CFCR.

110. This requirement seems to have provided much-needed hard currency to the revolutionary government. Ed Cony, "Cuba's New Exodus," *Wall Street Journal*, January 5, 1962, 1; Al Burt, "Legal Way Out of Cuba Isn't Easy," *Los Angeles Times*, April 2, 1965, C1.

111. Josiah Macy Jr. to Mr. Morrison, September 14, 1962, collection ASM0341, series 2, box 634, folder 3, Pan American World Airways Collection.

112. Cony, "Cuba's New Exodus"; William R. Frye, "Cuba Uncensored: Thousands Anxious to Escape from Isle," *Los Angeles Times*, August 18, 1964, 13.

113. Duany, "Cuban Migration." One 1965 estimate put the numbers at roughly 500 a month to Spain and another 700–800 to Mexico. See Burt, "Legal Way Out of Cuba Isn't Easy."

114. See García, *Havana USA*; Torres, *In the Land of Mirrors*.

115. Torres, *In the Land of Mirrors*, 37, 40.

116. See Rose, *Struggle for Black Freedom in Miami*, 212–40; Benson, *Antiracism in Cuba*, 122–52; Eckstein, *Cuban Privilege*.

117. See, for example, "Cuba Refugees Report Growing Escape Peril," *Baltimore Sun*, February 2, 1976, A6.

118. Philipson, *Freedom Flights*, 79.

119. Radio Cuba Libre, "Párrafos de carta de la Habana, Cuba, recibida en Octubre 25, 1966, firmada por Enrique, remitida a nuestro programa por la WWL, a través de un oyente en New Orleans," box 54, CFCR.

120. Fidel Castro (speech, Plaza de la Revolución, September 28, 1965), www.cuba .cu/gobierno/discursos/1965/esp/f280965e.html.

121. Joaquín Oramas, "Camarioca: Partió otra embarcación," *Granma*, October 11, 1965, 1, 3; Pecruz, "Un puerto llamado Camarioca. Dolor de cabeza yanqui," *Bohemia*, October 15, 1965, 48–53; Mario Kuchilan, "El Zafarrancho. El grito de Camarioca," *Bohemia*, October 15, 1965, 56–57.

122. "Bohemia en Camarioca," *Bohemia*, October 22, 1965, 58.

123. See also Guerra, *Patriots and Traitors in Revolutionary Cuba*, 401.

124. "Camarioca: 'No me voy, nada tengo que buscar en EE.UU,'" *Granma*, October 19, 1965, 1.

125. "Bohemia en Camarioca," 54.

126. *U.S. Apparatus of Assistance to Refugees throughout the World: Hearings Before the Subcommittee on Refugees and Escapees of the Committee on the Judiciary,* 89th Cong. 187 (1966).

127. "Miami Is Divided on Airlift's End," *New York Times,* September 5, 1971, 58, www.nytimes.com/1971/09/05/archives/miami-is-divided-on-airlifts-end -majority-of-cuban-refugees-have.html.

128. Joaquín Oramas, "Requisitos para la salida del país de los menores de 15 años: No abandonará la Revolución a los niños y ancianos que no quieren irse," *Granma*, October 28, 1965, 3. On related themes, see Casavantes Bradford, *Revolution Is for the Children.*

129. Soler and Pinares, "Camarioca: Puerto contra la mentira," *Cuba*, November 1965, 13. See also Guerra, *Patriots and Traitors in Revolutionary Cuba*, 401.

130. Beatrice Johnson, "Nadie ha llorado aquí por los que se han ido," *Granma*, November 2, 1965, 2. See, for example, Nuez, "Flora y fauna de Camarioca," *Granma* (revista), November 7, 1965, 16.

131. "Bohemia en Camarioca," 58.

132. Joaquín Oramas, "Funciona Camarioca como un puerto internacional," *Granma*, October 11, 1965, 3. On race and migration in the early 1960s, see Benson, *Antiracism in Cuba*, 122–52.

133. "Bohemia en Camarioca," 58.

134. See, for example, "Sigue proceso contra jóvenes de E.U. que visitaron Cuba," *Granma*, October 15, 1965, 1.

135. "En Cuba: El paraíso yanqui. Un clima de resentimiento y hostilidad," *Bohemia*, October 29, 1965, 54–61; Soler and Pinares, "Camarioca," 6. On tensions between Black Americans and Cubans, see García, *Havana USA*, 41; Rose, *Struggle for Black Freedom in Miami*, 212–40; Benson, *Antiracism in Cuba*, 122–52.

136. See Havana Domestic Television and Radio Services in Spanish, 0327 GMT 22, October 1965—F (Live speech by Prime Minister Fidel Castro at opening ceremonies of the national athletic games, closing event of the observances marking the fifth anniversary of the integration of the Cuban youth movement, from Havana's Pedro Marrero Stadium), http://lanic.utexas.edu/project/castro/db/1965/19651022 .html; Oramas, "Requisitos para la salida del país de los menores de 15 años," 3.

137. The United States would then combine the lists and give them to the Swiss embassy. See "El traslado de cubanos a Estados Unidos: Acuerdo y notas cruzadas sobre las negociaciones," *Bohemia*, November 12, 1965, 74–77; "308. Editorial Note," *Foreign Relations of the United States, 1964–1968*, 32, https://history.state.gov /historicaldocuments/frus1964-68v32/d308. The US government did not agree to restrictions on military-age men, professionals, and political prisoners, which were relegated to a footnote in the agreement. Memo from the President's Special Assistant (Rostow) to President Johnson, May 25, 1966, Johnson Library, National Security File, Country File, Cuba, vol. 2, 2/66–7/67, https://history.state.gov /historicaldocuments/frus1964-68v32/d309.

138. Philipson, *Freedom Flights*, 197.

139. Pedraza-Bailey, "Cuba's Exiles," 16; Dixon, "Cuban-American Counterpoint," 231.

140. Lockwood, *Castro's Cuba, Cuba's Fidel*, 284.

141. See Philipson, *Freedom Flights*, 82, 197.

142. Radio Cuba Libre, "Párrafos de carta de la Habana, Cuba, recibida en October 20, 1966, firmada por 'Alfonso 14' remitida a nuestro programa por la WWL, a través de un oyente en México"; "Párrafos de carta de la Habana, Cuba, recibida en 30 Enero 1966, firmada por Enrique, remitida a nuestro programa por la WWL, a través de un oyente en New Orleans," p. 1; "Párrafos de carta de la Habana, Cuba, recibida en Marzo 16, 1966, firmada por X-2615 enviada a nuestro programa por la WGBS, Miami," CFCR, box 54; Free Cuba Radio, "Excerpts from letter from Santiago de Cuba, received January 30, 1967, signed by "Q" forward to our program over WBGS, through a listener in Miami," box 53, CFCR.

143. Free Cuba Radio, "Excerpts from letter from Havana, Cuba, rcvd. March 28, 1966, signed 'Enrique,' forwarded to our program over WWL, through a listener in New Orleans"; "Excerpts from letter from Havana, Cuba, received March 26, 1966, signed 'Enrique,' forwarded to our program over WWL, through a listener in New Orleans"; Radio Cuba Libre, "Párrafos de carta de la Habana, Cuba, recibida en Marzo 16, 1966, firmada por X-2615," box 54, CFCR.

144. See Philipson, *Freedom Flights*, 82, 197.

145. Radio Cuba Libre, "Párrafos de carta de la Habana, Cuba, recibida en September 27, 1966, firmada por Mandy, remitida a nuestro programa por la WWL, a través de un oyente en Nebraska"; "Párrafos de carta de la Habana, Cuba, recibida en October 20, 1966, firmada por 'Alfonso 14.'" box 54, CFCR.

146. Untitled report (1967), p. 4, box 19, CFCR.

147. Radio Cuba Libre, "Párrafos de carta de la Habana, Cuba, recibida en September 26, 1966, firmada por Enrique, remitida a nuestro programa por la WWL, a través de un oyente en New Orleans," p. 3, box 54, CFCR.

148. "Editorial: Negociaciones," *Granma*, 2.

149. "Cuba: El paraíso yanqui," 54.

150. Johnson, "Nadie ha llorado aquí por los que se han ido," 2.

151. Havana Domestic Television and Radio Services in Spanish 0334 GMT 8 November 1965—F (Live speech by Prime Minister Fidel Castro at the dedication of the Lenin Hospital in Holguin, Oriente Province), http://lanic.utexas.edu/project/castro/db/1965/19651108.html.

152. Havana Domestic Radio and Television Services in Spanish 0125 GMT 16 Mar 68—F (Speech by Cuban Prime Minister Fidel Castro at the dedication of the Juan Manuel Marquez primary school in Boca de Jaruco, Havana Province—live).

153. Fidel Castro (speech, Plaza de la Revolución, September 28, 1971), www.cuba.cu/gobierno/discursos/1971/esp/f280971e.html.

154. See Bustamante, *Cuban Memory Wars*, 181–83.

155. W. E. Quantrill, confidential memo, "Discontent among Cuban Students," December 6, 1968, FCO/95/566, FCO—Records of the Foreign and Commonwealth Office and Predecessors, Division within FCO—Records of the Information Depart-

ments, Foreign Office and Foreign and Commonwealth Office: Information Research Department: Registered Files, National Archives at Kew, UK.

156. Law 1312, September 20, 1976, *Gaceta Oficial*, no. 19 (September 24, 1976): 257–59.

157. Philipson, *Freedom Flights*, 198.

158. See Philipson.

159. Torres, *In the Land of Mirrors*, 174.

160. Human Rights Watch, "World Report 2020: Cuba," www.hrw.org/world-report/2020/country-chapters/cuba.

161. These changes also spurred the diversification of Cuban migrant destinations. See Cearns, "The 'Mula Ring.'"

162. On US policy shifts, see Schoultz, *That Infernal Little Cuban Republic*; LeoGrande and Kornbluh, *Back Channel to Cuba*.

Chapter 5

1. Thomas, *Cuba*, 802.

2. Herminio Portell Vilá, radio script, January 2, 1963, Radio Free America, box 1, Herminio Portell Vilá Papers, CHC.

3. Monthly report, December 1964, box 44, CFCR.

4. Chastain and Lorek, introduction, 6.

5. See, for example, Solovey, *Shaky Foundations*; Oreskes and Krige, *Science and Technology in the Global Cold War*; Solovey and Dayé, *Cold War Social Science*.

6. Quinn, "Cuban Historiography in the 1960s." On the curtailment of such debates by 1970, see Ibarra Cuesta, "Historiografía y revolución."

7. See, for example, Yaffe, *"Che" Guevara*; Funes Monzote, *"Geotransformación"*; Funes Monzote and Palmer, "Challenging Climate and Geopolitics"; Ibarra, "Tropical Science and the Politics of Development."

8. See Casal, *El caso Padilla*; Reed, *Cultural Revolution in Cuba*; Rojas, *Tumbas sin sosiego*; Pogolotti, *Polémicas culturales de los 60*; Guanche, *El continente de lo posible*; Rojas, *El estante vacío*; Gallardo, *El martillo y el espejo*; Fornet, *El 71*; Gordon-Nesbitt, *To Defend the Revolution Is to Defend Culture*; Grenier, *Culture and the Cuban State*.

9. Guerra, *Patriots and Traitors in Revolutionary Cuba*, 285.

10. See Franco, *Decline and Fall of the Lettered City*; Iber, *Neither Peace nor Freedom*; Menand, *Free World*.

11. Valdespino, "Los castrologistas y el viaje de Fidel," 30.

12. Hoetink, "Cuba and the New Experts," 19. On US scholarly engagement with Cuba, see Valdés and Ibarra Zetter, "Senderos bifurcados."

13. Harbron, "Cuba," 217–18.

14. Hilton, "Castrofobia en los Estados Unidos," 507. For two relevant cases, see Stetson, "Academic Freedom"; Robertson, Pincoffs, and Randall, "Academic Freedom and Tenure."

15. See Chilcote, "The Cold War and the Transformation of Latin American Studies in the United States," 42–48.

16. See also Valdés, "Revolution and Paradigms."

17. Kapcia, "Does Cuba Fit Yet or Is It Still 'Exceptional'?," 630.

18. Rojas, *Fighting over Fidel*, 70.

19. Rojas, 64–68.

20. Artaraz, *Cuba and Western Intellectuals since 1959*, 6.

21. Rojas, *Fighting over Fidel*, 117.

22. Rojas, 132; Treviño, *C. Wright Mills and the Cuban Revolution*; Servín, "La experiencia mexicana de Charles Wright Mills," 1731. For two illustrative critiques of Mills's book, see Lino Novás Calvo, "Trucos, trampas y engañifas de los fidelistas americanos," *Bohemia Libre*, August 6, 1961, 22–23, 67, 79, 82; Hollander, *Political Pilgrims*, 223–67.

23. Servín, "La experiencia mexicana de Charles Wright Mills," 1763.

24. See Teel, *Reporting the Cuban Revolution*.

25. See also Lambe, "Communist Closet."

26. On the arc of Tannenbaum's engagement with Latin America, see Weinstein, "How to Become a Historian of Latin America."

27. Tannenbaum, "Castro and Social Change," 182. See also Servín, "Frank Tannenbaum entre América Latina y Estados Unidos en la Guerra Fría," 64–69.

28. Servín, Frank Tannenbaum entre América Latina y Estados Unidos en la Guerra Fría," 71.

29. John P. Rocha, "Committee for a Free Cuba," June 28, 1963, folder 6-11: Cuba: Citizens Committee for a Free Cuba, RFKAG-219-004-p0003, Papers of Robert F. Kennedy, Attorney General Papers, www.jfklibrary.org/asset-viewer/archives /RFKAG/219/RFKAG-219-004.

30. For a relevant contrast with "Soviet Studies," see Cohen, *Rethinking the Soviet Experience*, 3–37; Richmond, *Cultural Exchange and the Cold War*, 21–64; Engerman, *Know Your Enemy*; C. Kelly, "What Was Soviet Studies and What Came Next?"

31. See, for example, Reason et al., *Cuba Since Castro*; MacGaffey and Barnett, *Cuba: Its People, Its Society, Its Culture*; American University, *Special Warfare Area Handbook for Cuba*.

32. See Iber, *Neither Peace nor Freedom*, esp. 174–210.

33. Elliston, *Psywar on Cuba*, 177; Arguelles, "Cuban Miami"; Rodríguez García, *Crítica a nuestros críticos*, 3. See Gates, "CIA and the University." On academic recruitment by the CIA and Cuban intelligence, see Golden, *Spy Schools*, 52–83.

34. Cuban Economic Research Project, *Study in Cuba*, xv.

35. Memo, Donald Wilson, Deputy Director of USIA, to Brig. General Edward G. Lansdale, Assistant to the Secretary of Defense, July 20, 1962, p. 4, in Elliston, *Psywar on Cuba*, 108.

36. Christopher Lehmann-Haupt, "Theodore Draper, Freelance Historian, Is Dead at 93," *New York Times*, February 22, 2006, sec. New York, www.nytimes.com/2006 /02/22/us/theodore-draper-freelance-historian-is-dead-at-93.html.

37. Draper, *Roots of American Communism*, xvi–xvii.

38. Lehmann-Haupt, "Theodore Draper, Freelance Historian, Is Dead at 93."

39. Draper, *Roots of American Communism*, xi. A projected third volume was not completed.

40. Draper, 395.

41. For more on these connections, see F. S. Saunders, *Cultural Cold War*. On their intellectual footprint in Latin America, see Iber, *Neither Peace nor Freedom*.

42. Draper, "Castro's Cuba," 5; Draper, "Cuba and the Revolution of Our Time," 3.

43. Draper, "Cuba and the Revolution of Our Time," 4.

44. Draper, "Castro's Cuba," 13.

45. Draper, 11.

46. Draper, *Castro's Revolution*, 59–115.

47. Williams, "Cuba: Issues and Alternatives," 78.

48. Williams, "Historiography and Revolution," 102.

49. Hansen, *In Defense of the Cuban Revolution*, 7.

50. Hansen, 4.

51. Hansen, 8.

52. Hansen, 4. See also Norman Fruchter and Stuart Hall, "Notes on the Cuban Dilemma."

53. See, for example, Theodore Draper, "Cuba," letter to the editor, *New Left Review* 1, no. 11 (September–October 1961): 50.

54. Justo Carrillo to Theodore Draper, December 10, 1963, box 23, folder 2b [2], TDP.

55. Justo Carrillo to Theodore Draper, February 3, 1964, and Theodore Draper to Justo Carrillo, March 31, 1964, box 23, folder 2b [1], TDP; Theodore Draper to Orlando de Cárdenas, March 31, 1964, box 24, folder 6, TDP.

56. See Guerra, *Visions of Power in Cuba*, 136–37; Bustamante, *Cuban Memory Wars*, 67–74. On the discourse of betrayal in Cuban political culture, see Valdés, "Cuban Political Culture." For a critique of the betrayal thesis, see Morray, *Second Revolution in Cuba*. The paradigm of betrayal has surfaced in many revolutionary contexts, from France to Mexico and the Soviet Union—for example, Leon Trotsky, "The Revolution Betrayed" (1936); Adolfo Gilly, *La revolución interrumpida* (1971).

57. Carrillo book proposal, included in Justo Carrillo to Theodore Draper, February 25, 1964, box 23, folder 2b [1], TDP.

58. Justo Carrillo to Orlando de Cárdenas, February 14, 1964, box 23, folder 2b [1], TDP.

59. For another perspective on these questions, see Valdés, "Cuban Political Culture," 220.

60. O'Connor, *Origins of Socialism in Cuba*, 11, 6. O'Connor would later become a pioneer of political ecology. See "In Memory of James O'Connor (1930–2017)," January 12, 2018, www.versobooks.com/blogs/3560-in-memory-of-james-o-connor-1930-2017.

61. Baran, "Reflections on the Cuban Revolution," pt. 2, 521.

62. Rojas, *Fighting over Fidel*, 98.

63. For an instructive foil, see Seers et al., *Cuba*, v–xiii. The US funding source for Seers's project seems to have closed official doors in Cuba.

64. Mesa-Lago, *Breve historia económica de la Cuba socialista*, 17.

65. "Maurice Zeitlin (1958)," University of Berkeley Sociology Department, https://sociology.berkeley.edu/maurice-zeitlin-1958.

66. Zeitlin, *Revolutionary Politics and the Cuban Working Class*, 16.

67. Zeitlin, 227, 234.

68. Zeitlin, 75.

69. Zeitlin, 77, 73. Like O'Connor, Zeitlin would also continue to pursue many of these questions beyond Cuba, leading to important work on capitalism, class formation, and unionization in Latin America and the United States.

70. See also de la Fuente, *Nation for All*; Guerra, *Visions of Power in Cuba*; Benson, *Antiracism in Cuba*.

71. See, for example, A. Rodríguez, *Transitando por la psicología*; Yaffe, *"Che" Guevara*; Lambe, *Madhouse*, 174–84.

72. Karl, "Work Incentives in Cuba," 28–29; Mesa-Lago, *Breve historia económica de la Cuba socialista*, 84. Those who remained tended to frame their work in terms of providing support rather than intellectual direction. See the contributions of Ambrosio Fornet in "Diez años de revolución," *Casa de las Américas* 10, no. 56 (September–October 1969): 16–24.

73. Yaffe, *"Che" Guevara*, 164–65; Salém Vasconcelos, "Jacques Chonchol em Cuba," 87–88.

74. See also Seers et al., *Cuba*, 326. On kindred debates in Mexico, see Thornton, *Revolution in Development*.

75. Carmona, "Juan F. Noyola Vázquez, hijo fiel de la Escuela Nacional de Economía," 455–56.

76. Silva Herzog, "A manera de introducción," 10.

77. Bassols Batalla, "Al morir Juan F. Noyola Vázquez," 470; Bazdresch, "El pensamiento de Juan F. Noyola," 568.

78. Noyola, "Aspectos Económicos de la Revolución Cubana," 338.

79. García and Noyola, "Principales objetivos de Nuestro Plan Económico hasta 1965," 2. Emphasis in original. See also "Para planificar con éxito el poder político debe estar en manos del pueblo," *NH*, May 11, 1961, 5.

80. Noyola, "Aspectos Económicos de la Revolución Cubana," 339.

81. García and Noyola, "Principales objetivos de Nuestro Plan Económico hasta 1965," 12–15.

82. Carmona, "Juan F. Noyola Vázquez," 460; Bassols Batalla, "Al morir Juan F. Noyola Vázquez," 471.

83. Quoted in Carmona, "Juan F. Noyola Vázquez," 460.

84. Quoted in Carmona, 460–61.

85. García and Noyola, "Principales objetivos de Nuestro Plan Económico hasta 1965," 11.

86. C. R. Rodríguez, "Vida y obra de Juan F. Noyola," 601.

87. Rodríguez, 601.

88. Carmona, "Homenaje a Juan F. Noyola Vázquez," 131.

89. Felipe Pazos, "Comentarios a dos artículos sobre la Revolución Cubana," box 25, folder 8, TDP.

90. Chonchol, "Análisis crítico de la reforma agraria cubana," 69.

91. Salém Vasconcelos, "Jacques Chonchol em Cuba," 74.

92. Chonchol, "Análisis crítico de la reforma agraria cubana," 98, 141.

93. Chonchol, 1171–21; Salém Vasconcelos, "Jacques Chonchol em Cuba," 75–76; Salém Vasconcelos, "Reforma agrária e socialismo na América Latina," 7–8.

94. Chonchol, "Análisis crítico de la reforma agraria cubana," 135–42.

95. Chonchol, 142–43.

96. See also Funes Monzote and Palmer, "Challenging Climate and Geopolitics."

97. Dumont, "Une réforme agraire 'accélérée,'" 598.

98. Dumont, *Cuba: Socialism and Development*, 31, 53, 55–56, 99–102, 110, 119–20, 123, 164.

99. Dumont, "Une réforme agraire 'accélérée,'" 599; Dumont, *Cuba: Socialism and Development*, 164.

100. Dumont, *Cuba: Socialism and Development*, xii.

101. Dumont, 53.

102. Dumont, 91.

103. Dumont, 40.

104. Dumont, xiv.

105. Boorstein, *Economic Transformation of Cuba*, viii.

106. Boorstein, "Socialism and Development in Cuba," 621.

107. Boorstein, 622.

108. Boorstein, *Economic Transformation of Cuba*, 221.

109. Edward Boorstein, interview by Tana de Gamez, *Cuba Today*, WBAI, September 25, 1968, Pacifica Radio Archives, archive no. BB3155.

110. S. Díaz and Valdés Paz, *Charles Bettelheim en la Revolución Cubana*.

111. S. Díaz, "Cuba en Charles Bettelheim," 11.

112. Bettelheim, "Memorándum sobre la planificación económica en Cuba," 289.

113. S. Díaz, "Cuba en Charles Bettelheim," 11.

114. See also "'Producir más, mejor, y más económicamente': Una entrevista con el profesor Charles Bettelheim," *NH*, September 11, 1962, 5.

115. Bettelheim, "CUBA 1961. Artículo de Perspectiva, revista económica," 441.

116. See, for example, his interviews with Dorticós, reprinted as appendices in Díaz and Valdés Paz, *Charles Bettelheim en la Revolución Cubana*.

117. Cited in S. Díaz, "Cuba en Charles Bettelheim," 54.

118. See also Silverman, *Man and Socialism in Cuba*; Pericás, Sardenberg, and Binder, *Che Guevara and the Economic Debate in Cuba*; Yaffe, "Che Guevara and the Great Debate, Past and Present."

119. Cited in S. Díaz, "Cuba en Charles Bettelheim," 70.

120. Cited in Díaz, 29.

121. Cited in Díaz, 30.

122. Bettelheim letter of December 18, 1962, cited in S. Díaz, "Cuba en Charles Bettelheim," 34.

123. Cited in Díaz, 93.

124. Díaz, 95.

125. Mesa-Lago, *Breve historia económica de la Cuba socialista*, 43–49.

126. Mesa-Lago, 63.

127. Mesa-Lago, 61–62.

128. Years earlier, Dumont had advised that a 10-million-ton harvest was a realistic goal for 1975 and would only be possible in close coordination with the Soviet bloc. Dumont, *Cuba: Socialism and Development*, 150.

129. Dumont, *Is Cuba Socialist?*, 10.

130. Dumont, 10.

131. René Dumont, "Les cubains trouvent le temps long," *Le Monde*, December 9, 1969, 1; Guillermoprieto, *Dancing with Cuba*, 67.

132. Dumont, *Is Cuba Socialist?*, 118.

133. Petras, "Has the Cuban Revolution Failed?," 86n1, 90n3. See also Díaz and Valdés Paz, *Charles Bettelheim en la Revolución Cubana*; Artaraz, *Cuba and Western Intellectuals since 1959*.

134. See Guerra, "Gender Policing"; Sierra Madero, *El cuerpo nunca olvida*.

135. See Dopico Black, "Limits of Expression"; Reed, *Cultural Revolution in Cuba*, 76–97; Kapcia, *Havana*, 128–49; Gallardo, *El martillo y el espejo*, 107–35.

136. "Política con los intelectuales" (1967), folder Presidencia—Planes 1967, 17/6, CNC.

137. See Salkey, *Havana Journal*; Fernández Retamar, *Cuba defendida*, 265–89; Artaraz, *Cuba and Western Intellectuals since 1959*, 43; Gallardo, *El martillo y el espejo*, 145–64.

138. Artaraz, *Cuba and Western Intellectuals since 1959*, 41.

139. Artaraz, 130; Martínez Pérez, *Los hijos de Saturno*.

140. Artaraz, "Constructing Identities in a Contested Setting," 57.

141. Plá León and González Aróstegui, *Marxismo y revolución*; Kohan, "*Pensamiento Crítico* y el debate por las ciencias sociales en el seno de la revolución cubana"; Alonso Tejada, "Marxismo y espacio de debate en la revolución cubana"; Rojas, *Fighting over Fidel*, 180–94.

142. Andre Schiffrin, "Publishing in Cuba," *NYT*, March 17, 1968, BR40.

143. Artaraz, *Cuba and Western Intellectuals since 1959*; Fornet, *El 71*, 47.

144. Moore, *Castro, the Blacks, and Africa*, 307–10; Benson, "Redefining Mestizaje," 101–5.

145. Moore, *Castro, the Blacks, and Africa*, 309. See also Benson, "Redefining Mestizaje," 102.

146. Moore, *Castro, the Blacks, and Africa*, 310; Guerra, *Visions of Power in Cuba*, 256–89; Farber, "Cuba in 1968." See also Guerra, "*Poder Negro* in Revolutionary Cuba"; Benson, "Redefining Mestizaje."

147. Richard Fagen to René Vallejo, December 23, 1966; "Evaluation of Lee Lockwood, Castro's Cuba, Cuba's Fidel," included in Richard Fagen to René Vallejo, May 10, 1967, box 13, folder 6, RFP.

148. Betty Visley of Domestic Operations Division, Passport Office, Department of State, to US Department of Justice, FBI, "Richard Rees Fagen. Internal Security—Cuba," declassified May 30, 1989, box 13, folder 1, RFP.

149. These works include "Calculation and Emotion in Foreign Policy," *Cuba: The Political Content of Adult Education*, "Charismatic Authority and the Leadership of Fidel Castro," and "Mass Mobilization in Cuba."

150. See Richard Fagen, "Research: Plans, Problems, and Data," box 25, folder 7, TDP; Fagen, Brody, and O'Leary, *Cubans in Exile*.

151. Memo, Kalman H. Silvert to Harry E. Wilhelm, "Possible Foundation Activities Involving Cuban Affairs," October 10, 1967, pp. 2–4, box 4, folder: Cuba—Ford Programs—History, 1967–1989, FFR.

152. Memo, Kalman H. Silvert to Harry E. Wilhelm, "Possible Foundation Activities Involving Cuban Affairs," October 10, 1967, p. 4; memorandum, David E. Bell to McGeorge Bundy, "Small Program Actions vis-à-vis Cuba," 68–849, August 22, 1968, Request No. ID-235, box 4, folder: Cuba—Ford Programs—History, 1967–1989, FFR.

153. Karol, *Guerrillas in Power*, 477.

154. See Fagen, "Biographical Note on René Vallejo," and Richard Fagen to René Vallejo, March 30, 1967, box 13, folder 6, RFP.

155. René Vallejo to Richard Fagen, May 25, 1968, box 13, folder 6, RFP.

156. Halperin, "State of Latin American Studies," 99.

157. Fagen, *Transformation of Political Culture in Cuba*, 1.

158. Fagen, 2.

159. René Vallejo to Richard Fagen, April 5, 1969, box 13, folder 6, RFP.

160. Richard Fagen to Kalman Silvert (Ford Foundation), September 2, 1969, p. 2, box 14, folder 5, RFP.

161. Edwin McDowell, "Did Castro Double-Cross Oscar Lewis?," *NYT*, October 26, 1981, www.nytimes.com/1981/10/26/books/did-castro-double-cross-oscar-lewis .html; Guerra, "Former Slum Dwellers, the Communist Youth, and the Lewis Project in Cuba," 72.

162. Guerra, "Former Slum Dwellers, the Communist Youth, and the Lewis Project in Cuba," 68.

163. McDowell, "Did Castro Double-Cross Oscar Lewis?"

164. Guerra, *Patriots and Traitors in Revolutionary Cuba*, 215.

165. "An Exchange of Views: Ruth M. Lewis & José Yglesias," *Nation*, September 10, 1977, 220; Guerra, "Former Slum Dwellers, the Communist Youth, and the Lewis Project in Cuba," 71.

166. Guerra, "Former Slum Dwellers, the Communist Youth, and the Lewis Project in Cuba," 84.

167. Guerra, 68, 84.

168. Olga Chamero to Richard Fagen, August 16, 1971, box 14, folder 11, RFP; memo, Kalman Silvert to William D. Carmichael, "Narrative Report: FF Small Program Action vis-à-vis Cuba" (68–849), p. 3, December 17, 1973, box 4, folder: Cuba—Ford Programs—History, 1967–1989, FFR. Most US travelers were also denied Cuban visas in 1969 and 1970. See Thomas Skidmore (LASA Government Relations Committee), "Report on Scholarly Relations with Cuba," August 1, 1971, p. 3, box 14, folder 11, RFP.

169. Lee Lockwood, "A Former Friend of Fidel Has 'Let Cuba Down,'" *NYT*, January 24, 1971, www.nytimes.com/1971/01/24/archives/guerrillas-in-power-the-course-of-the-cuban-revolution-by-k-s-karol.html.

170. Karol, *Guerrillas in Power*, 476.

171. Karol, 484.

172. Karol, 459.

173. Karol, x.

174. Lockwood, "Former Friend of Fidel Has 'Let Cuba Down'"; Fornet, *El 71*, 50.

175. Fornet, *El 71*, 47–49.

176. Fidel Castro, "Año de los diez millones" (speech, Chaplin Theater, April 22, 1970), www.cuba.cu/gobierno/discursos/1970/esp/f220470e.html.

177. On this context, see Guerra, *Visions of Power in Cuba*, 290–316.

178. Fidel Castro (speech, Plaza de la Revolución, July 26, 1970), www.cuba.cu/gobierno/discursos/1970/esp/f260770e.html (my italics).

179. Heberto Padilla, "Intervención en la Unión de Escritores y Artistas de Cuba," April 27, 1971, *Casa de las Américas* 11, no. 65–66 (March–June 1971): 191–203, reprinted in Casal, *El caso Padilla*, 89. See also "Cuba, la C.I.A. et M. René Dumont," *Le Monde*, March 4, 1971, 3; Juan Arcocha, "Tribune internationale. Le poète et le commissaire," *Le Monde*, April 29, 1971, 2.

180. Cited in Besset, *René Dumont*, 327.

181. Reprinted in "Cuba: Revolution and the Intellectual," 82.

182. Luis García Peraza to Rolando Rodríguez, June 15, 1971, Biblioteca Nacional, Fondo del Ministerio de Cultura, bookcase 52, shelf 12, file 1, Caso Padilla: File y 3 folletos en un sobre (1971), note 9, transcription by Lillian Guerra, June–July 2005, Havana, Cuba, https://dloc.com/AA00019994/00001/pdf.

183. Cited in S. Díaz, "Cuba en Charles Bettelheim," 109.

184. S. Díaz, 110.

185. Travel journal, p. 57, box 12, folder 3, HMP.

186. Travel journal, p. 32, box 12, folder 3, HMP.

187. Léon Mayrand to Herbert Matthews, December 6, 1971, box 12, folder 6, HMP.

188. Norman Podhoretz, "Liberty and the Intellectuals," *Commentary Magazine* (November 1971), www.commentary.org/articles/norman-podhoretz/liberty-the-intellectuals/.

189. Memorandum, Howard R. Dressner to McGeorge Bundy, "Recommendation for Grant/DAP Action" (68–849), p. 5, March 12, 1979, box 4, folder: Cuba—Ford Programs—History, 1967–1989, FFR.

190. Domínguez, "Twenty-Five Years of Cuban Studies," 3.

191. Cited in Domínguez, 15.

192. Memorandum, Susan Cantor to William Carmichael, "Evaluation of Grants Given under the Small Programs Actions vis-à-vis Cuba" (68–849), p. 6, June 20, 1977, box 4, folder: Cuba—Ford Programs—History, 1967–1989, FFR.

193. Mesa-Lago, "Un futuro sin cortapisas para los intercambios académicos," 320.

194. See García, *Havana USA*, 198–207; Latner, *Cuban Revolution in America*, 153–98.

195. Skidmore, "Report on Scholarly Relations with Cuba," 4. See also Smith, "Status of Scholarly Exchanges with Cuba"; Fuller, "Fieldwork in Forbidden Terrain"; Martínez and Resende, "Academic Exchange between Cuba and the United States."

196. Alvarez, "The Dying Dialogue between US and Cuban Scholars," 65–68.

197. Memorandum, Susan Cantor to William Carmichael, "Evaluation of Grants Given under the Small Programs Actions vis-à-vis Cuba" (68–849), 1, June 20, 1977.

198. Mesa-Lago, "On the Objectives and Objectivity of Cubanology," 226–27.

199. Rodríguez García, *Crítica a nuestros críticos*, 8.

200. Rodríguez García, 8.

201. Mesa-Lago, "Revolutionary Empathy vs. Calculated Detachment in the Study of the Cuban Revolution," 91.

202. Kahl, *A Cuban Diary*, 67.

203. "Informe de la comisión cubana-alemana para estudios etnológicos," Havana, August 9, 1961, p. 1, and "Suplemento al informe de la comisión cubano-alemana para estudios etnológicos del 9 de agosto de 1961," Havana, August 28, 1961, p. 4, Folder Instituto de Etnología y Folklore, 17/1, CNC.

204. "Informe de la comisión cubana-alemana para estudios etnológicos," 4.

205. See A. Rodríguez, *Transitando por la psicología*.

206. "Suplemento al informe de la comisión cubano-alemana para estudios etnológicos del 9 de agosto de 1961," 4. See also Kahl, *A Cuban Diary*, 56–57.

Chapter 6

1. See, for example, Rosenfeld, *Revolution in Language*; O'Keeffe, *Esperanto and Languages of Internationalism in Revolutionary Russia*.

2. Pino, "Influence of the Revolution on Cuban Spanish"; Iglesias Utset, *Las metáforas del cambio en la vida cotidiana*.

3. Pino, "Influence of the Revolution on Cuban Spanish," 15.

4. Kotkin, *Magnetic Mountain*, 198–237.

5. Fagen, *Transformation of Political Culture in Cuba*, 7. See also Martínez, *Youngest Revolution*; Bunck, *Fidel Castro and the Quest for a Revolutionary Culture in Cuba*; Díaz Castañón, *Ideología y Revolución*; Serra, *"New Man" in Cuba*; Blum, *Cuban Youth and Revolutionary Values*; Guerra, *Visions of Power in Cuba*; Hynson, *Laboring for the State*; Guerra, *Patriots and Traitors in Revolutionary Cuba*. On Soviet precedents, see Hoffman, *Stalinist Values*.

6. Kharkhordin, *Collective and the Individual in Russia*, 231–79.

7. See Orejuela Martínez, *El son no se fue de Cuba*, 210–11; Bustamante, "Cultural Politics and Political Cultures of the Cuban Revolution."

8. Fidel Castro, *Granma*, September 29, 1967, 2, quoted in Fagen, *Transformation of Political Culture in Cuba*, 103.

9. "El libro a la calle: Festival del Libro Cubano," *NH*, September 11, 1959, 2.

10. R. Branly, "Cultura política para el pueblo," *La Calle*, June 15, 1960, 12. See also Smorkaloff, *Readers and Writers in Cuba*, 101–12.

11. Stanley Meisler, "Cuba's Frenzied Culture," *Nation*, December 25, 1960, 505.

12. [TV Program] Seminario y Revolución 1961, Folder Programas de TV 1961, 17/1, CNC.

13. Marcer, "Las bibliotecas del pueblo," 38.

14. Marcer, "Las bibliotecas del pueblo"; Nydia Sarabia, "El libro, compañero del obrero" (May 1963), 17/1, CNC.

15. Fagen, *Transformation of Political Culture in Cuba*, 54.

16. Fagen, 59. See also Bunck, *Fidel Castro and the Quest for a Revolutionary Culture in Cuba*; Blum, *Cuban Youth and Revolutionary Values*; Guerra, *Visions of Power in Cuba*; Guerra, *Patriots and Traitors in Revolutionary Cuba*.

17. Ángeles Periu, "Experiencias de la educación obrera y campesina en Cuba," 20–24, 33; Canfux and Mateja, "Brief Description of the 'Battle for the Sixth Grade,'" 227. In the early 1960s, the CTC was renamed the CTC-R (CTC Revolucionaria). For clarity's sake, I omit the "R" in the next two chapters.

18. Blum, *Cuban Youth and Revolutionary Values*, 60, 65; Huberman and Sweezy, *Socialism in Cuba*, 31–32.

19. Olga, phone interview by Laura Muñoz, January 2018.

20. Huberman and Sweezy, *Socialism in Cuba*, 47.

21. Quoted in Huberman and Sweezy, 31.

22. Huberman and Sweezy, 32–33.

23. Fagen, *Transformation of Political Culture in Cuba*, 106–7. See also Artaraz, *Cuba and Western Intellectuals since 1959*, 38; Blum, *Cuban Youth and Revolutionary Values*, 27.

24. Soto, "El nuevo desarrollo de la instrucción revolucionaria."

25. A. Castillo, "En el II Aniversario de la Imprenta Nacional," *Bohemia*, March 23, 1962, 64; Dirección Nacional de los CDR, *Los CDR en granjas y zonas rurales*; Fagen, *Transformation of Political Culture in Cuba*, 87.

26. Soto, "El nuevo desarrollo de la instrucción revolucionaria"; Fagen, *Transformation of Political Culture in Cuba*, 109–36.

27. Fagen, *Transformation of Political Culture in Cuba*, 136; Bunck, *Fidel Castro and the Quest for a Revolutionary Culture in Cuba*, 54. See also Plá León and González Aróstegui, *Marxismo y revolución*; Alonso Tejada, "Marxismo y espacio de debate en la revolución cubana." On Soviet party schools, see David-Fox, *Revolution of the Mind*, 24–82.

28. Fagen, *Transformation of Political Culture in Cuba*, 111.

29. Quoted in Soto, "Las Escuelas de Instrucción Revolucionaria en el ciclo político-técnico," *Cuba Socialista* 5, no. 41 (January 1965): 67.

30. Blum, *Cuban Youth and Revolutionary Values*, 53–55; Guerra, *Patriots and Traitors in Revolutionary Cuba*, 243–48.

31. See Bunck, *Fidel Castro and the Quest for a Revolutionary Culture in Cuba*, 185–215; Guerra, *Visions of Power in Cuba*, 139–40; Lambe, "Century of Work"; Schwall, "Prescribing Ballet."

32. On a kindred concept in the Soviet Union, see Volkov, "Concept of Kul'turnost.'"

33. Foucault, *Discipline and Punish*, 170.

34. See A. Rodríguez, *Transitando por la psicología*; Lambe, *Madhouse*, 180–84.

35. Castillo, "Artistas con el pueblo," *Bohemia*, November 2, 1962, 96–97.

36. "La cultura ya no es un privilegio," 99–100.

37. "La cultura ya no es un privilegio," 100; presentation by José Miguel Garófalo (Coordinador Provincial de La Habana), *Informe de la Coordinación Provincial a la Plenaria de Cultura*, November 25, 1962, 5–10, BNJM; Sánchez León, *Esa huella olvidada*, 82; Boudet, *Cuba*, 15.

38. Report, Maritza Alonso González (Jefe de la Sección de Cine, Televisión, y Radio) to Edith García Buchaca (CNC), May 16, 1962, 17/1, CNC; Garófalo, *Informe de la Coordinación Provincial a la Plenaria de Cultura*, 5–38.

39. Guerra, *Visions of Power in Cuba*, 80–81.

40. Report, Maritza Alonso González to Edith García Buchaca, 2.

41. R. D. Moore, *Music and Revolution*, 86.

42. See García Yero, "State within the Arts."

43. Villegas, "Origin, Development and Processes of Teatro Escambray in Cuba," 38; Ramos Ruiz, *Roa, director de cultura*; Boudet, *Cuba*, 11; Guzmán, "Actores gubernamentales de la política cultural cubana entre 1949 y 1961"; Schwall, *Dancing with the Revolution*, 27.

44. Sánchez León, *Esa huella olvidada*, 201–7; Schwall, *Dancing with the Revolution*, 71; "Manifiesto de la Sección Cultural de la Provincial del 26 de Julio, 3 de mayo de 1959," *Lunes de Revolución*, May 11, 1959, 5, cited in Sánchez León, *Esa huella olvidada*, 50.

45. "Narra Franqui su viaje a la Unión Soviética," *NH*, December 6, 1960, 2. See also Siegelbaum, "Shaping of Soviet Workers' Leisure"; Tsipursky, *Socialist Fun*.

46. See "Trabajos a realizar en el frente de cultura" (1962), p. 11, 17/1, CNC.

47. José Lorenzo Fuentes, "Primer festival de aficionados y Florencia la Cañabrava," *Bohemia*, September 28, 1962, 46–47.

48. Garófalo, *Informe de la Coordinación Provincial a la Plenaria de Cultura*, 39–40.

49. Reynold Rassi, "Festival Nacional de Aficionados: Campesinos y reeducados en el Festival Nacional," *Granma*, November 5, 1966, 7.

50. Angela Soto, "Barracón que se convierte en teatro," *Mella* 17, no. 192 (May 1961): n.p. (illegible).

51. Angela Soto, "En 84 y Mar. Un día con los instructores de arte," *Mella* 17, no. 199 (June 1961): 23.

52. Comisión Nacional de Aficionados, "Centro de Instructores Artísticos de Aficionados de cooperativas y Granjas" (1962?), p. 13, 17/1, CNC.

53. See speeches by Edith García Buchaca and Vicentina Antuña Tavlo in *Primer Congreso Nacional de Cultura*, 23, 51; Garófalo, *Informe de la Coordinación Provincial a la Plenaria de Cultura*, 41–42.

54. F.J., "Escuela para Instructores de Arte," *NH*, July 23, 1961, 12.

55. See speech by Edith García Buchaca in *Primer Congreso Nacional de Cultura*, 8.

56. Rosa Ileana Boudet, email message to author, December 13, 2021. See also Boudet, *Alánimo, Alánimo*.

57. Noelia González, email message to author, February 1, 2022.

58. Rafael Rojas, "Escuela para instructores de arte," June 27, 1964, folder: Presidencia—Planes 1964, 17/1, CNC.

59. See speech by Edith García Buchaca in *Primer Congreso Nacional de Cultura*, 24.

60. Felix Pita Rodríguez, "La graduación de los instructores de arte," *Pueblo y cultura*, no. 15 (1963): 24.

61. Boudet, email message to author, December 13, 2021.

62. E. S. Martínez, *Youngest Revolution*, 23–24.

63. Boudet, email message to author, December 13, 2021.

64. "Isla de Pinos: Buenos frutos del trabajo cultural ante un decidido afán de superación," *Revista del Consejo de Cultura*, 1963, 21, https://ctda.library.miami.edu/publications/1115/.

65. See "Isla de Pinos"; Consejo Municipal de Cultura, Isla de Pinos, August 18, 1962, "Informe de las actividades del consejo, de Enero de 1962 a la fecha (cine popular)" and "Informe del mes de octubre," Biblioteca Nacional, Fondo del Ministerio de Cultura, bookcase 47, shelf 28, file 16, Isla de Pinos, Informes, 1962, transcription by Lillian Guerra, https://dloc.com/AA00019994/00001.

66. Boudet, email message to author, December 13, 2021.

67. González, email message to author, February 1, 2022.

68. Augusto, interview by Eileen Artigas, October 2017.

69. CNC, "Trabajo de Aficionados, Dirección de Danza, [Planes?] para reorganizar y reorientar el Movimiento de Aficionados" [1964?], 17/1, CNC.

70. Schwall, *Dancing with the Revolution*, 142–57.

71. González, email message to author, February 1, 2022.

72. Sánchez León, *Esa huella olvidada*, 257.

73. "El bloqueo" (Nelson Rodríguez Leyva), Assessment of Amador Fernández, Concurso Literario 1963," Biblioteca Nacional, Fondo del Ministerio de Cultura, bookcase 03, shelf 25, file 44, CNC Coordinación Provincial Habana, Aficionados, Concurso Literario 1963, transcription by Lillian Guerra, https://dloc.com/AA00019994/00001/pdf.

74. Assessment of Amador Fernández, Concurso Literario 1963, Biblioteca Nacional, Fondo del Ministerio de Cultura, bookcase 03, shelf 25, file 44, CNC Coordinación Provincial Habana, Aficionados, Concurso Literario 1963, transcription by Lillian Guerra, https://dloc.com/AA00019994/00001/pdf.

75. Reynold Rassi, "Festival Nacional de Aficionados," 7.

76. Boudet, email message to author, December 13, 2021. See also Boudet, *Cuba*, 38–55.

77. González, email message to author, February 1, 2022.

78. Dirección Nacional de Extensión Cultural, "Movimiento de Aficionados," January 1971, p. 3; "Plan de trabajo del Movimiento de Aficionados para el año 1963"; and CNC, Dirección Nacional de Fomento de Grupos de Aficionados, "Planes para 1964," 17/1, CNC; Freddy Artiles, "Entrevista a Rigoberto Rodríguez y Hugo Fernández," *Granma*, June 24, 1964, 2; CNC, "Orientaciones sobre los planes concretos del Frente de Aficionados," 1966, folder: CNC—Aficionados—Planes de trabajo 1966, 17/1, CNC.

79. Edith García Buchaca, quoted in Manuel Navarro Luna, "Estampas de la Revolución: El Segundo Festival de Aficionados," *NH*, February 29, 1964, 2; Reynold Rassi, "La formación de los grupos selectivos: Un paso de avance en el movimiento de aficionados," *Granma*, February 11, 1967, 2; "Sobre el programa de aficionados del C.N.C. *El pueblo en escena*," folder: Programación ICRT 1967, 17/1, CNC.

80. Schwall, *Dancing with the Revolution*, 138.

81. Boudet, email message to author, December 13, 2021.

82. "Izan en obras del Parque Maceo la bandera que señala el primer lugar en la emulación," *NH*, June 8, 1961, 4.

83. Carlos Fernández R., "La emulación nacional," *NH*, June 9, 1961, 2.

84. See Guerra, *Patriots and Traitors in Revolutionary Cuba*, 225, 182.

85. See, for example, "Organizada una gran emulación para ayuda de nuestro periodico," *NH*, November 1, 1939, 1; "Concertaron una emulación los azucareros para el envío de delegados al congreso de Enero," *NH*, October 12, 1940, 3.

86. Siegelbaum, *Stakhanovism and the Politics of Productivity in the USSR*, 2.

87. Mesa-Lago, *Labor Sector and Socialist Distribution in Cuba*, 25; Siegelbaum, *Stakhanovism and the Politics of Productivity in the USSR*, 2.

88. Bunck, *Fidel Castro and the Quest for a Revolutionary Culture in Cuba*, 127–29.

89. Maurice Zeitlin, "Labor in Cuba," *Nation*, October 20, 1962, 238.

90. See Guerra, *Visions of Power in Cuba*, 32–170.

91. FORDC, *El trabajo en Cuba socialista*; Bunck, *Fidel Castro and the Quest for a Revolutionary Culture in Cuba*, 134–37.

92. Bunck, *Fidel Castro and the Quest for a Revolutionary Culture in Cuba*, 130.

93. GCIE, *Labor Conditions in Communist Cuba*, 53–55.

94. GCIE, 54n, 56; Jaime Gravalosa, "Visitan los héroes del trabajo el mausoleo de Lenin," *NH*, June 24, 1963, 3.

95. GCIE, *Labor Conditions in Communist Cuba*, 55–56.

96. Mesa-Lago, *Labor Sector and Socialist Distribution in Cuba*, 133.

97. GCIE, *Labor Conditions in Communist Cuba*, 57–58. See also "Reglamento para la organización de la emulación," *Gaceta Oficial: Año '62*, no. 19 (May 21, 1964): 445–83; "Un nuevo paso en el desarrollo de la emulación socialista," *Cuba socialista* 5 (August 1964): 107–11.

98. "Un nuevo paso en el desarrollo de la emulación socialista," 110.

99. "Reglamento para la organización de la emulación."

100. *Noticiero ICAIC Latinoamericano*, no. 197 (March 1964), dir. Santiago Álvarez, www.youtube.com/watch?v=w6aPkOvmxFw&list=PLxjJeycXohyr1wMfz9BP vyfYCl42lUxhp&index=21&ab_channel=CinecubanoICAIC.

101. Guerra, *Patriots and Traitors in Revolutionary Cuba*, 9.

102. Mirta Rodriguez Calderón, "El gran deseo realizado," *Granma*, January 17, 1966, 8.

103. See Pedro Rojas, "Reinaldo Castro corta ahora en una brigada de héroes," *NH*, January 17, 1964, 3; Fidel Castro (speech, CTC Theater, March 6, 1964); Norberto Fuentes, "Héroes," *Cuba*, April 5, 1964, 11; Luis Lara Espinosa, "Nuevas demostraciones de corte hace Reinaldo Castro en Oriente," *NH*, May 16, 1965, 3.

104. CMQ-Radio, Radio Progreso, Havana, April 13–17, 1965, as recorded by Carmelo Mesa-Lago, cited in FORDC, *El trabajo en Cuba socialista*, 74.

105. FORDC, *El trabajo en Cuba socialista*, 15; GCIE, *Labor Conditions in Communist Cuba*, 58.

106. GCIE, *Labor Conditions in Communist Cuba*, 58.

107. Quoted in FORDC, *El trabajo en Cuba socialista*, 90–91. See also Juan de Onís, "Cuban Economic Troubles Called a Break on Castro," *NYT*, April 14, 1964, 15.

108. FORDC, *El trabajo en Cuba socialista*, 17.

109. FORDC, 72.

110. Basilio Rodriguez, "El nuevo enfoque de la emulación socialista," *Granma*, May 23, 1966, 2.

111. Cited in Bunck, *Fidel Castro and the Quest for a Revolutionary Culture in Cuba*, 139.

112. See monthly reports, January and February 1965, box 44, CFCR.

113. FORDC, *El trabajo en Cuba socialista*, 6.

114. Radio Cuba Libre, "Copia de carta de Fomento, Las Villas, CUBA, recibida en Enero 3, 1966, firmada por 'Una Cubana,' remitida a nuestro programa por la WGBS, Miami," box 54, CFCR.

115. Onís, "Cuban Economic Troubles Called a Break on Castro," 1, 15.

116. Rodríguez, "El nuevo enfoque de la emulación socialista," 2; Mesa-Lago, *Labor Sector and Socialist Distribution in Cuba*, 121–28.

117. Carmen R. Alfonso, "Movimiento de avanzada, cantera de comunistas," *Granma*, October 25, 1967, 5; "Los movimientos de avanzada," *Granma*, May 27, 1968, 2.

118. Agustín García, "El movimiento de avanzada: Masa y vanguardia," *Granma*, February 22, 1969, 2.

119. Even so, vanguard workers continued to receive "full payment of their wages when becoming sick, disabled, or retired, and priority in lists to buy scarce goods such as refrigerators, or to obtain transfers in housing." See Hernández and Mesa-Lago, "Labor Organization and Wages," 237.

120. Hernández and Mesa-Lago, 237.

121. Bernardo, *Theory of Moral Incentives in Cuba*, 64.

122. Guerra, *Visions of Power in Cuba*, 291.

123. Alberto Pozo, "Una experiencia aleccionadora: El hombre; Factor decisivo," *Bohemia*, September 12, 1969, 6.

124. Pozo, 6.

125. Flor López, "La orientación revolucionaria en la Zafra de los 10 Millones," *Granma*, November 21, 1969, 2.

126. Pozo, "Una experiencia aleccionadora," 11, 6.

127. Lewis, Lewis, and Rigdon, *Living the Revolution*, 27n, 26.

128. Pérez Stable, "Whither the Cuban Working Class?," 67; Karl, "Work Incentives in Cuba," 36.

129. R. M. K. Slater to Miss E. R. Allcott, British Embassy, Havana, September 9, 1969, FCO/95/566, FCO—Records of the Foreign and Commonwealth Office and

Predecessors, Division within FCO—Records of the Information Departments, FCO 95—Foreign Office and Foreign and Commonwealth Office: Information Research Department: Registered Files, National Archives at Kew, UK.

130. Hernández and Mesa-Lago, "Labor Organization and Wages," 237; Bunck, *Fidel Castro and the Quest for a Revolutionary Culture in Cuba*, 147–52.

131. Nelson, *Cuba*, 124.

132. Salas, "Emergence and Decline of the Cuban Popular Tribunals," 604.

133. Domínguez, *Cuba*, 275–76.

134. Evelio Telleria, Jose Gabriel Gumá, Jaime Gravalosa, and Felix Pita Astudillo, "Franco debate obrero sobre ausentismo," *Granma*, September 8, 1970, 4–5.

135. McColl Kennedy, "Cuba's Ley Contra La Vagancia," 30n, 1188.

136. McColl Kennedy, 1188.

137. Bunck, *Fidel Castro and the Quest for a Revolutionary Culture in Cuba*, 158.

138. Though women aged seventeen to fifty-five were in principle required to work, no women were penalized because of the law. See Hynson, *Laboring for the State*.

139. Nelson, *Cuba*, 125; McColl Kennedy, "Cuba's Ley Contra La Vagancia," 1239, 1248; Bunck, *Fidel Castro and the Quest for a Revolutionary Culture in Cuba*, 158.

140. Jorge Luis González Suárez, "Yo tambien fui un 'vago' de la revolucion," March 29, 2017, www.cubanet.org/actualidad-destacados/yo-tambien-fui-un-vago -de-la-revolucion/.

141. Nelson, *Cuba*, 125.

142. Pérez-Stable, "Whither the Cuban Working Class?," 69–70; Karl, "Work Incentives in Cuba," 36.

143. Pérez-Stable, "Whither the Cuban Working Class?," 70.

144. Domínguez, *Cuba*, 277.

145. Bunck, *Fidel Castro and the Quest for a Revolutionary Culture in Cuba*, 153–63.

146. "1972: Año de la Emulación Socialista," *Granma*, January 3, 1971, 1; "¡Viva el año de la emulación socialista!," editorial, *Granma*, January 4, 1972, 1; Pérez-Stable, "Whither the Cuban Working Class?," 72.

147. Cited in Pérez-Stable, "Whither the Cuban Working Class?," 72.

148. Domínguez, *Cuba*, 278–79.

149. On emulation after 1980, see Córdova, *El trabajador cubano en el estado de obreros y campesinos*, 68–86; Bunck, *Fidel Castro and the Quest for a Revolutionary Culture in Cuba*, 168–79.

150. Mesa-Lago, *Labor Sector and Socialist Distribution in Cuba*, 149–50.

151. Report, "Cuba Revisited: 18 Years Later," 1978(?), p. 12, 009062 #1, box 4, folder: Cuba—Ford Programs—History, 1967–1989, FFR.

152. Bunck, *Fidel Castro and the Quest for a Revolutionary Culture in Cuba*, 184.

153. Miriam Leiva, "La emulación, otra falacia tronada por conveniencia," *Cuba Encuentro*, www.cubaencuentro.com/txt/cuba/articulos/la-emulacion-otra-falacia -tronada-por-conveniencia-277684.

154. Marisol, interview by author, February 2022.

155. "Tabla del desarrollo del movimiento de aficionados en los años 1965, 1968, 1971 y 1974," folder 4-1, Director Aficionados 1975, 17/1, CNC; Dirección de Cultura Masiva, "Antecedentes de la cultura popular masiva," 83.

156. "Plan a mediano plazo, 1976–1980," folder: Presidencia—Planes 1971, 17/6, CNC; Elvia Pérez Nápoles, "Casas de cultura no sólo actividades culturales," *Revolución y Cultura*, February 1981, 81, cited in Brill, "La Escuela Cubana," 224.

157. "Palabras pronunciadas por el Co. Luis Pavón, Presidente del Consejo Nacional de Cultura, en la Plenaria Provincial de Cultura de Oriente," January 23, 1972, folder: Presidencia—Planes 1971, 17/6, CNC.

158. "Plan de trabajo de la Dirección de Extensión Cultural, 1972," folder: Aficionados Prov. Hab. Planes de Trabajo 1972, 17/1, CNC.

159. "Tabla del desarrollo"; Brill, "La Escuela Cubana," 52.

160. "Palabras del Compañero Ivan Sihanouk, asesor soviético del Movimiento de Aficionados de Cuba" (1975), 17/1, CNC.

161. Valentín Puentes, "Informe sobre una experiencia—Regional Artemisa," July 11, 1972, 17/1, CNC.

162. "Analizan problemática del movimiento de aficionados al arte," *Granma*, November 25, 1979, 4; Evangelina Chió, "Aficionados: Presente y perspectivas," *Revolución y Cultura*, no. 128 (April 1983): 54–57; R. D. Moore, *Music and Revolution*, 86.

163. See Robbins, "Making Popular Music in Cuba," 157–73; Brill, "La Escuela Cubana," 56; Schwall, *Dancing with the Revolution*, 148–49.

164. Kapcia, *Havana*, 164.

165. Vienbenido Cárdenas to René Valdés Díaz, Delegado del Frente Campesino Nacional, Santa Clara, November 1974, 17/1, CNC.

166. Octavio Getino, "El teatro en la batalla del Escambray," in *Grupo Teatro Escambray*, 10.

167. "Al aire libre: Cinco años de experiencia sin experiencia previa," *Revolución y Cultura* 24 (August 1974): 12.

168. "Discurso pronunciado por el Compañero Sergio Corrieri . . . con motivo de la inauguración del Campamento 'La Macagua,'" December 30, 1972, in *Grupo Teatro Escambray*, 14; Rafael González and Rubén Medina, "Trabajo investigación-desarrollo Escambray, 1971–1972," *Universidad de La Habana* 198–199 (1973): 81–115.

169. "Al aire libre," 14, 17.

170. Laura Rodríguez Fuentes, "La dramaturgia abierta del GTE," *Vanguardia*, May 21, 2016, 6.

171. "Al aire libre," 20.

172. "Fragmentos de las palabras de la compañera Gilda Hernández . . . en una actividad política efectuada en La Macagua," April 12, 1974, in *Grupo Teatro Escambray*, 24.

173. Translation in appendix A of Villegas, "Origin, Development and Processes of Teatro Escambray in Cuba," 258.

174. *Y si fuera así*, in Leal, *Teatro Escambray*, 66.

175. "Entrevistas celebradas con posterioridad a la obra, con campesinos de El Abra, El Jíbaro, La Jutía y Los Cedros," in Leal, *Teatro Escambray*, 68.

176. Nicolás Chao, quoted in Séjourné, *Teatro Escambray,* 125.

177. González and Medina, "Trabajo investigación-desarrollo Escambray," 106, 93.

178. Séjourné, *Teatro Escambray,* 126.

179. Graziela Pogolotti, prologue to Leal, *Teatro Escambray,* 14–15.

180. "Al aire libre," 22

181. Pogolotti, prologue, 8.

182. Pogolotti, prologue, 15; Séjourné, *Teatro Escambray,* 272–80.

183. Séjourné, *Teatro Escambray,* 284.

184. Leal, *La dramaturgia del Escambray,* 22, 46; Albio Paz, cited in Séjourné, *Teatro Escambray,* 268.

185. Rodríguez Fuentes, "La dramaturgia abierta del GTE," 6.

186. Boudet, *Teatro nuevo,* 53.

187. Both cited in Séjourné, *Teatro Escambray,* 311, 313.

188. Villegas, "Origin, Development and Processes of Teatro Escambray in Cuba," 147–48.

189. See, for example, Garzón Céspedes, *Un Teatro de sus protagonistas*; Lauten, *Teatro La Yaya*; Herrero and Galich, *Teatro de relaciones*; Sánchez, *De pie!*; Sánchez, *Teatro de fuerza y candor.*

190. Frederik, *Trumpets in the Mountains,* 65.

191. Boudet, *Cuba,* 168.

192. Boudet, email message to author, December 13, 2021.

Chapter 7

1. Memorandum, Lisandro Otero to Manuel Stolik, July 1, 1967, Correspondencia, Vice-Presidencia, CNC.

2. The classic account is Adorno and Horkheimer, *Dialectic of Enlightenment* (1947); see also Pierre Bourdieu, *Distinction: A Social Critique of the Judgment of Taste* (1979). For critical perspectives, see Hall, "Notes on Deconstructing the Popular"; J. Franco, "What's in a Name?"

3. Martínez Furé, *Diálogos imaginarios,* 268.

4. See Hagedorn, *Divine Utterances*; Ayorinde, *Afro-Cuban Religiosity, Revolution, and National Identity*; Bustamante, "Cultural Politics and Political Cultures of the Cuban Revolution"; Schwall, *Dancing with the Revolution.*

5. See Schwall, "Between *Espíritu* and *Conciencia.*"

6. See, respectively, Tsipursky, *Socialist Fun*; Richthofen, *Bringing Culture to the Masses.*

7. See Vélez, *Drumming for the Gods,* 72; Díaz Ayala, *Música cubana,* 299–315; R. D. Moore, *Music and Revolution.* In 2021, the ICRT became the Institute of Information and Social Communication.

8. See Robbins, "Making Popular Music in Cuba," 48–156.

9. As of 1974, it became the Department of Revolutionary Orientation (DOR).

10. R. D. Moore, *Nationalizing Blackness,* 114–65. See also Acosta, *Otra vision de la música popular cubana,* 141–42; Pérez, *On Becoming Cuban*; Lane, *Blackface Cuba, 1840–1895.*

11. See Helg, "Race and Black Mobilization in Colonial and Early Independent Cuba"; de la Fuente, "Myths of Racial Democracy."

12. Juan René Betancourt, *El negro: Ciudadano del futuro* (Havana, 1959), 74, cited in Ayorinde, *Afro-Cuban Religiosity, Revolution, and National Identity*, 63. See also C. Moore, *Castro, the Blacks, and Africa*, 15–28; Benson, *Antiracism in Cuba*, 72–121.

13. Fidel Castro (speech, Plaza de la Revolución, March 22, 1959), www.cuba.cu /gobierno/discursos/1959/esp/f220359e.html.

14. Benson, *Antiracism in Cuba*, 54.

15. De la Fuente, *Nation for All*, 271.

16. "'Esta revolución no se hizo para conservar privilegios ni para acobardarse ante nadie en particular, ni para venderse a nadie en particular,' dijo Fidel Castro en la TV," *NH*, March 26, 1959, 3. Also discussed in Benson, *Antiracism in Cuba*, 54.

17. See, for example, de la Fuente, *A Nation for All*; Ayorinde, *Afro-Cuban Religiosity, Revolution, and National Identity*; Spence Benson, *Antiracism in Cuba*; Guerra, "Poder Negro in Revolutionary Cuba."

18. Gabriel Molina Franchossi, "Violencia integracionista," *Combate*, April 2, 1959, last page; "¿Barbas negras y barbas blancas?" *Combate*, April 15, 1959, 1; "A Guanajay no ha llegado la política justa de la integración nacional," *NH*, May 10, 1959, 1.

19. De la Fuente, *Nation for All*, 269. See also Benson, *Antiracism in Cuba*, 92–93.

20. "A este pueblo nuestro, de Maceo y de Marti, no lo volverán a oprimir," *NH*, March 24, 1959, 6; de la Fuente, *Nation for All*, 269.

21. Rafael Hernández Schumann, "Resuelto un angustioso problema: Ya el pueblo tiene sus playas," *Combate*, August 13, 1959, 2.

22. W. E. B. Du Bois, "The Color Problem of Summer," *Crisis*, July 1929, cited in Kahrl, *Land Was Ours*, 13.

23. José Vilasuso, "Playas para el pueblo," *Combate*, March 24, 1959, 2.

24. *Playas del pueblo* (dir. Juan José Grado, 1960). I am grateful to Luciano Castillo for locating a copy of this film. See also Kahrl, *Land Was Ours*.

25. R. Schwartz, *Pleasure Island*; Gustavsen, "Tension under the Sun"; Lane, "Smoking Habaneras"; Skwiot, *Purposes of Paradise*.

26. Rafael Sanchez Lalebret, "El Plan de Turismo Obrero Campesino: Encantadoras vacaciones garantiza el INIT a más de un millón de trabajadores," *Bohemia*, April 20, 1962, 21.

27. On efforts to cultivate African Americans as tourists, see Benson, *Antiracism in Cuba*, 153–97.

28. "Atraerá visitantes el INIT para el próximo 26 de julio," *La Calle*, June 3, 1960, 3; "Ya el turismo no es un lujo," *Trabajo* 2, no. 3 (1961): 45.

29. "El INIT," *Trabajo* 2, no. 19 (1961): 142; Vicente Cubillas, "El plan de vacaciones a obreros más barato del mundo," *Bohemia*, June 15, 1962, 70–71. On the environmental implications, see Herrera, "Protección de la naturaleza y turismo en la Revolución Cubana de 1959."

30. "INIT-CTC-R. Vacaciones . . . ¡de verdad!" *Trabajo* 3, no. 11 (July 1962): 12; Lalebret, "El Plan de Turismo Obrero Campesino," 22.

31. Leopoldo Paz, "En Varadero: Vacaciones obreras," *Cuba* 1, no. 5 (September 1962): 79, 82.

32. Toro, *La alta burguesía cubana*, 108–24.

33. Fariñas Borrego, *Sociabilidad y cultura del ocio*, 93.

34. Deschamps, "Sociedades"; Montejo Arrechea, *Sociedades negras en Cuba*; Barcia, *Capas populares y modernidad en Cuba*, 116–61; Pappademos, *Black Political Activism and the Cuban Republic*.

35. Pignot, "El asociacionismo negro en Cuba"; Guridy, "War on the Negro"; Benson, *Antiracism in Cuba*, 81; Fariñas Borrego, "El asociacionismo náutico en La Habana."

36. Pedro Luis Padrón, "Centros educativos y de recreación," *Revolución*, November 11, 1960, 10; "Un círculo social en cada pueblo," *Trabajo*, no. 7 (November 1960): 91–93; "300 Círculos Sociales Obreros e Infantiles," *Revolución*, December 17, 1960, 12.

37. "Los Círculos Sociales Obreros: Un privilegio de los humildes," *Trabajo* 2, no. 2 (1961): 84–87; Marta Rojas, "Los hijos del pueblo veranean en los Círculos Sociales Obreros," *Trabajo* 2, no. 6 (1961): 39.

38. Jaime Sarusky, "El alegre asalto a las bastillas de La Habana, *Revolución*, May 22, 1961, 8.

39. "Clubes aristocráticos se convierten en círculos obreros," *Revolución*, May 16, 1961, 12; Raúl Boschmonar, "Del 'Club Nautico de Marianao' al Circulo Social Obrero 'Felix Elmusa,'" July 2006.

40. Cited in Benson, *Antiracism in Cuba*, 99.

41. De la Fuente, *Nation for All*, 271–85; Benson, *Antiracism in Cuba*, 97–101.

42. Marquetti Torres, *Desmemoriados*, 285–88. See also Mayra Martínez, "Un baile sin igual. Entrevista con Enrique Jorrín," *Revolución y Cultura*, no. 129 (March 1983): 16–20; Díaz Ayala, *Música cubana*, 246–47.

43. C. Franqui, "Duelo en el pueblo, murió Beny Moré," *Revolución*, February 20, 1963, cited in Orejuela Martínez, *El son no se fue de Cuba*, 37.

44. R. D. Moore, *Music and Revolution*, 52.

45. Moore, 37–51, 52.

46. Fariñas Borrego, *Sociabilidad y cultura del ocio*, 92–93. Even so, the Casino Deportivo was unique in admitting Jewish members. Interview with members of the Círculo Social Obrero Otto Parellada (formerly Cubaleco) by author, January 2019.

47. Balbuena Gutiérrez, *El casino y la salsa en Cuba*, 39. On casino's varied influences, see Borges and Sardiñas, *Historia del baile y la rueda de casino-salsa*, 20–108.

48. Cited in Balbuena Gutiérrez, *El casino y la salsa en Cuba*, 43–44.

49. Juan "Juanito" Gómez, interview by author, January 2019.

50. L. Agüero, "Audiovideo," *Revolución*, October 12, 1960, 14, cited in Orejuela Martínez, *El son no se fue de Cuba*, 158.

51. Orejuela Martínez, *El son no se fue de Cuba*, 173.

52. For a close reading of this performance, see Vazquez, *Listening in Detail*, 186–90.

53. Tsipursky, *Socialist Fun*, 2.

54. Schwall, "Between *Espíritu* and *Conciencia*," 148–55.

55. Pedraza Ginori, "Salón Mambí," *Cuba* 5, no. 48 (April 1966): 30; Leonardo Acosta, "Eterna juventud de nuestra música popular," *Revolución y Cultura*, no. 66 (February 1988): 57.

56. A. Castillo, "Ritmo Oriental: Tambores en La Habana," *Bohemia*, March 2, 1962, 62–63; R. D. Moore, *Music and Revolution*, 178.

57. Rodríguez, "Apuntes sobre la creación musical actual en Cuba," 292; Díaz Ayala, *Música cubana*, 324.

58. R. D. Moore, *Music and Revolution*, 181, 181–85.

59. Moore, 184. As head of the CTC in the early 1960s, Lázaro Peña, among the few high-ranking Afro-Cuban officials and a known *santero*, was an enthusiastic promoter of both secular and religious Afro-Cuban culture. See Vélez, *Drumming for the Gods*, 87–88.

60. R. D. Moore, *Music and Revolution*, 185. See the banned short *Los del baile* (dir. Nicolás Guillén Landrián, 1966), which features one such performance.

61. INIT, "Programación de espectáculos presentados en el Cabaret 'La Trocha' de Santiago de Cuba durante los días del 14 al 17 de julio de 1967," 16/1, CNC; Enrique Valdés, "Pello: El twist cede el paso al mozambique en Europa," *Granma*, December 17, 1965, 10.

62. Jane, "Ensayo con Pello," *Mella*, July 23, 1965, 6.

63. R. D. Moore, *Music and Revolution*, 176. See also Orejuela Martínez, *El son no se fue de Cuba*, 200–258.

64. Rafael Sánchez Lalabret, "Festival de Música Popular Cubana," *Bohemia*, August 24, 1962, 29.

65. León, *Música folklórica cubana*, 13.

66. Schwall, *Dancing with the Revolution*, 38–52; Martínez Furé, *Diálogos imaginarios*, 193.

67. R. D. Moore, *Music and Revolution*, 200.

68. Vélez, *Drumming for the Gods*, 77–78.

69. See Barnet, *La fuente viva*; Martínez Furé, *Diálogos imaginarios*, 266–85; de la Fuente, *Nation for All*, 285–90; Ayorinde, *Afro-Cuban Religiosity, Revolution, and National Identity*, 105–11; R. D. Moore, *Music and Revolution*, 175–76, 204–7; Orejuela Martínez, *El son no se fue de Cuba*, 82, 179–240.

70. R. D. Moore, *Music and Revolution*, 185.

71. Martínez Furé, *Diálogos imaginarios*, 250.

72. R. D. Moore, *Music and Revolution*, 185–86; Ayorinde, *Afro-Cuban Religiosity, Revolution, and National Identity*, 113. See also Vélez, *Drumming for the Gods*, 75–87; Hagedorn, *Divine Utterances*; Schwall, *Dancing with the Revolution*, 77–94.

73. Schwall, *Dancing with the Revolution*, 77, 85, 94.

74. Blas Arrechea, "El factor racial y la nacionalidad," *Combate*, April 7, 1959, 2.

75. Catty Ruiz, Consejo Seccional de Cultura ORI (A. Apolo), to Carlos del Toro, Director de Consejos Seccionales, March 12, 1962, Biblioteca Nacional, Fondo del Ministerio de Cultura, bookcase 47, shelf 48, file 7, Carnaval 1962, transcription by

Lillian Guerra, https://dloc.com/AA00019994/00001/pdf. Also discussed in Guerra, *Visions of Power in Cuba*, 157.

76. See de la Fuente, *Nation for All*, 285–86; Guerra, *Visions of Power in Cuba*, 150–57; Benson, *Antiracism in Cuba*, 122–52.

77. On relevant Latin American parallels, see Zolov, *Refried Elvis*; Langland, *Speaking of Flowers*; Manzano, *Age of Youth in Argentina*; Cowan, *Securing Sex*; Dunn, *Contracultura*; Barr-Melej, *Psychedelic Chile*.

78. See Hall and Jefferson, *Resistance through Rituals*; Hebdige, *Subculture*; Frith, *Sound Effects*; Sanneh, *Major Labels*.

79. Orejuela Martínez, *El son no se fue de Cuba*, 261. See also Sierra Madero, *Del otro lado del espejo*, 81–137.

80. Waldo Fernández, "Los pepillos y los guapos." *Érase una vez un cubano* (blog), December 18, 2008, http://eraseunavezuncubano.blogspot.com/2008/12/los -pepillos-y-los-guapos.html; Orejuela Martínez, *El son no se fue de Cuba*, 261–62; Armando López, "Canciones viejas para el hombre nuevo," February 24, 2006, www .cubaencuentro.com/cultura/articulos/canciones-viejas-para-el-hombre-nuevo -12781. Robbins documented these divisions, virtually unaltered, in 1980s Santiago. See Robbins, "Making Popular Music in Cuba," 480–95.

81. See Casal, *El caso Padilla*; Dopico Black, "Limits of Expression"; Benítez Rojo, "Comments on Georgina Dopico Black's 'The Limits of Expression'"; Fornet, *El 71*; D. Díaz, *Palabras del trasfondo*; Grenier, *Culture and the Cuban State*, 61–104.

82. Guerra, "Gender Policing, Homosexuality and the New Patriarchy of the Cuban Revolution"; Cabrera Arús and Suquet, "La moda en la literatura cubana."

83. "Ocupa Gobernación el guión de un film por atentar contra Cuba," *Combate*, April 15, 1959, 1.

84. See film reviews in *Mella*, no. 179 (July 1960): 49.

85. "300 Círculos Sociales Obreros e Infantiles," 13.

86. "Americans Hang On in Cuba" [Reuters], *Christian Science Monitor*, July 31, 1962, 6; Juan de Onís, "In Castro's Cuba, What's at the Movies?" *NYT*, March 8, 1964, X9.

87. "Americans Hang On in Cuba," 6; "Cubans Prefer Old Yank Films to Red Ones," *Boston Globe*, September 3, 1962, 20. On related battles, see Pogolotti, *Polémicas culturales de los 60*, 145–61; Guanche, *El continente de lo posible*, 45–60.

88. See Jiménez-Leal and Zayas, *El caso "PM."*

89. Sierra Madero and García Buchaca, "'No se sabía dónde estaba la verdad y dónde estaba la mentira,'" 361–62.

90. See Guerra, *Visions of Power in Cuba*, 162–64, 342–43.

91. Marquetti Torres, *Desmemoriados*, 212–17.

92. "La música popular cubana" (n.d.), 17/1, CNC.

93. See Bertrand, *Race, Rock, and Elvis*; Altschuler, *All Shook Up*.

94. Cited in Manduley López, *Hierba mala*, 21–22.

95. Manduley López, 22. See also Castellanos, *John Lennon en La Habana*, 106–7.

96. Y. Rivero, *Broadcasting Modernity*, 93.

97. See Pacini Hernandez and Garofalo, "Between Rock and a Hard Place," 43–44.

98. Ryback, *Rock around the Bloc*; Ramet, *Rocking the State*; Cushman, *Notes from Underground*; Zolov, *Refried Elvis*; Poiger, *Jazz, Rock, and Rebels*; Pacini Hernandez, Fernández L'Hoeste, and Zolov, *Rockin' Las Américas*; Fenemore, *Sex, Thugs and Rock 'n' Roll*; Tsipursky, *Socialist Fun*.

99. Vilar, "De los Beatles a los Panchos," 115.

100. Castellanos, "La censura de Los Beatles," 143.

101. Castellanos, *John Lennon en La Habana*, 133.

102. Miami Radio Monitoring Service, Radio Rebelde transmission, April 12, 1963, CHC.

103. Manduley López, *Hierba mala*, 45. See also Guerra, "Gender Policing, Homosexuality and the New Patriarchy of the Cuban Revolution"; Cabrera Arús, "Thinking Politics and Fashion in 1960s Cuba."

104. ICR, "Informe sobre la política del ICR en torno a la música," November 1966, pp. 6–7, folder: CNC-Música-ICR 1966, 1968, 17/1, CNC.

105. ICR, "Informe sobre la política del ICR en torno a la música," 1.

106. A. López, "Canciones viejas para el hombre nuevo"; Pogolotti, *Polémicas culturales de los 60*, xvi–xvii; Orejuela Martínez, *El son no se fue de Cuba*, 231–32.

107. See *Los Zafiros: Music from the Edge of Time* (dir. Lorenzo DeStefano, 2007).

108. ICR, "Informe sobre la política del ICR en torno a la música," 3–6, 18–19.

109. ICR, 15.

110. Orejuela Martínez, *El son no se fue de Cuba*, 259.

111. Jane, "Ensayo con Pello," 7.

112. ICR, "Informe sobre la política del ICR en torno a la música," 7, 8.

113. *Maricón* is an epithet used across Latin America to refer to homosexual men. Castellanos, *John Lennon en La Habana*, 114.

114. ICR, "Informe sobre la política del ICR en torno a la música," 17.

115. ICR, 12.

116. Manduley López, *Hierba mala*, 178.

117. ICR, "Informe sobre la política del ICR en torno a la música," 19–20.

118. ICR, 17.

119. Michael Arkus, "Rock and Roll Rhythms Win Acceptance in Cuba," *Washington Post*, September 17, 1967, A23.

120. "¿Qué hay de nuevo?" *Juventud Rebelde*, September 21, 1967, 4, cited in Díaz Pérez, *Sobre la guitarra, la voz*, 102.

121. Acosta, "Eterna juventud de nuestra música popular," 56.

122. Veltfort, *Goodbye, My Havana*, 156.

123. "En paz descansen cabarets, cabaretuchos y similares," *Alma Mater*, March 1968, Ofensiva-suplemento especial), 4, in Veltfort, *Goodbye, My Havana*, 150.

124. Acosta, *Descarga número dos*, 139.

125. "Designan director del ICR al Comandante Jorge Serguera," *Granma*, May 26, 1967, 1; Pedraza Ginori, *Memorias Cubanas*, 2:17.

126. "La causa 108," *Cuba* (April 1966): 3–11; Castellanos, *John Lennon en La Habana*, 210–12.

127. Castellanos, *John Lennon en La Habana*, 210–12.

128. Pedraza Ginori, *Memorias Cubanas*, 2:17.

129. Jorge Serguera, interview by Ernesto Juan Castellanos, in Castellanos, *John Lennon en La Habana*, 212.

130. Silvio Rodríguez, interview by Ernesto Juan Castellanos, in Castellanos, 213, 238–41. See also R. D. Moore, *Music and Revolution*, 135–70.

131. Jorge Serguera, interview by Ernesto Juan Castellanos, in Castellanos, *John Lennon en La Habana*, 213, 218–19, 238–39.

132. Castro, "El diversionismo ideológico," 9. See also Guerra, "Gender Policing, Homosexuality and the New Patriarchy of the Cuban Revolution"; Baldacci, "Consumer Culture and Everyday Life in Revolutionary Cuba," 251–87.

133. Claude Regin, "Cuba Bans US Pop Music," *Jerusalem Post*, April 30, 1973, 9; "Quilapayún: Un arma contra la penetración cultural," *El Caimán Barbudo*, no. 46 (May 1971): 16–21.

134. Olavo Alén, "Música para colonizar," *El Caimán Barbudo*, no. 82 (September 1974): 14. See also Leonardo Acosta, "El colonialismo cultural en la música," *Revolución y Cultura*, February–March 1975, 60–66; Acosta, *Música y descolonización*.

135. A. López, "Canciones viejas para el hombre nuevo."

136. Eduardo López Morales [Director General de Literatura y Publicaciones] to Luis Pavón Tamayo [President, CNC], Asunto: Disposiciones del ICR, DGLP 52/73 [Limitado], April 25, 1973, folder ICR 73–74, 17/1, CNC (my italics).

137. Castellanos, *John Lennon en La Habana*, 216, 218–19.

138. Cited in Castellanos, 151.

139. ICR, "Informe sobre la política del ICR en torno a la música," 6.

140. Castellanos, *John Lennon en La Habana*, 216; Pedraza Ginori, *Memorias Cubanas*, 1:10.

141. Carmelo Mesa-Lago, quoted in Manuel, "Marxism, Nationalism and Popular Music in Revolutionary Cuba," 164.

142. Pedraza Ginori, *Memorias Cubanas*, 2:225, 235.

143. Curiously, his music was also deployed as torture against Pinochet's political prisoners. See Pedraza Ginori, *Memorias Cubanas*, 2:236; Chornik, "When Julio Iglesias Played Pinochet's Prison"; Chornik, "Memories of Music in Political Detention in Chile under Pinochet," 163; Julio Martínez Molina, "La viña de la ira," *Granma*, March 1, 2020, www.granma.cu/cultura/2020-03-01/la-vina-de-la-ira-01-03-2020-17-03-24.

144. Yoss, "Exorcizando fantasmas que vienen de Liverpool," in Castellanos, *Los Beatles en Cuba*, 133; Yoani Sánchez, "Julio and Enrique Iglesias, Two Moments in the Life of Cuba," *Generation Y* (blog), January 12, 2017, https://generacionyen.wordpress.com/2017/01/11/julio-and-enrique-iglesias-two-moments-in-the-life-of-cuba.

145. Río, "Hace cincuenta años (en 1972), *La vida sigue igual* apasionaba a los cubanos."

146. Ofelia, interview by Eileen Artigas, October 2017; Luisito, interview by Eileen Artigas, January 2018; Sara, interview by Laura Muñoz, November 2017; Manuel, interview by Jennifer Lambe, February 2022.

147. Río, "Hace cincuenta años (en 1972), *La vida sigue igual* apasionaba a los cubanos."

148. Pedraza Ginori, *Memorias Cubanas*, 1:220.

149. "Puntillazos," *Mella*, no. 177 (June 1960): 52.

150. Leonardo Acosta, "Musica de consumo," *Revolución y Cultura*, no. 32 (April 1975): 59.

151. A. López, "Canciones viejas para el hombre nuevo."

152. Juana, interview by Laura Muñoz, November 2017.

153. "Informe del Director General del ICR al Consejo de Dirección sobre el trabajo realizado en 1974 y los lineamientos principales para 1975," folder ICR 1975/76, 17/1, CNC.

154. Document, p. 4. The document is missing a title page and was found in incomplete form in a folder with other ICR materials from 1975 in 17/1, CNC.

155. See C. Moore, *Castro, the Blacks, and Africa*, 259–60. See also Vélez, *Drumming for the Gods*, 87–92; de la Fuente, *Nation for All*, 290–94; Ayorinde, *Afro-Cuban Religiosity, Revolution, and National Identity*; R. D. Moore, *Music and Revolution*, 213, 209–14; Guerra, *Visions of Power in Cuba*, 265–77; Guerra, "*Poder Negro* in Revolutionary Cuba"; Seidman, "Angela Davis in Cuba as Symbol and Subject."

156. Fernández Robaina, *Hablen paleros y santeros*, 46, 113.

157. R. D. Moore, *Music and Revolution*, 213.

158. See Komaromi, *Soviet Samizdat*.

159. Gabriel, "¿Qué hay de nuevo . . . ?" *Juventud Rebelde*, May 10, 1968, MM.

160. María del Carmen Mestas, "Formell: Del son al Changui-shake," *Romances*, May 1969, 98, MM.

161. Marlene Estrellas, "Juan Formell y Los Van Van: Otra juventud para el son," *Mujeres*, February 1971, 54, MM.

162. José Rivers García, "Escuchen nuestros discos y saquen conclusiones," *El caimán barbudo* no. 117 (September 1977): 2, 31, MM.

163. Acosta, "Eterna juventud de nuestra música popular," 57.

164. According to interviews in *Chucho Valdés and Irakere: Latin Jazz Founders* (dir. Ilena Rodríguez, 2005); R. D. Moore, *Music and Revolution*, 91.

165. *Chucho Valdés and Irakere: Latin Jazz Founders*. See also Igorra and Mosquera, *Perfiles culturales: Cuba, 1978*, 31; Acosta, *Del tambor al sintetizador*, 182.

166. Acosta, *Otra vision de la música popular cubana*, 108. See also interview by Zoila Gómez in Mayra Martínez, "Música popular: Sigue la encuesta," *Revolución y cultura*, no. 88 (December 1979): 65.

167. Díaz Pérez, *Sobre la guitarra, la voz*, 217–94; R. D. Moore, *Music and Revolution*, 135–69.

168. Guerra, *Patriots and Traitors in Revolutionary Cuba*, 298, 292–302.

169. Leonardo Acosta, "La nueva trova: ¿Un movimiento masivo?," and Alberto Faya, "Nueva trova y la cultura de la rebeldía," in Giró, *Panorama de la música popular cubana*, 342, 352, 358.

170. See interview by Helio Orovio in Mayra Martínez, "Música popular: Sigue la encuesta," *Revolución y Cultura*, no. 91 (March 1980): 75.

171. Acosta, "La nueva trova," 348–49.

172. See Baldacci, "Consumer Culture and Everyday Life in Revolutionary Cuba"; Cabrera Arús, "Material Promise of Socialist Modernity."

173. See Weiss, "Emergence of Popular Culture," 120–25.

174. See Domínguez, *Cuba: Order and Revolution*, 284–98; Ritter, "Los Organos del Poder Popular and Participatory Democracy in Cuba"; W. Kelly, "Promise of Home."

175. Kahl, *A Cuban Diary*, 57.

176. M.P.B., "Anibal Rodriguez responde a cuestionario," *Vida Universitaria*, December 1966, 35–36.

177. Renata Adler, "Cuba's Revolution of the Arts," *Chicago Tribune*, February 21, 1969, B13; Rolando Pérez Betancourt and Roberto Alvarez Quiñonez, eds., "Los espectadores hablan de 'El padrino,'" *Granma*, April 5, 1974, 4; Ted Morgan, "Cuba," *NYT*, December 1, 1974, 299; Linda Winer, "Castro's New Cuba Taps Its Cultural Roots," *Chicago Tribune*, December 15, 1974, E1.

178. Roberto Roque and Pablo Ramos, *Los jóvenes y el entretenimiento* (Havana: Sección de Investigaciones Centro de Información Cinematográfica, Ministerio de Cultura, 1980), BNJM.

179. Eugenio R. Balari, "Cinco años de trabajo del Instituto Cubano de Investigaciones y Orientaciones de la Demanda Interna," in ICIODI, *Investigaciones científicas de la demanda en Cuba*, 8–10.

180. See Richthofen, *Bringing Culture to the Masses*; Tsipursky, *Socialist Fun*, 78–102.

181. See Baldacci, "Consumer Culture and Everyday Life in Revolutionary Cuba," 209–19.

182. See Roque and Ramos, *Los jóvenes y el entretenimiento*; Comité Estatal de Estadísticas, Instituto de Investigaciones Estadísticas, *Encuesta nacional presupuesto de tiempo: Análisis comparativo de los resultados de 1985 y 1988* (Havana: Editorial Estadística, 1990), 33.

183. Equipo de Estudios de Opinión del Pueblo, Departamento de Orientación Revolucionaria del C.C., PCC, "Encuesta de Radio y Televisión" (1975), pp. 6, 26, folder ICR 1975/76, 17/1, CNC; "San Nicolás del Peladero: Pinelli nos cuenta la historia," *El Show de Carlucho*, www.univistatv.com/san-nicolas-del-peladero-pinelli-nos-cuenta-la-historia.

184. Departamento de Orientación Revolucionaria del Comité Central del Partido Comunista de Cuba, *Sobre los medios de difusión masiva: Tesis y resolución* (Havana, 1976), 13–23, folder INDER 1966/1975, 16/1, CNC.

185. "Informe del Director General del ICR al Consejo de Dirección sobre el trabajo realizado en el 1974 y los lineamientos principales para 1975," 9–13.

186. Bustamante, *Cuban Memory Wars*, 175; Guerra, *Patriots and Traitors in Revolutionary Cuba*, 289.

187. Bustamante, *Cuban Memory Wars*, 175.

188. Enrique del Risco, "El misterio de *Para bailar*," *Enrisco* (blog), October 6, 2019, http://enrisco.blogspot.com/2019/10/el-misterio-de-para-bailar.html; Igorra and Mosquera, *Perfiles culturales: Cuba, 1978*, 172.

189. Maria Elena Figueras, "Bailar . . . ¿es un problema?" *Opina*, no. 11 (May 1980): 38.

190. Leonardo Acosta, "¿Por qué *Para bailar*?" *Revolución y Cultura*, no. 85 (September 1979): 12–18.

191. Ivette Leyva Martinez, "*Para bailar* con Salvador," August 5, 2005, http://arch1.cubaencuentro.com/entrevistas/20050807/e3790f90775b06f63f1624c7d33fdc9f/printimg.html.

192. Mateo, interview by author, January 2017.

193. Armando López, "De Pumarejo a Castro," *Diario de Cuba*, October 24, 2010, https://diariodecuba.com/cultura/1287902622_2133.html.

194. Carlos Rafael Rodríguez to Eduardo Cáceres, December 18, 1978, in Enrique del Risco, "El misterio de *Para bailar*," 2019; Carlos Rafael Rodríguez, *Problemas del arte en la Revolución* (Havana, 1979), 71, cited in Guerra, "Gender Policing, Homosexuality and the New Patriarchy of the Cuban Revolution," 282.

195. Carlos Rafael Rodríguez to Eduardo Cáceres, December 18, 1978.

196. "Cachito Cáceres Manso: Talento y yunfa," *El blog de Pedraza Ginori*, August 15, 2015, http://elblogdepedrazaginori.blogspot.com/2015/08/cachito-caceres-manso-talento-y-yunfa.html.

197. The Centro de Investigación y Desarrollo de la Música Cubana (CIDMUC), established in 1978, conducted mostly unpublished surveys about musical taste. See Robbins, "Making Popular Music in Cuba," 185–92. On broader efforts in this vein, see Domínguez, *Cuba: Order and Revolution*, 303–4.

198. Armando López, interview by author, May 2022.

199. Gabriel Molina, "Gastronomía: Experiencias de un usuario," *Opina*, no. 1 (July 1979): 13–18.

200. López, interview by author.

201. "Critical Magazine a Sell-Out in Cuba," *Guardian*, January 2, 1980, 5.

202. See Leonardo Abarca, "American Gay of Life," *Opina*, no. 5 (November 1979): 8–9; "Gran oferta especial," *Opina*, no. 11 (May 1980).

203. In the words of *Opina*'s editor, cited in "Critical Magazine a Sell-Out in Cuba."

204. "Los lectores opinan sobre la televisión," *Opina*, no. 4 (October 1979): 2–5; "¿Qué hacer en vacaciones?" *Opina*, no. 5 (November 1979): 6–7.

205. Eugenio Pedraza Ginori, "La noche de los Girasoles de Opina," *El blog de Pedraza Ginori*, October 19, 2015, http://elblogdepedrazaginori.blogspot.com/2015/10/la-noche-de-los-girasoles-de-opina.html. On debates about polling methods and resulting modifications, see "El Girasol, ¿correcto?" *El Caimán Barbudo*, April 1984, 4; Omar Vázquez, "Entregan el lunes los Girasoles de Opina 1985," *Granma*, March 14, 1986, 4.

206. Pedraza Ginori, "La noche de los Girasoles de Opina"; Neysa Ramón, "Bienvenido un premio que decide un pueblo," *Juventud Rebelde*, February 13, 1983, in Pedraza Ginori, "La noche de los Girasoles de Opina."

207. "El Girasol, ¿correcto?," 4.

208. On differences between the singers' fan bases and musical styles, see Robbins, "Making Popular Music in Cuba," 439–45.

209. López, interview by author; Pedraza Ginori, "La noche de los Girasoles de Opina"; Omar Vázquez, "El Girasol de Cristal de Opina será entregado a 15 personalidades del arte y la literatura cubana," *Granma*, September 26, 1984, 4.

210. Víctor Rodríguez Núñez, "Silvio Rodríguez: No hacen falta alas," *El Caimán Barbudo* 19, no. 214 (September 1985): 25.

211. López, "Juan Formell en defensa de la música popular," 2. On the institutional distinctions between MNT, which was grouped along with classical music in the "auto-financed" cultural industries, versus dance music, which was governed by budgeted *empresas*, see Robbins, "Making Popular Music in Cuba," 91–120.

212. Neysa Ramón, "Querido Pablo," *El Caimán Barbudo* 19, no. 217 (December 1985): 10–11.

213. López, "Juan Formell en defensa de la música popular," 3.

214. Grupo de Programación para la TV y la Radio, S/F, 80.2.1, 1985, pp. 2, 4, 17/1, CNC.

215. Guillermo Cabrera, "Micarta," *Somos Jóvenes*, no. 35 (August 1982): 10.

216. Joseph B. Treaster, "Cuba Enlivens Radio as US Prepares a Challenge," *NYT*, August 5, 1984, 14.

217. López, interview by author; Pedraza Ginori, "¡Qué pista! ¡Qué revista! ¡Qué entrevista!" See also Hernández-Reguant, "Radio Taino and the Globalization of the Cuban Culture Industries."

218. See Perna, *Timba*; R. D. Moore, *Music and Revolution*; Baker, *Buena Vista in the Club*; Gámez Torres, "Hearing the Change"; U. Vaughan, *Rebel Dance, Renegade Stance*; Perry, *Negro Soy Yo*; T. L. Saunders, *Cuban Underground Hip Hop*; Zamora Montes, "Hip hop en Cuba"; Levine, "Sounding El Paquete."

Conclusion

1. Patrick Radden Keefe, *Wind of Change*, podcast audio, May–July 2020, https://crooked.com/podcast-series/wind-of-change/#all-episodes. The literature in this area is vast; for a representative survey, see Friedman, *Routledge History of Social Protest in Popular Music*; Kutschke and Norton, *Music and Protest in 1968*.

2. See, for example, "Diaz-Balart Submits Lyrics of Song 'Patria y Vida' to the *Congressional Record*," December 9, 2021, https://mariodiazbalart.house.gov/media-center/press-releases/diaz-balart-submits-lyrics-song-patria-y-vida-congressional-record. For a sample of island responses, see Teresa Melo, "¿Cuál patria y cuál vida?," *Granma*, February 18, 2021, www.granma.cu/cuba/2021-02-18/cual-patria-y-cual-vidacual-patria-y-cual-vida-18-02-2021-14-02-35; Pedro de la Hoz, "Cantar a la patria, no contra ella," *Granma*, February 18, 2021, www.granma.cu/cuba/2021-02-18/cantar-a-la-patria-no-contra-ella-18-02-2021-01-02-12; "Declaración de la UNEAC: Morir por la patria es vivir," *Cubadebate*, February 19, 2021, www.cubadebate.cu/noticias/2021/02/19/declaracion-de-la-uneac-morir-por-la-patria-es-vivir/?fbclid=IwAR1TqT3jhLxVWaBqQQ6RfP1qYI_giczOtZo6LLGiX2e1NqKueXxCavN12Fo; José Manzaneda, "Libertad de expresión en Miami? Con la pistola en la sien," *Cubadebate*, March 7, 2021, www.cubadebate.cu/opinion/2021/03/07/libertad-de-expresion-en-miami-con-la-pistola-en-la-sien-video.

3. Most notably, "Patria o muerte por la vida," featuring Raúl Torres, Annie Garcés, Dayana Divo, Karla Monier, and Yisi Calibre, www.ministeriodecultura.gob.cu /es/actualidad/noticias/en-estreno-la-cancion-patria-o-muerte-por-la-vida.

4. Miguel Díaz Canel (@DiazCanelB), Twitter post, March 11, 2021, 8:02 A.M. See also "Patria y vida de Fidel de los revolucionarios de Cuba," *Granma*, March 12, 2021, www.granma.cu/cuba/2021-03-12/patria-y-vida-de-fidel-y-de-los-revolucionarios -de-cuba-12-03-2021-02-03-45.

5. See Bustamante, "11J, 'Patria y Vida,' and the (Not So) New Cuban Culture Wars."

6. Decreto 349/2018, April 20, 2018, *Gaceta Oficial*, no. 35, Extraordinaria de 2018 (October 7, 2018), https://www.ministeriodecultura.gob.cu/images/jdownloads /pol%C3%ADticas_p%C3%BAblicas/marco_normativo/decreto349.pdf. See also Guerra, "Decree 349 and Today's History of Artistic Expression in the Cuban Revolution."

7. See Julyssa Lopez, "Cuba Isn't Banning Reggaeton, but a Law on Artistic Expression Is Still Worrying Activists," *Remezcla* (blog), March 1, 2019, https:// remezcla.com/music/cuba-decree-349-constitution/; Gámez Torres, "Hearing the Change."

8. Lillian Guerra, "The Return of Cuba's Security State," *NYT*, May 27, 2021, www.nytimes.com/2021/05/27/opinion/cuba-artist-luis-manuel-otero-alcantara .html.

9. See, for example, "Gente de Zona teme por sus familias en Cuba tras lanzar 'Patria y vida'" (EFE), www.14ymedio.com/cuba/Gente_de_Zona-Patria_y_vida_o _3043495633.html; Bustamante, "11J, 'Patria y Vida,' and the (Not So) New Cuban Culture Wars."

10. Coco Fusco, "Cuban Musicians and Artists Collaborate on Viral, Political Music Video," *Hyperallergic*, February 23, 2021, https://hyperallergic.com/624060 /patria-y-vida-music-video-cuban-artists/.

11. "Homofobia, difamaciones y mensajes de odio: Así responde el régimen a 'Patria y vida,'" *Diario de Cuba*, February 20, 2021, https://diariodecuba.com/cuba /1613780742_28969.html.

12. Pedro Jorge Velázquez, "Patria o muerte," *Granma*, February 17, 2021, www .granma.cu/cuba/2021-02-17/patria-o-muerte-17-02-2021-23-02-51.

13. See, for example, "Desinformaciones en el contexto de las protestas en Cuba," *El Toque*, July 15, 2021, https://eltoque.com/desinformaciones-sobre-las-protestas; Sarah March, "Fake News Muddies Online Waters during Cuba Protests," Reuters, July 16, 2021, www.reuters.com/world/americas/fake-news-muddies-online-waters -during-cuba-protests-2021-07-16/#:~:text=HAVANA%2C%20July%2016%20 (Reuters),Caracas%20was%20sending%20in%20troops.

14. "En vivo: Canciller cubano, Bruno Rodríguez, ofrece Conferencia de Prensa," *Radio Granma*, July 13, 2021, www.radiogranma.icrt.cu/en-vivo-canciller-cubano -bruno-rodriguez-ofrece-conferencia-de-prensa-video/; Oscar Figueredo Reinaldo and Abel Padrón Padilla, "Pueblo habanero toma La Piragua en defensa de la Revolución y el socialismo," *Cubadebate*, July 17, 2021, www.cubadebate.cu/noticias/2021 /07/17/pueblo-habanero-toma-la-piragua-en-defensa-de-la-revolucion/; Geisy Guia

Delis, "Desde Cuba, con VPN," *Periodismo de Barrio*, July 13, 2021, https://period ismodebarrio.org/2021/07/desde-cuba-con-vpn/.

15. Gustaf Kilander, "Miami Mayor Calls on Biden to Consider Airstrikes against Cuba," *Independent*, July 14, 2021, www.independent.co.uk/news/world/americas /us-politics/cuba-protests-airstrikes-miami-mayor-b1884238.html; Martin Koppel, Mary-Alice Waters, and Róger Calero, "Cuban Revolution: A Challenge to US Imperialism: Cuban Representative Speaks on US Economic War, Campaign of Lies against Socialist Revolution," *Militant*, October 25, 2021, https://themilitant.com /2021/10/16/cuban-revolution-a-challenge-to-us-imperialism/; José Manzaneda and Lázaro Oramas, "Cuba y el cerebro como territorio de conquista," December 13, 2022, www.cubadebate.cu/especiales/2022/12/13/cuba-y-el-cerebro-como-territorio -de-conquista-video/.

16. Black Lives Matters statement on Cuba, July 14, 2021, www.instagram.com /p/CRU5kYYp-UU/?img_index=2; Char Adams, "Black Lives Matter Faces Backlash for Statement on Cuba Protest," *NBC News*, July 16, 2021, www.nbcnews.com/news /nbcblk/black-lives-matter-faces-backlash-statement-cuba-protest-rcna1438; Jorge Felipe-Gonzalez, "Black Lives Matter Misses the Point about Cuba," *Atlantic*, July 17, 2021, www.theatlantic.com/ideas/archive/2021/07/black-lives-matter-misses-point -about-cuba/619471/.

17. For example, Guerra, *Visions of Power in Cuba*; Casavantes Bradford, *Revolution Is for the Children*; Benson, *Antiracism in Cuba*; Rojas, *Fighting over Fidel*; Lambe and Bustamante, "Cuba's Revolution from Within"; Bustamante, *Cuban Memory Wars*.

18. See, for example, Joseph and Nugent, *Everyday Forms of State Formation*; Halfin and Hellbeck, "Rethinking the Stalinist Subject"; Kotkin, *Magnetic Mountain*; Kharkhordin, *Collective and the Individual in Russia*; Volkov, "Concept of Kul'turnost'"; Brandenberger, *National Bolshevism*; Fitzpatrick, *Tear Off the Masks!*; Donahoe and Habeck, *Reconstructing the House of Culture*; Murat, *Man Who Thought He Was Napoleon*; Tsipursky, *Socialist Fun*; Sewell, *Capitalism and the Emergence of Civic Equality in Eighteenth-Century France*. For other relevant citations, see chapter 6 in this book.

19. Per introduction to Fitzpatrick, *Tear Off the Masks!*

20. See, for example, Fagen, *Transformation of Political Culture in Cuba*; E. S. Martínez, *Youngest Revolution*; Bunck, *Fidel Castro and the Quest for a Revolutionary Culture in Cuba*; Serra, *"New Man" in Cuba*; Blum, *Cuban Youth and Revolutionary Values*; Guerra, *Visions of Power in Cuba*; Hynson, *Laboring for the State*.

21. See also Díaz Castañón, *Ideología y Revolución*, 13–94.

22. See, for example, Grenier et al., "'¿Cuándo terminó la Revolución cubana? Una discusión'"; Grenier, "Cuban Studies and the Siren Song of La Revolución."

23. Decreto-Ley 35/2021: De las Telecomunicaciones, las Tecnologías de la Información y la Comunicación y el uso del Espectro Radioeléctrico (GOC-2021-759-O92), and Resolución 105/2021: Reglamento sobre el Modelo de Actuación Nacional para la Respuesta a Incidentes de Ciberseguridad (GOC-2021-762-O92), in *Gaceta Oficial*, no. 92 (August 2021): 2581, www.gacetaoficial.gob.cu/sites/default/files/goc-2021 -092.pdf.

24. See "#Falso: Desinformaciones en el contexto de las protestas en Cuba I," *El Toque,* July 15, 2021, https://eltoque.com/desinformaciones-sobre-las-protestas ?fbclid=IwAR2vKTkn7Jt6A7u31_f8m7NFQF2N0FZ4TZ52cgxgj4kYac9O4byyWmkI 5dSY; Ailynn Torres Santana, "J-11 in Cuba," *NACLA*, July 22, 2021, https://nacla.org /news/cuba-july-11-protests; Valerie Wirtschafter, "What Role Did the Internet Play in Fomenting Cuban Protests?," Brookings Institution, July 23, 2021, www.brookings .edu/techstream/what-role-did-the-internet-play-in-fomenting-cuban-protests/; Bastian, "From Facebook to the Streets."

Bibliography

Libraries and Archival Collections

Canada

Library and Archives Canada, Ottawa, Canada
   Department of External Affairs
   Frank and Libbie Park Fonds

Cuba

Archivo General del Ministerio de Cultura, Biblioteca Juan Marinello, Havana
Biblioteca Nacional José Martí, Havana
Centro de Documentación, Instituto Cubano de Radio y Televisión, Havana
Museo de la Música, Havana
   Álbum Los Van Van, 944-V

United States

Brown University, Providence, RI
   John Hay Library
      Hall-Hoag Collection
      Karen Brodkin Papers
Columbia University Libraries, New York
   Rare Book & Manuscript Library
      Herbert Lionel Matthews Papers
Duke University, Durham, NC
   David M. Rubenstein Rare Book and Manuscript Library
      Victoria Ortiz Papers
Hoover Institution Library & Archives, Stanford University
   Carlos Todd Newspaper Articles
   Cuban Freedom Committee Records
      Free Cuba Radio
   Richard Fagen Papers
   Theodore Draper Papers
John F. Kennedy Assassination Archives and Research Center
         (accessed at Mary Ferrell Foundation)
John F. Kennedy Presidential Library, Boston, MA
   Archival Collections
      Papers of John F. Kennedy
Lyndon B. Johnson Library, Austin, TX
   National Security Files

Rockefeller Archive Center, Sleepy Hollow, NY
   Ford Foundation Records
      Developing Countries Program, Latin America and the Caribbean,
         Office Files of Joan R. Dassin (FA660), Cuba, Series IV
University of Kansas, Lawrence
   Spencer Library
      Helen Simon Travis Papers
University of Miami, Coral Gables, FL
   Cuban Heritage Collection
      Antonio Maceo and Mackle Papers
      Bernardo Benes Papers
      Herminio Portell Vilá Papers
      Jay Mallin Papers
      Truth about Cuba Committee, Inc. Records
   Special Collections
      Pan American World Airways Collection
University of Michigan, Ann Arbor
   Bentley Historical Library
      Robert F. Williams Papers
University of the Pacific, Stockton, CA
   Holt-Atherton Special Collections and Archives
      Daniel James Papers
Wisconsin Historical Society, Madison
   Division of Library, Archives, and Museum Collections
      Dickey Chapelle Papers

Periodicals

Bohemia	*INRA/Cuba*
El Caimán Barbudo	*Juventud Rebelde*
La Calle	*Mella*
Chicago Daily Tribune	*El Mundo*
Combate	*New York Times*
El Crisol	*Opina*
Cuba Socialista	*Prensa Libre*
Diario de la Marina	*Pueblo y Cultura*
Gaceta Oficial	*Revolución*
Granma	*Revolución y Cultura*
Havana Times	*Somos Jóvenes*
Hoy	*Trabajo*

Published Sources

Acosta, Leonardo. *Del tambor al sintetizador.* Havana: Editorial Letras Cubanas,
   1989.

———. *Descarga número dos: El jazz en Cuba 1950–2000*. Havana: Ediciones Unión, 2002.

———. *Música y descolonización*. Havana: Editorial Arte y Literatura, 1982.

———. *Otra visión de la música popular cubana*. Havana: Ediciones Museo de la Música, 2014.

Agee, Joel. *In the House of My Fear*. Washington, D.C.: Shoemaker & Hoard, 2006.

Ahmed, Sara. *Complaint!* Durham, N.C.: Duke University Press, 2021.

Aldrich, Richard J. "American Journalism and the Landscape of Secrecy: Tad Szulc, the CIA and Cuba." *History* 100, no. 340 (2015): 189–209. https://doi.org/10.1111/1468-229X.12101.

Almeida, Thamyris. "Soul of a Modern Nation: Television in Cold War Brazil." Unpublished manuscript.

Alonso Tejada, Aurelio. "Marxismo y espacio de debate en la revolución cubana." In *El laberinto tras la caída del muro*, 216–37. Buenos Aires: Ruth Casa Editorial/CLACSO, 2009.

Altschuler, Glenn C. *All Shook Up: How Rock 'n' Roll Changed America*. Oxford: Oxford University Press, 2003.

Alvarez, José. "The Dying Dialogue between U.S. and Cuban Scholars." *Cuban Studies* 14, no. 2 (Summer 1984): 65–68.

American University, Foreign Areas Studies Division, and Armed Services Technical Information Agency (U.S.). *Special Warfare Area Handbook for Cuba*. Arlington, Va.: Armed Services Technical Information Agency, 1967.

Anderson, Benedict. *Imagined Communities: Reflections on the Origin and Spread of Nationalism*. London: Verso, 2016.

Ángeles Periu, María de los. "Experiencias de la educación obrera y campesina en Cuba." *Cuba Socialista* 5, no. 42 (February 1965): 18–38.

Arguelles, Lourdes. "Cuban Miami: The Roots, Development, and Everyday Life of an Emigré Enclave in the U.S. National Security State." *Contemporary Marxism*, no. 5 (1982): 27–43.

Aronson, James. *The Press and the Cold War*. 2nd ed. New York: Monthly Review Press, 1991.

Artaraz, Kepa. "Constructing Identities in a Contested Setting: Cuba's Intellectual Elite During and After the Revolution." *Oral History* 45, no. 2 (2017): 50–59.

———. *Cuba and Western Intellectuals since 1959*. London: Palgrave Macmillan, 2009.

Ayorinde, Christine Renata. *Afro-Cuban Religiosity, Revolution, and National Identity*. Gainesville: University Press of Florida, 2004.

Baiburin, A. K. *The Soviet Passport: The History, Nature, and Uses of the Internal Passport in the USSR*. Translated by Stephen Dalziel. Cambridge: Polity Press, 2021.

Baker, Geoffrey. *Buena Vista in the Club: Rap, Reggaetón, and Revolution in Havana*. Refiguring American Music. Durham, N.C.: Duke University Press, 2011.

Baker, Keith Michael. *Inventing the French Revolution: Essays on French Political Culture in the Eighteenth Century*. Cambridge: Cambridge University Press, 1990.

Balbuena Gutiérrez, Bárbara. *El casino y la salsa en Cuba*. Havana: Editorial Letras Cubanas, 2005.

Baldacci, Alexis. "Consumer Culture and Everyday Life in Revolutionary Cuba, 1971–1986." PhD diss., University of Florida, 2018.

Baran, Paul A. "Reflections on the Cuban Revolution." Pts. 1 and 2. *Monthly Review* 12, no. 9 (January 1961): 459–70; no. 10 (February 1961): 518–29.

Barcia, María del Carmen. *Capas populares y modernidad en Cuba, 1878–1930*. Havana: Fundación Fernando Ortiz, 2005.

Barnet, Miguel. *La fuente viva*. Havana: Editorial Letras Cubanas, 1983.

Barr-Melej, Patrick. *Psychedelic Chile: Youth, Counterculture, and Politics on the Road to Socialism and Dictatorship*. Chapel Hill: University of North Carolina Press, 2017.

Bassols Batalla, Angel. "Al morir Juan F. Noyola Vázquez." *Investigación económica* 23, no. 90 (1963): 469–72.

Bastian, Hope. "From Facebook to the Streets: Digital Infrastructures and Citizen Activism in Connected Cuba." American University. Accessed December 21, 2022. www.american.edu/centers/latin-american-latino-studies/cuba-after -the-july-11-protests-bastian.cfm.

Bazdresch, Carlos. "El pensamiento de Juan F. Noyola." *El trimestre económico* 50, no. 198(2) (1983): 567–93.

Beagarie, Max. "Who Went and How Did We Get There." In *New Cuba*, edited by Pieter Romayn Clark, 45–46. Chicago: Chicagoans for Freedom of Travel to Cuba, 1964.

Bengelsdorf, Carollee. *The Problem of Democracy in Cuba: Between Vision and Reality*. New York: Oxford University Press, 1994.

Benítez Rojo, Antonio. "Comments on Georgina Dopico Black's 'The Limits of Expression: Intellectual Freedom in Postrevolutionary Cuba.'" *Cuban Studies* 20 (1990): 171–74.

Benson, Devyn Spence. *Antiracism in Cuba: The Unfinished Revolution*. Chapel Hill: University of North Carolina Press, 2016.

———. "Redefining Mestizaje: How Trans-Caribbean Exchanges Solidified Black Consciousness in Cuba." *Small Axe: A Caribbean Journal of Criticism* 25, no. 2 (65) (July 1, 2021): 91–108. https://doi.org/10.1215/07990537-9384286.

Berg, Mette Louise. "'La Lenin Is My Passport': Schooling, Mobility and Belonging in Socialist Cuba and Its Diaspora." *Identities* 22, no. 3 (May 2015): 303–17. https://doi.org/10.1080/1070289X.2014.939189.

Bergmeier, H. J. P., and Rainer E. Lotz. *Hitler's Airwaves: The Inside Story of Nazi Radio Broadcasting and Propaganda Swing*. New Haven, Conn.: Yale University Press, 1997.

Bernardo, Roberto M. *The Theory of Moral Incentives in Cuba*. Tuscaloosa: University of Alabama Press, 1971.

Bernhard, Guillermo, and Alberto Etcheparo. *Reportaje a Cuba*. Montevideo: Ediciones América Nueva, 1961.

Bernhard, Nancy E. *U.S. Television News and Cold War Propaganda, 1947–1960*. New York: Cambridge University Press, 1999.

Bertrand, Michael T. *Race, Rock, and Elvis*. Urbana: University of Illinois Press, 2000.

Besset, Jean-Paul. *René Dumont: Une vie saisie par l'écologie.* Paris: Les Petits matins, 2013.

Bettelheim, Charles. "CUBA 1961: Artículo de Perspectiva, revista económica." In *Charles Bettelheim en la Revolución Cubana,* edited by Selma Díaz and Juan Valdés Paz. RUTH, 2016.

———. "Memorándum sobre la planificación económica en Cuba: Año 1960." In *Charles Bettelheim en la Revolución Cubana,* edited by Selma Díaz and Juan Valdés Paz. RUTH, 2016.

Blum, Denise F. *Cuban Youth and Revolutionary Values: Educating the New Socialist Citizen.* Austin: University of Texas Press, 2011.

Bon Tempo, Carl J. *Americans at the Gate: The United States and Refugees during the Cold War.* Princeton, N.J.: Princeton University Press, 2008.

Bonachea, Rolando E., and Nelson P. Valdés, eds. *Cuba in Revolution.* Garden City, N.Y.: Anchor Books, 1972.

Boorstein, Edward. *The Economic Transformation of Cuba: A First-Hand Account.* New York: Monthly Review Press, 1968.

———. "Socialism and Development in Cuba." Review of *Cuba, Socialisme et Développement* by René Dumont. *Monthly Review* 16, no. 10 (February 1965): 616–23. https://doi.org/10.14452/MR-016-10-1965-02_6.

Boorstin, Daniel. *The Image: A Guide to Pseudo-Events in America.* New York: Vintage, 1962.

———. "Television." *Life,* September 10, 1971.

Borges, Alan, and Alicia Sardiñas. *Historia del baile y la rueda de casino-salsa.* Havana: Artex, 2012.

Boudet, Rosa Ileana. *Alánimo, Alánimo.* Havana: Arte y Literatura, 1977.

———. *Cuba: Viaje al teatro en la revolución (1960–1989).* Santa Monica, Calif.: Ediciones de la Flecha, 2012.

———. *Teatro nuevo: Una respuesta.* Havana: Editorial Letras Cubanas, 1983.

Boudin, Leonard. "The Constitutional Right to Travel." *Columbia Law Review* 56 (January 1956): 47–75.

Brandenberger, David. *National Bolshevism: Stalinist Mass Culture and the Formation of Modern Russian National Identity, 1931–1956.* Cambridge, Mass.: Harvard University Press, 2002.

Brill, Deidre. "La Escuela Cubana: Dance Education and Performance in Revolutionary Cuba." PhD diss., University of Pennsylvania, 2007.

Bronfman, Alejandra. "'Batista Is Dead': Media, Violence and Politics in 1950s Cuba." *Caribbean Studies* 40, no. 1 (2012): 37–58.

———. "*El naciente público oyente*: Toward a Genealogy of the Audience in Early Republican Cuba." In *State of Ambiguity: Civic Life and Culture in Cuba's First Republic,* edited by Steven Palmer, José Antonio Piqueras, and Amparo Sánchez Sánchez Cobos , 251–68. Durham, N.C.: Duke University Press, 2014.

———. *Isles of Noise: Sonic Media in the Caribbean.* Chapel Hill: University of North Carolina Press, 2016.

Brown, Jonathan C. *Cuba's Revolutionary World.* Cambridge, Mass.: Harvard University Press, 2017.

Bunck, Julie Marie. *Fidel Castro and the Quest for a Revolutionary Culture in Cuba.* University Park: Pennsylvania State University Press, 1994.

Bustamante, Michael J. *Cuban Memory Wars: Retrospective Politics in Revolution and Exile.* Chapel Hill: University of North Carolina Press, 2021.

——. "Cultural Politics and Political Cultures of the Cuban Revolution: New Directions in Scholarship." *Cuban Studies* 47, no. 1 (2019): 3–18. https://doi.org /10.1353/cub.2019.0001.

——. "11J, 'Patria y Vida,' and the (Not So) New Cuban Culture Wars." American University. Accessed December 15, 2022. www.american.edu/centers/latin -american-latino-studies/cuba-after-the-july-11-protests-bustamante.cfm.

Cabrera Arús, María A. "The Material Promise of Socialist Modernity: Fashion and Domestic Space in the 1970s." In *The Revolution from Within: Cuba, 1959–1980*, edited by Michael J. Bustamante and Jennifer L. Lambe, 189–217. Durham, N.C.: Duke University Press, 2019.

——. "Thinking Politics and Fashion in 1960s Cuba: How Not to Judge a Book by Its Cover." *Theory and Society* 46, no. 5 (November 2017): 411–28. https://doi .org/10.1007/s11186-017-9299-x.

Cabrera Arús, María A., and Mirta Suquet. "La moda en la literatura cubana, 1960–1979: Tejiendo y destejiendo al hombre nuevo." *Cuban Studies*, no. 47 (2019): 195–221.

Cane, James. *The Fourth Enemy: Journalism and Power in the Making of Peronist Argentina, 1930–1955.* University Park: Pennsylvania State University Press, 2012.

Canfux, Jaime, and John A. Mateja. "A Brief Description of the 'Battle for the Sixth Grade.'" *Journal of Reading* 25, no. 3 (1981): 226–33.

Carmona, Fernando. "Homenaje a Juan F. Noyola Vázquez." *Problemas del desarrollo* 10, no. 39 (1979): 130–39.

——. "Juan F. Noyola Vázquez, hijo fiel de la Escuela Nacional de Economía." *Investigación económica* 23, no. 90 (1963): 451–67.

Casal, Lourdes. *El caso Padilla: Literatura y revolución en Cuba.* Miami: Nueva Atlantida, 1971.

Casavantes Bradford, Anita. *The Revolution Is for the Children: The Politics of Childhood in Havana and Miami, 1959–1962.* Chapel Hill: University of North Carolina Press, 2014.

Castellanos, Dimas, and Ted A. Henken. "Migration and Diaspora." In *Cuba*, edited by Ted A. Henken, Miriam Celaya, and Dimas Castellanos. Latin America in Focus, 242–60. Santa Barbara, CA: ABC-Clio/Greenwood, 2013.

Castellanos, Ernesto Juan. *John Lennon en La Habana: With a Little Help from My Friends.* Havana: Ediciones Unión, 2005.

——. "La censura de Los Beatles: ¿Mito o realidad?" In *Los Beatles en Cuba*, edited by Ernesto Juan Castellanos, 143–49. Havana: Ediciones Unión, 1997.

——, ed. *Los Beatles en Cuba.* Havana: Ediciones Unión, 1997.

Castillo, Luciano, ed. *Conquistando la utopía: El ICAIC y la revolución 50 años después.* Havana: Ediciones Instituto Cubano del Arte e Industria Cinematográfica (ICAIC), 2010.

Castro, Raúl. "El diversionismo ideológico: Arma sútil que esgrimen los enemigos contra la Revolución." *Verde Olivo*, June 6, 1972, 4–15.

Casuso, Teresa. *Cuba and Castro*. New York: Random House, 1961.

Cearns, Jennifer. "The 'Mula Ring': Material Networks of Circulation through the Cuban World." *Journal of Latin American and Caribbean Anthropology* 24, no. 4 (2019): 864–90. https://doi.org/10.1111/jlca.12439.

Chanan, Michael. *Cuban Cinema*. Minneapolis: University of Minnesota Press, 2003.

Chapelle, Dickey. *What's a Woman Doing Here? A Reporter's Report on Herself.* New York: William Morrow, 1962.

Chase, Michelle. *Revolution within the Revolution: Women and Gender Politics in Cuba, 1952–1962*. Chapel Hill: University of North Carolina Press, 2015.

———. "The Trials: Violence and Justice in the Aftermath of the Cuban Revolution." In *A Century of Revolution: Insurgent and Counterinsurgent Violence during Latin America's Cold War*, edited by Greg Grandin and Gilbert M. Joseph, 163–98. Durham, N.C.: Duke University Press, 2010.

Chastain, Andra B., and Timothy W. Lorek. Introduction to *Itineraries of Expertise: Science, Technology, and the Environment in Latin America's Long Cold War*, edited by Andra B. Chastain and Timothy W. Lorek, 3–29. Pittsburgh: University of Pittsburgh Press, 2020.

Chilcote, Ronald H. "The Cold War and the Transformation of Latin American Studies in the United States." In *Latin American Studies and the Cold War*, edited by Ronald H. Chilcote. Lanham, Md.: Rowman & Littlefield, 2022.

Chonchol, Jacques. "Análisis crítico de la reforma agraria cubana." *El trimestre económico* 30, no. 117(1) (1963): 69–143.

Chornik, Katia. "Memories of Music in Political Detention in Chile under Pinochet." *Journal of Latin American Cultural Studies* 27, no. 2 (April 2018): 157–73. https://doi.org/10.1080/13569325.2018.1450742.

———. "When Julio Iglesias Played Pinochet's Prison." *Guardian*, May 15, 2014. www.theguardian.com/music/2014/may/15/julio-iglesias-valparaiso-pinochet-chile.

Clark, Pieter Romayn. "I Saw Cuba—My Impressions." In *New Cuba*, edited by Pieter Romayn Clark, 7–24. Chicago: Chicagoans for Freedom of Travel to Cuba, 1964.

———, ed. *New Cuba*. Chicago: Chicagoans for Freedom of Travel to Cuba, 1964.

Cohen, Stephen F. *Rethinking the Soviet Experience: Politics and History since 1917*. Galaxy Books. New York: Oxford University Press, 1986.

Conte Agüero, Luis. *Héroes y mártires*. Havana: Editorial Cuba, 1959.

Cordero, Rodrigo, ed. *La sociedad de la opinión: Reflexiones sobre encuestas y cambio político en democracia*. Santiago: Ediciones Universidad Diego Portales, 2009.

Córdova, Efrén. *El trabajador cubano en el estado de obreros y campesinos*. Miami: Ediciones Universal, 1990.

Corner, John. "Performing the Real: Documentary Diversions." In *Reality TV: Remaking Television Culture*, edited by Susan Murray and Laurie Ouellette, 44–64. New York: New York University Press, 2009.

Cowan, Benjamin A. *Securing Sex: Morality and Repression in the Making of Cold War Brazil*. Chapel Hill: University of North Carolina Press, 2016.

Cozean, Jon D. *Cuban Guerrilla Training Centers and Radio Havana: A Selected Bibliography*. Washington, D.C.: American University, Center for Research in Social Systems, 1968.

"Cuba: Revolution and the Intellectual; The Strange Case of Heberto Padilla." *Index on Censorship* 1, no. 2 (June 1972): 65–88. https://doi.org/10.1080/03064227208532175.

Cuban Economic Research Project. *Cuba: Agriculture and Planning, 1964–1964*. Coral Gables: University of Miami Press, 1965.

———. *A Study in Cuba: The Colonial and Republican Periods, the Socialist Experiment, Economic Structure, Institutional Development, Socialism and Collectivization*. Coral Gables: University of Miami Press, 1965.

Cubillas, Vicente. "6 periodistas de países capitalistas visitan a Cuba. ¿Repetirán nuestra verdad?" *Bohemia* 54, no. 23 (June 1962).

Cullather, Nick. *Secret History: The CIA's Classified Account of Its Operations in Guatemala, 1952–1954*. Stanford, Calif: Stanford University Press, 1999.

Cummings, Richard H. *Cold War Radio: The Dangerous History of American Broadcasting in Europe, 1950–1989*. Jefferson, N.C.: McFarland, 2009.

Cushman, Thomas. *Notes from Underground: Rock Music Counterculture in Russia*. Albany: State University of New York Press, 1995.

Czaika, Mathias, Hein de Haas, and María Villares Varela. "The Global Evolution of Travel Visa Regimes." *Population and Development Review* 44, no. 3 (2018): 589–622.

Daston, Lorraine. "Objectivity and the Escape from Perspective." *Social Studies of Science* 22 (November 1992): 597–618.

David-Fox, Michael. *Revolution of the Mind: Higher Learning among the Bolsheviks, 1918–1929*. Ithaca, N.Y.: Cornell University Press, 2016.

Dayan, Daniel, and Elihu Katz. *Media Events: The Live Broadcasting of History*. Cambridge, Mass.: Harvard University Press, 1992.

De la Fuente, Alejandro. "Myths of Racial Democracy: Cuba, 1900–1912." *Latin American Research Review* 34, no. 3 (1999): 39–73.

———. *A Nation for All: Race, Inequality, and Politics in Twentieth-Century Cuba*. Chapel Hill: University of North Carolina Press, 2001.

DePalma, Anthony. *The Man Who Invented Fidel: Castro, Cuba and Herbert L. Matthews of the New York Times*. New York: Public Affairs, 2007.

Derby, Lauren. "In the Shadow of the State: The Politics of Denunciation and Panegyric during the Trujillo Regime in the Dominican Republic, 1940–1958." *Hispanic American Historical Review* 83, no. 2 (May 2003): 295–344.

Deschamps, Pedro. "Sociedades: La integración de pardos y morenos." *Cuba* 7, no. 71 (March 1968): 54–55.

Desnoes, Edmundo. "Los carteles de la Revolución Cubana." *Casa de las Américas* 51–52 (November 1968): 223–31.

Díaz, Duanel. "¿Gusanos?" *Cuba Encuentro*, March 2, 2006. www.cubaencuentro.com/opinion/articulos/gusanos-11649.

———. *Palabras del trasfondo: Intelectuales, literatura e ideología en la Revolución Cubana.* Madrid: Editorial Colibrí, 2009.

Díaz, Selma. "Cuba en Charles Bettelheim." In *Charles Bettelheim en la Revolución Cubana: Economía y socialismo,* edited by Selma Díaz and Juan Valdés Paz. RUTH, 2016.

Díaz, Selma, and Juan Valdés Paz, eds. *Charles Bettelheim en la Revolución Cubana: Economía y socialismo.* RUTH, 2016.

Díaz Ayala, Cristóbal. *Música cubana: Del areyto al rap cubano.* 4th. ed. San Juan, P.R.: Fundación Musicalia, 2003.

Díaz-Briquets, Sergio, and Lisandro Pérez. "Cuba: The Demography of Revolution." *Population Bulletin* 36 (April 1981): 1–41.

Díaz Castañón, María del Pilar. *Ideología y revolución: Cuba, 1959–1962.* Havana: Editorial de Ciencias Sociales, 2004.

———, ed. *Prensa y revolución: La magia del cambio.* Havana: Editorial de Ciencias Sociales, 2010.

———. "Revolución." In *Prensa y revolución: La magia del cambio,* edited by María del Pilar Díaz Castañón. Havana: Editorial de Ciencias Sociales, 2010.

———. "'We Demand, We Demand . . .': Cuba, 1959: The Paradoxes of Year 1." In *The Revolution from Within: Cuba, 1959–1980,* edited by Michael J. Bustamante and Jennifer L. Lambe, 95–116. Durham, N.C.: Duke University Press, 2019.

Díaz Pérez, Clara. *Sobre la guitarra, la voz.* Havana: Editorial Letras Cubanas, 1994.

"Diez años de revolución: El intelectual y la sociedad." *Casa de las Américas* 10, no. 56 (September–October 1969): 1–50.

Dimitrov, Martin K. "The Functions of Letters to the Editor in Reform-Era Cuba." *Latin American Research Review* 54, no. 1 (April 2019): 1–15. https://doi.org/10.25222/larr.232.

Dirección de Cultura Masiva, Ministerio de Cultura. "Antecedentes de la cultura popular masiva; Cuba: 1902–1978." In *La cultura en Cuba socialista,* 63–89. Havana: Editorial Letras Cubanas, 1982.

Dirección Nacional de los CDR. *Los CDR en granjas y zonas rurales.* Havana: Ediciones Con la Guardia en Alto, 1965.

Dixon, Heriberto. "The Cuban-American Counterpoint: Black Cubans in the United States." *Dialectical Anthropology* 13, no. 3 (1988): 227–39.

Doherty, Thomas. *Cold War, Cool Medium: Television, McCarthyism, and American Culture.* New York: Columbia University Press, 2003.

Domínguez, Jorge I. *Cuba: Order and Revolution.* Cambridge, Mass.: Belknap Press of Harvard University Press, 1978.

———. "Twenty-Five Years of Cuban Studies." *Cuban Studies* 25 (1995): 3–26.

Donahoe, Brian, and Joachim Otto Habeck. *Reconstructing the House of Culture: Community, Self, and the Makings of Culture in Russia and Beyond.* New York: Berghahn Books, 2011.

Dopico Black, Georgina. "The Limits of Expression: Intellectual Freedom in Post-revolutionary Cuba." *Cuban Studies* 19 (1989): 107–42.

Downton, James V. *Rebel Leadership: Commitment and Charisma in the Revolutionary Process.* New York: Free Press, 1973.

Draper, Theodore. "Castro's Cuba: A Revolution Betrayed?" *New Leader*, supplement, March 27, 1961, 1–27.

———. *Castro's Revolution: Myths and Realities*. New York: Frederick A. Praeger, 1962.

———. "Cuba and the Revolution of Our Time." *New Leader*, July 4–11, 1960, 3–4.

———. *The Roots of American Communism*. New York: Viking Press, 1957.

Duany, Jorge. "Cuban Migration: A Postrevolution Exodus Ebbs and Flows." *Migration Information Service*, July 6, 2017. www.migrationpolicy.org/article /cuban-migration-postrevolution-exodus-ebbs-and-flows#:~:text=In%20 1959%2C%20the%20Cuban%20Revolution,by%20Fidel%20Castro's%20 guerrilla%20fighters.

Dubois, Jules. *Fidel Castro: Rebel—Liberator or Dictator?* Indianapolis: Bobbs-Merrill, 1959.

———. *Freedom Is My Beat*. Indianapolis: Bobbs-Merrill, 1959.

Dumont, René. *Cuba: Socialism and Development*. New York: Grove Press, 1970.

———. *Is Cuba Socialist?* Translated by Stanley Hochman. London: Deutsch, 1974.

———. "Une réforme agraire 'accélérée.'" *Esprit*, April 1961, 585–600.

Dunn, Christopher. *Brutality Garden: Tropicália and the Emergence of a Brazilian Counterculture*. Chapel Hill: University of North Carolina Press, 2001.

———. *Contracultura: Alternative Arts and Social Transformation in Authoritarian Brazil*. Chapel Hill: University of North Carolina Press, 2016.

Eckstein, Susan Eva. *Cuban Privilege: The Making of Immigrant Inequality in America*. New York: Cambridge University Press, 2022.

Ehrlich, Ilan. *Eduardo Chibás: The Incorrigible Man of Cuban Politics*. London: Rowman & Littlefield, 2015.

Elliston, Jon. *Psywar on Cuba: The Declassified History of U.S. Anti-Castro Propaganda*. Melbourne: Ocean Press, 2005.

Engerman, David C. *Know Your Enemy: The Rise and Fall of America's Soviet Experts*. New York: Oxford University Press, 2012.

———. "Social Science in the Cold War." *Isis* 101, no. 2 (2010): 393–400. https://doi .org/10.1086/653106.

Ernest, Jeanne. "A Snapshot of the 'Radical Middle': On the Life and Labels of Extremist-Watcher Gordon D. Hall, 1946–1969." Undergraduate thesis, Department of History, Brown University, 2021.

Fagen, Richard R. "Calculation and Emotion in Foreign Policy: The Cuban Case." *Journal of Conflict Resolution* 6, no. 3 (1962): 214–21.

———. "Charismatic Authority and the Leadership of Fidel Castro." *Western Political Quarterly* 18, no. 2 (1965): 275–84.

———. *Cuba: The Political Content of Adult Education*. Hoover Institution Studies 4. Stanford, Calif.: Hoover Institution on War, Revolution, and Peace, Stanford University, 1964.

———. "Mass Mobilization in Cuba: The Symbolism of Struggle." *Journal of International Affairs* 20, no. 2 (1966): 254–71.

———. *The Transformation of Political Culture in Cuba*. Stanford, Calif.: Stanford University Press, 1969.

Fagen, Richard R., Richard A. Brody, and Thomas J. O'Leary. *Cubans in Exile: Disaffection and the Revolution*. Stanford, Calif.: Stanford University Press, 1968.

Farber, Daniel A. "National Security, the Right to Travel, and the Court." *Supreme Court Review* 1981 (1981): 263–90.

Farber, Samuel. "Cuba in 1968." *Jacobin Magazine*, April 29, 2018. https://jacobinmag.com/2018/04/cuba-1968-fidel-castro-revolution-repression.

———. *The Origins of the Cuban Revolution Reconsidered*. Chapel Hill: University of North Carolina Press, 2006.

Fariñas Borrego, Maikel. "El asociacionismo náutico en La Habana: Desde las élites hasta las capas populares (1886–1958)." *Catauro*, no. 19 (2009): 39–55.

———. *Sociabilidad y cultura del ocio: Las élites habaneras y sus clubes de recreo (1902–1930)*. Havana: Fundación Fernando Ortiz, 2009.

Feinberg, Melissa. *Curtain of Lies: The Battle over Truth in Stalinist Eastern Europe*. New York: Oxford University Press, 2017.

Fenemore, Mark. *Sex, Thugs and Rock 'n' Roll: Teenage Rebels in Cold-War East Germany*. New York: Berghahn Books, 2007.

Fernandes, Sujatha. *Cuba Represent! Cuban Arts, State Power, and the Making of New Revolutionary Cultures*. Durham, N.C.: Duke University Press, 2008.

Fernández, Waldo. *La imposición del silencio: Cómo se clausuró la libertad de prensa en Cuba, 1959–1960*. Madrid: Hypermedia Ediciones, 2016.

Fernández Retamar, Roberto. *Cuba defendida*. Havana: Editorial Letras Cubanas, 2004.

Fernandez Robaina, Tomas. *Hablen paleros y santeros*. Havana: Editorial de Ciencias Sociales, 2008.

Ferrer, Ada. *Insurgent Cuba: Race, Nation, and Revolution, 1868–1898*. Chapel Hill: University of North Carolina Press, 1999.

Feuer, Jane. "The Concept of Live Television: Ontology as Ideology." In *Regarding Television*, edited by E. Ann Kaplan. Los Angeles: University Publications of America, 1983.

Field, Thomas C., Stella Krepp, and Vanni Pettinà, eds. *Latin America and the Global Cold War*. Chapel Hill: University of North Carolina Press, 2020.

Fitzpatrick, Sheila. *Tear Off the Masks! Identity and Imposture in Twentieth-Century Russia*. Princeton, N.J.: Princeton University Press, 2005.

FORDC (Frente Obrero Revolucionario Democrático Cubano). *El trabajo en Cuba socialista*. Ediciones FORDC, no. 5. Miami, 1965.

Fornet, Jorge. *El 71: Anatomía de una crisis*. Havana: Letras Cubanas, 2013.

Foucault, Michel. *Discipline and Punish: The Birth of the Prison*. New York: Vintage Books, 1995.

Francis, Michael J. "The U.S. Press and Castro: A Study in Declining Relations." *Journalism Quarterly* 44, no. 2 (Summer 1967): 257–66.

Franco, Jean. *The Decline and Fall of the Lettered City: Latin America in the Cold War*. Cambridge, Mass.: Harvard University Press, 2002.

———. "What's in a Name? Popular Culture Theories and Their Limitations." In *Critical Passions: Selected Essays*, 169–81. Durham, N.C.: Duke University Press, 1999.

Franco, Victor. *The Morning After: A French Journalist's Impressions of Cuba under Castro*. New York: Praeger, 1963.

Franqui, Carlos. *Family Portrait with Fidel: A Memoir*. Translated by Alfred MacAdam. Random House: New York, 1984.

Frederick, Howard H. *Cuban-American Radio Wars: Ideology in International Telecommunications*. Norwood, N.J.: Ablex, 1986.

Frederik, Laurie Aleen. *Trumpets in the Mountains: Theater and the Politics of National Culture in Cuba*. Durham, N.C.: Duke University Press, 2012.

Free, Lloyd A. *Attitudes of the Cuban People toward the Castro Regime in the Late Spring of 1960*. Princeton, N.J.: Institute for International Social Research, 1960.

Freije, Vanessa. *Citizens of Scandal: Journalism, Secrecy, and the Politics of Reckoning in Mexico*. Durham, N.C.: Duke University Press, 2020.

Fried, Amy. *Pathways to Polling: Crisis, Cooperation and the Making of Public Opinion Professions*. New York: Routledge, 2012.

Friedman, Jonathan C., ed. *The Routledge History of Social Protest in Popular Music*. Routledge Histories. New York: Routledge, 2013.

Friedrich, Carl J. "Political Leadership and the Problem of the Charismatic Power." *Journal of Politics* 23, no. 1 (1961): 3–24.

Frith, Simon. *Sound Effects: Youth, Leisure, and the Politics of Rock 'n' Roll*. New York: Pantheon Books, 1981.

Fruchter, Norman, and Stuart Hall. "Notes on the Cuban Dilemma." *New Left Review of Books* 1, no. 9 (May–June 1961): 2–12.

Fuller, Linda. "Fieldwork in Forbidden Terrain: The U.S. State and the Case of Cuba." *American Sociologist* 19, no. 2 (1988): 99–120.

Funes Monzote, Reinaldo. "*Geotransformación*: Geography and Revolution in Cuba from the 1950s to the 1960s." In *The Revolution from Within: Cuba, 1959–1980*, edited by Michael J. Bustamante and Jennifer L. Lambe, 117–45. Durham, N.C.: Duke University Press, 2019.

Funes Monzote, Reinaldo, and Steven Palmer. "Challenging Climate and Geopolitics: Cuba, Canada, and Intensive Livestock Exchange in a Cold War Context, from the 1960s to the 1980s." In *Itineraries of Expertise: Science, Technology, and the Environment in Latin America's Long Cold War*, edited by Andra B. Chastain and Timothy W. Lorek, 137–59. Pittsburgh: University of Pittsburgh Press, 2020.

Gallardo, Emilio J. *El martillo y el espejo: Directrices de la política cultural cubana (1959–1976)*. Madrid: Consejo Superior de Investigaciones Científicas (España), 2009.

Gámez Torres, Nora. "Hearing the Change: Reggaetón and Emergent Values in Contemporary Cuba." *Latin American Music Review* 33, no. 2 (2012): 227–60. https://doi.org/10.7560/LAMR33203.

García, Francisco, and Juan F. Noyola. "Principales objetivos de Nuestro Plan Económico hasta 1965." *Cuba Socialista* 2, no. 13 (September 1962): 1–16.

García, María Cristina. *Havana USA: Cuban Exiles and Cuban Americans in South Florida, 1959–1994*. Berkeley: University of California Press, 1996.

García Yero, Cary Aileen. "The State within the Arts: A Study of Cuba's Cultural Policy, 1940–1958." *Cuban Studies* 47 (2019): 83–110. https://doi.org/doi:10.1353/cub.2019.0006.

Garth, Hanna. "Things Became Scarce: Food Availability and Accessibility in Santiago De Cuba Then and Now." *NAPA Bulletin* 32, no. 1 (2009): 178–92. https://doi.org/10.1111/j.1556-4797.2009.01034.x.

Garzón Céspedes, Francisco. *Un teatro de sus protagonistas: El teatro de participación popular y el teatro de la comunidad.* Havana: Unión de Escritores y Artistas de Cuba, 1977.

Gates, Robert M. "CIA and the University." Speech presented at the Association of Former Intelligence Officers National Convention, Tysons Corner, Va., October 10, 1987. Declassified January 31, 2014, and available online, www.cia.gov/readingroom/docs/CIA-RDP89G00720R000500070019-9.pdf.

GCIE (Grupo Cubano de Investigaciones Económicas). *Labor Conditions in Communist Cuba.* Coral Gables: Cuban Economic Research Project, University of Miami, 1963.

Giró, Radamés, ed. *Panorama de la música popular cubana.* Havana: Editorial Letras Cubanas, 1998.

Gleijeses, Piero. *Shattered Hope: The Guatemalan Revolution and the United States, 1944–1954.* Princeton, N.J.: Princeton University Press, 1991.

Golden, Daniel. *Spy Schools: How the CIA, FBI, and Foreign Intelligence Secretly Exploit America's Universities.* New York: Picador, 2018.

González, Patricia Calvo. "Enrique Meneses, un periodista español en Sierra Maestra." *Semata: Ciencias sociais e humanidades,* no. 24 (2012): 471–87.

———. "Percepciones de la Sierra Maestra. La visión de la insurrección cubana (1957–1958) a través de los periodistas latinoamericanos." *Revista internacional de Historia de la Comunicación,* no. 7 (2016): 92–115.

González de Bustamante, Celeste. *"Muy buenas noches": Mexico, Television, and the Cold War.* Lincoln: University of Nebraska Press, 2012.

Gordon-Nesbitt, Rebecca. *To Defend the Revolution Is to Defend Culture: The Cultural Policy of the Cuban Revolution.* Oakland, Calif.: PM Press, 2015.

Gorsuch, Anne E., and Diane P. Koenker, eds. *The Socialist Sixties: Crossing Borders in the Second World.* Bloomington: Indiana University Press, 2013.

———, eds. *Turizm: The Russian and East European Tourist under Capitalism and Socialism.* Ithaca, N.Y.: Cornell University Press, 2006.

Gosse, Van. *Where the Boys Are: Cuba, Cold War America and the Making of a New Left.* London: Verso, 1993.

Green, James N. "'Who Is the Macho Who Wants to Kill Me?' Male Homosexuality, Revolutionary Masculinity, and the Brazilian Armed Struggle of the 1960s and 1970s." *Hispanic American Historical Review* 92, no. 3 (2012): 437–69.

Green, Melanie C., Timothy C. Brock, and Geoff F. Kaufman. "Understanding Media Enjoyment: The Role of Transportation into Narrative Worlds." *Communication Theory* 14, no. 4 (November 2004): 311–27.

Grenier, Yvon. "Cuban Studies and the Siren Song of La Revolución." *Cuban Studies*, no. 49 (2020): 310–30.

———. *Culture and the Cuban State: Participation, Recognition, and Dissonance under Communism*. Lanham, Md.: Lexington Books, 2017.

Grenier, Yvon, Jorge I. Domínguez, Julio César Guanche, Jennifer Lambe, Carmelo Mesa-Lago, Silvia Pedraza, and Rafael Rojas. "'¿Cuándo terminó la Revolución cubana? Una discusión.'" *Cuban Studies* 46 (January 2018): 143–65.

Gronbeck-Tedesco, John A. *Cuba, the United States, and Cultures of the Transnational Left, 1930–1975*. New York: Cambridge University Press, 2015.

Grupo Teatro Escambray. Villa Clara: Editoria Política. http://ctda.library.miami .edu/publications/1396/.

Guanche, Julio César. *El continente de lo posible: Un examen sobre la condición revolucionaria*. Havana: Instituto Cubano de Investigación Cultural Juan Marinello, 2008.

Guede, Emilio. *Cuba: La revolución que no fue*. Eriginal Books, 2013.

Guerra, Lillian. "Decree 349 and Today's History of Artistic Expression in the Cuban Revolution: A Review Article." *Cuban Studies* 50, no. 1 (2021): 333–45. https://doi.org/10.1353/cub.2021.0029.

———. "Former Slum Dwellers, the Communist Youth, and the Lewis Project in Cuba, 1969–1971." *Cuban Studies* 43, no. 1 (August 2015): 67–89.

———. "Gender Policing, Homosexuality and the New Patriarchy of the Cuban Revolution, 1965–70." *Social History* 35, no. 3 (August 2010): 268–89.

———. *Heroes, Martyrs, and Political Messiahs in Revolutionary Cuba, 1946–1958*. New Haven, Conn.: Yale University Press, 2018.

———. *Patriots and Traitors in Revolutionary Cuba, 1961–1981*. Pittsburgh: University of Pittsburgh Press, 2023.

———. "*Poder Negro* in Revolutionary Cuba: Black Consciousness, Communism, and the Challenge of Solidarity." *Hispanic American Historical Review* 99, no. 4 (November 2019): 681–718. https://doi.org/10.1215/00182168-7787175.

———. "Searching for the Messiah: Staging Revolution in the Sierra Maestra, 1956–1959." In *The Revolution from Within: Cuba, 1959–1980*, edited by Michael J. Bustamante and Jennifer L. Lambe, 67–94. Durham, N.C.: Duke University Press, 2019.

———. *Visions of Power in Cuba: Revolution, Redemption, and Resistance, 1959–1971*. Chapel Hill: University of North Carolina Press, 2014.

Guillermoprieto, Alma. *Dancing with Cuba: A Memoir of the Revolution*. New York: Pantheon Books, 2004.

Gumbert, Heather L. *Envisioning Socialism: Television and the Cold War in the German Democratic Republic*. Ann Arbor: University of Michigan Press, 2014.

Guridy, Frank Andre. *Forging Diaspora: Afro-Cubans and African Americans in a World of Empire and Jim Crow*. Chapel Hill: University of North Carolina Press, 2010.

———. "'War on the Negro': Race and the Revolution of 1933." *Cuban Studies*, no. 40 (2010): 49–73.

Gustavsen, John Andrew. "Tension under the Sun: Tourism and Identity in Cuba, 1945–2007." PhD diss., University of Miami, 2009.

Guzmán, Jorgelina. "Actores gubernamentales de la política cultural cubana entre 1949 y 1961." *Revista Latinoamericana de Ciencias Sociales, Niñez y Juventud* 10, no. 1 (2012): 257–70.

Habermas, Jürgen. *The Structural Transformation of the Public Sphere: An Inquiry into a Category of Bourgeois Society.* Translated by Thomas Burger and Frederick Lawrence. Cambridge, Mass.: Harvard University Press, 1989.

Hadley, David P. *The Rising Clamor: The American Press, the Central Intelligence Agency, and the Cold War.* Lexington: University Press of Kentucky, 2020.

Hagedorn, Katherine J. *Divine Utterances: The Performance of Afro-Cuban Santería.* Washington, D.C.: Smithsonian Institution Press, 2001.

Halfin, Igal, and Jochen Hellbeck. "Rethinking the Stalinist Subject: Stephen Kotkin's 'Magnetic Mountain' and the State of Soviet Historical Studies." *Jahrbücher Für Geschichte Osteuropas* 44, no. 3 (1996): 456–63.

Hall, Stuart. "Encoding/Decoding." In *Culture, Media, Language,* edited by Stuart Hall, Dorothy Hobson, Andrew Love, and Paul Willis, 128–38. London: Hutchinson, 1980.

———. "Notes on Deconstructing the Popular." In *People's History and Socialist Theory,* edited by R. Samuel, 227–40. London: Routledge & Kegan Paul, 1981.

Hall, Stuart, and Tony Jefferson. *Resistance through Rituals: Youth Subcultures in Post-War Britain.* London: Harper Collins Academic, 1976.

Halperin, Ernst. "The State of Latin American Studies." *Washington Quarterly* 1, no. 2 (April 1978): 99–111. https://doi.org/10.1080/01636607809450228.

Hamilton, Carrie. *Sexual Revolutions in Cuba: Passion, Politics, and Memory.* Chapel Hill: University of North Carolina Press, 2012.

Hansen, Joseph. *In Defense of the Cuban Revolution: An Answer to the State Department and Theodore Draper.* New York: Pioneer, 1961.

Harbron, John D. "Cuba: Bibliography of a Revolution." *International Journal* 18, no. 2 (1963): 215–23. https://doi.org/10.2307/40198790.

Hebdige, Dick. *Subculture: The Meaning of Style.* New Accents. London: Methuen, 1979.

Helg, Aline. "Race and Black Mobilization in Colonial and Early Independent Cuba: A Comparative Perspective." *Ethnohistory* 44, no. 1 (Winter 1997): 53–74.

Herbst, Susan. *Numbered Voices: How Opinion Polling Has Shaped American Politics.* Chicago: University of Chicago Press, 1993.

Hernandez, Andres R. "Filmmaking and Politics: The Cuban Experience." *American Behavioral Scientist* 17, no. 3 (January 1974): 360–88. https://doi.org/10.1177/000276427401700303.

Hernández, Robert E., and Carmelo Mesa-Lago. "Labor Organization and Wages." In *Revolutionary Change in Cuba,* edited by Carmelo Mesa-Lago, 209–49. Pittsburgh: University of Pittsburgh Press, 1971.

Hernández-Reguant, Ariana, ed. *Cuba in the Special Period: Culture and Ideology in the 1990s.* Basingstoke: Palgrave Macmillan, 2010.

———. "Radio Taino and the Globalization of the Cuban Culture Industries." PhD diss., University of Chicago, 2002.

Herrera, Claudia Martínez. "Protección de la naturaleza y turismo en la Revolución Cubana de 1959: El caso de la Ciénaga de Zapata." *Historia Ambiental Latino-americana y Caribeña* 1, no. 2 (March 2012): 193–217.

Herrero, Ramiro, and Manuel Galich. *Teatro de relaciones.* Havana: Editorial Letras Cubanas, 1983.

Hess, Carol A. *Representing the Good Neighbor: Music, Difference, and the Pan American Dream.* New York: Oxford University Press, 2013.

Hilton, Ronald. "Castrofobia en los Estados Unidos." *Foro internacional* 4, no. 4 (16) (April–June 1964): 498–516.

Hinckle, Warren, and William W. Turner. *The Fish Is Red: The Story of the Secret War against Castro.* New York: Harper & Row, 1981.

Hoetink, H. "Cuba and the New Experts," *Caribbean Studies* 1, no. 2 (1961): 16–21.

Hoffman, Barry, and Roul Tunley. "Red Junket to Cuba." *Saturday Evening Post,* October 5, 1963, 25–28.

Hoffman, David L. *Stalinist Values: The Cultural Norms of Soviet Modernity, 1917–1941.* Ithaca, N.Y.: Cornell University Press, 2003.

Hoffmann, Bert. "Charismatic Authority and Leadership Change: Lessons from Cuba's Post-Fidel Succession." *International Political Science Review* 30, no. 3 (June 2009): 229–48.

Hoganson, Kristin L. *Fighting for American Manhood: How Gender Politics Provoked the Spanish-American and Philippine-American Wars.* New Haven, Conn.: Yale University Press, 1998.

Hollander, Paul. *Political Pilgrims: Western Intellectuals in Search of the Good Society.* New York: Oxford University Press, 1981.

Horowitz, Irving Louis. *Party Charisma.* 2nd ed. St. Louis: Social Science Institute, Washington University, 1965.

Horten, Gerd. *Radio Goes to War: The Cultural Politics of Propaganda during World War II.* Berkeley: University of California Press, 2002.

Houghton, Neal D. "The Cuban Invasion of 1961 and the U.S. Press, in Retrospect." *Journalism Quarterly* 42, no. 3 (Summer 1965): 422–32.

House Committee on Foreign Affairs and Subcommittee on International Organizations and Movements. *Winning the Cold War: The U.S. Ideological Offensive: Hearings Before the Subcommittee on International Organizations and Movements of the Committee on Foreign Affairs, House of Representatives, Eighty-Eighth Congress.* Washington, D.C.: Government Printing Office, 1963.

Huberman, Leo, and Paul M. Sweezy. *Socialism in Cuba.* New York: Monthly Review Press, 1969.

Hulme, Peter. "Seeing for Themselves: U.S. Travel Writers in Early Revolutionary Cuba." In *Politics, Identity, and Mobility in Travel Writing,* edited by Miguel A. Cabañas, Jeanne Dubino, Veronica Salles-Reese, and Gary Totten. London: Routledge, 2015.

Hunt, Lynn. *Politics, Culture, and Class in the French Revolution.* Berkeley: University of California Press, 1984.

Hynson, Rachel. *Laboring for the State: Women, Family, and Work in Revolutionary Cuba, 1959–1971*. Cambridge: Cambridge University Press, 2019.

Ibarra, Clare. "Tropical Science and the Politics of Development: Cuban-Soviet Scientific Collaboration Post-1960." *Cuban Studies* 51, no. 1 (2022): 68–85. https://doi.org/10.1353/cub.2022.0018.

Ibarra Cuesta, Jorge. "Historiografía y revolución." *Temas* 1, no. 3 (1995): 5–17.

Iber, Patrick. *Neither Peace nor Freedom: The Cultural Cold War in Latin America*. Cambridge, Mass.: Harvard University Press, 2015.

ICIODI. *Investigaciones científicas de la demanda en Cuba*. Havana: Editorial ORBE, 1979.

Iglesias Utset, Marial. *Las metáforas del cambio en la vida cotidiana: Cuba, 1898–1902*. Havana: Editorial Unión, 2003.

Igorra, Rosalina, and Gerardo Mosquera, eds. *Perfiles culturales: Cuba, 1978*. Havana: Editorial ORBE, 1980.

Imre, Anikó. *TV Socialism*. Durham, N.C.: Duke University Press, 2016.

James, Daniel. *Cuba: El primer satélite soviético en América*. Translated by José Meza Nieto. Mexico, D.F.: Libreros Mexicanos Unidos, 1962.

James, Raymond C. "The Right to Travel Abroad." *Fordham Law Review* 42, no. 4 (1974): 837–51.

Jiménez-Leal, Orlando, and Manuel Zayas. *El caso "PM": Cine, poder y censura*. Madrid: Editorial Colibrí, 2012.

Johnson, A. Ross. *Radio Free Europe and Radio Liberty: The CIA Years and Beyond*. Stanford, Calif: Stanford University Press, 2010.

Joseph, Gilbert M., and Daniel Nugent, eds. *Everyday Forms of State Formation: Revolution and the Negotiation of Rule in Modern Mexico*. Durham, N.C.: Duke University Press, 1994.

———. "Popular Culture and State Formation in Revolutionary Mexico." In *Everyday Forms of State Formation: Revolution and the Negotiation of Rule in Modern Mexico*, edited by Gilbert M. Joseph and Daniel Nugent, 3–23. Durham, N.C.: Duke University Press, 1994.

———. "What We Now Know and Should Know: Bringing Latin America More Meaningfully into Cold War Studies." In *In from the Cold: Latin America's New Encounter with the Cold War*, edited by Gilbert N. Joseph and Daniela Spenser, 3–47. Durham, N.C.: Duke University Press, 2008.

Joseph, Gilbert M., Anne Rubenstein, and Eric Zolov, eds. *Fragments of a Golden Age: The Politics of Culture in Mexico since 1940*. Durham, N.C.: Duke University Press, 2001.

Kahl, Joseph. *A Cuban Diary*. St. Louis: Dept. of Sociology, Washington University, 1969.

Kahrl, Andrew W. *The Land Was Ours: African American Beaches from Jim Crow to the Sunbelt South*. Cambridge, Mass.: Harvard University Press, 2012.

Kami, Hideaki. *Diplomacy Meets Migration: US Relations with Cuba during the Cold War*. Cambridge: Cambridge University Press, 2018.

Kane, Brian. "The *Radio Free Dixie* Playlists." *Resonance* 1, no. 4 (December 2020): 344–70. https://doi.org/10.1525/res.2020.1.4.344.

Kapcia, Antoni. "Does Cuba Fit Yet or Is It Still 'Exceptional'?" *Journal of Latin American Studies* 40, no. 4 (November 2008): 627–50. https://doi.org/10.1017/S0022216X08004690.

———. *Havana: The Making of Cuban Culture*. Oxford: Berg, 2005.

———. *A Short History of Revolutionary Cuba: Revolution, Power, Authority and the State from 1959 to the Present Day*. London: Bloomsbury, 2020.

Karl, Terry. "Work Incentives in Cuba." *Latin American Perspectives* 2, no. 4 (1975): 21–41.

Karol, K. S. *Guerrillas in Power: The Course of the Cuban Revolution*. New York: Hill & Wang, 1970.

Keller, Renata. "Fan Mail to Fidel: The Cuban Revolution and Mexican Solidarity." *Mexican Studies/Estudios Mexicanos* 33, no. 1 (2017): 6–31.

———. "The Revolution Will Be Teletyped: Cuba's Prensa Latina News Agency and the Cold War Contest over Information." *Journal of Cold War Studies* 21, no. 3 (August 2019): 88–113.

Kelly, Catriona. "What Was Soviet Studies and What Came Next?" *Journal of Modern History* 85, no. 1 (2013): 109–49. https://doi.org/10.1086/668800.

Kelly, William. "The Promise of Home: Housing, Everyday Life, and Revolution in Cuba, 1959–1988." Cambridge: Cambridge University Press, forthcoming.

Kharkhordin, Oleg. *The Collective and the Individual in Russia: A Study of Practices*. Berkeley: University of California Press, 1999.

Kneitel, Tom. "Inside the CIA's Secret Radio Paradise." Pts. 1 and 2. *Popular Communications* November 1985, 16–20; December 1985, 18–22.

Kohan, Néstor. *"Pensamiento Crítico" y el debate por las ciencias sociales en el seno de la revolución cubana*. In *Crítica y teoría en el pensamiento social latinoamericano*, 389–437. Buenos Aires: CLACSO, 2006. https://biblioteca-repositorio.clacso.edu.ar/bitstream/CLACSO/10848/2/C07NKohan.pdf.

Komaromi, Ann. *Soviet Samizdat: Imagining a New Society*. Ithaca, N.Y.: Cornell University Press, 2022.

Kotkin, Stephen. *Magnetic Mountain: Stalinism as a Civilization*. Berkeley: University of California Press, 1997.

Kutschke, Beate, and Barley Norton, eds. *Music and Protest in 1968*. Cambridge: Cambridge University Press, 2013.

"La cultura ya no es un privilegio." *Trabajo Cuba*, no. 8 (December 1960).

Laguna, Albert Sergio. *Diversión: Play and Popular Culture in Cuban America*. New York: New York University Press, 2018.

Lam, Rafael. *Esta es la música cubana*. Serie Biblioteca cubana. Madrid: Editorial Verbum, 2019.

Lambe, Jennifer L. "A Century of Work: Reconstructing Mazorra, 1857–1959." *Cuban Studies* 43 (2015): 90–117.

———. "The Communist Closet: Secrecy, Sexuality, and Ideology in the Cuban Cold War." *Hispanic American Historical Review*, December 28, 2023. https://doi.org/10.1215/00182168-11085469.

———. "Cuban Leaders Have Long Relied on Anti-Imperialist Anger. This Time, It's Not Working." *Politico*, July 15, 2021. www.politico.com/news/magazine/2021/07/15/cuba-protest-blame-government-imperialism-revolution-499760.

———. "Drug Wars: Revolution, Embargo, and the Politics of Scarcity in Cuba, 1959–1964." *Journal of Latin American Studies* 49, no. 3 (2017): 489–516. https://doi.org/10.1017/S0022216X16001851.

———. *Madhouse: Psychiatry and Politics in Cuban History.* Chapel Hill: University of North Carolina Press, 2017.

———. "The Revolution's Fourth Face on the Fourth Network: Feuding over Cuba on U.S. Educational Television, 1959–1970." *Journal of American History* 107, no. 3 (December 1, 2020): 636–57. https://doi.org/10.1093/jahist/jaaa341.

Lambe, Jennifer L., and Michael J. Bustamante. "Cuba's Revolution from Within: The Politics of Historical Paradigms." In *The Revolution from Within: Cuba, 1959–1980*, edited by Michael J. Bustamante and Jennifer L. Lambe, 3–32. Durham, N.C.: Duke University Press, 2019.

Lane, Jill. *Blackface Cuba, 1840–1895.* Philadelphia: University of Pennsylvania Press, 2005.

———. "Smoking Habaneras, or A Cuban Struggle with Racial Demons." *Social Text* 28:3, no. 104 (2010): 11–37.

Langland, Victoria. *Speaking of Flowers: Student Movements and the Making and Remembering of 1968 in Military Brazil.* Durham, N.C.: Duke University Press, 2013.

Latner, Teishan. *Cuban Revolution in America: Havana and the Making of a United States Left, 1968–1992.* Chapel Hill: University of North Carolina Press, 2017.

Lauten, Flora. *Teatro La Yaya.* Havana: Editorial Letras Cubanas, 1981.

Lazo, Rodrigo. *Writing to Cuba: Filibustering and Cuban Exiles in the United States.* Chapel Hill: University of North Carolina Press, 2006.

Leal, Rine. *La dramaturgia del Escambray.* Havana: Editorial Letras Cubanas, 1984.

———, ed. *Teatro Escambray.* Havana: Editorial Letras Cubanas, 1978.

Ledeneva, Alena V. "Between Gift and Commodity: The Phenomenon of *Blat*." *Cambridge Anthropology* 19, no. 3 (1996): 43–66.

Lekus, Ian Keith. "Queer Harvests: Homosexuality, the U.S. New Left, and the Venceremos Brigades to Cuba." *Radical History Review* 89, no. 1 (June 2004): 57–91.

Lenoe, Matthew E. *Closer to the Masses: Stalinist Culture, Social Revolution, and Soviet Newspapers.* Cambridge, Mass.: Harvard University Press, 2004.

LeoGrande, William M., and Peter Kornbluh. *Back Channel to Cuba: The Hidden History of Negotiations between Washington and Havana.* Chapel Hill: University of North Carolina Press, 2015.

León, Argeliers. *Música folklórica cubana.* Havana: Ediciones del Departamento de Música de la Biblioteca Nacional "José Martí," 1964.

Levine, Mike. "Sounding El Paquete: The Local and Transnational Routes of an Afro-Cuban Repartero." *Cuban Studies*, no. 50 (2020): 139–60.

Lewis, Oscar, Ruth M. Lewis, and Susan M. Rigdon. *Living the Revolution: An Oral History of Contemporary Cuba*. Urbana: University of Illinois Press, 1977.

Light, Matthew A. "What Does It Mean to Control Migration? Soviet Mobility Policies in Comparative Perspective." *Law and Social Inquiry* 37, no. 2 (2012): 395–429.

Lockwood, Lee. *Castro's Cuba, Cuba's Fidel*. New York: Vintage Books, 1969.

López, Oscar Luis. *La radio en Cuba*. Havana: Letras Cubanas, 2002.

López, Rick Anthony. *Crafting Mexico: Intellectuals, Artisans, and the State after the Revolution*. Durham, N.C.: Duke University Press, 2010.

López Fresquet, Rufo. *My Fourteen Months with Castro*. Cleveland: World, 1966.

López Rivero, Sergio. *El viejo traje de la revolución: Identidad colectiva, mito y hegemonía política en Cuba*. Valencia: Universitat de València, 2007.

Lovelace, H. Timothy. "William Worthy's Passport: Travel Restrictions and the Cold War Struggle for Civil and Human Rights." *Journal of American History* 103, no. 1 (June 2016): 107–31.

Lueck, Simone. *Cuba TV*. Brooklyn: Mark Batty, 2011.

Luis-Brown, David. *Waves of Decolonization: Discourses of Race and Hemispheric Citizenship in Cuba, Mexico, and the United States*. Durham, N.C.: Duke University Press, 2008.

MacGaffey, Wyatt, and Clifford R. Barnett. *Cuba: Its People, Its Society, Its Culture*. Westport, Conn.: Greenwood Press, 1962.

Mahler, Anne Garland. *From the Tricontinental to the Global South: Race, Radicalism, and Transnational Solidarity*. Durham, N.C.: Duke University Press, 2018.

Major, Patrick. *Behind the Berlin Wall: East Germany and the Frontiers of Power*. Oxford: Oxford University Press, 2010.

Malitsky, Joshua. *Post-Revolution Nonfiction Film: Building the Soviet and Cuban Nations*. Bloomington: Indiana University Press, 2013.

Mallin, Jay. *Adventures in Journalism: A Memoir*. Washington, D.C.: Kelbrenjac, 1998.

Manduley López, Humberto. *Hierba mala: Una historia del rock en Cuba*. Holguín: Ediciones La Luz, 2015.

Manuel, Peter. "Marxism, Nationalism and Popular Music in Revolutionary Cuba." *Popular Music* 6, no. 2 (1987): 161–78.

Manzano, Valeria. *The Age of Youth in Argentina: Culture, Politics, and Sexuality from Perón to Videla*. Chapel Hill: University of North Carolina Press, 2014.

Marcer, Manuel. "Las bibliotecas del pueblo." *INRA* 2, no. 7 (July 1961): 34–39.

Marinari, Maddalena, Madeline Yuan-yin Hsu, and María Cristina García, eds. *A Nation of Immigrants Reconsidered: US Society in an Age of Restriction, 1924–1965*. Urbana: University of Illinois Press, 2019.

Marquetti Torres, Rosa. *Desmemoriados: Historias de la música cubana*. Barranquilla: Editorial La Iguana Ciega, 2016.

Marrero, Juan. *Dos siglos de periodismo en Cuba: Momentos, hechos y rostros*. Havana: Editorial Pablo de la Torriente, 2018.

Martínez, Elizabeth Sutherland. *The Youngest Revolution: A Personal Report on Cuba*. London: Pitman, 1970.

Martínez, Milagros, and Sheryl Lutjens, eds. *Historia de los intercambios académicos entre Cuba y Estados Unidos.* Havana: Editorial de Ciencias Sociales, 2018.

Martínez, Milagros, and Rosana Resende. "Academic Exchange between Cuba and the United States: A Brief Overview." *Latin American Perspectives* 33, no. 5 (2006): 29–42.

Martínez Furé, Rogelio A. *Diálogos imaginarios.* Havana: Editorial Letras Cubanas, 1997.

Martínez Pérez, Liliana. *Los hijos de Saturno: Intelectuales y revolución en Cuba.* Mexico, D.F: FLACSO, 2006.

Martínez Victores, Ricardo. *7RR: La historia de Radio Rebelde.* Havana: Editora Política, 2008.

Matthews, Herbert Lionel. *Revolution in Cuba: An Essay in Understanding.* New York: Scribners, 1975.

McColl Kennedy, Ian. "Cuba's Ley contra la Vagancia." *UCLA Law Review* 20, no. 6 (August 1973): 1177–1268.

McEnaney, Tom. *Acoustic Properties: Radio, Narrative, and the New Neighborhood of the Americas.* Evanston, Ill.: Northwestern University Press, 2017.

McLuhan, Marshall. *Understanding Media: The Extensions of Man.* Toronto: McGraw-Hill, 1964.

Menand, Louis. *The Free World: Art and Thought in the Cold War.* New York: Picador, 2020.

Merritt, Richard L., and Anna J. Merritt, eds. *Living with the Wall: West Berlin, 1961–1985.* Durham, N.C.: Duke University Press, 1985.

Mesa-Lago, Carmelo. *Breve historia económica de la Cuba socialista: Políticas, resultados y perspectivas.* Madrid: Alianza Ed., 1994.

———. *The Labor Sector and Socialist Distribution in Cuba.* New York: Praeger, 1970. Published for the Hoover Institution on War, Revolution, and Peace.

———. "On the Objectives and Objectivity of Cubanology: A Response to a Critic from Cuba." *Cuban Studies* 16 (1986): 225–34.

———. "Revolutionary Empathy vs. Calculated Detachment in the Study of the Cuban Revolution: A Reply to Fitzgerald." *Cuban Studies* 11, no. 1 (1981): 90–92.

———. "Un futuro sin cortapisas para los intercambios académicos." In *Historia de los intercambios académicos entre Cuba y Estados Unidos,* edited by Milagros Martínez and Sheryl Lutjens. Havana: Editorial de Ciencias Sociales, 2018.

Meyer, Karl E., and Tad Szulc. *The Cuban Invasion: The Chronicle of a Disaster.* New York: Praeger, 1962.

Mickelson, Sig. *America's Other Voice: The Story of Radio Free Europe and Radio Liberty.* New York: Praeger, 1983.

———. *The Electric Mirror: Politics in an Age of Television.* New York: Dodd, Mead, 1972.

Miller, Ivor L. "Religious Symbolism in Cuban Political Performance." *TDR/The Drama Review* 44, no. 2 (June 1, 2000): 30–55.

Miller, Warren. *90 Miles from Home: The Truth from Inside Castro's Cuba.* New York: Crest Books, 1961.

Mislan, Cristina. "'In the Spirit of '76 Venceremos!': Nationalizing and Transnationalizing Self-Defense on *Radio Free Dixie*." *American Journalism* 32, no. 4 (October 2015): 434–52. https://doi.org/10.1080/08821127.2015.1099265.

———. "Transnationalism, Revolution and Race: The Case of Cuba's *Radio Free Dixie*." PhD diss., Pennsylvania State University, 2013.

Mittell, Jason. *Television and American Culture*. New York: Oxford University Press, 2010.

Modleski, Tania. "Femininity as Mas(s)querade: A Feminist Approach to Mass Culture." In *High Theory, Low Culture: Analysing Popular Television and Film*, edited by Colin MacCabe, 37–52. Manchester: Manchester University Press, 1986.

Monahan, James, and Kenneth O. Gilmore. *The Great Deception: The Inside Story of How the Kremlin Took Over Cuba*. New York: Farrar, Straus and Girous, 1963.

Montejo Arrechea, Carmen Victoria. *Sociedades negras en Cuba, 1878–1960*. Havana: Editorial de Ciencias Sociales, 2004.

Moore, Carlos. *Castro, the Blacks, and Africa*. Afro-American Culture and Society. Los Angeles: UCLA Center for Afro-American Studies, 1988.

———. *Pichón: A Memoir; Race and Revolution in Castro's Cuba*. Chicago: Lawrence Hill Books, 2008.

Moore, Robin D. *Music and Revolution: Cultural Change in Socialist Cuba*. Berkeley: University of California Press, 2006.

———. *Nationalizing Blackness: Afrocubanismo and Artistic Revolution in Havana, 1920–1940*. Pittsburgh: University of Pittsburgh Press, 1997.

Morray, J. P. *The Second Revolution in Cuba*. New York: Monthly Review Press, 1962.

Morton, Ward McKinnon. *Castro as Charismatic Hero*. Occasional Publications 4. Lawrence: University of Kansas, Center of Latin American Studies, 1965.

Muller, Dalia Antonia. *Cuban Émigrés and Independence in the Nineteenth-Century Gulf World*. Chapel Hill: University of North Carolina Press, 2017.

Murat, Laure. *The Man Who Thought He Was Napoleon: Toward a Political History of Madness*. Chicago: University of Chicago Press, 2014.

Nelson, Lowry. *Cuba: The Measure of a Revolution*. Minneapolis: University of Minnesota Press, 1972.

Nelson, Michael. *War of the Black Heavens: The Battles of Western Broadcasting in the Cold War*. Syracuse, N.Y.: Syracuse University Press, 1997.

Nerey Obregón, Boris. "Hoy." In *Prensa y revolución: La magia del cambio*, edited by María del Pilar Díaz Castañón. Havana: Editorial de Ciencias Sociales, 2010.

Novick, Peter. *That Noble Dream: The "Objectivity Question" and the American Historical Profession*. Cambridge: Cambridge University Press, 1988.

Noyola, Juan F. "Aspectos económicos de la Revolución Cubana." *Investigación económica* 21, no. 82 (1961): 331–59.

Nuez Carrillo, Iván de la. *Fantasía roja: Los intelectuales de izquierdas y la Revolución cubana*. Barcelona: Debolsillo, 2010.

O'Connor, James R. *The Origins of Socialism in Cuba*. Ithaca, N.Y.: Cornell University Press, 1970.

O'Keeffe, Brigid. *Esperanto and Languages of Internationalism in Revolutionary Russia*. London: Bloomsbury Academic, 2021.

Orejuela Martínez, Adriana. *El son no se fue de Cuba: Claves para una historia, 1959–1973*. Caracas: Fundación Celarg, 2013.

Oreskes, Naomi, and John Krige. *Science and Technology in the Global Cold War*. Cambridge, Mass.: MIT Press, 2014.

Ortega, Gregorio. *La coletilla: Una batalla por la libertad de expresión, 1959–1962*. Havana: Editora Política, 1989.

Oyen, Meredith. *The Diplomacy of Migration: Transnational Lives and the Making of U.S.-Chinese Relations in the Cold War*. Ithaca, N.Y.: Cornell University Press, 2015.

Pacini Hernandez, Deborah, Héctor Fernández L'Hoeste, and Eric Zolov, eds. *Rockin' Las Américas: The Global Politics of Rock in Latin/o America*. Pittsburgh, Penn.: University of Pittsburgh Press, 2004.

Pacini Hernandez, Deborah, and Reebee Garofalo. "Between Rock and a Hard Place: Negotiating Rock in Revolutionary Cuba, 1960–1980." In *Rockin' Las Americas: The Global Politics of Rock in Latin/o America*, edited by Deborah Pacini Hernandez, Héctor Fernández L'Hoeste, and Eric Zolov, 43–67. Pittsburgh: University of Pittsburgh Press, 2004.

Pappademos, Melina. *Black Political Activism and the Cuban Republic*. Chapel Hill: University of North Carolina Press, 2011.

Pedraza-Bailey, Silvia. "Cuba's Exiles: Portrait of a Refugee Migration." *International Migration Review* 19, no. 1 (1985): 4–34. https://doi.org/10.2307/2545654.

Pedraza Ginori, Eugenio Antonio. *Memorias Cubanas*. Vol. 1, *Eugenito quiere televisión*. Self-published, CreateSpace, 2016.

———. *Memorias Cubanas*. Vol. 2, *Quietecito no va conmigo*. Self-published, CreateSpace, 2016.

Pérez, Louis A. *On Becoming Cuban: Identity, Nationality, and Culture*. Chapel Hill: University of North Carolina Press, 1999.

———. "The Cuban Revolution Twenty-Five Years Later: A Survey of Sources, Scholarship, and State of the Literature." In *Cuba: Twenty-Five Years of Revolution, 1959–1984*, edited by Sandor Halebsky and John M. Kirk, 393–412. New York: Praeger, 1985.

———. *The War of 1898: The United States and Cuba in History and Historiography*. Chapel Hill: University of North Carolina Press, 1998.

Pérez Salomón, Omar. *Estrellas en la frente: Comunicaciones, electrónica e informática, 1959–2008*. Havana: Editora Política, 2009.

Pérez-Stable, Marifeli. "Charismatic Authority, Vanguard Party Politics, and Popular Mobilizations: Revolution and Socialism in Cuba." *Cuban Studies* 22 (1992): 3–26.

———. *The Cuban Revolution: Origins, Course, and Legacy*. New York: Oxford University Press, 1993.

———. "Whither the Cuban Working Class?" *Latin American Perspectives* 2, no. 4 (1975): 60–77.

Pericás, Luiz Bernardo, Rodrigo Sardenberg, and Vanessa Binder. *Che Guevara and the Economic Debate in Cuba*. New York: Atropos Press, 2009.

Perna, Vincenzo. *Timba: The Sound of the Cuban Crisis*. Aldershot, Hants, England: Ashgate, 2005.

Perry, Marc D. *Negro Soy Yo: Hip Hop and Raced Citizenship in Neoliberal Cuba*. Durham, N.C.: Duke University Press, 2015.

Petras, James. "Has the Cuban Revolution Failed?," *Science and Society* 36, no. 1 (1972): 86–90.

Pettinà, Vanni. *Historia mínima de la guerra fría en América Latina*. Mexico: El Colegio de México, 2018.

Pflaum, Irving Peter. *Tragic Island: How Communism Came to Cuba*. Englewood Cliffs, N.J: Prentice-Hall, 1961.

Philipson, Lorrin. *Freedom Flights: Cuban Refugees Talk about Life under Castro and How They Fled His Regime*. 1st ed. New York: Random House, 1980.

Phillips, R. Hart. *The Cuban Dilemma*. New York: I. Obolensky, 1962.

Piccato, Pablo. *The Tyranny of Opinion: Honor in the Construction of the Mexican Public Sphere*. Durham, N.C.: Duke University Press, 2010.

Pignot, Elsa. "El asociacionismo negro en Cuba: Una vía de integración en la sociedad republicana (1920–1960)." *Revista de Indias* 70, no. 250 (December 2010): 837–62. https://doi.org/10.3989/revindias.2010.027.

Pino, Octavio. "The Influence of the Revolution on Cuban Spanish." Paper presented at the Annual Colloquium on Hispanic Linguistics (2nd, Linguistic Institute, University of South Florida, Tampa, July 17–19, 1975).

Plá León, Rafael, and Mely González Aróstegui, eds. *Marxismo y revolución: Escena del debate cubano en los sesenta*. Havana: Editorial de Ciencias Sociales/Centro de Investigación y Desarrollo de la Cultura Cubana Juan Marinello, 2006.

Playa Girón: Derrota del imperialismo. Vol. 4. Havana: Ediciones Revolución, 1962.

Pogolotti, Graziella, ed. *Polémicas culturales de los 60*. Havana: Editorial Letras Cubanas, 2007.

Poiger, Uta G. *Jazz, Rock, and Rebels: Cold War Politics and American Culture in a Divided Germany*. Berkeley: University of California Press, 2000.

Polanyi, Michael. "Knowing and Being." *Mind* 70, no. 280 (1961): 458–70.

Porbén, Pedro P. *La revolución deseada: Prácticas culturales del hombre nuevo en Cuba*. Madrid: Editorial Verbum, 2014.

Primer Congreso Nacional de Cultura: Discursos. Havana: Ediciones del Consejo Nacional de Cultura, 1963.

Puddington, Arch. *Broadcasting Freedom: The Cold War Triumph of Radio Free Europe and Radio Liberty*. Lexington: University Press of Kentucky, 2000.

Quinn, Kate. "Cuban Historiography in the 1960s: Revisionists, Revolutionaries and the Nationalist Past." *Bulletin of Latin American Research* 26, no. 3 (July 2007): 378–98. https://doi.org/10.1111/j.1470-9856.2007.00230.x.

Quintana Suárez, Raúl Osvaldo. *Recuerdos no olvidados: Memorias periodísticas*. Saarbrücken: Editorial Academica Española, 2013.

Quintero García, Santiago R. *La hegemonía mediática contra Cuba, 1959–1964*. Havana: Casa Editorial Verde Olivo, 2014.

Quiroga, José. *Cuban Palimpsests*. Minneapolis: University of Minnesota Press, 2005.

Quiza, Ricardo. "Sujetos olvidados: Los trabajadores en la historiografía cubana." In *La historiografía en la Revolución cubana: Reflexiones a 50 años*, edited by Rolando Julio Rensoli Medina, 313–47. Havana: Editorial Historia, 2010.

Radio Habana Cuba. *¡Cuba estamos contigo! Cartas y mensajes de solidaridad con la Revolución cubana*. Havana, 1961.

Radway, Janice A. *Reading the Romance: Women, Patriarchy, and Popular Literature*. Chapel Hill: University of North Carolina Press, 1984.

Ramet, Sabrina P. *Rocking the State: Rock Music and Politics in Eastern Europe and Russia*. Boulder, Colo.: Westview Press, 1994.

Ramos Ruiz, Danay. *Roa, director de cultura: Una política, una revista*. Havana: Centro de Investigación y Desarrollo de la Cultura Cubana Juan Marinello, 2006.

Reason, Barbara, Margaret B. Mughisuddin, and Bum-Joon Lee Park. *Cuba Since Castro: A Bibliography of Relevant Literature*. Washington, D.C.: Research Division. Special Operations Research Office, American University, 1962.

Reed, Roger. *The Cultural Revolution in Cuba*. Geneva: Latin American Round Table, 1991.

Rey, Carmelina. *¿Adónde va la televisión cubana?* Havana, 1959.

Ribadero, Martín, and Grethel Domenech Hernández, ed. "Presentación del Dossier: Visiones, entusiasmos y disidencias de la Revolución cubana en la escena intelectual latinoamericana de los años sesenta." *Cuban Studies* 52 (2023): 257–64. https://doi.org/10.1353/cub.2023.a899803.

Richmond, Yale. *Cultural Exchange and the Cold War: Raising the Iron Curtain*. University Park: Pennsylvania State University, 2010.

Richthofen, Esther Von. *Bringing Culture to the Masses: Control, Compromise and Participation in the GDR*. New York: Berghahn Books, 2009.

Riera, Pepita. "Datos sobre autora." In *Servicio de inteligencia de Cuba comunista*. Miami: Florida Typesetting of Miami, 1966.

———. *Servicio de inteligencia de Cuba comunista*. Miami: Florida Typesetting of Miami, 1966.

Río, Joel del. "Hace cincuenta años (en 1972), *La vida sigue igual* apasionaba a los cubanos." *Revista Cine Cubano*, March 3, 2022. www.revistacinecubano.icaic.cu/hace-cincuenta-anos-en-1972-la-vida-sigue-igual-apasionaba-a-los-cubanos/.

Ritter, Archibald R. M. "Los Organos del Poder Popular and Participatory Democracy in Cuba: A Preliminary Analysis." *Social and Economic Studies* 29, no. 2/3 (1980): 193–219.

Rivero, José Ignacio. *Contra viento y marea: Periodismo y mucho más*. Miami: Ediciones Universal, 2004.

Rivero, Yeidy. *Broadcasting Modernity: Cuban Commercial Television, 1950–1960*. Durham, N.C.: Duke University Press, 2015.

Roa, Raúl. *Bufa subversiva*. Havana: Ediciones La Memoria, Centro Cultural Pablo de la Torriente Brau, 2006.

Robbins, James Lawrence. "Making Popular Music in Cuba: A Study of the Cuban Institutions of Musical Production and the Musical Life of Santiago de Cuba." PhD diss., University of Illinois, 1990.

Robertson, William van B., Edmund L. Pincoffs, and Charles H. Randall. "Academic Freedom and Tenure: The University of Arizona." *AAUP Bulletin* 49, no. 4 (1963): 336–43. https://doi.org/10.2307/40223039.

Rockefeller, Nelson A. *The Rockefeller Report on the Americas: The Official Report of a United States Presidential Mission for the Western Hemisphere*. Chicago: Quadrangle Books, 1969.

Rodríguez, Aníbal. *Transitando por la psicología: Antes y después de la revolución*. Havana: Editorial de Ciencias Sociales, 1990.

Rodríguez, Carlos Rafael. "Vida y obra de Juan F. Noyola." *El trimestre económico* 50, no. 198(2) (1983): 595–605.

Rodríguez, Victoria Elí. "Apuntes sobre la creación musical actual en Cuba." *Latin American Music Review / Revista de Música Latinoamericana* 10, no. 2 (1989): 287–97. https://doi.org/10.2307/779954.

Rodríguez García, José Luis. *Crítica a nuestros críticos*. Havana: Editorial de Ciencias Sociales, 1988.

Rodríguez Gómez, Katya. "Diario de la Marina." In *Prensa y revolución: La magia del cambio*, edited by María del Pilar Díaz Castañón. Havana: Editorial de Ciencias Sociales, 2010.

Rojas, Rafael. *El estante vacío: Literatura y política en Cuba*. Barcelona: Anagrama, 2009.

———. *Fighting over Fidel: The New York Intellectuals and the Cuban Revolution*. Translated by Carl Good. Princeton, N.J.: Princeton University Press, 2016.

———. *Historia mínima de la Revolución Cubana*. Mexico, D.F.: El Colegio de México, 2015.

———. "The New Text of the Revolution." In *The Revolution from Within: Cuba, 1959–1980*, edited by Michael J. Bustamante and Jennifer L. Lambe, 33–46. Durham, N.C.: Duke University Press, 2019.

———. *Tumbas sin sosiego: Revolución, disidencia y exilio del intelectual cubano*. Barcelona: Editorial Anagrama, 2006.

Romay, Zuleica M. *La opinión pública en el ocaso de la neocolonia cubana*. Havana: Editora Política, 2003.

Rose, Chanelle Nyree. *The Struggle for Black Freedom in Miami: Civil Rights and America's Tourist Paradise, 1896–1968*. Baton Rouge: Louisiana State University, 2015.

Rosendahl, Mona. *Inside the Revolution: Everyday Life in Socialist Cuba*. Ithaca, N.Y.: Cornell University Press, 1997.

Rosenfeld, Sophia A. *A Revolution in Language: The Problem of Signs in Late Eighteenth-Century France*. Stanford, Calif.: Stanford University Press, 2001.

Routon, Kenneth. *Hidden Powers of State in the Cuban Imagination*. Gainesville: University Press of Florida, 2010.

Ryback, Timothy W. *Rock around the Bloc: A History of Rock Music in Eastern Europe and the Soviet Union*. New York: Oxford University Press, 1990.

Salado, Minerva. *Censura de prensa en la revolución cubana.* Madrid: Verbum, 2016.

Salas, Luis. "The Emergence and Decline of the Cuban Popular Tribunals." *Law and Society Review* 17, no. 4 (1983): 587–612. https://doi.org/10.2307/3053489.

Salém Vasconcelos, Joana. "Jacques Chonchol em Cuba: Reforma agrária e revolução em 1961." *Revista Mouro* 7 (2012): 72–88. www.mouro.com.br /Jacques%20Conchol%20em%20Cuba_JoanaVasconcelos.pdf.

———. "Reforma agrária e socialismo na América Latina: Cuba e Chile." Paper presented at the 29th Simpósio Nacional de História, Universidade de São Paulo, 2017. www.snh2017.anpuh.org/resources/anais/54/1489583445 _ARQUIVO_JSV,ReformaagrariaesocialismonaAmericaLatina.pdf.

Salkey, Andrew. *Havana Journal.* Pelican Books, A 1303. Harmondsworth: Penguin, 1971.

Salwen, Michael Brian. *Radio and Television in Cuba: The Pre-Castro Era.* Ames: Iowa State University Press, 1994.

Sánchez, Herminia. *De pie!* Havana: Ediciones Unión, 1984.

———. *Teatro de fuerza y candor.* Havana: Ediciones Unión, 2019.

Sánchez León, Miguel. *Esa huella olvidada: El Teatro Nacional de Cuba, 1959–1961.* Havana: Letras Cubanas, 2001.

Sanneh, Kelefa. *Major Labels: A History of Popular Music in Seven Genres.* New York: Penguin, 2021.

Saunders, Frances Stonor. *The Cultural Cold War: The CIA and the World of Arts and Letters.* New York: New Press (Distributed by W. W. Norton), 2000.

Saunders, Tanya L. *Cuban Underground Hip Hop: Black Thoughts, Black Revolution, Black Modernity.* Austin: University of Texas Press, 2015. https:// doi.org/10.7560/302378.

Schlesinger, Stephen C., and Stephen Kinzer. *Bitter Fruit: The Story of the American Coup in Guatemala.* Boston, Mass.: Harvard University, David Rockefeller Center for Latin American Studies, 1999.

Schlosser, Nicholas J. *Cold War on the Airwaves: The Radio Propaganda War against East Germany.* Urbana: University of Illinois Press, 2015.

Schoultz, Lars. *That Infernal Little Cuban Republic: The United States and the Cuban Revolution.* Chapel Hill: University of North Carolina Press, 2011.

Schudson, Michael. *Discovering the News: A Social History of American Newspapers.* New York: Basic Books, 2011.

Schwall, Elizabeth. "Between *Espíritu* and *Conciencia*: Cabaret and Ballet Developments in 1960s Cuba." In *The Revolution from Within: Cuba, 1959–1980,* edited by Michael J. Bustamante and Jennifer L. Lambe, 146–69. Durham, N.C.: Duke University Press, 2019.

———. *Dancing with the Revolution: Power, Politics, and Privilege in Cuba.* Chapel Hill: University of North Carolina Press, 2021.

———. "Prescribing Ballet: A History of Gender and Disability in Cuban Psicoballet." *Gender and History* 32, no. 2 (May 2020): 373–92. https://doi.org /10.1111/1468-0424.12479.

Schwartz, Abba P. *The Open Society.* New York: W. Morrow, 1968.

Schwartz, Rosalie. *Pleasure Island: Tourism and Temptation in Cuba*. Lincoln: University of Nebraska Press, 1997.

Scott, Joan W. "The Evidence of Experience." *Critical Inquiry* 17, no. 4 (1991): 773–97.

Seers, Dudley, Andrés Bianchi, Richard Jolly, and Max Nolff. *Cuba: The Economic and Social Revolution*. Chapel Hill: University of North Carolina Press, 1964.

Seidman, Sarah J. "Angela Davis in Cuba as Symbol and Subject." *Radical History Review* 2020, no. 136 (2020): 11–35.

———. "Tricontinental Routes of Solidarity: Stokely Carmichael in Cuba." *Journal of Transnational American Studies* 4, no. 2 (2012). https://escholarship.org/uc/item/0wp587sj.

———. "Venceremos Means We Shall Overcome: The African American Freedom Struggle and the Cuban Revolution, 1959–79." PhD diss., Brown University, 2013.

Séjourné, Laurette. *Teatro Escambray: Una experiencia*. Havana: Editorial de Ciencias Sociales, 1977.

Serra, Ana. *The "New Man" in Cuba: Culture and Identity in the Revolution*. Gainesville: University Press of Florida, 2007.

Servín, Elisa. "Frank Tannenbaum entre América Latina y Estados Unidos en la Guerra Fría." *A contracorriente: Una revista de estudios latinoamericanos* 13, no. 3 (May 2016): 50–76.

———. "La experiencia mexicana de Charles Wright Mills." *Historia Mexicana*, April 1, 2020, 1729–72. https://doi.org/10.24201/hm.v69i4.4056.

Sewell, Jr., William H. *Capitalism and the Emergence of Civic Equality in Eighteenth-Century France*. Chicago: University of Chicago Press, 2021.

Shibusawa, Naoko. "Femininity, Race and Treachery: How 'Tokyo Rose' Became a Traitor to the United States after the Second World War." *Gender and History* 22, no. 1 (2010): 169–88. https://doi.org/10.1111/j.1468-0424.2010.01584.x.

Shils, Edward. "Charisma, Order, and Status." *American Sociological Review* 30, no. 2 (1965): 199–213.

Siegelbaum, Lewis H. "The Shaping of Soviet Workers' Leisure: Workers' Clubs and Palaces of Culture in the 1930s." *International Labor and Working-Class History*, no. 56 (1999): 78–92.

———. *Stakhanovism and the Politics of Productivity in the USSR, 1935–1941*. Cambridge: Cambridge University Press, 1988.

Siegelbaum, Lewis, and Andrei Sokolov, eds. *Stalinism as a Way of Life: A Narrative in Documents*. New Haven, Conn.: Yale University Press, 2008.

Sierra Madero, Abel. *Del otro lado del espejo: La sexualidad en la construcción de la nación cubana*. Havana: Fondo Editorial Casa de las Américas, 2006.

———. *El cuerpo nunca olvida: Trabajo forzado, hombre nuevo y memoria en Cuba (1959–1980)*. Rialta, 2022.

Sierra Madero, Abel, and Edith García Buchaca. "'No se sabía dónde estaba la verdad y dónde estaba la mentira': Entrevista a Edith García Buchaca, 30 de abril de 2012." *Cuban Studies*, no. 45 (2017): 359–71.

Silva Herzog, Jesús. "A manera de introducción." In *La economía cubana en los primeros años de la Revolución y otros ensayos*, by Juan Noyola, 9–23. Mexico: Siglo Veintiuno, 1978.

Silverman, Bertram. *Man and Socialism in Cuba: The Great Debate.* New York: Atheneum, 1973.

Simpson, Christopher. *Science of Coercion: Communication Research and Psychological Warfare, 1945–1960.* New York: Oxford University Press, 1996.

Sirvén, Pablo. *El rey de la TV: Goar Mestre y la pelea entre gobiernos y medios latinoamericanos, de Fidel Castro a Juan Perón; A 40 años de la estatización de los canales de TV.* Buenos Aires: Sudamericana, 2013.

Skwiot, Christine. *The Purposes of Paradise: U.S. Tourism and Empire in Cuba and Hawai'i.* Philadelphia: University of Pennsylvania Press, 2011.

Smith, Benjamin T. *The Mexican Press and Civil Society, 1940–1976: Stories from the Newsroom, Stories from the Street.* Chapel Hill: University of North Carolina Press, 2019.

Smith, Lois M., and Alfred Padula. *Sex and Revolution: Women in Socialist Cuba.* New York: Oxford University Press, 1996.

Smith, Wayne S. "Status of Scholarly Exchanges with Cuba," *LASA Forum* 17, no. 3 (Fall 1986): 14–16.

Smorkaloff, Pamela María. *Readers and Writers in Cuba: A Social History of Print Culture, 1830s–1990s.* New York: Garland, 1997.

Soley, Lawrence C., and John Spicer Nichols. *Clandestine Radio Broadcasting: A Study of Revolutionary and Counterrevolutionary Electronic Communication.* New York: Praeger, 1987.

Solovey, Mark. *Shaky Foundations: The Politics-Patronage-Social Science Nexus in Cold War America.* New Brunswick, N.J.: Rutgers University Press, 2013.

Solovey, Mark, and Christian Dayé, eds. *Cold War Social Science: Transnational Entanglements.* Cham, Switzerland: Palgrave Macmillan, 2021.

Somerville, Keith. *Radio Propaganda and the Broadcasting of Hatred: Historical Development and Definitions.* New York: Palgrave Macmillan, 2012.

Sontag, Susan. "Some Thoughts on the Right Way (for Us) to Love the Cuban Revolution." *Ramparts*, April 1969, 6–19.

Soto, Lionel. "El nuevo desarrollo de la instrucción revolucionaria." *Cuba Socialista* 1, no. 12 (August 1962): 32–45.

———. "Las Escuelas de Instrucción Revolucionaria en el ciclo político-técnico." *Cuba Socialista* 5, no. 41 (January 1965).

Soules, Marshall. *Media, Persuasion and Propaganda.* Edinburgh: Edinburgh University Press, 2015.

Spigel, Lynn. *Make Room for TV: Television and the Family Ideal in Postwar America.* Chicago: University of Chicago Press, 1992.

———. "Our TV Heritage: Television, the Archive, and the Reasons for Preservation." In *A Companion to Television*, edited by Janet Wasko, 67–102. Malden, Mass.: Blackwell, 2005.

Spigel, Lynn, and Michael Curtin, eds. *The Revolution Wasn't Televised: Sixties Television and Social Conflict.* New York: Routledge, 1997.

Stetson, Damon. "Academic Freedom." *New Leader*, January 7, 1963.

St. George, Andrew. "A Revolution Gone Wrong." *Coronet*, July 1960, 111–19.

Sweig, Julia E. *Inside the Cuban Revolution: Fidel Castro and the Urban Underground.* Cambridge, Mass.: Harvard University Press, 2002.

Szulc, Tad. "Cuban Television's One-Man Show." In *The Eighth Art: Twenty-Three Views of Television Today,* edited by Eugene Burdick and Robert Lewis Shayon, 97–107. New York: Holt, Rinehart and Winston, 1962.

Tannenbaum, Frank. "Castro and Social Change." *Political Science Quarterly* 77, no. 2 (June 1962): 178–204. https://doi.org/10.2307/2145869.

Teel, Leonard Ray. *Reporting the Cuban Revolution: How Castro Manipulated American Journalists.* Baton Rouge: Louisiana State University Press, 2015.

Thomas, Hugh. *Cuba: The Pursuit of Freedom.* New York: Harper & Row, 1971.

Thornton, Christy. *Revolution in Development: Mexico and the Governance of the Global Economy.* Oakland: University of California Press, 2021.

Toro, Carlos del. *La alta burguesía cubana: 1920–1958.* Havana: Editorial de Ciencias Sociales, 2003.

Torres, María de los Angeles. *In the Land of Mirrors: Cuban Exile Politics in the United States.* Ann Arbor: University of Michigan Press, 1999.

Treviño, A. Javier. *C. Wright Mills and the Cuban Revolution: An Exercise in the Art of Sociological Imagination.* Chapel Hill: University of North Carolina Press, 2017.

Trouillot, Michel-Rolph. *Silencing the Past: Power and the Production of History.* Boston: Beacon Press, 2015.

Tsipursky, Gleb. *Socialist Fun: Youth, Consumption, and State-Sponsored Popular Culture in the Cold War Soviet Union, 1945–1970.* Pittsburgh: University of Pittsburgh Press, 2016.

Tyson, Timothy B. *"Radio Free Dixie": Robert F. Williams and the Roots of Black Power.* 2nd ed. Chapel Hill: University of North Carolina Press, 2020.

Umezaki, Toru. "Breaking through the Cane-Curtain: The Cuban Revolution and the Emergence of New York's Radical Youth, 1961–1965." *Japanese Journal of American Studies* 18 (2007): 187–207.

United States Congress, House Committee on Un-American Activities. *Violations of State Department Regulations and Pro-Castro Propaganda Activities in the United States: Hearings, Eighty-Eighth Congress, May 6, 1963–September 28, 1964.* Washington, D.C.: U.S. Government Printing Office, 1963.

United States Information Agency. *Cuba: External Information and Cultural Relations Programs.* Washington, D.C.: Research Service, Office of Research and Assessment, U.S. Information Agency, 1972.

Urfé, Odilio. "Factores que integran la música cubana." *Islas* 2, no. 1 (1959): 7–21.

Valdés, Nelson. "Cuban Political Culture: Between Death and Betrayal." In *Cuba in Transition: Crisis and Transformation,* edited by Sandor Halebsky and John M. Kirk, 207–28. Boulder, Colo.: Westview Press, 1992.

———. "Revolution and Paradigms: A Critical Assessment of Cuban Studies." In *Cuban Political Economy: Controversies in Cubanology,* edited by Andrew Zimbalist, 182–212. Boulder, Colo.: Westview Press, 1988.

———. "The Revolutionary and Political Content of Fidel Castro's Charismatic Authority." In *A Contemporary Cuba Reader: Reinventing the Revolution,* edited by Philip Brenner, Marguerite Rose Jiménez, John M. Kirk, and William M. LeoGrande, 27–41. Lanham, Md.: Rowman & Littlefield, 2008.

Valdés, Nelson, and Karol Ibarra Zetter. "Senderos bifurcados: Los estudios sobre Cuba y la cubanología." *Temas* 91–92 (July–December 2017): 75–80.

Valdés-Dapena, Jacinto. *Piratas en el éter: La guerra radial contra Cuba, 1959–1999.* Havana: Editorial de Ciencias Sociales, 2006.

Valdespino, Andrés. "Los castrologistas y el viaje de Fidel." *Bohemia Libre Puertorriqueño* 54, no. 7 (May 1963): 30–39.

Vaughan, Mary Kay. *Cultural Politics in Revolution: Teachers, Peasants, and Schools in Mexico, 1930–1940.* Tucson: University of Arizona Press, 1997.

———. *The Eagle and the Virgin: Nation and Cultural Revolution in Mexico, 1920–1940.* Durham, N.C.: Duke University Press, 2006.

Vaughan, Mary Kay, Gabriela Cano, Jocelyn H. Olcott, and Carlos Monsivais, eds. *Sex in Revolution: Gender, Politics, and Power in Modern Mexico.* Durham, N.C.: Duke University Press, 2007.

Vaughan, Umi. *Rebel Dance, Renegade Stance: Timba Music and Black Identity in Cuba.* Ann Arbor: University of Michigan Press, 2012. https://doi.org/10.3998/mpub.3355867.

Vazquez, Alexandra T. *Listening in Detail: Performances of Cuban Music.* Durham, N.C.: Duke University Press, 2013.

Vélez, María Teresa. *Drumming for the Gods: The Life and Times of Felipe García Villamil, Santero, Palero, and Abakuá.* Philadelphia: Temple University Press, 2000.

Veltfort, Anna. *Goodbye, My Havana: The Life and Times of a Gringa in Revolutionary Cuba.* Stanford, Calif.: Stanford University Press, 2019.

Vilar, Guille. "De los Beatles a los Panchos." In *Los Beatles en Cuba,* edited by Ernesto Juan Castellanos, 111–17. Havana: Ediciones Unión, 1997.

Villegas, Alma. "The Origin, Development and Processes of Teatro Escambray in Cuba from 1968 to 1985." PhD diss., New York University, School of Education, 1995.

"Voice of Castro," *Time,* August 10, 1962. http://content.time.com/time/subscriber/article/0,33009,873690,00.html.

Volkov, Vadim. "The Concept of Kul'turnost': Notes on the Stalinist Civilizing Process." In *Stalinism: New Directions,* edited by Sheila Fitzpatrick, 210–30. London: Routledge, 2000.

Warner, Michael. "Publics and Counterpublics." *Public Culture* 14, no. 1 (2002): 49–90.

Watson, Mary Ann. *The Expanding Vista: American Television in the Kennedy Years.* New York: Oxford University Press, 1990.

Webb, Sheila. "Radical Portrayals: Dickey Chapelle on the Front Lines." *American Periodicals: A Journal of History and Criticism* 26, no. 2 (2016): 183–207.

Weber, Max. *The Theory of Social and Economic Organization.* Translated and edited by A. M. Henderson and Talcott Parsons. New York: Free Press, 1947. First published in German in 1922.

Weinstein, Barbara. "How to Become a Historian of Latin America: The Extraordinary Career of Frank Tannenbaum." *Americas* 80, no. 3 (2023): 383–94.

Weiss, Judith A. "The Emergence of Popular Culture." In *Cuba: Twenty-Five Years of Revolution, 1959–1984*, edited by Sandor Halebsky and John M. Kirk, 117–33. New York: Praeger, 1985.

Welch, David, ed. *Propaganda, Power and Persuasion: From World War I to Wikileaks.* London: I.B. Tauris, 2014.

Williams, Raymond. *Television: Technology and Cultural Form.* Hanover, NH: University Press of New England, 1992.

Williams, William Appelman. "Cuba: Issues and Alternatives." *Annals of the American Academy of Political and Social Science* 351, no. 1 (January 1964): 72–80. https://doi.org/10.1177/000271626435100109.

———. "Historiography and Revolution: The Case of Cuba; A Commentary on a Polemic by Theodore Draper." *Studies on the Left* 3, no. 3 (Summer 1963): 78–102.

Willner, Ann Ruth. *The Spellbinders: Charismatic Political Leadership.* New Haven, Conn.: Yale University Press, 1984.

Wise, David, and Thomas B. Ross. *The Invisible Government.* New York: Random House, 1964.

Woodard, Blair. "Intimate Enemies: Visual Culture and U.S.-Cuban Relations, 1945–2000." PhD diss., University of Albuquerque, 2010. https://digitalrepository.unm.edu/hist_etds/87.

XV Annyversary [sic] of Radio Havana Cuba. Havana: Department of Revolutionary Orientation, Central Committee, Communist Party of Cuba, 1977.

Yaffe, Helen. "Che Guevara and the Great Debate, Past and Present." *Science and Society* 76, no. 1 (2012): 11–40.

———. *"Che" Guevara: The Economics of Revolution.* Basingstoke: Palgrave Macmillan, 2009.

Yurchak, Alexei. *Everything Was Forever, until It Was No More: The Last Soviet Generation.* Princeton, N.J.: Princeton University Press, 2013.

Zamora Montes, Alejandro. "Hip hop en Cuba: Logros y desafíos de una cultura de resistencia." *Cuban Studies*, no. 48 (2019): 159–62.

Zeitlin, Maurice. *Revolutionary Politics and the Cuban Working Class.* New York: Harper & Row, 1970.

Zeitlin, Maurice, and Robert Scheer. *Cuba: Tragedy in Our Hemisphere.* New York: Grove Press, 1963.

Zhou, Taomo. *Migration in the Time of Revolution: China, Indonesia, and the Cold War.* Ithaca, N.Y.: Cornell University Press, 2019.

Zolov, Eric. *Refried Elvis: The Rise of the Mexican Counterculture.* Berkeley: University of California Press, 1999.

Index

www.ingramcontent.com/pod-product-compliance
Lightning Source LLC
Chambersburg PA
CBHW020454270326
41926CB00008B/595